Louis XIII: The Making of a King

Bust of Louis XIII as a child. Musée de Versailles. Photo courtesy of the
Musées Nationaux.

ELIZABETH WIRTH MARVICK

Louis XIII: The Making of a King

Yale University Press
New Haven and London

Designed by Nancy Ovedovitz and set in Bembo type by Eastern Graphics, Binghamton, New York. Printed in the United States of America by The Alpine Press, Inc., Stoughton, Massachusetts.

Library of Congress Cataloging-in-Publication Data

Marvick, Elizabeth Wirth.
    Louis XIII: the making of a king.
    Bibliography: p.
    Includes index.
    1. Louis XIII, King of France, 1601–1643—Childhood and youth. 2. Louis XIII, King of France, 1601–1643—Psychology. 3. France—Court and courtiers—History—17th century. 4. France—History—Louis XIII, 1610–1643—Psychological aspects. 5. France—Kings and rulers—Biography. I. Title.
DC123.8.M36 1986   944'.032'0924 [B] 86–9187
ISBN 0–300–03703–1

The paper in this book meets the guidelines for permanence and durability of the Committee on Production Guidelines for Book Longevity of the Council on Library Resources.

10   9   8   7   6   5   4   3   2   1

Ce petit monde pouvoit mieux que toute
autre chose enseigner à connoître le monde.

Guido Bentivoglio from the court of Louis XIII

Contents

Acknowledgments

It was at the suggestion of my husband, Dwaine Marvick, that I began the research that led to this book. As always, I am gratefully indebted to him for every kind of support.

Probably the study would not have been started without the contribution made to my knowledge and interests by my sons. For this they are not responsible, but for their help in later years I am grateful to Louis Marvick for expert advice on translations of French and Italian texts and to Andrew Marvick for giving me the benefit of his experience in iconographic research.

For many years it has been my good fortune to have the friendship of Nathan Leites, enabling me to call upon his erudition and incomparable critical powers that have contributed so much to psychopolitical understanding. His encouragement was decisive in my undertaking of the present inquiry and my debt to him in it is pervasive.

I owe special thanks to Orest Ranum for invaluable advice when I first entered the field of early modern studies. His hospitality to approaches different from his own and his generosity with his learning are an example to scholars. I have also benefitted greatly from the expert knowledge of Ruth Kleinman, Andrew Lossky, Alfred Soman and Dr. Micheline Guiton.

A grant and a fellowship from the American Council of Learned Societies were of assistance in the early stages of work.

Illustrations

Preface: Methods and Sources

The time is certainly past when it can be claimed of a potentate, as it was claimed of Louis XIII when he was thirteen years old, that "it is not with kings as with ordinary men. They do not grow with the passing of time, but are born complete—nurtured, reared, educated, and accomplished . . . children of the gods . . . men and kings at the same moment. . . . Their childhood is short, . . . their minds being in flower when those of others are still in bud."[1] Whatever weight one attaches to it, childhood is now generally agreed to be a stage that everyone—even the great and the powerful—goes through. Nor would many deny that powerful persons sometimes act toward those who are subject to their power in ways influenced by feelings that originated in childhood experiences.

Today's readers of life histories expect some account of the subject's early years. Many would probably even raise questions if a present-day biographer were to dismiss without description, as John Morley did with Gladstone, "one or two juvenile performances in no way differing from those of any other infant."[2] But I am not certain that everyone who is curious about the formation of politically influential people will be prepared for the amount of detail offered here on the earliest years of Louis XIII. As it happens, however, there are no current sources that provide as much information on the childhood origins of political tastes and tendencies as is afforded by the documentation on the childhood of this king. I hope, therefore, that the politically curious will decide, like Plunkitt of Tammany Hall, to accept their opportunities where they find them.

It may seem that Louis's childhood milieu and the conditions under which he was to exercise power are so different from those of today's rulers that the connection between then and now is difficult to make. However, as I shall indicate through some prefatory remarks on the methods I have followed in this study, one can successfully make this connection by means of contemporary psychological knowledge. The exceptional sources available for this inquiry also call for some words of introduction, for their very peculiarity has to be taken into account in weighing the evidence they offer.

METHODS

This work is not presented as "psychohistory"; it is history—an account of what happened in one important public figure's life from birth to adolescence. No principle should distinguish good method in writing such an account from good method in writing the history of an institution, a group, or an aspect of culture. Any history consists of statements of fact; good method requires the making of meaningful statements of fact, each supported by the preponderance of reliable evidence. In history, meaningful statements are those that enhance subjective understanding of what happened; reliable evidence is firsthand evidence, tested and weighed for what it contains of the reporter or the recorder as well as of the matters reported or recorded.

That the principal subject of this study is the development of an individual from birth to maturity is not a distinguishing feature so far as method is concerned. Just as a history of an institution such as the British Parliament may describe how, through time, changes in the interior arrangements of that body interacted with the exterior setting—with king and country, for example—so the inner life of our present subject, a dauphin who became king of France, was changed through time by what was done to him by others. What he did in turn affected those others and the world beyond. This work, then, is a history of the interaction between the inner and outer worlds of Louis XIII.

Whatever the subject, some kinds of statements about what happened in its history raise fewer questions than do others. Statements like "The king dismissed Parliament" or "The dauphin was whipped" usually refer to events sufficiently public for their veracity to be easily accepted. On the other hand, statements like "Many in Parliament despaired of the monarch's adaptability to reality" or "The dauphin repressed his rage at his father's treatment" refer to invisible feelings as well as visible responses. In these statements subjective events are inferred from what is reported or recorded to have been said or done by performers in the story. They are, nevertheless, statements of fact like the first kind—that is, either they happened or they did not. In all such cases the reader must evaluate the historian's inferences on the basis of the evidence presented for them.

In this book, most of the evidence is given in the text. We may have, for example, the testimony of several persons that Louis ceased to show feelings of rage toward his father on several occasions where he had shown it before and instead showed signs of fear or apathy—or presented symptoms such as stuttering or an upset stomach. We can observe how patterns of such responses change over periods of weeks, months, and years; and the inferences that are made about the interconnection of outside stimuli, outward responses, and inner states can be evaluated for their meaningfulness and on the evidence for them.

Most of the notes I have provided refer to the sources of evidence, so that the interested reader can judge, and perhaps inquire further into, how ample the documentation for statements concerning such patterns may be. Other references, however, aim to set the documented behavior in a wider context. They are not, therefore, intended to be necessary for understanding or evaluating the links between events that have been narrated in the text. These contextual references are mostly of two kinds. One describes the contemporary cultural or social setting of the behavior reported; the other offers cases of behavior recorded in the clinical literature of psychoanalysis with which to compare the behavior described in my narrative.

References to the social and cultural setting are included to indicate the extent to which particular practices or beliefs were typical. They are largely confined to notes because whatever the typicality of these practices and beliefs, it is one individual's experience of them that is the primary concern of this book. When atypicality reveals something about the personality of someone around Louis, it is appropriately treated in the text itself as a factor in the prince's experience.

Contextual references to psychoanalytic literature are no more necessary than those to the social and cultural milieu for understanding the main body of this work or for evaluating the evidence presented in it. Most such references are to reports of clinical research. They are included because they have helped suggest to me some inferences I draw in the text or because they suggest further inferences for which there is at present insufficient evidence. In addition, the studies that are cited for these reasons are characteristic of a literature that has contributed to my own perspectives on the etiology and dynamics of human feelings and thoughts.

The research findings on which I have mostly relied are founded on the hypotheses Freud developed as a result of his basic discoveries. They are generally representative of what has come to be called "classic psychoanalysis," although what they exemplify are the elaboration, enrichment, and revision of early psychoanalytic theory that have come about as a result of a half century of research into infant and child behavior. The literature that has resulted from this research represents a variety of directions taken in recent years by psychoanalytic inquiries. Investigators as different as Donald Winnicott (who has been grouped by some with a so-called object-relations school) and Phyllis Greenacre (considered to be in a direct line of descent from the Vienna school founded by Freud) have both, separately, reported findings about child development based mainly on observations of children or adults in a private, one-to-one therapeutic context. Others, like René Spitz, Selma Fraiberg, Margaret Mahler, and Anna Freud, have worked with colleagues in making controlled observations of children in institutional settings. The case material produced by all these inquirers includes a careful testing of new hypotheses against observed stages of normal child development. In this their reports contrast with those of Melanie Klein, for example, in which theory-building often outstrips its supposed basis in observed child behavior, and of Heinz Kohut, whose later work, at least, seems neither based on child observation of his own nor linked explicitly to that of others.

Given the frequent appearance of references to *The Psychoanalytic Study of the Child* in my notes, I conclude that the annual, now in its forty-first year of publication, represents rather well my perspective on child-development research. It is, nevertheless, but one source of the psychoanalytic literature upon which I have drawn. Furthermore, the inquirers mentioned above comprise only a few of those whose findings I have cited—a few who are representative of pioneers in child study, separated from Freud's seminal work by no more than one generation. In any case, the psychoanalytic reports cited in the notes are intended to exemplify the same standards for making and testing factual statements about the world that are applicable to historical or any other scientific inquiry into human behavior.

SOURCES

At all stages in this book a persistent effort has been made to consult original historical documents listed in the bibliography. A good many notes contain discussion of differences between manuscript and published versions, or among various manuscript accounts, and explain my reasons for preferring the ones cited. Something should be said here, however, about a major source employed for the daily life of Louis XIII over the period covered by this study. This is the diary kept by his physician, Jean Héroard, from Louis's birth through his twenty-sixth year.

Historians became aware of the existence of Héroard's record almost as soon as he began to make daily entries on the life of the infant with whose health he was entrusted in 1601. Charles Bernard, for example, was appointed royal historiographer in 1621, but he had been *lecteur ordinaire de la chambre du roy* since Louis was about five years old and as such had the task of reading aloud to the young prince. He became familiar with Héroard and includes a short eulogy of "that good man" in his *Histoire de Louis XIII* (1646). Information in this and his other works suggests that he was one of the many who were allowed to consult the doctor's daily *registre*. It is virtually certain that Gédéon Tallemant Des Réaux (1619–1692) at some time had access to Héroard's manuscript: his description of it as "several volumes in which you will find nothing except what time he [Louis] awakened, breakfasted, spat, pissed, crapped, etc." ("Louis Treiziesme" in *Les histori-ettes*) is so accurately graphic as to convince one that he had firsthand knowledge. These and other contemporary allusions to the diary's contents or its author indicate some awareness of its extraordinary nature: no other document in Western literature gives as complete a record of the development of an individual.

How Héroard's manuscript found its way into the library of Jean-Baptiste Colbert, Louis XIV's minister, is not known, but when, in 1732, Colbert's collection was acquired by the royal library, the diary was in it. By this time, as Baluze's catalogue shows, the first three-and-a-quarter years of Héroard's original record had been lost.[3] The remainder, comprising six thick folio volumes, finally came to be designated as 4022–4027 of the *fonds français* in the Département des Manuscrits of the Bibliothèque Nationale. The first volume begins on January 1, 1605—the start of the year in which Louis, then dauphin of France, would be four years old.

Despite this lack, a number of historians consulted the document over the years, though it was never transcribed and published—for the very reasons to which Tallemant called attention: roughly three-quarters of the text was concerned with just such matters pertaining to Louis's body as the anecdotist claimed. In 1868, however, two seventeenth-century specialists, Eudore Soulié and Edouard de Barthélemy, prepared a well-annotated two-volume abridgment of Héroard's manuscript for publication under the title of *Journal de Jean Héroard sur l'enfance et la jeunesse de Louis XIII*. These editors naturally wished to begin at the beginning of the dauphin's life, and to supply the record that was missing from the original they turned to a version of it that had been produced by a physician, Simon Courtaud, who was Héroard's nephew and had had the complete manuscript in his possession long enough to make a four-volume handwritten abridgment of it. This document was in private hands in the nineteenth century, but Barthélemy and Soulié were able to use it for their diary edition.

The published work reflected the editors' high standard of scholarly exactness, their sensitivity to colorful human details, and their interest in cultural and political history. It was very readable, and historians began to rely upon it rather than the original manuscript.

Readability, however, was achieved at a certain cost. Soulié and Barthélemy suppressed almost all the details on the dauphin's physical care and development that figured so largely in Héroard's record. In making use of Courtaud's version, moreover, they compounded the tendency of this editorial policy, for Courtaud himself had also reduced the original by eliminating most of the thousands of details on Louis's bodily treatment and processes that Héroard had diligently collected. The great bulk of these were concerned with those matters Tallemant had found so tedious: the conditions of the prince's sleeping and awakening; what, when, and how he ate or otherwise took substances into his body; his digestion, defecation, urination, and other excretions.

This nineteenth-century version was full of "pictures and conversation," for the editors kept much of what the original diary contained on how the dauphin looked and what he said. Nor did Soulié and Barthélemy allow any prudery of their own milieu to deter them from publishing many details on the dauphin's genital experiences and responses, which Héroard had reported along with other physical information on his patient. These editors, like Héroard's physician nephew, found such material more interesting than the far greater quantity of oral and anal information he had recorded.

This published version of Héroard's record became a basic resource for later historians of the period and also aroused new French interest in the life and times of Louis XIII. The comte de Beauchamp drew upon the publication for his work on *Louis XIII d'après sa correspondance avec le cardinal de Richelieu* (1902); Louis Vaunois used it extensively in two works on the king (1932, 1943); it was a fundamental source for Louis Batiffol's many books on the reign of Louis XIII. But these, like even so recent a biography as Pierre Chevallier's *Louis XIII* (1979), gave few signs that their authors had consulted Héroard's original manuscript.

While French writers and editors were interested in the *Journal* mainly for general political and cultural history, English-language authors soon became aware of its value as a record of one child's development. In 1902 Ida A. Taylor's *The Making of a King: The Childhood of Louis XIII* and in 1930 Lucy Crump's *Nursery Life 300 Years Ago* reflected an appreciation of the diary as a description of the childhood of an individual. Despite its title, however, Taylor's work in no way aimed to relate Louis's early experiences to his behavior as adult king, and Crump's book was explicitly devoted to the more picturesque details of child-rearing in the court of Henri IV.

The first French author to turn his attention to such details was Philippe Ariès. In 1960 *L'enfance et la ville familiale* (published in English as *Centuries of Childhood*) used the Soulié and Barthélemy edition as a principal source to support hypotheses concerning the transformation of family attitudes since early modern times. Ten years later David Hunt used the same source, among others, for *Parents and Children in History*, in which he took issue with Ariès's general theme that the early modern French child's experience, as exemplified by the dauphin's, was integrated into the adult world rather than regarded as a condition apart from it. Guiding the attention of each author was a position on the relative value of historical child-rearing practices and attitudes: Ariès implicitly criticized a present-day child-centered morality by contrasting it with early modern community life; Hunt found methods of child-rearing in Louis's nursery "inhumane and wrong" (p. 157).

With *Parents and Children*, however, Hunt became the first writer to train psychoanalytic perspectives on the dauphin's treatment and responses. Using Erik Erikson's elaborations of Freud's essays on infantile sexuality, he followed Louis through the oral, anal, and genital stages of childhood development, both to illustrate what he considered salient in child-rearing methods of the time and to demonstrate Ariès's error in believing that Louis XIII's experience exemplified a conflict-free pattern of growing up that had prevailed in pre-modern Europe.

Both Ariès and Hunt extrapolated from Héroard's account of Louis's rearing to contemporary childhood in general. They were little interested in the diary for the light it threw on the development of one individual—in particular, the individual who would be the authoritative source of a transformation of state power in France. Both, moreover, imposed on their material a model of Louis's family structure that seemed to have little relation to how the prince himself actually experienced it: Ariès conceived of that part of the court that comprised Louis's nursery setting as a sort of undifferentiated extended family; Hunt tried to make the same setting fit a father-mother-baby model in which hired servitors—and even siblings—played only a peripheral role. And, of course, both relied for their information about Louis's upbringing on the doubly edited 1868 version of Héroard's diary.

This study of Louis XIII's development was begun in 1965. Consulting the surviving portion of Héroard's manuscript in order to trace the child's experience in as much detail as possible, I was surprised to discover the prominent part played in his life by the doctor himself. Rather than the usually silent, benevolent, and objective witness that he seems to be in Soulié's and Barthélemy's version, Louis's first physician emerges in the original diary as a morally, intellectually, and politically confident figure with high ambitions and powerful means for implementing them through the child in his care. In this full version of the text, even though it begins only in Louis's fourth year of life, the peculiarity of Héroard's concerns with physical input and output is striking, as is the persistence of his own constant intervention in that process. Seeking further information, I found that the Bibliothèque Nationale's Département des Manuscrits had acquired, between 1946 and 1950, that privately owned abridgment of the diary made by Courtaud on which Soulié and Barthélemy had relied for Louis's first three-and-a-third years. Beginning at the beginning with this apparently completely neglected document—neither it nor Héroard's original had yet been microfilmed—I found that Héroard's intrusions into his patient's bodily functions had begun in Louis's very first days of life, and that they were of such a nature as to help account for some of the unexpected behavior that the infant prince began very early to show.

I soon concluded that any use of Héroard's diary as a source on Louis's development would require a better-informed estimate of the diarist's own part in that development. Accordingly, my first publication using this material (1974) was a historiographical essay on the apparent influence of

Héroard's character and behavior on the character and behavior of the child whose unfolding nature he was recording. Most of this influence will become evident in the narrative ahead. At every point, moreover, I attempt to weigh the doctor's special perspectives against contemporary evidence from other sources.

Jean Héroard presents himself as the devoted, understanding, and appreciative champion of Louis and Louis's interests in a competitive environment and represents the prince as developing daily towards a condition in which he will be preeminently worthy of this valuable support. This perspective shapes Héroard's concerns in several ways that distort his picture of reality. For example, he often gives the impression that Louis is alone at the center of the stage or, perhaps, surrounded just by respectful servants. Only occasionally do we glimpse the scramble for favors and benefits among the many adults in and around the child's household—a melee in which Louis himself was often a pawn or a victim of exploitation. The crowd in whose midst Louis was raised included noble attendants as well as lowly servants of all kinds, and many of these nobles were well connected or centers of influence in their own right. Some were Louis's rivals—often successful rivals—for favors of the king and queen.

By and large Héroard focuses exclusively on Louis; the behavior, including the words, of others are far more rarely reported, and then only to explain a response from the young prince. Apparently, the doctor's biological training had no effect in alerting him to the floral and faunal setting in which he and Louis lived—unless it was a question of something the child ate, rode, or shot. Héroard also tends whenever possible to idealize Louis's sentiments, as well as those of his parents and siblings toward him— though the feelings of the supporting players in Héroard's story are usually ignored.

The best corrective to Héroard's biases is to be aware of them through understanding his personal history and interests and to subject his accounts constantly to controls from reports of other witnesses to the matters he describes. Fortunately, the courts of Henri IV and of Marie de Medici were exceptionally open. They not only contained letter writers, diarists, and memoir writers but were surrounded, and often penetrated, by journalistic observers whose records and correspondence have also been preserved.

In the course of the inquiry that led to this volume, a number of firsthand reports that seem to have been unknown or neglected turned up—not only on obscure matters but also on so well-worked-over a subject as the murder of Concino Concini. These are fully cited in the notes. But even sources well known to earlier historians take on a new aspect when we focus not on the broad march of history or on a cultural and social milieu but rather on how a particular child experienced these in his own immediate world and how he responded to this experience.

CHAPTER ONE

Introduction

"There is no king more difficult to understand in French history," writes Gérard de Contades, a nineteenth-century scholar of Louis XIII. "The most commonly accepted laws of physiology, psychology, and heredity are powerless to explain the peculiarities and contradictions of this extraordinary, . . . morose, and mysterious prince whose want of energy allowed so many heads to fall."[1] Contades's perplexity was not new: one of Louis's contemporaries remarked that anomalies in the monarch's character had earned him the secret designation of the Incomprehensible One at court.[2] Puzzlement over the contradictions presented by this ruler has persisted to the present day.

Louis XIII, son of the energetic Henri IV and the robust Marie de Medici, inherited a sturdy physique that reflected the good health of both parents. Yet the physical vigor and stamina he showed from birth onward alternated with bouts of utter lassitude, and illnesses that became chronic in his childhood killed him before he had finished his forty-second year. Further, although the strong will, high intelligence, and clear understanding that many noticed in Louis as a boy never left him, no French monarch was more dependent on others to initiate and pursue policies. Even though Louis's inclinations were fully as autocratic as his predecessor's and successor's, his reign, unlike either of theirs, was rarely one of personal rule.

And was this King Louis a good man? In his lifetime it was often affirmed that he was, though other contemporaries bore witness to his capacity for cruelty. While he would sometimes show, by word or deed, a humane concern for some of his subjects' well-being, he could on occasion take aim and fire upon a pair of rebellious peasants, killing them with the same apparent satisfaction he showed at bagging game birds or shooting a stag. On the level of international politics, this Very Christian King seems to have been exempt from the horror that many of his contemporaries felt at the bloody destruction visited by France on other Christian populations—a horror that

1

has been evoked anew in our own time by writers who have contemplated the Thirty Years' War. Within France itself, the heads of Louis's intimates that were allowed to fall by his orders—or by lack of them—were many indeed: executions under his regime were far more frequent than under the rule of his father or his son. This volume concludes with an account of young Louis's exultation at the murder of his mother's adviser, the maréchal d'Ancre, of the complacency with which he allowed a court to contrive that his mother's dearest friend, Ancre's widow, be decapitated, and of the obduracy with which he withstood the banishment of his mother herself.

But if the contradictions in Louis XIII's character are as obvious today as they have ever been, the laws of psychology, at least, no longer seem so inadequate to explain them. Contades expressed his helplessness before the mystery of this king in 1889, at the very time that Freud's first inquiries were opening the way to a new understanding of personality. Among the various paths taken by psychoanalytic research since then, those that have focused directly upon infant and child development have perhaps provided the most illuminating insights into the structure and dynamics of character. Not surprisingly, a growing number of scholars have sought to apply these insights to the study of important actors on the political stage.

Few will argue against making an effort to understand a political leader's feelings and behavior by tracing their manifestations from the earliest possible moment. All too often, however, the forces that shaped the leader's character are obscure, the data that would reveal them scarce or disputable. Missing or dubious evidence obstructs progress toward discovering links between personal history and public performance.

The case of Louis XIII is conspicuously different. No ruler's (and probably no individual's) childhood has been chronicled with such care and completeness as his. This gives the historian a resource the psychoanalyst rarely enjoys. The process of psychoanalytic discovery, like archeology, usually strives to bring the long-buried and mutilated relics of infantile feelings to the light of day and to reconstruct from such fragments some idea of the original experience of a living patient. But in the exceptional case of Louis XIII, the record is more nearly complete for the early years of life than for the later, and we can follow in detail the formation of the adult king's mental life from its beginnings in the experience of the neonate. When Louis is unaware at a conscious level of the roots of his recent behavior, the reader can reach into the past, as it were, to supply what has been forgotten by the subject himself. Since the events of this king's long and momentous reign are also abundantly and reliably reported, no leader's early history seems to offer a better foundation for examining the relationship between personality and political decision making.

In seeking the sources of Louis XIII's distinctive traits, one first becomes aware that his earliest experiences were only indirectly shaped by his progenitive parents. His mother, Marie de Medici, felt herself well acquitted of immediate responsibility for her firstborn child once she had delivered him to a rejoicing France. The great king Henri IV was rarely present in the dauphin's early months, but his selection of Héroard as his son's first physician may have had a fateful import for Louis's development. The Protestant doctor had ambitions, it appears, that were gratified by controlling his infant patient according to his own lights. Héroard contributed to Louis's subjection to surgical intervention in the mouth and, independently of this, to the failure of Louis's first nursing relationship (see chapter 2 below, "First Months"). The future king's morose pessimism, his sense that life lacked joy, and his severe speech impediment cannot, of course, have been set by these first experiences alone: symptoms, personality traits, and, still more, perspectives on the world are surely determined by a multitude of influences, from infancy to late in life. Nevertheless, there seems little reason to doubt that the more primitive the early sensations of pain and disappointment, the more pervasive they may be for later development, and the more likely to color reactions to later joys and sorrows.

Joys were not late in coming to the infant prince, in the form of a gratifying nurse who was to be the main love of his childhood. But the satisfaction he felt at a seemingly complete possession of this nurturing figure was marred, as he became a toddler, by extreme anxiety that she would be torn from him or slip from his grasp. It seems plausible that Héroard's exceptional assiduity in controlling the eating, digestion, and bowel movements of his young charge were connected with this anxiety over losing beloved possessions—not only persons but parts of his body and things inside and outside it.

As the heir to a powerful throne, Louis was treated with deference by many, with reverence by some, and with circumspection by most of those close to him. Nominally, he was master of all but the king; in practice, however, his helplessness was like that of any baby boy, and there were many around him eager to exploit his dependency for their own purposes. The child was encouraged in unrealistic visions of his powers at the same time that he was exposed to seductive, threatening, and belittling treatment. In particular, in the bawdy court of Henri IV there was exaggeration of the phallic grandeur of the baby who was supposed eventually to generate successors to secure the new dynasty of his popular father. He was, in fact, both master and slave.

Before Louis was two, Henri IV reentered his life (see chapter 3 below). The father began to take a leading part in engendering a fear in the child that was the more powerful for the love that he was also able to inspire in his son. For the dauphin, taking punishment from the king became pleasurable; yet it also evoked rage, which had its precursors in earlier reactions to physical control. Pleasure—whether from yielding to Henri's seductiveness or

to his whip—was an obvious danger to Louis's developing sense of autonomy; danger as obvious lay in yielding to rage against this father whose
power to damage his son seemed unlimited. Thanks to exceptionally detailed descriptions, we can detect in Louis's accounts of his own dreams
how tempting the sexual blandishments of his father were, and how such
temptation was excluded from consciousness. The same firsthand accounts
allow us to be present at dramatic contests between father and son: we
watch Louis's rage explode and then follow his struggle to divert it to less
threatening objects or to turn it inward.

As the dauphin confronted this nursery version of a prisoner's dilemma,
we can observe him developing the coping techniques that he would later
exhibit as a ruling monarch (see chapter 5 below). His fears of being damaged, so unacceptable in a future ruler, were visibly transformed into their
opposite—aggressively warlike tastes—and he developed skills that would
make him appear an intrepid military leader. Yet these new tastes and skills
retained signs of their origins. He increasingly made use of those props for
which early inner conflicts had given him an affinity—drums and guns,
certain animals and types of persons—and neglected or rejected others of
less emotional value to him.

When, at the age of seven, Louis left the hands of women, his world became peopled with new relatives, servants, noble aides, clerics, and public
figures. We can see how his mode of relating to a widened cast of characters
reproduced, with growing complexity, qualities of his ties to nursery
personnel.

Had Henri lived through Louis's adolescence, it is possible that conflicts
in the son that impeded his development of feelings of autonomy and im-
paired his capacity to take pleasure in his adult role might have been worked
through. Instead, Henri's sudden, violent death dramatically revived, without resolving, longings and fears in the eight-year-old prince that had earlier
been so intense. At the same time, the new king was plunged into a milieu
in which he himself was the prize in a struggle among competing forces
whose political significance he was unable to understand.

At this turning point in Louis's life, it is possible to identify (as I do in
chapter 7) the personal significance for him of important political symbols
in his environment. His words and behavior show how he interpreted the
norms he was asked to meet and what choices he tended to make among
them when this seemed necessary.

At the age of thirteen Louis was proclaimed an adult, ruling monarch.
Although the youth's real opportunity to act independently had not yet arrived, his reactions to political constellations in court and country were becoming more meaningful for possible political action. With the help of the
diligent Héroard's diary and other intimate reports, we are still able to follow the way in which the king's responses to public actors and events were

linked to, and given meaning by, the vicissitudes of his early development. His mother and her counselors, court factions, diplomatic coups, and distant battles now evoke in Louis sentiments whose origins in childhood can be identified with some confidence.

With adolescence, Louis's history merges with the history of France. It does not become the less personal for that. The fourteen-year-old helped to ward off a conspiracy, he became a bridegroom, he took part in a coup d'état sponsored by his mother against his cousin, Condé. Greatly expanded documentation is now added to the intimate testimony that has hitherto been the principal source for understanding how the prince's personality affected the outcome of these events.

Few youths can have had the opportunity to participate in the destruction of a man who was felt to have usurped a murdered father's position. Fifteen-year-old Louis had this opportunity, and took it. The assassination of the maréchal d'Ancre, Marie de Medici's powerful counselor, seems to have helped Louis to discharge, without guilt, the anger he still felt toward his dead father against a man who almost certainly represented that father in his unconscious mind. The plotting, execution, and aftermath of the maréchal's murder form a fitting denouement to the present study, a story rarely encountered except in fiction—one in which the strongest passions of the protagonist are at once plainly exposed and deeply gratified.

Yet this ending was also a beginning: it was the political debut of Louis XIII. His character had for the most part been formed. Titular king for seven years and monarch in his own right for more than two, he still had a long reign ahead. A short epilogue can only sketch some of its critical events, but in all of them the past that is traced here speaks through the monarch's actions, touching the lives of many.

CHAPTER TWO

The First Family of Louis XIII

He was jealous of those who belonged to him [les siens] *and had always been so, even as the tiniest child.*[1]

Almost as soon as the future Louis XIII was born, on September 27, 1601, those appointed to care for him began to affect his development in important ways. During his earliest months his significant family consisted not of his kin but of hired caretakers who supplied the objects for his drives, the controls put upon them, and the models for his conduct.[2]

Nevertheless, the infant's appointive family was chosen by the king and queen of France, his progenitive parents. Not only did they make the important initial choice of the baby's household; they also set the conditions of his care and attempted to supervise the administration of their orders by these servants. Moreover, much that Louis's appointive family did during the first year was done in anticipation of the wishes or interests of his father or mother, on whose approval the caretakers were completely dependent.

PROGENITORS

Few genealogies are more complete than those of European rulers in the early modern era, and the antecedents of Louis XIII are known on both sides for many generations. His father, Henri IV, king of France, was descended on his father's side from a younger son of the sainted Louis IX. Less remotely, ancestors on Henri's maternal side included rulers of Navarre and the Valois king, Charles V. Jeanne d'Albret, Henri's mother, was the niece of François I.

Louis's mother, Marie de Medici, was the descendant of Florentine merchant princes and Habsburg emperors. Her mother was a daughter of emperor Ferdinand of Austria and sister of the queen of Spain. On the Medici side, Marie was related to cardinals and popes. Her father, Grand Duke Francesco II of Tuscany, was one of the richest men in Europe and an important Italian ally of France. Both parents died in Marie's childhood, leaving only two surviving children. Marie was reared by her uncle as a valuable property, since her wealth and pedigree qualified her for a princely hand.[3] A most attractive suitor became available when, at the end of 1599, Henri's childless marriage to Marguerite de Valois was annulled, and the French king became free to remarry in the interest of continuing his new Bourbon dynasty.

Although Henri was already one of France's most popular kings, his recent profession of Catholicism was shadowed, for some, by his former Protestantism, and his conciliation of the Huguenots was a potential pretext for rival princes to revolt. In negotiating a marriage with Marie even before his divorce became final, he hoped through this Tuscan alliance to reaffirm his new Catholic affiliation, thus warding off dangerous foreign challenges and pacifying domestic enemies.

Most important in Henri's calculations was his hope, at forty-eight, of producing a legitimate heir to stabilize his regime. The bride's robustness and her family history gave promise of high fertility. Even before Henri met the Tuscan princess he wrote her that he hoped she would conserve this good health so "that we may make a beautiful child, causing our friends to laugh and our enemies to cry."[4]

The new queen of France was married by proxy in Florence on April 10, 1600, a few days before her twenty-seventh birthday.[5] She met her husband for the first time in Lyons eight months later, on December 9. Anne d'Este, the queen's attendant, wrote to Marie's sister in Mantua that the couple "were constantly together, day and night." This, she hoped, would produce the effect desired by everyone: "May it please God to give them a Dauphin." She pronounced the union "the happiest marriage in the world."[6]

This sunny picture notwithstanding, the royal couple were mismatched in personality. Henri, a warrior-king, spurned formality and was graceful, amiable, and shrewd. His national goal of reuniting and reconciling antagonists under his rule paralleled a private side that was eager for affection, slow to take offense, and quick to forgive. On the domestic as on the national level, Henri aimed at the creation of "one big happy family." His heterosexual demands were omnivorous, insatiable, and fruitful, and he indulged them freely. To the progeny that resulted from these liaisons he extended the same all-embracing impulses that had helped him unite a bitterly divided realm, even requiring Marie to welcome his mistresses and his bastards at court. He symbolized his conciliatory impulses with names: one illegitimate daughter was named after a beloved dead mistress (not her mother), and this child's brother after Henri himself. Perhaps he had also hoped to provide consolation in naming his sons by Gabrielle d'Estrées after the emperors Caesar and Alexander,[7] since they could not be heirs to the throne so long as Henri was married to Marguerite.

The king, an athlete and passionate hunter, prided himself aggressively and often coarsely in his masculinity. Although he was well educated for a man of his epoch and rank, some of the finer arts were lost on him. "The king knows many things," Cardinal Du Perron is said to have remarked, "but he understands nothing either of music or of poetry."[8] The stable-room atmosphere of this warrior-king's court was partly responsible for the exodus of more delicate souls to private houses for social contacts toward the beginning of the seventeenth century. Moreover, though Henri was liberal with his affections, he was tight with money, a combination inimical to social refinement.

In contrast to her husband, Marie was stout, stiff, stubborn, and proud. She was extravagant with money but had little spontaneous affection to give. One of her deepest attachments was to Leonora Galigai, an Italian lady-in-waiting with whom she had had a close relationship since childhood and who had accompanied her to France from Florence. Marie had grown quite dependent on this bright, lively, somewhat older woman.

The new queen's French was rudimentary and heavily accented, a handi-cap at court that was probably compounded by an intellect limited by the isolated and narrowly circumscribed conditions of her rearing. But Marie's taste was cultivated, and she possessed some artistic talent.[9] She was inter-ested in acquiring fine objects—jewels, clothes, paintings, dogs—and she continued in France the Medicis' enthusiasm for palace building, an avoca-tion she shared with Henri. Unlike her open-hearted husband, however, she was suspicious, sensitive to slights, and persistent in harboring resent-ment. Although she stood much on the dignity of her rank and the correct-ness of ceremony, she was occasionally unable to control outbursts of rage. Some of these were directed at her husband, whom she came to blame bit-terly for humiliating her by flaunting his many affairs. He, in turn, re-proached her for making him uncomfortable and for not appreciating him. Henri's success in reconciling antagonistic forces was far greater on the wide national canvas than it was around the hearth over which the jealous Marie presided. *Brouilleries* between the two came to be known to all the court and even to interested foreign powers.[10]

In spite of these differences, barely nine months after their marriage had been consummated Marie presented Henri with a son, the first of six chil-dren born to the couple in the ten years of their marriage. The queen's labor was long, but delivery was not difficult, and the baby was robust and vigor-ous. Immediately after giving birth the queen sought reassurance on the most important point: "Is it male?" she asked several times in Italian, and af-ter being shown that it was, gave it a benevolent glance.[11] The midwife re-ports that when she expressed her concern to the king at the throng flocking into the delivery room, he replied: "Shut up, shut up, Midwife! Don't worry about it! That child belongs to everybody: everyone must enjoy him!"[12] Louis was the first dauphin to be born to France in eighty years—

a cause for rejoicing not only by Henri's and Marie's friends but by the general populace.

Once reassured as to his sex, the queen left her infant to the care of others. During his early months she saw him infrequently and did not once embrace him until he was nearly six months old.[13] The king was initially more demonstrative but gave up holding the baby after a week, when Louis nearly fell to the floor while being presented to his father on a velvet cushion.[14] Thus, to trace this child's earliest development, it is necessary to turn to the household appointed by the king and queen to supply the prince's intimate needs. Louis's significant family for his first months consisted primarily of his nurses and the first physician, Jean Héroard, who had effective control of his conditions of life in the beginning weeks.

THE FIRST PHYSICIAN

A striking medallion portrait of Jean Héroard, probably designed by the engraver Dupré, appeared not long after Louis's accession to the throne in 1610. It shows the strong features of a self-assured man in the prime of life.[15] The representation is accurate: Héroard was no mere court physician. He had a high opinion of himself, confirmed by the views of others, as a scholar and political advisor. He also had strong ambitions for influence. The origins, history, and character of this man who was so important in shaping Louis's own character have been described in some detail elsewhere;[16] it will suffice here simply to sketch them briefly.

Héroard was born in Montpellier in 1551 (about two years before Henri IV) and was descended from a line of influential Protestant doctors and surgeons with international reputations and contacts. Even before receiving his medical training he entered service in princely circles; in about 1567 he became attached to the household of the great Italian lord Louis Gonzaga, duc de Nevers, and his German wife, the princess Henriette de Clèves. Here Héroard was, according to his own report to this couple, a sort of general factotum, employed "in the management of your most important affairs which I may say I know more about than anyone else of my status [*qualité*]."[17] Perhaps special linguistic abilities initially qualified him for this post; on the other hand, he may have acquired from travels with the Gonzagas the skills in Italian and German that he later displayed at the royal court. While still with these patrons he matriculated at the Montpellier medical school in 1571 and became qualified to follow in the footsteps of the many graduates of that famous center who had been physicians to the rulers of Navarre and of France. Continuing in the service of the Gonzagas, in about 1574 he also became attached to the royal court as a part-time physician in the service of Charles IX, for whom his duties may have been mainly veterinary. His appointment was renewed by Henri III, and he was kept on the staff of court doctors under the Bourbon Henri IV. The king himself selected Héroard, in the last month of Marie de Medici's first pregnancy to serve as physician to what Henri predicted would be "my son, the dauphin."[18]

By the time Henri offered this new opportunity to Héroard, the doctor's high estimation of himself was already well developed. In a report of 1581 he complained to the Gonzagas that the civil wars were causing distractions from his "more serious occupations and studies." These included a study of the anatomy of the horse, a work commissioned by Charles IX. Héroard's "Hippostéologie"—a manuscript on the bones of the horse—was presented in 1579, but the author anticipated that it would be merely the first part of a "*grand oeuvre,* truly worthy of a king." How seriously he took its value is shown by the preface, addressed to Henri III. He intended that the finished treatise would comprehend "the entire veterinary art" and would be far "superior to any other treatment of the matter in your kingdom." He considered his abilities inimitable: it would be impossible, he said, for this "edifice" to be achieved by any other "in the form and manner that I shall execute it."[19]

Héroard's claims to expertise extended even to poetic composition. In 1579 he published a flowery quatrain as tribute to the physician Laurent Joubert.[20] In 1609 he provided a laudatory Latin epitaph for the tomb of Ronsard.[21] During the same year the queen's midwife, a respected practitioner and the wife of a noted surgeon, published a handbook on obstetrics, gynecology, and pediatrics, which she prefaced with a poem honoring Héroard as an author:

> Your writings will engrave your happy memory,
> Building an altar in your praise.[22]

Marie de Medici herself apparently thought Héroard an appropriate person to draft an appreciation of Henri IV after the king's assassination.[23] Louis's doctor was esteemed "like my father" by the illustrious *amateur* and scholar Peiresc and was one of those at court who was expected to be a link between intellectuals and the chief ministers of state.[24]

Furthermore, Héroard considered himself qualified to appraise political values. His work on the house of Nevers purports to establish the Gonzagas' claims "in the Duchies of Brabant, Lembourg, and . . . Antwerp . . . usurped by the House of Austria." In his preface to the "Hippostéologie" he exhorts the king to cultivate the sciences, citing the examples of Caesar Augustus and François I. The epitaph for Henri IV goes into considerable political detail.

The work that most reveals Héroard's political ambition, however, is a pedantic essay on the education of princes, *L'institution du prince,* published in 1609. Cast in the form of a conversation prolonged over six days between the doctor and the dauphin's governor, Gilles de Souvré, the work gives advice not only on the early physical training and care of the prince but also on the moral and intellectual qualities that should be instilled in him to prepare him for kingship. In this imaginary dialogue Héroard pictures himself as a sage teaching his deferential colleague the best techniques for training the potential monarch who was their common charge. Clearly, Héroard saw his own role in state affairs as central. In one passage he has Souvré consult him on political matters, on the grounds that expertise in the body of man may be extrapolated to the body politic. The doctor recalls with approval the role of another doctor, Nichomachus, in the court of Philip of Macedon.[25] Indeed, he later hints that it is Louis's mission to carry France's glory beyond its borders, as Alexander had spread the culture of Hellas. This fantasy of Louis as a crusader is reflected in Héroard's report of a conversation between the three-year-old dauphin and his half brother, a chevalier of Malta:

Dauphin: What cross is that?
Chevalier: It's a cross of Malta.
D.: Where is that?
C.: It's very far away.
D.: (Showing his own [cross]) I have one I shall carry much farther away.[26]

In the margin of this account the doctor twice appends the word "*Nota*" to signify its importance.

Evidently, then, the baby born on September 27, 1601, embodied not only the hopes of Henri IV for the survival of his dynasty but also those of Jean Héroard to fashion a philosopher-king. In the earliest months of Louis's life it was the doctor who had by far the greater direct influence.

FIRST MONTHS

When the midwife servered the umbilical cord of Marie de Medici's first-born son, it was the signal to Héroard to assume direct responsibility for the infant's physical care. He ordered wine to stimulate the child, followed by bathing, oiling, and swaddling—usual practices of the time. Here, however, the unexceptional nature of Louis's neonatal care ended; from then on the doctor constantly subjected the baby to unusual control and manipulation.[27]

In spite of the favorable life signs Louis showed, Héroard was not content to let nature take its course. On the second day of the infant's life the doctor decided he was "having trouble sucking" and called in the surgeon to cut "in three places" the membranes at the base of the tongue that were thought to be impeding Louis's nursing.[28] This, too, was a common practice of the time, but in the dauphin's case it may have been applied with more thoroughness and zeal because of a professional surgeon's intervention. Louis could well have experienced traumatic effects from this treatment, lacking as he did at this stage the awareness of various parts of his body necessary to localize sensation. Recent research in comparable cases suggests that flooding the neonatal sensory system with such a stimulus is likely to be a setback to normal development.[29]

Louis's feeding experiences in the first three months compounded the injury. Héroard's apparent lack of experience with infants did not prevent him from intervening in the nursing process. That Louis continued to suck after feedings was attributed by the doctor to hunger persisting on account of insufficient milk in his nurse, Hotman. The "great gulps" with which he sucked, "so that he swallowed more in one than another would have done in three,"[30] would seem, on the contrary, to indicate that he ingested milk so quickly that his hunger was appeased before his sucking drive was satisfied. This interpretation is supported by Héroard's observation that the baby was "racked by cramps" after feeding.[31] Further evidence that he was overfed is the fact that one night when the nurse, in the well-founded fear of losing her job, had overeaten so much that she vomited, Louis himself later "vomited great quantities of milk." But to Héroard this was proof that the milk of Louis's nurse caused a "fury in his stomach."[32]

If overfeeding was part of the infant's problem, the doctor promptly exacerbated it: he ordered the administration of boiled pap and auxiliary feedings from supplementary wetnurses. In addition, he supervised the suckling process with intense attention. These measures no doubt aggravated the nurse's nervousness, with further adverse effects on her nursling. On the occasion when the king awkwardly tried to take Louis in his arms, she nearly dropped the infant.[33] It is no wonder that the baby "never suckled Hotman without its disagreeing with him," as Héroard said later.[34] Louis developed every sign of an unsatisfactory nursing relationship: cramps and severe rash heralded a general failure to thrive. By the age of three months he was getting thinner, he was red all over, and "his stomach looked like a skinned rabbit."[35]

Héroard seems to have sought complete control of the physical inputs and outputs of his infant charge. Just as he intervened continually and disruptively in Louis's earliest nursing relationship, so he attempted to manage the baby's excretory functions. On the tenth day of Louis's life the doctor observed that it had been a "long time since he had voided." Thereupon he induced evacuation by suppository. This practice soon became habitual: before the baby was a month old, we learn, his bowels were "emptied . . . in the usual manner."[36] Héroard appears to have made it impossible from the very beginning for Louis to develop spontaneously a sense of control over this important bodily process.

The "benign circle" by which a child repeatedly experiences, actively and passively, the ingestive, digestive, excretory cycle was interfered with in Louis's care at two crucial points.[37] Héroard's control through the rectum not only prevented the baby from gaining a sense of power over his own internal process; it probably also helped determine the importance of the anal zone as a later focus for the prince's relationship to the outside world. Such rectal intervention, at a stage when an infant first becomes aware of the boundaries of his body and develops his earliest sense of potency, can significantly alter the child's outlook on life.[38] Héroard's part in the failure of Louis and his first nurse to make a stable mutual adjustment may also have influenced the prince's character formation, contributing to a sense that he harbored bad substances within himself and confirming anxiety about damaging the nurturing object.[39] These setbacks could have reinforced impressions of injury from the early surgical trauma.

Héroard managed to secure the banishment of Hotman—although her successor, sent by the queen, was not the candidate he sponsored. The new nurse, Antoinette Joron (Madame Bocquet), arrived at the end of December, 1601. Her intimacy with Louis would endure into his adulthood.

DOUNDOUN AND NURSING

Louis's relationship with this new nurse flourished—thanks partly, no doubt, to the fact that Héroard went on a short vacation soon after her arrival, and baby and nurse were allowed to establish a rapport without interference from him. When he returned in mid-February 1602, he was delighted to observe the baby's improvement. He found him "very cheerful" and reports that, as he stood over Louis's crib, "he watched me for a long time and smiled at me for a quarter of an hour without being disturbed."[40] The baby's ability to fix his gaze on a human face and to respond with a smile, though delayed, had finally appeared.[41]

By the time the king and queen paid a visit to their son at Saint-Germain en Laye in March 1602, they found him "big and white," his physical health seemingly restored. Nevertheless, various features of this household, which was the setting for Louis's early rearing, reinforced the groundwork for pathological development that had been laid in his first weeks and helped prepare the scene for new problems in his later maturation.

Doundoun, as Louis was to call his new nurse, was "docile" and "timid," according to Héroard.[42] She gave complete scope to her nursling's oral drives. "Within a period of seven or eight hours she changed the breast she offered him fifteen or twenty times," an account of the time related, "sucking him the better part of each day."[43] The nurse had no duties other than this and was always available on demand. In this basic nurturing function, therefore, Doundoun was the dauphin's mother. Once he had acquired the powers of speech, Louis himself expressed as much: "I wasn't in Mother's stomach; I was in Mother Doundoun's stomach. *That's* who my mother is!" To a half sibling seeking Doundoun's attention the dauphin shouted: "Get away from there! I don't want you to be next to my mother!" Héroard explains, "It was of his nurse" that he spoke.[44]

There was, however, a difference between this nurse and an ordinary mother: Joron's function was one of complete yielding and indulgence in these early months; she was Louis's possession. Furthermore, her monopolization by this firstborn child was unaffected by the regular arrival of new siblings in the nursery: she was Louis's exclusively. Restrictions and deprivations that the ordinary mother imposes on her baby were not part of Doundoun's role. Another female figure, Louis's governess, Madame de Montglat, was responsible for imposing restrictions on the prince and administering discipline. Like a real mother in her "bad" persona, this woman was in charge of all the children in the nursery and often had to impose deprivations on Louis for the protection or advantage of a growing number of siblings. Although she had little physical contact with Louis during these first months, later, when whippings were commanded by the king or orders issued to restrict Louis's activity, it was she who had them carried out.

A long nursing period had distinctive effects on Louis's behavior. Since he was not weaned until he was nearly twenty-five months old, his symbiotic relationship with his nurse-mother was maintained intact at the same time that he achieved several forms of physical autonomy—walking, talking, opening doors by himself, and so forth. His view of Doundoun as another person separate from himself was slow to develop. For a long time he regarded her as an adjunct to himself, a sort of "tail." In fact he sometimes used this word affectionately to name her. As a four-year-old sitting on her lap, "he caresses her, kisses her: 'Hey, my mad one, my ass [*cul*]! My mother Doundoun; it's Doundoun who gave me to suck!' "[45] He fantasizes himself as part of her—perhaps as her faeces: "I'll enter by your mouth, Doundoun; then I'll go in your stomach. You'll say you're pregnant and then you'll make me!"[46]

The characteristic need of babies for transitional objects to hold or to suck in place of the mother's skin, in order to fend off outside dangers or provide a bridge to meet them, was partly satisfied by the active young child through possession of Doundoun herself. Both before and after weaning he would cry to her, "Take me! Take me!" in moments of stress. He habitually fell asleep in her arms and was often taken into her bed on waking in the morning. Thus, weaning was for Louis less of a separation of the nurse from his own body than it usually is;[47] and she continued to be a refuge from the challenges and threats in the world beyond the enclosure formed by the two of them.

As Louis began to run about in garden or palace, he would fly into a rage if he discovered that Doundoun had not followed closely behind him. At the age of three-and-a-half it was exceptional for him to permit any distance between himself and his nurse. On one rare occasion, Héroard notes, "he even left his nurse behind—that being one of his greatest passions, to have her with him."[48] Once, when the dauphin finds himself separated from Doundoun in the garden, he is "angry, in a fury, beside himself—there is no way to pacify him." As he waits for her to return to him, he "conducts her with his eye . . . without saying a word, watching her coldly as she comes up, then when she is next to him," he exclaims: "'Ha! Next time, always follow me!'"[49]

It is against this stable background of intimacy with his nurse that others who were important to the dauphin in his first two years must be considered. Of these, Jean Héroard was the most significant in the earliest symbiotic "family" surrounding Louis, occupying a role different from that of the child's nurse—his "good" mother—and that of his governess—the "bad" Madame de Montglat.

HÉROARD AND "HATCHING"

For a man with Héroard's ambition to influence a future king, the position of first physician to the dauphin was ideal. Such an officer was required by law to "be always near" his master, "at dinner, supper, on awakening, retiring, as well as at other times."[50] A courtier later appreciated the significance of this access to a somnolent child. Héroard, he perceived, was able "from the moment of awakening" to imprint his "pretensions and advice on a mind not yet engaged in the activities of the day."[51]

During the first two years of Louis's life, Héroard was omnipresent, and his physical contact with the baby was extensive and intimate. He felt Louis's pulse every morning ("found the little bird," as the child later said), handled his head and body for temperature and other signs of health or illness, held his hand all night when he suffered from teething pains,[52] and monitored and controlled, as far as he could, the baby's intake of food and output of waste. In these months too he frequently prescribed and administered lotions, potions, unguents, compresses, and—regularly—suppositories. It was as though Louis's body belonged to him.[53]

In addition to dominating and manipulating Louis's physical process—functions sometimes fulfilled by a mother—Héroard mediated, as a mother does, between the maturing child's inner and outer worlds. Like a parent, he aimed to be protective or educational. He warded off dangers, real or imagined, to the dauphin's health and safety and instructed him on what precautionary measures to take.

As Héroard's journal unfolds, it becomes clear that Louis was dependent on the doctor's presence in important ways. Although Héroard's role was very different from the nurse's, like hers it resembled that of a mother who remains partly physically merged with her child. At an early age Louis reacted to the doctor's returns after absences as a baby does to the return of a mother who has temporarily abandoned him. Louis's separation from Héroard, as from Doundoun, was slow, painful, and incomplete.

The dauphin's progress in "hatching" from the symbiotic shell[54] provided by Héroard can be observed in the journal from day to day. When the baby is one-and-a-half, we find the two experimenting in dealing with separation. Héroard writes: "I pretend to leave, telling him, 'Goodbye.' He starts to cry. I stop. He is pacified." A year later boy and doctor are playing "individuation games" together—a kind of play frequently seen between babies and their mothers at this age. "He said to me," records Héroard, "'Mithter 'éouad, call me Mithter 'éouad and I'll call you Mithter doffin."[55]

Louis's close physical relationship with Héroard promoted not only dependence on the doctor but also defensive efforts to keep his physician at some distance from himself. Louis felt both an attraction and a revulsion toward Héroard. Very different from his seeking of solace through intimate physical contact with Doundoun was his keeping of his doctor at arm's length. This is illustrated by an occasion on which Héroard reports Louis's anger toward him. The child threatens to beat him up. The doctor counters, "Goodbye, Sir," adding, "I refuse to be beaten," and leaves the room. Sure of the three-year-old's inability to tolerate his departure, Héroard waits in the anteroom. He is soon rewarded when Louis sends for him and, "promising not to drive me away any more, gives me his hand for kissing."[56]

Only in desperation does Louis volunteer closer contact. In one instance he has scratched Héroard, who is holding the child to prevent his running after his nurse. The doctor pretends to be annoyed and says:

> "Sir, do as you please—I no longer belong to you." He is taken aback, as though stunned. Finally he says to Monsieur de Ventelet, "Have him come here; I'll embrace him." I come near, asking him, "Sir, what is it you plan to command me?" He comes to face me with open arms and does me the honor of hugging me . . . and crying, says to me, "Mithter 'éouad, I like you a lot. I don't want you to go away"—squeezes me while saying this. I promise him to serve him well. Right away his heart relaxes and his face cheers up.[57]

Though the dauphin's need for the doctor's presence was great—clearly he was in terror lest he lose an adjunct—normally he could tolerate it only so long as Héroard kept himself outside a certain boundary. Thus during one of Héroard's absences Louis takes his place, assigning to his own page the role of sick patient. Saying that "he is going to cure him, he takes up his pen to write."[58] In spite of the fact that Héroard often handled Louis's body, doctor and patient tacitly maintained that it was the services of the former's mind that were valuable. His healing powers were supposed to lie in his prescriptions and other writings.

Although there is no report that Louis ever said Héroard was *merde,* as he did of some other close supporters, the association of the doctor with the child's anal impulses may account for the quality of the prince's occasional outbursts of distaste for Héroard. This is confirmed by the testimony of a onetime tutor of Louis, Nicolas Vauquelin, who suggests that Héroard actually smelled bad to the child—a reason for Louis's holding him at a distance whenever he could. The former tutor advises the mother of Louis XIV that everyone attending a prince should have "a mouth as pure and clean as his mind so that he does not hesitate to draw near to His Majesty, nor the king to him—as I remember that the late king his father did to his first physician, about whom he often used to complain to me."[59]

Héroard was certainly not exempt from Louis's fury. The following exchange illustrates the vicissitudes of the boy's feelings by showing a kind of minuet he danced with the older man, and it suggests that such episodes may have occurred more frequently than Héroard cared to record. The physician has refused to allow the six-year-old prince to be served wine at dinner:

He begins to heat up with anger: "You're a snow man; you're ugly."

"Yes, Sir. But you will not drink wine because it will do you harm."

Upon this refusal he takes a knife and, all flushed with fury, threatens me with it. I tell him, "Adieu, Sir, I am going away for good." I leave and go into my room. He sends for me several times and after several refusals I come back. He says that he's very sorry for what he did and that he will never do it again. . . . Asks for something to drink. . . . He still wants wine. . . . I still resist him.

"I don't like you at all," [says Louis,] "You're a real snow man."[60]

"Sir, I'll write that to the king, or I'll go tell him about it."

"I don't care."

"Well then, Sir, since I'm no further use to you, goodbye. I'm really going to find the king." I leave. He sends for me several times. He comes to my room . . . enters. I greet him wordlessly. Finally he comes to me:

"I beg you, don't go away."

"Sir, what do you want me to do here with you? Since you don't want to do that which is for your health, I am of no further use."

"I won't do it any more" [says he]. . . .

And peace was made.[61]

No embrace concludes this successful negotiation: the doctor's presence is essential to the dauphin's well-being—but at arm's length.

Like the nurse, Héroard had no responsibility for explicitly disciplining

Louis in his earliest years. Not until the prince is nearly six does the diarist report that the king has "done him the honor to command him" to "reprove" the child "when he commits some fault."[62] Héroard's power lay in manipulation. From the beginning he offered moral judgments on Louis's actions and responded freely, on many topics, to questions put to him by the child or by those around him. In many silent ways, too, he reinforced in his patient traits that were prominent in himself. Recording an occasion when Louis was playing with books in Héroard's study, the doctor notes in his journal that the prince, only two-and-a-half, "never messed anything up" and always restored everything to its place "if there were some disorder."[63]

The journal—which Héroard first called his "register" and later his "collection" (*recueil*)—was itself an influence in Louis's life. Occasionally, when the child proposed some dubious course, Héroard deterred him by reminding him that the behavior would be recorded. But, more important, the diary shows how Héroard strove, both in writing and in real life, to hold the growing boy together and present him, to himself as well as to the outside world, in the best possible light. In the margins the doctor interprets, almost always favorably, traits of the dauphin illustrated in his text— for example, "admirable memory," "loves justice," "a taste for command," "humane." When Louis misbehaves—is stubborn or violently punitive, or throws a tantrum—Héroard emphasizes the child's feelings rather than dramatizing the misconduct: "extreme anger," irritable," or "they got the dauphin in such a bad humor that he almost burst from crying so hard."[64]

Other observers, by contrast, described the dauphin as a true enfant terrible. Even the apothecary charged by Héroard with recording Louis's behavior in the doctor's absence offered an objective description of one of Louis's bouts of arbitrary imperiousness as a two-year-old: "Wants to dine; dinner brought. Has it taken away; then brought back. Naughty; whipped good and hard."[65] Within his intimate circle, the dauphin's reputation grew for being an exceptionally stubborn child, anything but compliant with adult demands.

Héroard had a habitual explanation for Louis's recalcitrance: stubbornness or ill temper arose from "bad humors" inside the child. For example, the doctor records that the three-year-old Louis had been "peevish," talking back to his governess. When accused of stubbornness he denies his "fault," saying, "It's not I who is stubborn—it's . . .[another]." Héroard understands the cause as physical: Louis has been keeping bad things inside himself that he must be helped to be rid of. "[Louis] makes caca—tannish, much. Peevish, short-tempered as he always was when he retained such humors."[66]

Héroard concludes his rather peculiar work on the bones of the horse as follows: "Now, that we may restore everything to him [the horse] that we have ripped out of and dismembered from him," proceeding to list all the bones he has previously described.[67] Similarly, to put Louis back together, Héroard considered it necessary first to extract what was pernicious from within him. Extraction and "dismemberment" were followed by restitution—both through the doctor's "register" and in his prescriptions for what was to be ingested by the child.

Louis's growing stubbornness coincided with a growing obduracy to intrusions from Héroard. When the baby was in his eighth month, the doctor reports, "I put my little finger in his mouth" in order to take "out of him" a piece of bread he was chewing that had stuck to his palate. "He bit me, clenching his teeth firmly on my finger twice."[68]

It is clear that by the time Louis began to acquire the power of speech, food and excrement were often equivalent in his mind. Watching a little rabbit that had a blade of grass on its rear end he exclaimed, "Hey! It eats through its anus!" When he was getting dressed for the day he was asked, "Through what does one eat?" He replied, "Through there," showing, Héroard tells us, "his back end with his hand and smiling." When Doundoun tried to cajole him out of an angry mood by playfully offering him a nipple to suck he responded crossly, "Suck my ass!" When she asked him teasingly, "Little gallant, what did you eat for supper?" He replied smiling, "as though joking, 'Some *merde*.'"[69] A year later he had the following conversation with his nurse:

Louis: Give me a little rabbit. . . . I'll eat it.
Nurse: And when you've eaten it what will you do with it?
Louis: I'll make caca out of it.[70]

The following year found Madame de Montglat trying to discourage the little prince from the habit of eating *ordures* that he had picked from his nostrils and ears. When scolded he nonchalantly replied, "What? Is it poison?"[71] At the same time Louis showed that he resisted coprophagic inclinations: for a time he avoided other children who were "snotty" (*morveux*) and, according to Héroard, described everything as "scabrous" (*galeux*). The aversion extended, as might be expected, to money.[72] He became fastidious at the sight of sloppy behavior and slimy foods, showing increased finickiness at table and occasional reluctance to eat. His temperamental digestion impressed his doctor: "He had a very sensitive stomach opening," writes Héroard when Louis at the age of three-and-a-half vomits part of his supper.[73] He approved of the boy's discrimination, yet pressured him to eat what was good for him.

Héroard insisted not only on the types of food to be eaten but also on the order and quantities in which they were to be consumed. As the child's diet became more varied, the doctor's preoccupation with detailing the quantities of everything he ate, down to the exact numbers of mouthfuls, grains, or units of weight, became more and more apparent. He even specified how each item was seasoned and prepared. None of those who filled in for Héroard during his occasional brief absences was able to equal him in describing fully what the prince ingested. If Louis resisted his prescriptions from time to time, it was a losing battle.[74]

Héroard was equally specific in reporting and evaluating the appearance and form of the child's excretions. Here, however, his attempt at control was less effective: the little boy resisted the doctor's intrusions with growing persistence.

Except for its mention of the perpetual suppository, Courtaud's abridgement of Héroard's diary—the only form of the journal available for Louis's first three-and-a-quarter years—does not enable us to follow the beginnings of what was to become a prolonged struggle over bowel control. But it does show that during the child's first year he was given many preparations designed to promote evacuation and that he was often kept seated on a toilet chair for long periods without producing the desired results. It may have been this adamancy that prompted administration of the "first laxative medicine"—a purgative—when he was twenty-seven months old.[75]

At the beginning of Louis's fourth year (according to the original version of Héroard's diary) he was still unwilling to perform on the "pierced chair" provided for him. Instead he obliged his entourage to produce the "*bassin*" at a moment's notice. Here too his performance was the subject of argument and resistance: he "promised to go caca on his chair," Héroard writes, "in exchange for some chestnuts"—a fair exchange for faeces!—and "laughingly called for it in order to get them."[76] If the adults were hopeful at the promised bargain, they were disappointed on this occasion. In fact, it was more than two years before Louis delivered on his promise. Finally, when he was five-and-a-half-years old, Héroard reports the banner event: "Makes caca in the *bassin,* seated in his chair." A note in the margin emphasizes, "It is the first time."[77]

Louis often overtly resisted these adult attempts to toilet train him by refusing to give up, at the place and time desired, what others attempted to extract from him or by compelling them to accept his faeces when and where they did not wish to do so—defecating at inconvenient times or obliging others to clean him afterward. Less obviously, however, he expressed his obduracy to manipulation and intrusion into his digestive tract by developing traits and symptoms such as teeth gnashing, tongue chewing and biting, making staccato ("drum") sounds with his tongue against the palate or with other instruments, and stuttering to express the anal focus of conflicts going on inside him. "In his imagination he finds a drum in everything and makes of everything a drum," Héroard observes of the three-year-old. Louis himself seemed half-consciously to have recognized the anal significance of these compulsions. On being reproved for gnashing his teeth, he explained: "It's because I want to make caca." Scolded for farting, he replied: "It's my ass that spoke."[78] His most conspicuous symptom, a severe stutter, seems to be in part a legacy of conflicts connected with this cathexis of the anal zone.

It is two days after the administration of the first purgative that Héroard explicitly notes this speech impediment, which was severe from the outset. A few days later, although the dauphin replied to one question promptly, "as he used to do," when he asked for his drumsticks the sounds that came out instead of the word needed were "a a a a a a." He became vexed at not being able to articulate it—"can't say it"—then finally succeeded.[79] Héroard mentions the stutter frequently in the next few days but rarely thereafter; he never again reproduces it in this way—at least, not so far as his transcriber shows us. It did not, however, abate. A tutor describes how Louis, unable to pronounce a word during a lesson, "grabbed his face with his hands,"[80] and a witness of the adult Louis describes him as "so extreme a stutterer that he would sometimes hold his tongue outside his mouth a good while before he could speak so much as one word,"[81] a picture that is consistent with Héroard's single description.

The inability to release words except with the explosive staccato rhythm of the stutterer was but the most obvious residue of Louis's anal phase of development. It is clear that, as he grew older his conflict over releasing or retaining his faeces colored many other aspects of his relationship with the world surrounding him.

BELONGINGS: PEOPLE AND THINGS

At first only by his actions and later also by his words, Louis showed that he assimilated objects around him to faeces. These then became parts of himself, to be treasured and cared for or expelled or cut off. Such objects were *"les siens"* (possessions), whether things or persons—property, servants, and kin—that belonged to him or owed him obedience. Salient among the persons cast in this role were soldiers. From the time that the prince first beat out a marching cadence in his cradle, imitating the drum with his tongue on his palate, he was passionately interested in marshaling, arranging, and commanding troops. As a baby, he played with his silver toy soldiers or chessmen while seated on his "little seat" for long periods at a time while silently resisting adult demands for toilet performance. From early childhood these toys, as well as real soldiers, played a significant part in his imagination.

The infant dauphin was attended by personal guards, and throughout childhood he periodically developed an infatuation for one or another of them. Héroard notes that even before Louis could walk he would anxiously look behind himself to make sure that his precious soldiers were still in his suite.[82] "Everything he sees and handles are his soldiers," observes the doctor of the three-year-old. Louis's associations of soldiers with his anus is obvious by this time, as this typical fantasy suggests: "He is playing with bean pods of various colors. He calls them his 'so'ders.' He lines them up, makes them come and go. Some of them drop into his bed. . . . He finds [them] under his back end. 'Hey, they want to kiss my ass! They're the kiss-ass so'ders!' He plays on, talking to himself—all war talk."[83]

Collapse of the child's resistance to adult demands was sometimes signaled by his giving up precious possessions, as when he decides to "'send all these infantrymen to Papa,' speaking with ardor." Héroard continues: "He loaded my hands with all his chessmen, one after another, 'to take to Papa!'" At the age of five, imagining himself going to war, "he dreams while walking about, his hands on his back end."[84]

Louis's interest in firearms was as great as his interest in soldiers. Bribing the three-year-old prince with a promise of a musket, Héroard comments: "It was a means to pacify him in his most difficult moods, so great was his inclination for everything to do with the métier of war—men as well as instruments. . . . He is highly drawn to that profession. All his talk, his songs, his actions, consist of drums, soldiers, arms, and war."[85] As a boy of eight, Louis "plays with little round lead bullets, which he makes roll the length of the canal of a flat taper holder, saying they are soldiers."[86] Similarly, bullet-shaped objects are soldiers; he "enjoys playing with the rosary—everything on it is a soldier."[87] Henri IV recognized his son's predilection, writing to the duc de Beaumont at the time of Louis's fourth birthday: "It seems that he has a mind more given to arms than to anything else."[88] For Louis, anal processes were aggressive, like using firearms. Héroard records him farting "near the nose" of an attendant. "Sir, you must fire your musket again," said the servant. "But it's not loaded," said Louis. "Sir, what is it loaded with?" "With *merde,*" the dauphin replied.[89]

Louis's passion for military matters was certainly approved of by his doctor, who considered preoccupation with martial arts suitable for a future king. But it was less through his manifest approval than through his unconscious influence that Héroard shaped the interests Louis was to show in later life. Both conscious encouragement of military concerns and a tacit stress on different matters are revealed in an exchange that took place as the four-and-a-half-year-old dauphin watched his doctor record his deeds for the day: "'This book, Sir,' I tell him, 'is your pissing history.' He replies, 'No!' 'It is your defecating history.' He replies, 'No!' 'It is the history of your arms.' 'Yes!' he replies."[90]

Héroard's persistent intrusion contributed to the anal focus of much of the child's imagery and attention and evoked the symptoms Louis showed. In his *Institution du prince* the doctor discusses the need for the instructor to empathize with his pupil, commenting: "One must stammer with little children."[91] In fact, his was the first of the influences that were to make a stutterer of Louis.

During the months in which Louis came to rely on his nurse for food and comfort and to expect his doctor to hover at his side, monitoring his digestion and supplying support, he was also subjected to powerful stimuli from other persons around him. Most significant among these were some of his close kin, with whom he formed early and important links that had permanent effects on his development. Before his first year was over, several of Louis's relatives had begun to play crucial roles in his maturation.

CHAPTER THREE

Becoming Papa's Little Valet: Temptations and Fears

> *The king says to him, "My son, I want you to make*
> *a baby with the infanta."*
> *"Ho! ho! No, Papa."*
> *"I want you to make a little dauphin like yourself."*
> *"No, if you please, not, Papa," he says, taking his hat in his*
> *hand and making a bow.*[1]

The procreativity of kings and their heirs has always been a central concern of their families and subjects. In the family headed by Henri IV and Marie de Medici the frequent appearance of new offspring did not lessen this concern, for the previous dynasty had been extinguished in the space of thirty years by the deaths of Henri II and all four of his childless sons. For the legitimate Bourbon line, the dauphin Louis's fertility was second in importance only to the continued generation of male successors by Marie and Henri.[2] Much depended on the sexual inclinations and progenitive powers of the baby born in September 1601.

It was customary to admire the phallus of a newborn prince:

> Madame la duchesse de Bar, sister of the king, who was looking at the parts, so well formed, of this beautiful body, having cast her gaze on those that made him be dauphin, turned toward Madame de Panjas, her lady-in-waiting, and remarked to her that he was well equipped. These words were received with a laughter that carried them to the ears of the king, who was with the queen.[3]

This attention to the parts that made Louis "be dauphin" became more intense as the weeks and months passed.

ENCOURAGING GENITALITY

In Louis's first year many of those around him stimulated his interest in his genitals by tickling, teasing, or seductive behavior and suggestive words.

The baby was responsive to this stimulation, as a typical experience at nine months reveals: "He takes pleasure and bursts out laughing when the maid who dresses him wiggles his cock with the end of her finger." The king's mistress made less innocent advances: "He has himself put on his nurse's bed, where she plays with him, often putting her hand up under his dress." Exhibition was encouraged, and some courtiers apparently amused themselves by training the one-year-old Louis to offer his *guillery* instead of his hand for kissing.[4] Masturbation was regarded with complacency—the baby's pleasure in his own genitals apparently indicated a healthy interest. Héroard records of the twenty-two-month-old: "While nursing he scratches his 'merchandise,' erect and hard as wood. He often took great pleasure in handling it and in playing with the tip of it with his fingers."[5]

The courtiers' delight was greatest when Louis seemed to exhibit heterosexual aims. They were eager to demonstrate them to Henri, who appeared just as eager to have them confirmed: "They had His Majesty shown the caresses he had already given Tinette Clergeon . . . chambermaid of Mademoiselle his Nurse, the king himself having had her approach, and presenting her to him."[6]

A few weeks after this Héroard reported the one-year-old's response to the visit of a nobleman and his young daughter: "He laughed hard at him, pulled up his dress and showed his cock to him; but above all to his daughter. Because, while holding it and laughing his little laugh, he shook his whole body, people remarked that he understood what it was all about." The visit of a little girl later in the day inspired a similar demonstration in his crib, performed "with such ardor that he was beside himself," as Héroard notes. "He lay down at the wrong end to show it to her."[7]

Many at court took it upon themselves to enlighten the prince on "what it was all about." Marriage and copulation with the Spanish infanta, who was born about the same time as Louis, were often the imaginary focus for his supposed genital aims. Before Louis is a year old, Héroard reports: "He listens to stories that a lady-in-waiting told him about the infanta, that he will sleep with her. He laughs at that." A few months later he is more knowledgeable: "Where is the infanta's darling?" Héroard asks the fourteen-month-old boy. "He puts his hand on his cock." By the age of three he knows more clearly what is expected of him. Héroard tells us that in bed Louis "crosses his legs, asking, 'Will the infanta do this?'" A lady-in-waiting answers: "'Sir, when you go to bed together she will put her legs in that position.'" The prince replies "promptly and cheerfully, 'And I, I will put them like *that!*' spreading his legs apart with his hands."[8]

Since Héroard confined his descriptions to aspects of the dauphin's behavior that he had observed directly and described what Louis saw only when the child's reaction was clear, it is impossible to know for certain whether the prince witnessed sexual intercourse in his first two or three years. However, it seems likely that he did. He was often taken into the bed of a married couple and may have watched coitus between his nurse and her husband or, more probably, between his governess and the baron de Montglat. Observing a Judith doll belonging to his sister lying on a miniature Holofernes "with its head separate"—a toy with rather ominous suggestions—the three-year-old asked, "Shouldn't the woman be underneath the man?"[9]

Considering Henri's sexual exhibitionism, Louis may even have witnessed intercourse between his parents—or between the king and one of his many women. A frightening dream he related to Héroard at the age of six-and-a-half suggests an early experience. In it he saw a "man dressed in white" (possibly a memory of undergarments or nightclothes worn by his father or another man in bed[10]) who was a "*sot*," a word designating not only a foolish person but also, in early modern usage, one deceived by a woman.[11]

It is more likely still that Louis witnessed, at an early age, intercourse between servants in his household. Furnishings were sparse, even in the royal establishment, and most beds (except those for the highly privileged) were used by several persons, often by day as well as at night. Attendants slept where they could—under the beds of the great, on pallets laid down in odd places—and privacy was minimal. As a baby, Louis was regularly guarded at night by women who slept on straw mats on the floor.[12]

Héroard seems to have suspected that Louis had observed the primal scene; he recounts how the dauphin, not yet one-and-a-half, reacts excitedly to play between a young lady of the court and his governess's husband, who is pursuing her and spanking her on the rump. The girl "cries out loudly; the dauphin . . . points them out to everyone." A little later, Louis takes the role of Montglat with a younger child: "[He] plays with little Marguerite, kisses her, hugs her, drags her down, throws himself on her, jumping with his whole body and gnashing his teeth . . . and gets so warmed up that he is transported with delight, having been a good quarter of an hour . . . flinging himself with abandon upon her, like a person who understood the joke."[13] The teeth-gnashing in this scene suggests a sadistic interpretation of adult lovemaking, as do those anal associations that had become so prominent in Louis's mental life.

On another occasion Louis imagined intercourse with the infanta, telling Héroard:

> "She will sleep with me and I'll make a little baby for her."
> "Sir, how will you do that?"
> "With my cock," he says shyly, in a whisper.
> "Sir, will you kiss her a lot?"
> "Yes, like that," he says, flinging his body down with abandon, his face against the bolster.[14]

Whether or not these episodes show that Louis had witnessed sexual encounters, it seems certain that by the time he was three-and-a-half he "understood the joke." Héroard reports that, in response to Madame de Montglat's question "What will the bride do?" (on her wedding night), Louis "puts his pike between his legs and raising one end shook his buttocks."[15]

ELISABETH

Contributing to the dauphin's sexual enlightenment was the birth of his sister Elisabeth on December 20, 1602. A few months after Louis's first birthday, just at the time when he was beginning to explore the palace on foot, the little "Madame" was installed in an apartment next to his. She was his first full sibling, the only other child who was, like himself, "from the stomach of Maman." Louis apparently recognized the significance of this and regarded her as a sure ally against Henri's other children, especially since, being a girl, she could not become his rival. He was her master, and she learned to call him "Little Papa." "One day," Héroard told Louis, "everything she possesses will be your gift to her."[16]

The prince was often rough and demanding with his siter, but she became his adoring slave, willing to surrender everything she had to him. At table, for example, "he asks for Madame's dessert, which she pushes over to him right away, saying, 'Take it, Little Papa!' . . . She was so happy when she could oblige him."[17]

The relationship of brother and sister was reinforced by their strong physical resemblance. Contemporary portraits show a striking likeness between the two, and Héroard notes that Elisabeth "resembled Monsieur le Dauphin greatly."[18] Much of their affectionate play entailed acting out their imagined adult roles as bride and bridegroom of foreign partners. Thus, Elisabeth was a stand-in for Louis's infanta. Visiting her in her room one evening, Louis heard someone say, "There is Madame, who will one day go to Spain or England; we shall see her no more." The dauphin protested: "I don't want her to go—I want her to stay here." As he played a game of waiting upon her at table, he said: "She's my little wife." Héroard approved: "There never was anything as nice as that."[19]

Their father encouraged the intimacy of the two children, perhaps regarding it as good training for their future conjugal roles. During the summer of 1605, for example, he has them both undressed and put to bed with him, "entirely naked, where they kiss each other, chatter, and give much pleasure to the king." Héroard continues:

> The king asks him, "My son, where is the infanta's package?"
> He shows it, saying, "It has no bone, Papa!" Then, as it was stiffening a bit, "Now it has one—it does have sometimes."[20]

Louis's sister was in many ways a mirror image of himself, but in one crucial respect she was different: she lacked the organ so highly valued by him and by everyone at court.

When Elisabeth came to the nursery, Louis had ample opportunity to examine her anatomy. He was often present while she was being dressed and, although he could not yet talk, he had daily occasion to note the absence in her of the precious *guillery*. Only after he was able to speak, did he show directly how he coped with his observation of a lack that was especially threatening in one otherwise so like himself: he denied it. Thus, at three-and-a-half, he plays with the two-year-old girl as she lies in her cradle, "kisses her, hugs her, troubles himself to help her pass the time." Returning to his room at bedtime "he calls for his pot" and jokes:

> "Ho! Ho! Mr. Pot, there you are! I think I'll piss in you!"
> Then he says that his cock is not like Madame's.
> "Mine is pointed," he says.[21]

In the following winter and spring, however, he already gave signs that he was not entirely oblivious to the awful truth. He began, on occasion, to be afraid of Elisabeth, to avoid her or attack her. As early as the preceding June, Héroard recorded a clue as to the reason for this change: "As they were taking Madame to make Ka Ka they pulled up her dress. He sees this and begins to yell, 'Ha! Take her away! I refuse to see Madame's ass! Take her away!'" The following November Louis caused consternation in the nursery by injuring Elisabeth with a spoon that he threw at her. Héroard's notes in the margin from about this time comment on the change in the dauphin's behavior: "aversion to Madame"; "throws out Madame"; "great aversion." On one occasion Louis would "really have injured her severely" with the blow of a racquet had her nurse not parried his assault.[22]

From Héroard's description it is clear that Louis's "aversion" was a response to specific fears, as this December entry testifies:

> His nurse, playing, lays him down on her lap, pulls up his clothes and pats him on the buttock with her hand. He laughs at this. Madame slaps him gently with hers; he gets up.
> "Ha!" he says angrily, "I don't want Madame to hit me!"
> To appease himself he spanks Madame's buttock, but Madame is right away back on his. There he is, instantly furious, and trying to hit her. One could never persuade him to let Madame do this, even as a game.

When on another occasion he was persuaded to lend his sister the bottle out of which he was drinking, he expressed the fear that she was going to break it.[23]

Soon after, when he tried to strike Elisabeth with his pike as she entered the room, Héroard records:

> Madame de Montglat scolds him, asking, "Sir, why did you want to hit Madame?"
> "I'm annoyed with her because she wanted to eat my pear."

But, Héroard admits,

> These were made-up excuses. The almoner asks him the same thing.
> . . . He answers:
> "Because I'm afraid of her."
> "Sir, why is that?"
> "Because she's a girl."[24]

Only a short time after this last discussion Louis articulated an observation he must have made as a one-year-old. In March he conceded, as Héroard tells us, "that the infanta has a little vagina like Madame's." He made the disclosure "in a whisper," the doctor writes, "ashamed to say it out loud."[25] Despite Héroard's interpretation, however, Louis's expressions rarely seem to convey shyness or shame. Neither as a child nor as an adult was he sensitive to the dangers of humiliation or often exposed to ridicule. Appearances meant little to him, possessions much. And the most prized of these possessions was also the most endangered.

The arrival of Elisabeth when Louis was fifteen months old did a great deal to stimulate both his pride in and his fear for his precious organ.[26] But even before the birth of his sister another highly stimulating force entered Louis's life—his father, the king. Already a semilegendary figure to his people, Henri IV was never to inspire more emotion in anyone than in his baby son at Saint-Germain.

HENRI AND TEMPTATION

Louis's father first became a frequent visitor to the dauphin's household in the summer of 1602. His rekindled personal interest in his son was signaled later that year in a letter written from Saint-Germain to his minister, Villeroy: "I found my son entirely changed since I last saw him. He is in the best possible shape—not recognizable."[27]

The king's customary powerful effect on his subjects was even stronger on Louis. The dauphin became infatuated with Henri, who was delighted and responded sensually, encouraging the child's devotion in a way that was alternately tender and teasing. Having dined with the king, Louis "cries on seeing him leave." Later, returning from the hunt, "the king caresses him, kisses him, kisses his breast." But, at about the same time, "he meets the king, who pretends not to see him. He cries; the king turns back, goes to him and embraces him."[28]

As Louis began to walk on his own, he followed his father as best he could or had himself carried or led in search of him. "On a walk he meets the king, laughs at him and holds out his arms; goes into the queen's bed chamber. They have him search for the king in the queen's bed; not finding him he gets very angry. He goes into the king's bedroom, who puts him to bed with him, with infinite caresses."[29]

The king alternated between demonstrations of fondness and of force toward the dauphin. On one occasion the eighteen-month-old boy was treated to a romp in bed with the king and queen. Afterward, waiting on the king at table, "he wants to cry; the king threatens him with the whip; he is calmed down."[30] At about this time, a rise in Louis's inner conflicts was outwardly indicated by the first appearance of his stutter.[31]

At the age of twenty-five months the dauphin was weaned. This milestone coincided with another: his first whipping.[32] The king was a strong believer in the salubrious effects of this form of punishment, writing to Louis's governess, "I wish and command you to whip him every time he is stubborn or does something bad . . . there is nothing in the world that will do him more good."[33]

Héroard does not usually specify the acts of "stubbornness" *(opiniâtreté)* for which the dauphin was first whipped, in the autumn and winter of 1603. But his increasingly frequent references to this trait coincide with Louis's growing resistance to toilet-training demands. The first administration of laxative medicine—a rhubarb infusion—was apparently ineffective, since during the following days additional doses were prescribed, and the baby's "liver" and stomach were rubbed with oils and ointments as he lay in bed at night. In spite of Héroard's tactics, the child's "bad humors" and resistance to control persisted, as in scenes like the following: "The king comes to see him and plays with him gaily. They got the dauphin in such a bad humor that he almost burst from crying and everything was in such great confusion until six o'clock that I didn't have the courage to notice what he did, except that he wanted to hit everyone, crying incessantly; whipped for a long time afterward."[34]

As Henri's sexual stimulation of Louis continued, the dauphin, who had begun to talk plainly, stuttered more and more. Héroard reports: "The dauphin stutters in speaking; it is observed that this has been so since two days ago when the king, lying in bed, amused himself by having him banter with the little Frontenac boy, who was stuttering."[35] Louis's stutter accompanied his physical resistance to anal intrusions from Héroard. It could only have been intensified by his anxiety over whippings and by this exciting play in bed with the king and another child.

In his third year, Louis emerged as a headstrong, imperious child, prone to tantrums and sudden rages in which he attacked his servants and companions. At the same time, he sometimes submitted to whippings with apparent enjoyment.

Since no servant wanted to be personally responsible for chastising the difficult child, he was doubtless told from the start that his whippings were commanded by his father and were therefore to be welcomed rather than resisted. Moreover, they were administered to Louis as he lay in a prone position. He would be "seized by the chambermaids," often soon after he awoke, "taken and laid down on the bed and whipped." The bundle of switches that was applied to his bare or covered buttocks was called the *verges*—a word that also means penis. Thus the whippings recalled the sexual advances made to Louis by Henri's mistress. Not surprisingly, he seems to have enjoyed them in the same way, as is evident in this example: "Awakens at eight, starts out in a bad humor; cries, is whipped, puts his hand on his back end, saying, 'Tickle me! Tickle me!' Cries out of spite, pacified."[36]

FEARS

During 1604 Louis not only learned to take pleasure in submitting to punishment but also experienced a surge in his active genital strivings. He became gallant toward his sister and developed an interest in other girls and ladies of the court. He was delighted to be allowed to wear masculine dress such as spurs and boots, and he proudly showed his nurse the *brayette* he had been given to wear, in the style of the Swiss guards, to protect his penis.[37]

Yet the dangers presented by his masculinity were also impressed upon him by many of those around him. Castration threats, implicit and explicit, were widespread in this court, where the royal heir's phallus was the focus of so much concern.

Reluctant to discipline the dauphin, who had become a holy terror, courtiers often tried to win his compliance by threatening intervention by outside persons or forces. The implicit threats to his organ were especially noticeable on occasions when terror was casually invoked to solve routine problems of discipline. Does the child give trouble to those trying to comb his hair? "They have the *charbonnier* come to frighten him."[38] Does he wake up inconveniently early? The *lavandier* is sent for to carry him off. Is he slow to rise? Bongars (the mason with frightening pincers) will come in, Héroard tells him, and "take away" his stockings—a threat to which Louis responds by crying, "Get me up!" Is he unwilling to eat his soup? The huge cook enters to tell him that he has put the head of La Barge, a court page, in the casserole and will do the same to the prince himself if he remains obdurate.[39]

Is he irritable? "They have the mason come," clanking his dreaded tentacles, in search of "stubborn boys." "Hey! Don't let him come in!" cries the terrified child.[40]

Louis feared the *lavandier* and the *charbonnier* because they might put him in the sacks they carried over their shoulders and take him off. Once, after Madame Héroard had given him a little knife to be worn on a ribbon around his neck, he had an agitating dream and cried out in his sleep: "Take away my sack—I don't want what you've given me."[41] This may suggest a struggle not to succumb to the invitation to become like a girl, who has, instead of the precious *guillery,* a "sack" or receptacle.

Bogeymen were ubiquitous. To ward off a host of dangers at bedtime, the four-year-old prayed, "Guard me from all my enemies, visible and invisible." Louis added ("on his own," Héroard notes approvingly), "and from Bongars and Thomas . . . from the one-eyed one, from the hunchback, from the *charbonnier* . . . !"[42] The child could well have added many more forces—non-human as well as human—that had been cited to intimidate him when he was "stubborn," "naughty," or merely refractory.

Héroard was prominent among those who pointed out hazards, and the means for escaping them, to the dauphin. Thus he mediated in explaining an act of God: when Louis was informed that lightning had struck near the cradle of an infant half brother, the doctor told him that this was because the room was "full of stubborn people."[43]

Above all, however, the first physician used fear to develop in Louis habits deemed necessary to the health and integrity of the dauphin's body. Every output and input carried a risk—either the loss of something healthful or the ingestion of something harmful—on which Héroard considered himself an expert.

On the loss side, the doctor was attentive not only to defecation, as we have seen, but also to all the other means by which the body's contents might escape. Compared with his contemporary professional colleagues, he was very conservative in prescribing enemas, purgatives, and bleedings. He thought of himself as manipulating with "gentle" strategies.[44] To him, any loss of body fluids was a serious matter. For example, when Louis cut himself slightly at the age of fifteen months, the doctor observed in the margin: "First blood to come out of him."[45] When the three-year-old dauphin pricked his finger and shed a few drops of blood, Héroard perceived him to be severely shaken and to become faint.[46] Hérard went so far in his conservationist attitude, according to one hostile contemporary, that he opposed sweating and nose blowing.[47] When Louis "spits on the ground in the queen's garden" at the age of three, Héroard noted in the margin, "First time he has spit."[48]

As for ingestion, Louis used to consult his doctor before sampling any new food that appeared on his table, and Héroard was usually ready with definite suggestions about how to eat it without incurring harm. He felt, for example, that there was a risk if certain amounts of bread did not accompany certain quantities of other foods, if drinking and eating were not ordered in precise ways, and so on.

Louis was encouraged by his caretakers to fear being eaten as well as eating improperly. One morning he witnessed a wolf hunt, actually seeing the wolf "taken right in front of him." He commented in his still-babyish pronunciation, "They put a big thick thtick in his mouf." At bedtime that night, Héroard told him playfully of the wolf, "For dinner he ate two stubborn children." Louis asked, "Who had him come?" Héroard replied that Bongars had called him. "Bongars?" Louis asked anxiously. "Tell him I'm not stubborn any more."[49]

Louis sometimes associated the threat of being attacked by wild animals with staying out in the "*serain*"—the evening mist. In the following scene this danger from the *serain* is used to get the child to come indoors at twilight: "He wants to play on the tennis court. They tell him that the *serain* was in the net. La Barge pretends to have been bitten by it." The dauphin's reaction is instantaneous: he leaves the scene hastily, "half-stunned," according to Héroard.[50]

It seems that at this stage of Louis's development, his fear of attack by wild animals focused on the anal region. One morning after excited talk about killing a boar, servants tried to subdue him by making him fear the "*venelle*," a word he had never heard. The dauphin's terror, as Héroard describes it, seems disproportionate:

> He thought it was some new kind of beast.
> "Hey! My God!" I say, "There it is!"
> He runs instantly to his nurse. . . .
> "Oh!" says he, "You frightened me."
> "Sir," say I, "It's grabbed you by the fanny [*cul*]."
> "Eek! My God! Take it off me! Take it off me!"
> His nurse, pinching him slightly on the buttocks, says, "There it is,
>   Sir, taken off."
> "Kill it!"[51]

These fears of bodily harm were often explicitly associated with the loss of his penis. Even the beloved Doundoun warned the child of dangers to this organ. "Sir," she once said, in an obvious allusion to the advances of the king's mistress, the Marquise de Verneuil, "don't let anyone touch your nipples or your cock—they'll cut them off." Héroard noted that the child was suddenly anxious when the marquise subsequently approached him. "He remembered," wrote the doctor.[52] Héroard himself, the authority on threats to health, gave casual warnings of the same kind. Once, when Louis suggested that a too-long ribbon on his coat be trimmed, the doctor remarked, "Then, Sir, we must cut off your cock." The child demurred, "Oh no! It's not too long—it's short!" On another occasion, when he feared the child might slip and fall against a croquet mallet, he suddenly announced, "Sir, your cock is gone." Louis answered, "What? Isn't it there?" anxiously "showing" the doctor "the place for it." Héroard's explanation for this frightening announcement is that, "he was leaning against the handle, and I wanted to scare him about it."[53]

CONFLICTING PASSIONS

As Louis's anxieties about his penis mounted, his relationship with his father grew more intense. During the summer and fall of 1604, his relations with Henri came to resemble a stormy love affair. The little boy was alternately warmly affectionate and furiously angry with his father. Héroard records this response as Henri returns from the hunt:

> He goes running with open arms to meet the king, who blanches with happiness and pleasure, kisses and hugs him for a long time, and leads him into his office [cabinet]. Takes him for a walk holding him by the hand, changing hands as he turns without saying a word. . . . Can't let go of the king nor the king of him. . . . The king extremely happy.

But the next day, when "the king wants to force him to kiss him," Louis's behavior is very different:

> Here he is in such a bad humor that he is whipped for it by His Majesty. He defends himself, scratches him on the hands, grabs at his beard. The king asks him, showing him the *verges*, "My son, who is that for?" He replies angrily, "For *you!*" The king was obliged to laugh. This lasted more than three-quarters of an hour, the king having picked him up and put him down several times. The king leaves. "I want Papa," he says. The king returns, kisses him.[54]

While Henri could on occasion blanch with pleasure at his son's infatuation with him or be "obliged to laugh" at the little boy's fearless anger, he could also oppose Louis's masculine assertions by variously teasing, deprecating, or physically maltreating him, often capriciously. At table, for example, the king once threw meat juice in the face of the two-and-a-half-year-old child. Héroard noted that, although Louis started to cry, he "would have been further mistreated" had the king not been restrained by a companion.

A more critical scene occurred at Fontainebleau at the height of the dauphin's pride in his new masculine attire. Booted, "like the king," and carrying his little drum ("one of his greatest delights"), Louis went to show himself to his father:

The king says, "Take off your hat." He has trouble getting it off; the king takes it off him. He gets mad at that; then the king takes away his drum and his sticks; that was still worse. "My hat! My drum! My sticks!" To spite him the king puts the hat on his own head. "I want my hat!" The king whacks him on the head with it. That makes him furious, and the king with him. The king takes him by the wrists and raises him in the air, arms extended as on a cross. "Hey! You're hurting me! Hey! My drum! My hat!" . . . Carried off . . . bursting with anger. . . . Cried a long time without subsiding . . . finally whipped . . . crying, "Hey! Whip me up higher!"[55]

In this confrontation Louis's self-assertion and rage were dangerous to himself. He finally controlled them only by turning them against himself, winning out in the end by deriving pleasure from a punishment he himself commanded.

Such a pattern became habitual. After this scene Héroard noticed increased lassitude and passivity in the dauphin's behavior. The doctor writes that at the sight of Henri, Louis "no longer wears that bold, gay expression he used to have."[56]

More generally, the child's customary hyperactivity began to alternate with bouts of enervation. Héroard had been proud of Louis's remarkable energy, noting how at tea time he took his repast standing, because "between the time he got up in the morning until he went to sleep . . . he didn't sit down except at dinner and supper."[57] Although this observation was made in April 1604, as early as February of that year Héroard had noticed a lapse into fatigue after a contest with the king: "He wanted to leave the room against the king's wishes. The king threatens him with the whip, but he is stubborn . . . carries on. The king commands that he be whipped." Louis is enraged—"wanted to hit and scratch"—and is led back by Henri, who "handles him roughly." Afterward the child "falls asleep in the arms of his nurse," although his supper is still on the table untouched.[58]

After another day of stormy scenes with the king in which whippings alternate with passionate reconciliations, "the king returns, kisses him." Héroard continues: He is pacified, but now and then releases great sighs. . . . At mass he leans against his chair like a tired person.[59] Louis would sometimes even drop off to sleep unexpectedly at inappropriate times or ask to be put to bed early.

Waking one morning soon after the hat episode, Louis "enjoys being in bed, says nothing of getting up, unlike his usual habit . . . occasionally has the expression of one slightly dazed." On his way to chapel three weeks later, he turns back: "He says he is tired," Héroard writes. "Never before did he say he was tired."[60]

Sometimes Louis remained inactive on purpose, thereby revealing one explanation for his apparent lack of energy—inertia and apathy countered angry feelings toward his father too dangerous to express directly. In one instance, instead of rushing as usual to the windows with everyone else to see Henri go off to the hunt, he was "firm" and "resolute" in remaining where he was. Héroard silently supported him by staying with him.[61]

In the midst of Louis's intermittent lassitude, his former high level of physical activity reasserted itself sporadically. Now, however, it often seemed involuntary. At table, Héroard noted, "he always jiggles his legs or his hands or his head, often even while he is drinking."[62] These repetitive movements seem inappropriate to the stimuli that apparently triggered them.

On some occasions Héroard was aware that such movements represented the dauphin's anger, as when Louis, whose governess had compared him unfavorably with Elisabeth, had a temper tantrum—"a furious rage"—that lasted more than an hour-and-a-half. Prevented from attacking his sister, he was removed to his bedroom, where he "goes back and forth, extremely agitated and trembling all over with rage, in body and speech."[63] The repetitive movements of his body thus seem to have the same meaning as his stuttering.

Similar fury may have underlain Louis's apparently harmless, involuntary movements, such as those at table, where "he is always in motion while he eats . . . tapping his feet." Héroard interpreted such energetic action as a favorable sign in the young prince, as in the remark that "he can't retire, so active and avid for exercise is he."[64] It is as if the doctor—recognizing that Louis's only alternatives to overt anger were passivity or purposeless motion—shared the pateint's efforts to defend himself against relapsing into a passive state.[65]

Yet Héroard noted that often the dauphin was submissive and compliant when Henri appeared after the early scenes of conflict. "Who is the dauphin?" the child would be asked. "Papa's little valet," he would respond, serving his father obediently. To Henri's commands he would reply, "At your service," and would comply with alacrity. When the king, playing catch with his son, hit him on the forehead with a ball, Louis, instead of protesting, "almost weeps, restrains himself out of respect for the king."[66]

It seems as though the king had become too dangerous an object for Louis's rage; the dauphin could express his anger at his father only indirectly. For example, he could make his violent feelings explicit toward the husband of his nurse, "Maman" Doundoun. The day after being hit with the ball by his father, he heard Doundoun's husband threaten her with a beating. He responded furiously, "showing him the scissors he was holding and saying, 'And I'll castrate you; here's what I'll use to chop off your penis!'"[67]

Another indirect expression of anger toward his father occurred upon

Louis's return to Saint-Germain after the dramatic hat scene at Fontaine-bleau, which he reenacted in a morning ritual: "He goes to bid good morning to the portraits of the king and queen that hang in his bedroom. Holds in his hands his white velvet cushion; puts it on his head using it as a hat. Takes if off, saying, 'Bonjou' Papa, Bonjou' Mama!' All of a sudden, throws the cushion to the floor."[68]

The child's anger could also take a somatic form, such as the bodily symptoms of aggression that accompany his words in the following episode. Louis had been invited to dine with the king. Héroard writes that at the meal the dauphin was "very nice, obedient, timid, and respectful," and a note in the margin reads, "very compliant with the king." But, "immediately after the king left," the doctor reports, Louis "asked to 'make caca.'" At supper later he lacked appetite and told Héroard, by way of explanation: "'My cock hurts me.' Then pissed . . . pulse a little fast. . . . Didn't want to say his prayers; 'I want to say the *Sancta*, I don't want to say, "Our Father." '"[69] The compliance and timidity that Louis showed his father in person seem to conceal a rage that was subsequently turned against people or things representing Henri or against his own body.

The ordinary ambition of a little boy to become like a father who is admired and loved as well as feared was made exceptionally problematic for Louis. It was, moreover, repeatedly discouraged by Henri, who rarely lost an opportunity to make his son feel weak in comparison with himself. To the little boy who sought to emulate him, the king said, according to Héroard:

> "My son, you're a little calf."
> "And you too, Papa" (because he thought he was the same as the king).
> "*I'm* a bull!"[70]

Henri could be pettily childish in demonstrating his superiority over his small son. As Louis shoots a bow and arrow in the garden,

> The king takes it in order to shoot.
> "Papa, do you want me to show you?"
> The king says to him, "I know how to shoot better than you."
> "Excuse me, Papa," he answers, sweetly and calmly.[71]

At times the king seemed to embody Freud's legendary patriarch who claims sexual dominion over all the females in the tribe. Henri openly preened himself in front of Louis on the powers of his generative organ (to Héroard's embarrassed regret).[72] As one of the king's mistresses passed by in the palace garden, he boasted to the little boy, "I have made a baby with that beautiful woman." During one after-hunt siesta he reclined on Madame de Montglat's bed.[73]

Henri even violated Louis's tenderest feelings by setting his son's submission to himself as the condition under which he would refrain from making love to the child's sister and nurse. One day the three-year-old Louis "doesn't want Elisabeth to dance, nor the king to kiss her," writes Héroard. "He is annoyed with the king for it, who, to appease him, tells him, 'Kiss me, my son, I won't kiss her any more.' He lets himself be kissed, pacified. . . . Very nice until the king wants to lie down on the green bed. 'Get off that! Get off that!' he says, and gets into a bad humor."[74]

About a year later the king, "returning from the hunt, kisses him, embraces him." At seven o'clock, Louis joins his father for supper. "While he was eating the king asked if he wanted to have Henri sleep with him, telling him, 'If you won't let me sleep with you, I'll sleep with Maman Doudoun.' "[75] It is as though allowing himself to be seduced by his father was the boy's only alternative to Henri's seduction of those nearest and dearest to him.

The manly, defiant acts that challenge the father and bring on whippings and submission also entail the danger of castration. For example, as the prince plays with the king and queen, "the king makes him take off his hat and go bareheaded," a recurrent assertion of paternal supremacy. The queen, as though in support of her husband, "putting her hand on [Louis's] . . . cock, says, 'Son, I've taken your pecker.' " The little boy, in doubt, "puts his hand there too," saying, "I still have it."[76] The threat seems more than a child of three can contend with. The boy, who has not yet resolved his unusual difficulty in relinquishing his bowel contents, has been plunged into a particularly threatening oedipal stage, which he cannot resolve by becoming like his father, since the king's behavior is simultaneously seductive and menacing.

The kind of vengeance Louis believed his father capable of is suggested by a surmise the boy made two years later. One of Henri's mistresses, the comtesse de Moret, had borne him a son, and the king arranged an annulment of her pro forma marriage on grounds of the count's impotence. Overhearing this matter discussed, Louis said, "No, it's not that; it's because he is castrated!"[77]

Given such dangers and temptations, it is little wonder that no hope of replacing the king was allowed to enter the child's consciousness, even in play. When, during the traditional Twelfth Night ceremony of the *galette* in 1606, the dauphin draws the crown and the company propose the toast "The king drinks!" Louis "suddenly lets go of his goblet, saying, 'No—I don't want to!' " Two years later he still refused this salute. "Never did he want to permit that they cry, 'The king drinks!' " observes Héroard.[78] On the same occasion in the following year, 1609, Louis showed that, rather than nurture a forbidden ambition to replace his father, he took pleasure in servility. This time Elisabeth had drawn the token and was crowned queen.

She appointed Louis her *grand écuyer*, but he declined: "'No,' says he, 'I want to be footman [*valet de pied*]. I'm good at running!'" This thought was no doubt prompted by the court entertainment planned for the evening, a play that featured Verdelet, the king's footman, in a leading role.[79]

Instead of challenging his father, Louis aimed to be Papa's "little valet," the faithful servant of the king. During one of Henri's absences Héroard and the dauphin together worked out a set of alluring, yet safe aspirations for the boy:

D.: I'll go hunting. I'll kill a wild boar with my sword . . . then I'll chop its head off.

H.: You'll catch a deer, have its foot cut off. You'll bring it to Papa, who'll caress you, call you his darling, take you into his beautiful hall at the Louvre.

D.: Monsieur de Verneuil [his half brother] won't get in—*he's* stubborn. . . . Then Papa will give me a little pistol. What will he tell me?

H.: He'll tell you, Sir, "My son, I give you this pistol. Go out to war against my enemies. . . . "

D.: (Getting animated) I'll kill them all, ratatatat. (He was getting warm as though he were in the thick of battle.)

H.: When you return Papa will kiss you, call you his darling.

Even in fantasy the dauphin needed external support:

"Salignac [a favorite soldier] will be with me . . . When Papa goes away, Salignac will stay with me.[80]

Doctor and child told each other one version or another of this story over and over again.

Attached to Louis's desire for his father's love, however, was the fear of becoming his passive object rather than his faithful valet, brave lieutenant, or bold hunter. Furthermore, for the dauphin to become the king's loyal servant, the anger Henri so often inspired had to be directed elsewhere. The household at Saint-Germain offered a considerable range of persons on whom Louis could vent his destructive feelings with less danger and toward whom he could express his longing for love.

CHAPTER FOUR

Mixed Feelings: Loves and Hates

*His loves were strange loves; there was nothing of the lover
about him except jealousy.*[1]

In the spring of 1606 Louis was given a few months' respite from his conflicts over his father. "Going off to besiege Sedan," the king comes to bid
him goodbye, "kisses him, embraces him," and says: "'Adieu, my son,
pray God for me; adieu, my son, I give you my blessing.' 'Adieu, Papa,' replies the dauphin. He was completely stunned—as though at a loss for
words."[2]

Héroard is always at pains to depict Louis as devoted to his father. But
the dauphin's spirits lifted as soon as the king departed. Moreover, during
Henri's absence there was an upsurge in Louis's genital curiosity and in his
heterosexual desires. Perhaps the recent arrival of a second baby sister[3] renewed the force of observations he made concerning Elisabeth when she
was a baby and revived the romantic feelings he had felt for his first sister.
In any case, the spring and early summer of that year were for him a time of
sexual excitement and exploration.

OLD LOVES

With his nurse, who, as we have seen, seemed to be as much a part of himself as a separate person, Louis was able to act on his aspirations to be manly
with little anxiety: "Seated at the head of his bed, playing, shows his cock,
says, 'Hey, take it, there's my handsome piece!' . . . Plays with his nurse on
the rug, jumps on her neck, 'Hey, kiss me, my mad one!' Wants to kiss her
on the breast, undoes her blouse; she prevents it. He gets down on all fours
and tries to pull up her skirt." Héroard is delighted at this exhibition of virility; he finds his patient to be "vigorous, ardent, robust in all his actions—
strong of body, strong of mind."[4]

In these days, Louis often went to sleep in his nurse's bed; when waking in his own bed, he asked to be put back there. But his aims were not only of the genital kind: "Awakened, has himself put in bed with his nurse, plays with her, kisses her, makes her kiss his ass, bringing up both his legs around her neck." Returning from a visit to his baby sister, in whose nurse he had also developed a romantic interest (which everyone encourages), he kissed and hugged his own nurse once again, saying, "I love you, my mad Doun-doun, I think that I am mad about you."[5]

Disappointments as well as dangers necessarily accompanied this rise in Louis's erotic interests. Both are manifest in Héroard's account of a tender scene between him and his sister Elisabeth, one of the last such occasions the doctor will observe:

> He conceives the notion of having Madame sleep with him. When they make excuses for her he gets angry, saying "Good grief, how slow she is in undressing," cries about it, doesn't want to go to sleep. . . . Finally they bring her; he has her lie down next to him. She looked like a young, dazed [*étonnée*] bride, and he, strangely resolute, kissed her. Then, his nurse having whispered in his ear that she [Elisabeth] would piss in the bed, he says, "Take her—take her away to bed in her room!"[6]

The danger represented by a *pisseuse*—as women were often called by Louis—was less when advances were directed toward an object once or twice removed, such as the nurse of his younger sister. Louis courted this young woman ardently, kissing her, Héroard reports, "on the mouth, the eyes, the forehead, the nose, the nipples, saying in a transport, 'I'll kiss you forever.'" The following day having failed to catch her while she was still in bed, he resolved to rise early the next morning for that purpose.

But on that day, June 8, 1606, the king returned from the wars, accompanied by Marie. Henri's first words to the dauphin were, "Well, son, have you been whipped?" Louis replied, "Not every day, Papa."[7] In fact, he had not been whipped at all since the king's last visit, almost three months before—an immunity that may well account for his bold lovemaking and high spirits in the interim.

REENTER HENRI

Significantly, the king's first move was to ascend with his son to the baby sister's bedroom, scene of Louis's courtship of the nurse. There Henri and the boy conversed for a "very long time," according to Héroard. That evening there was a return of the lassitude Louis had formerly shown after such encounters with his father: he simulated sleep in his nurse's lap to escape Henri and the rest of the company, saying, "I was so hot."[8] A few days later the old response of actively accepting punishment reappeared when Louis was whipped for "being naughty" in chapel: "He wanted afterward to keep the *verges*," Héroard notes, "saying to them, 'You're my darling.' "[9]

In the next few days Henri's chastening and seductive effect upon Louis was reestablished. On June 26 the two went into Madame de Montglat's little bedroom, where the king went to bed and had his son put in a night shirt to play there with him "in a very familiar way." Afterward, when Henri is about to leave, Louis "reddens, and the tears come to his eyes." The king pacifies him by kissing him and embracing him and promising to return forthwith. Later, we are given a hint of what their familiarity in bed may have involved. On the rug with the governess's two young daughters, "he said some new words and phrases that were shameful and unworthy of his upbringing, saying that Papa's was lots longer than his, that it was as long as *that*—showing half the length of his arm."[10]

Henri's reassertion of dominance over Louis was reinforced by this commanding Mamanga[11] to whip the dauphin if need be until, as she informed the child, she drew blood.[12] Thus the erotic component in the child's submission to his father was once again fused in his mind with physical and moral pain. There is a consciously self-demeaning element in his "kissing and embracing" of a hideous poodle with which the king presented him: "I love," he says, "everything that comes from Papa."[13]

While the self-abnegating, self-punitive aspect of submission to Henri was conscious, the erotic pleasure associated with it was unconscious. When it threatened to become conscious it produced anxiety, as, for example, when Louis awoke with a start after a nightmare in which he has dreamed that "a beast was biting him on the right buttock."[14]

The anxiety produced by the fantasized pleasure of yielding to his father's seduction was intensified by increased awareness of the dangers inherent in the feminine role. Since March of the preceding year, when he acknowledged the existence of Madame's "little vagina," the female anatomy that he had observed long before had been impressed more and more upon his consciousness. A few months later he was asked, at bedtime, what the difference is between a boy and a girl. He reflected, then said, "I'll say what it is tomorrow; I don't know, I want to think about it in bed." His explorations of the matter show him acting out a picture of the marriage-bed encounter as a sadistic one:

Mademoiselle Mercier [one of his maids who stood vigil at night] was still in the bed next to him. He plays with her, has her put her legs up. . . . Sends for the switches to whip her, then does so. His nurse then asks, "Sir, what have you seen in Mercier?"
"I have see her ass" (coolly).
Is it very skinny?" . . .

"No, it's pretty fat."

"What else did you see?"

"I've seen her vagina"—coolly, and without laughing.[15]

Although by this time Louis has reached a more realistic view of female anatomy than in the days when he denied the difference between boys and girls, his feelings about this difference show genital aims overlain by those anal sadistic strivings so important in his development. The "coolness" that Héroard now discerns in the dauphin as he regards Mercier's *conin* is supported by his aggressive actions toward her.

The conscious aims of those at court, not least among them Henri and Héroard, were to encourage Louis's heterosexual interests and to foster in him a bold virility. But Héroard, as we have seen, played a significant part in preventing the dauphin from becoming autonomous. He also contributed to the predominance of anal components in Louis's erotic and aggressive aims and fantasies. And Henri was foremost among those who unintentionally encouraged the little boy to adopt a passive homosexual role.

The danger of castration entailed in this role that Henri often implicitly offered Louis caused the child to react against it, repressing the desires his father aroused in him. At the same time, too, the king provoked rage in the little boy. The rage was as dangerous as the desire. Freud writes that "the child's first years are governed by grandiose overestimation of his father. Kings and queens in dreams and fairy tales always represent, accordingly, the parents."[16] How much more grandiose must have been the estimation of a father like Henri, a powerful and admired king who vaunted his genital superiority over his son at almost every opportunity and imposed fearsome sanctions for insubordination. And how dangerous the threat of losing such a father's support, perhaps leaving oneself open to surprise attacks of the kind already perpetrated by him and those in his service. Thus the little boy enjoined a departing soldier, "Go give Papa good service so the enemies don't come and kill us."[17] If these were the dangers, a man like Henri was not to be challenged but rather was either to be avoided or conciliated. Targets for the rage as well as for the forbidden love he inspired were better sought elsewhere.

HOUSEHOLD TARGETS

Montglat

One habitual object of Louis's rage was his governess, Madame de Montglat. A "violent and annoying" woman, according to L'Estoile,[18] she was frequently the target for verbal and physical abuse by the prince. Héroard often shows her to have been crude of speech and manners.[19] If Mamanga's personality was unpleasant, her fate as Louis's caretaker was unenviable: she was forced to play the role of "bad" mother opposite the cherished Maman Doundoun.[20] Indeed, one morning the child jokingly saw his governess as a devil. Having climbed into bed beside her, he started hitting her on the head as he sang a little jingle. "There's the horned mother," he said, "gently" batting her head with his hand.[21]

In the hat scene Louis's rage against his father was finally transferred to others, especially to his governess. As she punished him he cried, "Whip me up higher!"—an invitation accompanied by actions apt to provoke further whipping, such as "scratching her face and striking her with feet and hands." Shortly afterwards the dauphin was again in "extreme anger," saying, "Kill Mamanga! Mamanga is naughty!"[22] And a few days later, "imperious in all he commands," as Héroard says with seeming admiration, the boy told Mamanga, "Ha! I'll kill you!" But this time, according to the doctor, he spoke "altogether softly, as though it was a thing that would have cost nothing to do."[23]

Abuse of his governess could have seemed to Louis a low-cost indulgence. The king encouraged his son to direct his rage at the unfortunate woman, attributing to her the responsibility for his own punitive acts.[24] Once, when Louis has been willful, Henri remarked to the governess in front of the child, "One day you'll be the cause of my skinning him alive."[25]

Not surprisingly, Mamanga was not eager to punish this vengeful and violent boy. In the second half of his fourth year the provocativeness of Louis's invitations to punishment seems to have risen sharply:

> Made caca next to Madame de Montglat's chair. . . . Won't allow her to clean his behind with her handkerchief. . . . On his way to his room he meets her coming out of the dressing room, gets into peevish humor: "Go through by the other door!" Madame de M. is reluctant and goes as far as the table with him pulling her by her dress, crying and screaming, bursting with rage. She is obliged to give in and does so. He conducts her as far as the door. She scolds him and leads him into the room, he screaming all the while and beside himself. Does his best to bite her finger with extreme fury. Approaches the table, threatening her, "I'll kill you if you go through by way of the dressing room again! . . . Get to your knees, Mamanga!" Then, when she's done this, "Put your face down on the ground!"

Even this tantrum does not seem to have provoked punishment. The dauphin was not whipped for what Héroard calls his "imperious" behavior.[26]

Punishment was, of course, more probable when the King was present. Later in the same year, Louis was once again enraged at Madame de Montglat. "Suddenly he becomes angry," writes Héroard: "'I'll hit you, Mamanga,' and goes for her, hits her: 'I'll kill you, Mamanga.' The king spanks him on the buttocks with his hand; since he doesn't keep still, hits him once again—then leaves." But here the pleasure the dauphin has taken in the episode is shown by his facetiousness: "He throws himself to the ground, then pretends to be unable to walk, goes along hobbling, crying, screaming, 'Hey, Mamanga, Papa broke my thigh! Put some ointment on it!' "[27]

By spring of the following year outrageous behavior, inviting whippings, recurred regularly and often. At chapel he was "peevish" to his governess because she had prevented his leaving in order to watch the changing of the guard. "He insults her with a vulgar gesture [*lui fait les cornes*] and says, 'Fie, how ugly you are!' . . . He gets on her back, tries to make her fall, throws his book at her head . . . whipped . . . but doesn't cry at all, only shouts, 'That's enough! That's enough!'"[28] This time Mamanga satisfies Louis's apparent demand for punishment. His reaction has also changed.

There is little in Louis's behavior toward his governess to suggest that he entertained any affection for her. When there was talk of his transfer to the hands of male tutors, "the queen asked him if he would be sorry when he was no longer with Mamanga"—a disingenuous query, perhaps, since Marie knew the baroness to be Henri's "creature" and had herself frequently tried to circumvent her. Héroard reports, probably also with satisfaction, that the dauphin replied with an unqualified "No!"[29]

Sometimes the dauphin showed feelings of revulsion for his governess's lack of fastidiousness. For example, while he and his half brother were playing a kissing game with the girls (an exceptional activity for Louis, as Héroard notes), Louis kissed Montglat, "to flatter her," Héroard explains. But no sooner had he done this than the child cried, "Yech! You smell of dog shit, Mamanga!" Another time, when she touched him, he said: "Yech! Change my shirt, filthy ugly one! Don't touch me! . . . I wish you were dead!"[30] When Louis's departure was imminent and he was flinging insults at Mamanga—"Ugly one! Bitch!"—an attendant warned, "Sir, you must not be angry with her, not having long still to be with her here." He replied, "I wish I were already out!"[31]

The quality of Louis's hostility to his governess deserves notice. It is indicated by this fantasy of destroying her that he confided to his half sister: "Sissy [*Soeu-soeu*] Vendôme, I'll take a hollow stick, I'll fill it up with gunpowder, and then . . . I'll light the powder that will burn up her whole ass."[32]

In her visits and letters to Louis in the years that followed, the former governess often expressed affection for her highborn ward, but it is impossible to detect the slightest spark of tender feeling for her in Louis.[33] While his subordination to her rule gave him masochistic satisfaction, it appears to have been consciously accompanied by unalloyed detestation.

Whipping Boys

With another sort of attendant Louis's apparent feelings were more variable. From the first the dauphin was waited upon by boys and men, some gentlemen, others servants. Those who were assigned to serve him were *les siens*—his jealously guarded, sometimes loved, possessions. They were also often targets for his rage. Before he was four he was capable of threatening a lackey with the words: "I'll chop off your head with a larding fork and lard your ass and your nose with it."[34] In contrast to his angry feelings toward his father, which were dangerous to express in word or deed, the dauphin was given much freedom to act out his rage toward these attendants.

Thus, while playing war games with his age-mates in May 1606, Louis starts to whip Roger de Frontenac on the hand: "Warming up to the game, asks for the switches; they don't bring them. He throws himself on his valet to beat him up, in a rage, chewing his tongue as was his habit."[35] A year later we see him unleash his fury in the same way on a servant boy who has accompanied him on a walk with the king in the gardens at Fontainebleau. Back in his apartment afterward, "he wants to beat up Bompar, his page, saying it was for not having followed him." But Héroard knows this is a subterfuge. Louis is "not mentioning" his real motives: "The reason was for his having followed the king, holding over him the dauphin's parasol. He holds on to [*retient*] this vengefulness for a long time. Bompar arrives; he goes for him with lashes of the whip, which he held in his hand, and with kicks, unwilling to forgive him no matter what was said to him; remains cold and firm in his resolve." Despite Louis's opposition, Bompar is sent on an errand by Madame de Montglat, and after he leaves the dauphin falls back on his notion of vengeance: " 'When he returns I'll really beat him up. I'll give him a hundred blows of the cane, then I'll send him to the kitchen.' He says all this coldly; he could not forget his animosity."[36]

There was a sense, however, in which these paroxysms were self-damaging as well as injurious to their targets. Such servants were alter egos—literally stand-ins for their master. Thus, when Louis was naughty, "they threatened to whip La Barge"—another page—if the prince did not ask pardon for a misdeed. A few days later, when Louis had again misbehaved, he was reminded by others of La Barge's whipping-boy status and whipped the page himself. Bompar, given to Louis by the king when the dauphin was only three-and-a-half, was also eligible to play the role of whipping boy.[37] Hence, when Louis raged against Bompar and treated him cruelly, as in the scene above, he might have been receiving the punishment as well as inflicting it.

The dauphin would sometimes put such servants in other situations in which they replaced him. It was, for example, considered whimsical of

Louis to arrange for the unwilling Bompar to take horseback-riding lessons from the dauphin's own equestrian tutor. The prince would then derive pleasure from watching the page demonstrate his ineptitude.[38] But more often Louis sought to replace the servant in some lowly capacity—to be himself the one who was commanded and debased. He would repeatedly play the lackey, valet or footman—making his own bed, setting his place at table, joining in the work required by the frequent displacements of his household. On one trip he told his servant, "I want to be the footman." He helped his little suite of attendants into his carriage and then walked alongside it, "swinging his arms and walking in the manner of a lackey." Then, says Héroard, he had himself called "Little Louis."[39] Thus did Papa's little valet volunteer to serve others as well.

BROTHERS

In the dauphin's first years his male rivals for Henri's favor were his half brothers. Louis was nearly six before Marie produced a second son, and that child, apparently congenitally ailing and short-lived, took little part in the everyday life of the nursery. Gaston, the brother who was to figure importantly in later political concerns, was not born until the dauphin was almost seven. News of his arrival was welcomed—it meant a cannonade (silence greeted the birth of princesses) and "another servitor for Papa." But its principal significance for Louis was that it strengthened the "party" of the legitimate heir in the nursery. "Now we are three," said Louis.[40] His more important ties were still to his half brothers and to his sisters.

The Vendômes

While Marie de Medici was in labor with her first child in September 1601, a seven-year-old boy tried to peek into her bedchamber where his father, Henri IV, in the company of many courtiers, was awaiting the arrival of a dauphin. When Louis was finally delivered and put on exhibit, he became the focus of the throng's attention. His half brother, little César de Vendôme, complained to Marie's midwife, "A little while ago everyone was talking to me; . . . now no one says anything at all to me any more." Louise Boursier reported this remark to the queen. Marie, "whose kindness was always marvelously great," took pity on the child and commanded that he "be caressed as much as or more than usual."[41]

Marie's command was probably superfluous so far as Henri was concerned. César, Henri's elder son by Gabrielle d'Estrées, his most beloved mistress, had long been the king's preferred child. Born in 1594 and legitimated a year later, the boy had also been, while his mother lived, a potential heir to the throne. He was close to his father. When Henri went to visit his ill sister, for example, he would take his infant son with him, holding him in his arms as he chatted at her bedside. With Henri's marriage to Marie after Gabrielle's death in 1599, the young duc de Vendôme was much in the company of his father, waiting upon his new stepmother as well.[42] His presence was to affect Louis in several important ways.

The dauphin shared the nursery at Saint-Germain in his earliest years with César and two other Vendôme children, Catherine, born in 1596, and Alexandre (as a child called "Alexandre Monsieur" and later "Monsieur le Chevalier"), born in 1598. As the eldest, César was probably the most conspicuous of the three, yet his presence during this period is least often noted in Héroard's record. Perhaps the omission is due to Héroard's partiality for his own patient; it was obvious even to an onlooker like the British representative at court that César was Henri's "most loved" son.[43] Even if Héroard was jealous, on the dauphin's behalf, of César's relationship with the king, he allowed bits of evidence to slip through in his diary that throw light on the young duke's place in court and reveal that the example of this older, more accomplished son of the *vert galant* influenced Louis's maturation. These clues suggest that, in many respects, César's role was for Louis the prototype of one that would be played by several others later in his life.

By the time "Monsieur de Vendôme" began to figure with some frequency in Héroard's record, he had apparently already been put into the hands of men and was no longer living at Saint-Germain with Louis and the other children. César's tutor was Nicolas Vauquelin, Sieur Des Yveteaux, who in 1609 would be assigned by Henri to perform the same function for the dauphin himself. According to the king, the older boy had been "well instructed" by Vauquelin, although L'Estoile, among others, disagreed. Evidently, however, Henri was satisfied with César's progress and would have been content to see Louis follow in his footsteps.[44]

By 1604 César was frequently in the company of his father in adult pursuits—able to go hunting on horseback with the king and perhaps accompany him in the pursuit of less innocent aims. Indeed, Des Yveteaux himself many years later declined responsibility for César's education, saying that he had been put in charge of it "a little too late," the king having already given the boy "an important place in sharing his most secret pleasures."[45] The suggestion seems to be that César was his father's confidant and an accomplice to Henri's vices. Whatever the degree of his complicity, he preceded Louis as "Papa's darling."

From time to time the young duke reappeared in Louis's quarters, and Héroard depicts his entries as an intrusion. On one such occasion he writes that César "puts himself next to him on the left; . . . [Louis] repulses him twice with the hand, saying, 'Get farther away!' Monsieur de Vendôme kisses the back of his hand unexpectedly. 'Ha!' he says, showing himself to be annoyed, 'You kiss my hand!'—and rubs it on his dress."[46]

The doctor was alert to signs of self-advancement in this half sibling. Ten days later he noted that César visited Louis "heavily attended," an affront, as he saw it, to the legitimate heir, whose retinue was still small. This was the summer of stormy conflict between Louis and his father. After one of their quarrels Henri sent César as his emissary to invite the three-year-old to rejoin the king. Louis was unwilling, not trusting himself with his father. "Monsieur de Vendôme," Héroard recorded, reported "very crudely" to Henri that Louis "did not want to see him." Henri, expectedly, was irritated and blamed Madame de Montglat. But Héroard held César responsible for jeopardizing the younger son's favor with his father.[47]

It is clear that Louis was encouraged by his doctor, and perhaps also by others in his entourage, to assert his precedence over César. When he ordered the older boy, "Put on my boots," he was no doubt imitating the commands he had heard Henri give the young duke. "Go away!" the dauphin ordered him peremptorily in the following spring.[48]

Yet Héroard does not prevent us from perceiving that Louis by no means dominated his eldest half brother. As we have seen, Henri called Louis a "little calf." César's superior status seems to be acknowledged in the three-year-old dauphin's exclamation, on catching sight of the young duke, "There's a big calf!"[49] In the many war games the troop of children played together, it seems that César was usually in command: his role was that of captain to Louis's guard. On one occasion when these assignments were in force, the king reminded Louis that he, as a mere musketeer, should not give commands; this was the prerogative of the captain. The doctor tells how Louis, nearly seven, "makes himself musketeer; Monsieur de Vendôme was the captain"—and obviously still the leader.[50] Even out of the nursery the dauphin remained subordinate to his half brother. On guard at Fontainebleau, Louis was the company drummer; Vendôme deployed the troops. The king, says Héroard, took a "singular pleasure" in watching these games.[51]

Signs of the devotion Henri felt for his firstborn son occasionally emerge from the diarist's pages. In 1606, for example, when the carriage of the king and queen overturned in a flash flood at the Neuilly crossing, César, traveling with the royal couple, was the first to be rescued by Henri.[52]

Héroard's references to César usually convey Louis's animosity. Thus, the dauphin waited for César to return from dinner with Henri, "out of jealousy because he was not dining there himself." When the same slight was later repeated by Henri, the doctor considered Louis to be "inwardly piqued." The dauphin was apprehensive that the guards may have stood at attention for César when he returned ahead of the king after the two had been on a hunt together. When Louis visited the Louvre as a six-year-old, Henri seemed to indicate the respective ranks of the two boys in his affections by assigning César's room to the dauphin and taking the elder child to his own bed.[53] Henri may have been making invidious comparisons again

when, in a conversation he is reported to have had with his friend Lesdiguières, he commented that César's excellent upbringing equipped him
well to perform future services for the state.[54]

Competition between the brothers for their father's love took the form of
which could better perform the services of "Papa's little valet." Thus, when
Louis learned of the unexpected return of Henri from the hunt and heard
someone suggest that César order the king's supper, he cried "with passion
[*ardeur*]," as Héroard writes: "No! No! It's I who want to give him supper.
Let them put four capons on the spit—let them put them all on!"[55] And
when Louis himself was about to graduate to the Louvre and acquire a
household of his own, he was rueful that César was not under Gilles de
Souvré as he himself was to be. The young duke, moreover, "has more
than I of everything," he complained. "He has six lackeys and I have only
two." Héroard comments, "He had heard this said, and he always compared himself with Monsieur de Vendôme."[56]

But if Héroard stresses Louis's jealous animosity toward César, he also
allows us to glimpse the younger boy's admiration and envy—as when the
dauphin longed to see the ballet César was to perform before the king. The
duke seems to have been accomplished at dancing, whereas Louis, Héroard
frequently tells us, had little aptitude or liking for it. In spite of this the dauphin threw himself into a dance led by César, "below Monsieur de Vendôme," although César begged him to take the station appropriate to his
rank. We may suspect that Louis wished to take the place of this other "darling of Papa" when he put his page, Bompar—that alter ego we have met
before—not on his own horse but on his half brother's.[57]

César's sexual precocity was also likely to inspire a wish in Louis to emulate him, especially since, if Des Yveteaux is correct, César had been initiated into the "secret pleasures" of his father. When at the age of six-and-a-
half Louis was reproached for showing his penis to the little daughter of his
maître d'hôtel, he told Madame de Montglat that César had taught him to
do this—which was possibly true, though Héroard attributes the accusation
to Louis's spiteful feelings toward César.[58] If the king—who was himself
not above such conduct—trained his eldest son in his own ways, it would
not be surprising if that child, in turn, initiated the younger one.

In 1609 César's status as an adult male was confirmed for Louis in a painful way. Marie de Medici, in labor with her last child, was attended as usual
by a host of great noblemen, including the young duc de Vendôme. Louis
pleaded also to be admitted to Marie's chamber: "My brother Vendôme is
allowed in there," he told the king, but Henri was adamant, and the child
was not allowed in.[59] In the following year César was married, and before
he was eighteen he had sired a son. The record of his sexual performance
was far more like the *vert galant's* than Louis would be able to manage.

Héroard's implicit denial that Louis had any positive feelings for César is belied by some evidence he gives us suggesting that the first of Papa's darlings was not only envied and hated but also admired and loved by the dauphin. For example, the doctor relates a scene that took place in Madame de Montglat's room at Fontainebleau during the court's summer sojourn there. César, whom the dauphin had not seen "the entire day," entered to this response from Louis: "Where have you been? Go away! Go away! You've been with Sissy Vendôme the whole day! You didn't come to see me. Get out of here! Go back to her!"[60]

Héroard gives us another glimpse of this side of Louis's feelings for César five months after their father's death: "There was a young boy named César who had been a lackey. He made him the coachman of his little pony cart, and loved him; he spoke of him often. He was asked why he loved him and he replied immediately, 'Because he is a good man.' "[61] The incongruity of this description with the status and age of this César suggests that he was an object for feelings the prince bore his eldest half brother. As with César de Vendôme, who often played valet to Papa but captain to Louis's musketeer, Louis played footman to the former lackey, César's namesake, who now commanded the horse and carriage.

Héroard makes Alexandre, the younger Vendôme brother, more visible to us. Closer to Louis in age, he was, according to the diarist, a consistent object of Louis's hatred in his earliest years. When the dauphin was only sixteen months old Alexandre presented him with his undershirt (a court ritual), whereupon, Héroard says of Louis, "suddenly, having taken it, he aimed a blow of his hand at him in order to hit him," The doctor explains, "He couldn't abide him."[62]

That Héroard did not discourage violent detestation of the Vendôme half brothers is further evident in this conversation about Alexandre. The doctor has bent close to the three-and-a-half-year-old dauphin, who is in bed:

> Talking of Monsieur le Chevalier. . . .
> "He says *he's* the dauphin but I know exactly what *I'll* do."
> I ask him, "Sir, what will you do to him?"   "I don't want to tell," and after several refusals to tell, he burrowed down in his bed saying he would tell me inside it—says in a very low voice . . . "I'd castrate him." Then asks me, "Did you hear what I said?"
> "Yes, Monsieur le Dauphin."
> "Well, what did I say?"
> "That you would castrate him."
> "Yes, I'd chop off his penis."[63]

Héroard seems to share Louis's damaging thoughts.

Yet the dauphin certainly entertained warm feelings as well as hostile ones for Alexandre, just as he did for César. Unlike his brother the duke, the younger Vendôme was no pacesetter for the dauphin. Compared with

Louis, he was incompetent at games. By the dauphin's own description, he was a "little gosling" to César's "big calf."[64] He was apparently smaller in size than Louis and no rival for the king's favors.[65] While Louis might abuse him and speak abusively of him, it appears that he also harbored possessive feelings for him. L'Estoile reports that soon after Henri's death Alexandre de Vendôme seemed to be the only prince or *seigneur* of the court to whom Louis was greatly attached. This opinion was shared by a foreign observer.[66] Héroard himself describes a deep attachment: when Alexandre was supposed to accompany César to Bretagne, the doctor writes, Louis "started to cry so hard that the chevalier's trip was cancelled and he remained with him." (Thus, of course, Louis also prevented César from seizing what belonged to him.) In 1611, when Alexandre was to be sent off on a voyage to Malta, the two boys wept together as they contemplated the separation. Louis complained, "They want to take him away from me because I love him."[67] He feared the loss of a valued possession.

Lesser Breeds

It was Henri's wish to have his many offspring treated equally, when possible. His pretended achievement of this aim was belied, however, by Louis's frequently successful sabotage, as even a foreigner could see: "He sheweth to those youths who are brought up with him, somewhat a cruel and vindictive disposition, though the king one day pained himself to tell me many pretty stories, that argued the meekness of his nature."[68] Although the three Vendôme children had shared the nursery with Louis from the beginning, only direct orders of the king induced the dauphin to allow them equal status, according to what Héroard shows us. Unless Henri commanded it, none of these half siblings dined with Louis. Even the form of address the prince used for them—"*Fé-fé* [for *frère*] Vendôme" and "*Soeu-soeu* Vendôme"—was changed to "My brother," and "My sister" only on explicit instruction from their father.[69]

The Vendôme children had been removed to Saint-Germain for rearing when their mother died, before Louis was born. But Henri de Verneuil, the first of Henri's bastards by Henriette d'Entragues, Marquise de Verneuil, spent his first three years in his mother's household. Although he was born at about the same time as Louis, his earliest relationships with the king were not visible to his half brother. Reports of them may have reached the dauphin's entourage: they had certainly reached the ears of the Tuscan ambassador to the court. That emissary wrote to his master, the grand duke (Marie de Medici's uncle), that the king had visited his Verneuil children at the home of their mother and had publicly compared his son by Henriette to Louis, to the disadvantage of the dauphin. "In front of the princes and lords who were around him," Henri had remarked: "See how good-natured this son is and how much he resembles me. *He* is not a stubborn child like the dauphin."[70] Somewhat later the king observed to Lesdiguières that Henri de Verneuil was "a very nice soul [*fort gentil esprit*]" and very obliging, who would "make himself welcome with everyone."[71] It was apparently this half brother's docility that his father appreciated—a docility Louis could never show without conflict.

The king introduced the Verneuil children into the Saint-Germain establishment in June 1604, a time when, as we have seen, Louis's intense, conflicted feelings toward his father were rising to a climax. This was the same month in which César reappeared as his father's favored companion, and the presence of Henri de Verneuil gave the dauphin still another cause for jealousy. Héroard helped intensify his feelings by adding to Louis's anxiety that he might lose his father's love: "I tell him, 'Monsieur, get dressed quickly; you're going to the park to see Papa. He'll give you a beautiful cannon. . . . Otherwise Monsieur de Verneuil will get there first and he'll get it instead.'" Louis replied, "*Fé-fé* Vaneuil is still sleeping," but Héroard did not relent. He rejoined, "Sir, I beg your pardon, but he's got up and has gone to find Papa."[72] Thus Louis's constant fear that his prized possessions would be stolen from him found confirmation in Héroard's warnings.

In the spring of 1607 courtiers reported to Louis yet another dereliction of the king, his father:

"Sir, you have still another brother."
"Who? Who is he?" he asks, as though stunned.
"Sir, Madame la Comtesse de Moret has delivered a son."

Louis is disdainful:

"Ho! He's not Papa's!"
"Sir, whose is he then?"
"He is his mother's."

But his scorn is mixed with dismay. Héroard continues:

"He didn't want to say another word about it, all disturbed and looking as though he would have liked to cry."[73]

At this age it was rare that Louis was brought near to tears. In early spring of the following year, Henri dispatched Héroard to examine this latest of his progeny, a mission that upset the dauphin, who, the doctor noted on this occasion, was "jealous of his servitors."[74]

Henri's numerous illegitimate progeny were not only competitors for what belonged to Louis. I have pointed out that, taught to address the dauphin as "*mon maître*," they were also his possessions—humble servants and future subjects. As such they were, if not loved for themselves, at least *les siens*. To his jealousy of what they might steal from him was added the fear that they themselves might be stolen from him.

The precedence of the dauphin over his half brothers was based on his mother's position. He had been made to understand very early that his status was dependent on his mother's relationship with his father. At the age of six Louis was told that his father loved Madame Des Essarts, another mistress. He commented, "But if I don't love her, she's only a whore."[75] At three he was shown his parents' marriage bed and told, "That's where you were made." His response: "With Mother." Two years later he was quite explicit: "I love my little sister more than *Fé-fé* Chevalier, because he was not in Mama's stomach with me as she was."[76] Thus Elisabeth is like himself, but the others?

The following exchange is suggestive; it takes place while the dauphin is seated on his toilet chair after the guard has announced the arrival of his Vendôme half brothers:

Héroard: Sir, they are your brothers.
Dauphin: Ho! They're another breed of dogs.
H.: And Monsieur de Verneuil?
D.: Ho! Still another breed. . . . I'm a different breed, together with my brother Orléans, my brother Anjou, and my sisters.
H.: Which is the best?
D.: Mine; then the Vendômes, then brother Verneuil.

But where, Héroard asks, should one put the latest arrival, the comte de Moret? Louis replies, "He's the last and he comes after the *merde* I've just made."[77]

Like his *merde*, Louis's half brothers belonged to him, and he was unwilling to relinquish them. On the other hand, he would, if allowed, sometimes cast them out ruthlessly, expel them with disgust and hatred, or cut them off without mercy.

MUCH IN A NAME

Louis's struggles with his brothers centered partly on his longing for his father's love, partly on his striving to become like that great man. As the child grew older the second wish did not seem to become any more attainable than it had been when he was an infant.

In a boy's experience, bearing the father's given name is often a support for strivings to become like him. It was therefore natural that the dauphin should hope to be named Henri. In the French royal family it was the practice to baptize princes formally when they had reached a stage at which they were able to respond in public to questions about their religious creed. For such occasions godparents were assigned and names chosen to symbolize the aspirations of the dynasty. Thus, after the dauphin's baptismal ceremony at Fontainebleau, Henri wrote to his own godfather, the constable of

France, to explain his reasons (no doubt already plain to Montmorency) for the choice of name: "We have given the name of Louis to my son the Dauphin in order to renew the memory of the king Saint Louis from whom our house issues."

To Henri, this choice had been solemnized "very happily and to my satisfaction."[78] But to Louis the naming was painful and disappointing. More than a year before the event, Héroard reports, the child had been asked by courtiers:

"Sir, when you are baptized, what will you be named?"
"Henri" [he replies] and then, turning toward me, "Let them name me like that."[79]

Later in the same year "they were talking about . . . his baptism":

Madame de Montglat asks him, "Sir, what do you wish to be named?"
"Henri."
I ask him why.
"Papa is named that; I don't want to have the name of Louis."[80]

Nevertheless, on September 14 in the following year he was baptized Louis in the chapel of the palace at Fontainebleau. In the ceremony Cardinal de Joyeuse stood in for the official godfather, Pope Paul V. The pontiff's participation had been a plum for Henri, negotiated by his representatives in Rome. He was able to announce to Parlement that the head of the Roman Catholic church intended to "honor and render more illustrious the baptism of our very dear son the dauphin,"[81] and ordered the news to be published throughout France. By reaffirming his link to the pope, the ex-Protestant Henri hoped to strengthen his dynasty.[82]

Soon after, Louis showed himself trying to make the best of this naming. He wrote to his governess and the brothers and sisters at Saint-Germain, "I am feeling much better than I did before my baptism." He signed his letter "Ludovicus," which perhaps indicates no more than a half-acceptance of his new name.[83]

Louis's tribulations over his desire to be his father's namesake were not yet ended, however. A year after his baptism, insult was added to injury when he learned that, by order of the king, his half brother Verneuil was now to receive the name of Henri. He was tested still further by the role he was to play in the affair: it was Louis who was to be godfather to the child who would be required to bestow the name himself:

They tell him that Monsieur de Verneuil would be named Henri. He replies, "I don't want to, I don't! I won't name him Henri—that's Papa's name. He would be more than I am, and I'm called Louis."

He stuck to that resolve for a long time. They tried to make him change his mind, above all by telling him that was the way the king wanted it."[84]

Of course the adults prevailed and Louis eventually bestowed on his half brother the name of the father for whose favors the two boys competed.

Even this action, however, did not put to rest Louis's wish to possess this important attribute of the king. In the following month when a portrait of his paternal grandfather was identified on the wall of his room, he asked:

"What is his name?"
"Sir, he was called Antoine."
"Then I'm very put out that I don't have the name of Antoine."[85]

Louis often seemed to feel that his efforts to emulate his father were puny; in the matter of names they were given little support.

STRANGE LOVES

As Louis emerged from the chapel where his baptism had taken place, he was excited by the sight of a different object of love and emulation: "Passing onto the terrace he notices Descluseaux, who was among the company of guards. . . . He calls him, 'Hey! My darling [*mignon*]! Come here, my darling!' Going to his room he takes a fancy to put himself on guard, has his pike handed to him, his high collar put on." Louis's passion for this guard was of several months' standing. In the preceding June, when Descluseaux had entered after dinner, Louis cried out: "Hey! There's my darling! Come here my darling Dec'useaux!" Héroard explains, "This soldier had made a practice of playing with him."[86] "My darling" was, of course, an endearing term Henri sometimes used for the dauphin.[87] Louis, in turn, acted toward his guardsman as a solicitous lover might. Listening to a story in the garden, "he scatters rose petals on the bench where Descluseaux was seated . . . and says, 'That's so your place smells good.' He loved this soldier."[88]

It is not clear whether or not Héroard regarded Louis's form of address with misgivings or whether he attempted to discourage Louis's passionate attachments to such young guards. But it is certain that the doctor was apprehensive about advances that might be made to the dauphin from some of his other male servitors. A note in the margin of his journal describes as "bold and impudent" the baron de Montglat's embrace of the five-year-old dauphin: "He takes him in his arms, lifts him, has himself hugged and kisses him hard on the mouth." Presumably Louis gives no sign of objecting, but a few months later Héroard again notes the baron's "signal impudence" in putting the dauphin to bed between him and his wife.[89]

The doctor's worries about such liberties rarely appear in his diary. There is, however, another source for determining his concern that young members of Louis entourage would take advantage of their physical proximity to the dauphin. A memoir of Nicolas Vauquelin, Louis's onetime tutor, warns that in order to avoid "importunities" a governor's eyes must be "continually upon the actions of the prince, especially at the siesta hour, when the children of honor and pages have the most freedom with their master." Louis once experienced such an importunity—"a small discommodity," as Vauquelin calls it—in the Bois de Vincennes. The tutor, Héroard, and Beringhen, a favorite attendant of the dauphin, were the only ones aware of the danger. A similar event, Vauquelin writes, had occurred earlier at Chantilly and had "greatly astonished and angered" Henri, who had commanded that care in surveying the children's behavior be redoubled.[90] These precautions seem designed to ward off homosexual intimacies.

Avoidance of similar encounters also seems to be behind Héroard's marginal note, "to be corrected," when Louis later shows a taste for privacy in the company of some of his young attendants: "Going into his office, he orders the *huissier* not to admit anyone without asking his name and coming to him to give it. He liked sometimes to be in private."[91] This "inclination [*humeur*]," of Louis, as Héroard terms it, may have worried the doctor because it reminded him of a similar taste on the part of Henri III, the effeminate king who liked to shut himself off from public view and enjoy the company of a few *mignons* against the advice of his mother, the dowager queen.[92] Both as dauphin and as a boy king, Louis was supposed to live his intimate life in full view; concealment from the court was considered a danger signal.

At about the time that Henri IV was himself exerting such a stimulating sexual influence on Louis, he made a decision likely to have contributed to Louis's inclination to accept, with unconscious pleasure, assaults and intrusions from other men. Henri assigned to Louis's beloved Descluseaux the task of holding the prince while he was being whipped.[93] If Henri was "astonished and angered" to hear of the kind of events at which Vauquelin hints, he would no doubt have been more astonished still to learn that his own behavior encouraged Louis to take pleasure in masochistic homosexual reveries.

CHAPTER FIVE

Becoming Brave: Fortitude and Skills

> *He is yet . . . timorous and dastardly in his courage, at the which the king hath been much troubled, when he hath seen or heard the tokens of it, saying,* Fault il donc que je soy père d'un poltron? *but his education is like to . . . amend . . . these faults.*[1]

For any gentleman to command respect in seventeenth-century France it was necessary for him to appear indifferent to physical danger. For a king the requirement was absolute: "In such a society, bravery . . . is as valued as it is necessary. Kings all possessed it to a high degree; it is the only obligatory attribute."[2]

The dangers threatening noblemen, and kings in particular, were omnipresent. Assassination plots against the French monarch were constantly suspected, often with good reason. In 1602 Henri IV always kept a physician at his side to administer an antidote in case he was poisoned. In 1603 Marie de Medici feared that Henri's mistress was conspiring with his enemies to murder the dauphin.[3] In 1609 Héroard himself, aware of the frequent threats to Henri, regarded the preservation of the king's life thus far as a sign of God's special care.[4] In Paris especially, rumors of assassination abounded. On September 21, 1612, for example, soldiers trying to halt a counterfeiter "in the name of the king" were misunderstood to have said that the fugitive had killed the king. "In the first reaction," according to the Tuscan resident, "there were very few who did not believe the truth of this report."[5]

Fearlessness was a quality so essential in French kings that it was taken for granted and rarely mentioned. Those grooming the dauphin to be king did not think it necessary to emphasize bravery explicitly as a required characteristic. They were not wrong; like his predecessors, Louis became a king noted for this "obligatory attribute": "The most politically mediocre like François I, the most frivolous like Henri II, the most depraved like

Henri III were as valorous as the wise ones like Louis XII or the men of genius like Henri IV. And in this respect, Louis XIII ceded nothing to his predecessors."[6]

Yet, as we have seen, Louis was anything but brave as a little boy. At the age of three, Héroard observes, "He cries at the slightest injury."[7] And, a bit later, "He was greatly afraid of getting hurt and of doing himself harm in any way whatever."[8] The young dauphin's list of fears was long and varied. How did this fearful child become the brave king that tradition required him to be?

REPRESSION AND DENIAL

When Louis was not quite five he occasionally began to show the apparent indifference to danger that was typical of his adult behavior. For example, he was prepared to brave the elements, even though rain, thunder, and lightning (along with the *serain*) were among his early fears. Héroard records him boldly crossing the courtyard in stormy conditions "for love of Papa," who was waiting for him. When warned of the bad weather he had replied, "It makes no difference, it makes no difference." In the fall of the same year he insisted on walking with the king in the rain "I'm not afraid of the rain," he asserted, but Héroard knew better: "He did it on account of the love he bore his father, for he feared going out in the rain."[9]

Like thunder, gunfire also inspired fear in the little boy at first. In the silence of that seventeenth-century rural world, the discharge of firearms—cannons, muskets, or rifles—was a heart-stopping sound. Becoming inured to this noise, however, was essential for a king's son, who would later be expected to defend his realm at the head of his armies.

At the age of three Louis was still afraid when the *harquebusiers* fired their weapons, and Héroard regreted that he had been "intimidated by women, and above all by his nurse." Before the child was four, though, Héroard noted that he denied his fright: when the captain fired seven or eight volleys Louis said, "I'm not afraid." A short time later, as several riflemen and musketeers fired under the great gate at once, "he turns back and cries loudly, 'I'm not afraid!'"[10] A few days later, Héroard writes, the dauphin showed himself to be "cunning and wary [*rusé et avisé*]" when he gave no sign of fear as the cannon went off after he himself had lit the fuse "for the first time." But a few weeks later he hid his head in his governess's lap (an extreme measure!) at the sound of a sudden volley. Still, such fears were considered appropriate only for women and Louis was emboldened when his nurse said, "Good Lord, how I fear war!" Shaking his head, according to Héroard, he replied: "Ho! Not I! *I* don't fear it!"[11]

Louis did not need to dissimulate his nervousness concerning the apparatus of war or his fear of firearms for very long: they were soon turned into opposite feelings—avidity for battle, love of weapons, and a delight in manipulating and discharging guns of all kinds. When almost seven he announced to his governess' daughter, Madame de Vitry, at bedtime: "When I grow up I want to go to war all the time!" Apparently to emphasize the portent of this remark, Héroard ends his day's entry with it, omitting the usual details on the time and circumstances of Louis's retirement and sleep.[12]

The alleged timidity of women[13] also helped Louis deny another fear—that inspired by his sense of genital puniness compared with his powerful father and by the seemingly ubiquitous threats to his penis. Both these impressions were partly countered by courtiers who helped the little boy exaggerate the size and power of his phallic equipment. The girls and women around him in particular supported his grandiose view.

First among the admiring young females in Louis's household was his respectful and adoring sister Elisabeth. At the very time that Henri was particularly assertive of his phallic superiority over the dauphin and the boy's own fear of girls was becoming visible, the two-year-old princess regarded her brother with "incredible fear."[14] Her fear, witnessed repeatedly by Héroard in the ensuing months, may have encouraged Louis to think that his male organ inspired terror in females. As we saw earlier, he reinforced this notion by threatening, abusing, and disdaining the docile little girl. The gratifying results led him to generalize to other women the cowing effect he had on Elisabeth. After Madame de Vitry handed him the chamber pot, he asked, "Mamanga, is my friend Vitry afraid of my cock?"[15] Thus, at the age of four he affirmed that it was not *he* who feared the loss of his genital and becoming like a girl; it was the girls who were afraid of *him*. Nor was his penis endangered; rather, it inspired fear in others. When in fun a chambermaid accused Louis of being a girl, Héroard encouraged him to confound her with the overwhelming truth: "He is furious. . . . I say to him, 'Monsieur, show her that there's nothing in [what she says]'. . . . He gets up and, smiling, pulls up his clothing all the way to his face."[16] This kind of denial, as we have seen, was not always effective against terror.

Louis graduated from the nursery to the hands of men in the beginning of 1609, after he had passed his seventh birthday. As the change approached, Héroard became increasingly attentive to signs of the child's growing courage, noting for example, how Louis ascended fearlessly into the dark attic of the Louvre."[17]

When the time finally came it meant leaving his two younger sisters and most of his female entourage behind at Saint-Germain en Laye. Louis's rapid assimilation of the new masculine culture is reflected in a letter to Elisabeth from Paris announcing his prospective visit to the scene in which he had passed his earliest years. "My sister," he writes, "Get ready to see me in eleven days at Saint-Germain. However, I must let you know there is a rumor all over this city that in the month of August a beast is to be born with

twelve heads and twenty-four feet. I shall remain even if this happens."[18]
The tone is one of confident masculinity. The once fearful little boy has,
with the help of his feminine audience, become steadfast in the face of
threats from unknown beasts that lurk.

REASSURANCE AND SUPPORT

Although Louis sometimes belied anxiety with bravado, it was uncommon
for him to conceal his emotions deliberately. Héroard and others in his
household encouraged him to express his feelings freely and fully, and the
child frequently used his first physician as a confidant, especially at bedtime.
We have already seen how Héroard was indulgent of Louis's fantasies about
enjoying his father's favor at the expense of his half brothers, the doctor
serving as a depository for the prince's bad thoughts about rivals. Héroard
was also hospitable to Louis's expressions of fear. More than once, for example, Louis revealed to him in bed that he always kept his hands on his penis at night:

> "Monsieur Héroard, can you guess where I put my hands?"
> "Sir, between your legs?"
> "I always put them on my cock."[19]

Héroard seems to have received such information with equanimity—
perhaps half understanding why Louis might feel such precautions to be
necessary.

The court abounded, as we have seen, in threats to the young dauphin,
who could not always count on the support of those who thought themselves most devoted to his interests; we recall how his fear of castration was
sometimes reinforced by warnings from his doctor and his nurse. But
sometimes Héroard would offer protective strategies or reassurances worthy of Doctor Spock or Doctor Bettelheim. Here, for example, he encourages the child to express his fears and then gives him reasons to discount
them:

> [He is] playing with his ninepins . . . on the bed . . . I say, putting my
> hand on his cock, "Here's another good ninepin." He starts to rumi-
> nate. . . . "It's the tailor. . . . I struck him a blow with my hunting
> crop. He said he wanted to cut it off me—and I was only playing!" It
> had been a long time since this happened, yet he starts to cry. I tell him
> that [the tailor's] scissors could cut only fabric and suiting and were ab-
> solutely unable to cut off his cock.[20]

Héroard also seems to have helped protect Louis from another feared
injury—to his tongue. It was characteristic of French medicine at the time
to attribute speech defects to physical imperfections. Hence the cause of

Louis's worsening stutter was sought in the persistence of some of the *filet* under his tongue. When he was eight years old there was talk of renewed surgery in this region, and Héroard accompanied the child to the queen's apartment for an inspection of his mouth: "He feared they wanted to cut his tongue off when they pulled it out. He says, "What? Do they want to cut it off?' and begins to cry."[21] "They" presumably included Louis's mother, some of her physicians, and, perhaps, surgeons, who merely executed the others' directives. "It was decided that there was no need for it," Héroard tells us, in what is probably a record of his own advice to Marie against further surgery.

Gilles de Souvré assumed his duties as Louis's governor when the child was seven years old. A faithful servitor of Henri IV, he had a reputation for bravery dating back to the days of Henri III.[22] He had been familiar to Louis from childhood, both as a frequent attendant and as the father of Courtenvaux, an early favorite of the prince. He served, on the whole, as a further support to the dauphin. Héroard clearly felt Souvré's presence in the dauphin's entourage to be benign, and he has flattering words for him in *L'institution du prince*.

In spite of the governor's new powers over Louis and his position as representative of the king, the child seems not to have feared him, as a rather realistic sketch by the six-year-old suggests (see fig. 1). Once, for example, when the prince had upset his suite by concealing himself in a bush during an excursion, Souvré threatened to whip him. Louis is said to have replied that "if he whipped him for that, he would not like him any more."[23] Such threats were apparently telling on the venerable governor.

Though Souvré may have been pliable, he did bolster Louis's confidence in his masculine capacities. At three-and-a-half, as we have seen, the dauphin was adamant at the prospect of one day becoming a father himself as well as uncertain of the procedures involved. When arrangements were made to marry him to the Spanish infanta at the age of ten, however, he felt that Souvré had initiated him adequately into men's secrets. The queen questioned her son:

Queen: My son, I want to marry you [off]. Are you willing?
Dauphin: I'm very willing, Madame.
Q.: But you won't know how to make babies.
D.: I beg your pardon, Madame.
Q.: And how do you know how?
D.: Monsieur de Souvré has taught me.[24]

It takes more than realistic instructions and reassurances, though, to control fears of injury. Indeed, as I have shown, many strategies designed for Louis's sexual education inspired anxiety rather than confidence, and dangerous unconscious wishes, usually aggravated by his father's visits, gave

Figure 1. Six-year-old Louis's sketch of his governor, Gilles de Souvré. October 30, 1607. (BN, fr. 4022, fol. 495v.) Photo courtesy of the Bibliothèque Nationale, Paris.

rise to conflict that expressed itself in lassitude, malaise, and physical symptoms. So long as Louis was still in the nursery, and especially when his father was absent, he was allowed relatively free reign to counter such anxiety and threatening stimuli. For example, his toilet habits, made possible by the numerous servants at his beck and call, enabled him to express his recalcitrance to external controls and intrusions until he was nearly six years old. His regressive oral fantasies had a ready object in his nurse, who sometimes even offered a nipple for the growing boy, long since weaned, to suck. Few four-and-a-half-year-olds can have had so indulgent a setting in which to reenact a scene of infancy as the following: "He wants to have himself swaddled, and tells Mademoiselle Piolant [his dresser] so. 'Pretend I'm a tiny baby. Say, "Oh, you're crying!"' Then, imitating a tiny baby's voice, 'Waaa . . . waaa!' he sends for his Maman Doundoun. When she comes she asks him, 'Well, Sir, What do you want of me?' 'I want to kiss you.'"[25]

Once Louis was in the hands of men, such freedom to regress was restricted. Though some of the resources of the nursery continued to be available (if often in a changed form), babyish behavior of the kind just described was no longer indulged by those around the dauphin. Female attendants, notably his nurse, his sisters, and his governess, ceased to be readily available; although his nurse accompanied him to the Louvre, she was not included among his sleeping attendants. His immediate entourage consisted exclusively of boys and men, who offered new occupations to replace those older ones that, as children's play, were now disapproved of.

MASTERY THROUGH ACTIVITY

Weapons

The dauphin was given playthings that make even the most modern therapeutic milieu seem meagerly equipped. Did the mason threaten him with ominous pincers? He receives a pair of small ones with which to experiment. Did he fear that the tailor would cut off his precious *guillery* with his scissors? He is provided with a pair of tiny scissors. Given his own knife to wear on a cord around his neck, he exclaims: "There is my little knife—it cuts where I want it to!"[26] As a small boy he was often presented with finely crafted toy cannons, harquebuses, muskets, and pistols, which he treasured and played with, acting out his desires to become a brave soldier:

> He asks for his arms—musket, bandoleer, whip, and sword. Sends for the harquebuses of the guard corps. He makes a musketeer of himself, Monsieur de Verneuil close to him. . . . Mortemart and several other little ones and the pages of the small stable. His ensign was a yellow scarf . . . he had the guard corps' drum. They go like that across the terrace in battle formation to the ballroom, line up, and charge . . . The

king and queen come in to watch them. . . . After several reviews and
salvoes of harquebuses—rat-a-tat-tat—he addresses Monsieur de Sully
. . . [for] money to pay the soldiers. . . . He does another . . . review
and salvo . . . then retires in battle formation to his bedchamber.[27]

Though Louis was at first frightened by the sound of gunfire, he had always
been fascinated by firearms and weapons of all kinds. We have already
noted the association in his mind between anal processes and the expulsive
action and sound of guns and their missiles. Other gratifications connected
with the exercise of anal sphincter controls also seem to be involved in his
fantasies about shooting. For example, the three-year-old devised a violent
strategy for entering the chapel if the door was closed when he was late for
mass:

Dauphin: I'll open it with my harquebus. I'll fire a great coup—rat-a-tat-
  tat—and break it down.
Nurse: If you've broken it down, won't God be annoyed?
D.: (Shaking his head and speaking softly like someone fearful that he was
  not being good in saying what he did) Ha! I'll shoot him! (lifting his
  hands and opening and closing his fingers.)[28]

The next day the object of his aggressive designs was a more usual one—
his half brother and age-mate, Henri de Verneuil. Playing with "things he
enjoys the most, his firearms," the dauphin "takes up his firing posture, left
foot in front, with incredible grace, then, 'rat-a-tat-tat,' and comes over to
Madame. 'Madame, I've shot him,' he says softly. 'I've got the stag right in
the middle of the head,' because he had said to Monsieur de Verneuil, 'You
be the stag.'"[29]

A few months later he was allowed to fire a real gun for the first time.
Under the falconer's supervision he pulled the trigger. "It made a great
noise; his finger was caught in it," says Héroard. "He was afraid, pulled it
back, trembling, crying: 'I was scared.' Then he suddenly calmed down,
squeezing it again, by himself."[30] In the following spring he was allowed,
on his own, to light a fuse that discharged one of his harquebuses. Now he
enjoyed the smell of gunpowder as well as the action of discharge. "How I
love that smell," he confided to Héroard much later.[31]

With Louis's transfer to the Louvre, exercises in handling weapons and in
other military arts became a regular part of his training. It was typical of the
prince's growing vigor that, when his instructor proposed to show him the
correct stance for firing "while advancing and while retreating," he impressed Héroard by replying, "Advancing—not retreating."[32]

Eventually, at Monsieur de Souvré's request, the queen allowed Louis to
fire his loaded revolver-type harquebus on his own. At the age of ten he already had seven of these weapons. On the appointed day he rose at five in

the morning and had them all brought to him while he was still in his dress-
ing gown. "He says to me," Héroard reports, "'If enemies come, here's
really something to give them a good salvo with!'" After marching about in
excited anticipation with one of the guns on his shoulder, he asked to be
given an enema (which he then refused). In the afternoon he fired his first
bullet and then discharged the gun once more. The next morning he shot a
jay in the head from his bedroom window and killed yet another in the
afternoon.

The young king was on his way to becoming a crack shot. "He had never
been so happy," says Héroard.[33]

Birds and Beasts

Any picture of Louis XIII's childhood setting must include a large animal
population. All the royal palaces in which he lived were in country that
teamed with wildlife, and the barrier between indoors and outdoors was in-
definite. Undomesticated beasts often entered the palace precincts: on one
occasion or another living quarters were penetrated by badgers, bears,
boars, foxes, wolves, various hooved animals including a giraffe, and, of
course, rats. There were bats in Louis's bedroom at Saint-Germain.[34] The
more or less tame animals that normally slept in the palace included monkeys as well as dogs and birds of many varieties.

Louis's relations with animals were so intimate that we may understand
his serious puzzlement when his nurse was telling him the story of "the little
frog." "Do animals talk?" he asked, since this did not square with his customary experience.[35] Animals took part in most of his activities and accordingly figured importantly in his mental life.

Birds were the first creatures Louis showed awareness of, and they became one of his most profound and abiding interests. This fascination can
probably be traced back to Héroard's practice of feeling the child's pulse
every morning, a ritual that the doctor, and later the child, called "feeling
the little bird." The first recorded scene involving an actual flying creature
took place when he was three-and-a-half. The sieur de Courtenvaux,
Souvré's son and a favorite of the dauphin (as well as an intimate retainer
and messenger of Henri IV), returns after an absence.[36] Louis rejoices to see
him, Héroard knows, but he does not show his pleasure directly: "He
blushes deeply and is overcome with delight. Without glancing at him he
says, 'There's a bat!' Looking up and pointing with his finger: 'I've caught
it!'"[37]

The meaning of this is uncertain but, it seems, his excitement at seeing
Courtenvaux is somehow associated with the flying creature in the rafters.

Louis's earliest drawings depict birds. Héroard appended them to one of
his journal entries, noting that the child, not yet four, could already represent birds recognizably, with the "bodies, legs, feet, and other parts in the

right places." On this occasion Louis was so absorbed in his work that a court bogeyman had to be summoned in order to frighten him into bed.[38]

Both Louis's drawings and his remarks suggest that, in his imagination, he sometimes took the place of birds or felt them to be part of himself. One of his pictures, for example, reveals an association between birds and his nurse (see figure 2). He first sketches in a bird, then proceeds to draw a naked Doundoun, working his way from her head downward, as Héroard tells us.[39]

The bird representing himself seems most often to be female. Thus, in play with Doundoun, "You be the rooster and I'll be the hen. I'll make a little cackle." Then, as Héroard relates, he starts to sing: "Cock-a-doodle-doo! Look, Maman Doundoun, the hen has cackled!"[40]

The identity between bird and little boy is further indicated in an exchange between Héroard and the dauphin. The child has just awakened, and the doctor, feeling his pulse, asks:

"Little bird, have you slept well?"
"Yes! Yes!"
"Where do you come from, little bird?"
"(Speaks in nonsense words) then he says: "From Barbary in Tartary."[41]

This ritual continued over the years. When Héroard is about to leave the Louvre on vacation, the dauphin, who has gone to bed, "gives me his arm and says to me, 'Look at the little bird before you leave.' It was his pulse."[42] In this context the bird is a part of himself. On one occasion, eating on the run, Louis says to his nurse:

"Doundoun, I'm going off to find something for my little birds to eat," and goes over to her with meat in his mouth, shows it to her, then swallows it, then drinks. Says that he's giving it to his little birds. Then, "More drink—There's a little bird who has not drunk!"—It was himself.[43]

Louis often refers to his penis in terms associated with birds. His "cock" is a *guillery*—literally, a "pecker"—and also a little bird or beak (*bec*). Still in bed after the "Barbary in Tartary" exchange with Héroard, "he looks at his cock in the mirror and says, 'Hey! There's Mademoiselle!' smiling to himself."[44]

Whatever birds may have represented to Louis in his imagination, during the following year he was able to take an active role with them. He was initiated into the secrets of falconry, a sport that was to fascinate and delight him for years, and developed the habit of going about with a falcon on his hand. A courtier presented him with a shrike—the "butcher bird"—which kills and devours smaller birds after impaling them on sharp objects. It was

trained to hunt sparrows. After the dauphin had put on his falconer's gaunt-
let he released the shrike "exactly right" in the *salle,* and it performed as it
should.[45]

When at last he was allowed to go on his first hunt, two partridges were
caught, one by his own sparrow hawk, as well as five or six quails and various other animals. Louis told Héroard the whole story with zest at supper
time.[46] The next day, however, the corpse of his shrike was brought to
him. Although the boy "did not want to show his grief," Héroard knew
that he was upset by the sight of the dead bird, for "he used to take great delight in it."[47]

Birds taken as prey by other birds, or brought down with arrows or gun-
shot, often turned up on Louis's table the next day, evoking pride, pleasure,
or other, mixed feelings. When, for example, he was served some little pigeons, he exclaimed: "'Oh! How little it is! It makes me feel sorry for it!'
. . . almost with a tear in his eye—and then he doesn't want to eat any
more." This description is a note in the margin of Héroard's textual account
of how Louis declined a serving of liver, calling it *merde.* The association between the two aversions suggests that the eating of these birds was both
pleasurable and disgusting.[48]

The military associations of the names Louis gave his pet birds further
suggest the basis of their appeal for him: "Is it not curious to see him make
himself a little military company of birds from the lesser aviary? Here is his
Ardennes finch, which he calls the *captain,* another *lieutenant,* and another
ensign. There is a lark, which is the *drummer,* and a goldfinch, which is the
fife."[49] The avian military hierarchy had a deadly order that was attractive
and amusing to the young prince: "While at supper he spoke of birds; of a
shrike that he possessed. He says that he wanted to train it to fly after sparrows, and a sparrow after a wren, and a wren after a fly. I ask him, 'And the
fly, Sire, what will you have it fly after?' 'I shall make it fly after a gnat.'"[50]

With the transfer to the Louvre, Louis's surroundings acquired some aspects of an aviary. Small birds flew about in his bedchamber or perched on
roosts he had constructed himself. Merlins were caged in his office. One
night he complained of being awakened by chickens that were being fat-
tened in the room above his own for the queen's table.[51] As for falconry,
Louis speedily became an adept. His falconer later wrote of him, "There is
no falconer in the world who has anything to teach him about that science."[52] His ready skills reflected his keen interest in the sport: "This taste
soon became a passion," judges one historian, "the only one that gave a bit
of excitement to the youthful life of the prince."[53] Héroard agrees as to the
passion: "At supper he talks about falconry, which he loves with a passion.
He speaks of it with a knowledge and intelligence beyond his years."[54]

According to the child, it was the birds themselves that he loved. While
conversing at dinner as a ten-year-old with a group of noblemen, he ob-

jected when one of them remarked that no one loved birds more than the late cardinal de Guise. "Ah," said Louis, "On that point I cede to no one. I get up at four in the morning to groom them." Héroard concludes, "He loved them extremely."[55]

Louis's falconer exalted the relationship between the prince and birds: "It seems as though [he] . . . has some secret intelligence of birds and a power unknown to men . . . for besides the great inclination with which he loves them [he has] an inimitable skill in managing them, whether in luring them or in making them fly."[56]

In addition to his pleasure in training birds to prey on one another and his delight in midair captures, Louis loved the menial aspects of physically caring for the birds: "He goes in robe and slippers before breakfast to his birds to groom them. Works at it himself, and with such ardor that he sometimes takes off his robe when it gets in his way."[57] He attended to them in the evening, too, both before and after he had done his "business" [*affaires*] on the little toilet seat.[58] Just as Héroard cared for the "little bird" Louis, so the prince attended to the grooming of his own birds, large and small. This activity and the sport of falconry itself helped him master anxieties created by the doctor's intrusions and other dangers.

Such anxieties were no doubt revived at about this time by the illness of Louis's four-year-old brother. This child, an invalid all his life, was now dying of a kind of sleeping sickness at Saint-Germain, where the prince was visiting, and the sight of his helpless passivity could well have been disturbing. After supper, Héroard tells us, Louis went to his apartment, where, "being seated at his *affaires*," he let fly his *pie grièche*, "has it kill a bird in the torches." Perhaps the doctor is half aware of Louis's struggle, by this means, to keep active; he notes in the margin, "never idle."[59]

Devising original ways to capture and kill prey was a specialty with the boy, whose falconer describes one such *vol*. Louis had servants fix nets over the Tuileries gardens; when beaters then flushed the tiny birds out of the dense hedges bordering the way, the birds were unable to escape Louis's falcons. This strategy so swelled the day's bag that the falconer warned the prince that the supply of victims for his "pleasure" would soon be exhausted. Whereupon "His Majesty, opening his hand, showed the six heads of his take for the morning, and, that done, he went off to hear mass."[60]

Through his passion for birds and falconry, Louis developed specialized knowledge and skills unusual even in his own royal circle, where riding with hounds after stags, boars, foxes, or wolves was more usual. The dauphin's attendants encouraged early mastery of fears associated with these animals, and from infancy he was exposed to the bloody rituals connected with the hunt. When he was nine months old his father had him watch as the entrails of a stag taken near Rueil were given to the dogs—a traditional dénouement to a successful chase. Héroard, always eager for the dauphin to show his mettle before the king, notes proudly that the baby "is not at all disturbed by it." Two years later Louis is taken to watch a boar hunt: "He sees the boar go back and forth before him" at close quarters and exclaims, "It has big teeth!"[61] As we have seen, biting animals figured in Louis's dreams at least as soon as he was able to give an account of them.

Wild animals were pursued and trapped with the aid of dogs, which were so plentiful in Louis's surroundings that it occasioned little comment when a lady visitor presented him with a dozen at one time.[62] His contact with them in the nursery was constant and intimate. "He loves dogs extremely," Héroard remarks of his three-and-a-half-year-old patient.[63] This conclusion is usually confirmed by the doctor's description of Louis's relationship with them.

But dogs were not always benign and obliging; sometimes they inspired terror. Occasionally a rabid dog would be encountered in the neighborhood, and Louis had to be protected by his attendants, who would try to kill it. Some of the household pets were gigantic, barely tamed mastiffs unused to children, and a large dog that habitually accompanied Henri IV was bad-tempered with Louis. Héroard records it jumping on the six-year-old child, "surprising him"; "he cries," but Henri is unsympathetic, "scolds him for having been afraid and tells him he must fear nothing. He replies, 'It's just that I wasn't thinking.'"[64] Louis spoke truthfully. Indeed, at this age he was for the most part confident with dogs, using them to master his own fears rather than allowing them to inspire fear in him. An early demonstration of such mastery occurred when, though not yet three, he chased a dog from the dining room in disgust. "He ate some *merde*," Louis explained.[65] This "disgusting" feature of dogs was perhaps one basis for the child's attraction to them.

In Louis's play with dogs we see him reenacting in a dominant role experiences that inspired fear when he was their victim. Once, for example, he has been sticking out his own tongue and chewing on it, "out of habit"—a habit that was disapproved of. "They try to scare him by telling him he'll have to kiss the ass of his dog, Cavalon," Héroard reports. "He laughs at that and starts playing with it. He makes love to it in the manner of a dog, kisses it, nuzzles his face in its ears."[66]

As his skills grew, Louis was able to control dogs more and more effectively, a reassurance against whatever dangers they threatened. He sometimes hitched them to carts that were part of his games or managed them in other ways. Watching two foxes being hunted down by dogs in the Fontainebleau courtyard, Héroard writes, the five-year-old dauphin addresses the master of hounds from the window: "'Release this white dog,' he orders, then this one, or that one, naming them by name. He commanded magisterially and appropriately."[67]

A week later Louis is taken by the king to the ballroom to see a fight between mastiffs and a bear and bull. "The bear having got a mastiff beneath him," Héroard relates, "he starts to scream, 'Kill the bear! Kill the bear!'" After witnessing this combat, the dauphin plays a game in which he takes the place of the victimized dog. He puts on one of his old dresses with leading strings and "has himself held by the *lisières* to imitate the mastiffs that he had seen straining at the leash in order to hurl themselves on the bear."[68]

Families of dogs, with which Louis lived in such intimate contact, could also be used to act out feelings that were more troublesome in the context of his own family. In an early letter to Elisabeth the promise of a dog expresses his tender feelings for her: "My sister . . . I have a bitch that is in heat, out of which I hope to give you the offspring. . . . Your most affectionate brother."[69] Relationships in his real family that caused pain or anxiety are the cause of gleeful confidences when they concern his dog families: "Talking about his dogs, he says he has six pregnant bitches: 'I married them.' . . . In a lowered voice: 'I have one dog that made a cuckold of another—he slept with his wife, the bitch—but you must tell no one else.'"[70] Murderous feelings toward family members could also be expressed through dogs. We have seen how in play Louis would pretend to be a hound in pursuit of a stag. Often it was his rival half brother, Henri de Verneuil, who was cast as the stag-victim.

As I mentioned earlier, hunting on horseback figured in Louis's daydreams from his first years. As the four-and-a-half-year-old tells Héroard his fantasy at bedtime, the doctor amends it to make it more realistic and exciting:

Louis: I'll go hunting; I'll kill a boar with my sword.
Héroard: Sir, you will go hunting and carry your sword. Then the boar, coming straight at you, will impale himself on it. After you give him a sword's blow, he will die.
L.: Then I'll chop off his head.
H.: No, Sir, then you'll have the huntsmen cut it off.
L.: Won't I be the huntsman?
H.: Sir, you will command the huntsmen who will cut off the head, and you'll take it to Papa who will embrace you—he'll love you so much. Then you'll go off and take a stag, give him a sword's blow on the hamstring. He'll fall, and you'll have his foot cut off. You'll take it to Papa, who will caress you, call you his darling, take you to his beautiful gallery in the Louvre.[71]

More than a year later hunting figures in a nightmare: "He wakes with a start at one a.m. with an extremely loud, terrifying scream. . . . 'Hey! Papa's going without me!' crying and bursting into tears. 'Hey, I want to go with Papa! Wait for me, Papa!'" Later he tells his nurse: "I dreamed I went hunting with Papa. I saw a great big wolf that wanted to eat Papa and another that wanted to eat me and I pulled out my sword and then I killed them both."[72] Thus his desire for and his terror at surrender to the king ("being eaten by the wolf"?) have been countered by protecting Papa through killing the wolf.

As we have seen, this was a time of conflict for Louis in which he often felt helpless against self-destructive desires to surrender to his father. It was, therefore, a significant change for the child when, just before his seventh birthday, he was at last able to play in real life the bold role he had imagined in dreams. When he mounted a horse for the first time Héroard commented proudly, "I have never seen a man better seated on a horse, body erect, legs as though he were fully trained." The very next day, he noticed, Louis was already "bold and well seated."[73] The child's deep inclination now coincided both with his capacities and with a highly approved activity.

From then on Louis was given every material and instructional support needed to become an expert horseman and marksman. Soon he was able, side by side with his father, to hunt down stags and boars in a sport considered eminently suitable for kings. What had been possible only in dreams—mounting a horse and killing the wolves that threatened to devour—now became a daily opportunity.

As was the case with birds, dogs, and weapons, Louis became a passionate collector of horses, though Héroard tells us less of the prince's attachment to them, perhaps because they were not kept in the palace. Nevertheless, his journal does reveal that horses, too, were among Louis's jealously guarded possessions—like *les siens*, to be shared as little as possible with others. So strong was this sentiment that as a ten-year-old he would deprive himself of the joy of horseback riding in order to keep his horses to himself, as in this exchange:

> At four o'clock he got into the carriage to go hunting. . . . Having arrived, Monsieur de Souvré asks him if he doesn't want to mount a horse and [indicates] that there are two hackneys from which he may choose.
> "For whom is the other?" [Louis asks.]
> [Souvré:] "It will be for me."
> "I'm perfectly satisfied to remain in the carriage"—he didn't want to get out. This was deliberate, so that Monsieur de Souvré would not mount his hackney—it was one of his strongest jealousies.[74]

Lesser Skills

Horsemanship, hunting, and practicing the arts of war certainly aided Louis's efforts to overcome his anxieties, gratify his desires, and win the approval of adults, particularly his father. But the dauphin also had other pastimes that, though less appreciated at court, enabled him to master his fears or use substitute objects for forbidden gratifications.

From his earliest months Louis was sensitive to music: "Nothing captured his mind so much," writes Héroard. He took great pleasure in listening to the many court musicians perform on various instruments, responding especially to the rhythmic, rather than the melodic or harmonic, qualities of the music. The young prince soon mastered military drum rolls and was given to beating out these and other patterns with his tongue on the roof of his mouth, with his hand, a spoon, or other implements. The attraction that percussive rhythm had for him was connected, as we have seen, with the motives that contributed to his stutter. He seems to have had some aptitude for the lute and had a few lessons on it, but such proficiency was discouraged by Henri IV. The King's limited taste aside, playing musical instruments was regarded as a low skill, inappropriate for a future French monarch.[75] In later years, Louis's musical activities were mostly confined to directing choral or instrumental groups. Not surprisingly, in view of his taste for order, the arrangement of vocal parts appealed to him as a task. There is no indication in Héroard's record that Louis had a gift for composition, and the works attributed to him, such as the music for the ballet *Merlaison*, are most likely the products of court professionals.[76]

The prince's considerable talents in the plastic arts, if not greatly valued by anyone except Héroard, were at least regarded as innocuous by those responsible for his training. His drawing began at the age of four as he held a pencil in his hand after a writing lesson. He had little aptitude for calligraphy: his writing was always cramped and labored. Sometimes, too, he repeated words, apparently inadvertently, reflecting the same impediment that inhibited his speech. But, as we have seen, he was soon able to draw recognizable birds.

Louis seems to have used his skill in drawing to master certain anxieties. At the age of nearly six, after beginning with representations of a bird, he sketches in a naked Doundoun, working his way down from her head (see figure 2). "Finishing the navel, he sketches what is lower down and, having made it, says, 'And there is what I don't want to say,' starting to laugh."[77] The drawing, included in Héroard's manuscript journal, shows that he has clearly represented the female genitals, and this at a time when he was struggling to overcome fears inspired by what appeared to be a dangerous lack in the bodies of the girls and women around him.

As he grew older his drawing skill increased. He also enjoyed mixing his paints himself, with knife and palette. In 1609 his newly appointed tutor was surprised to find that the prince painted "like a painter."[78]

Louis had other fine motor skills, and a liking and aptitude for all manual activities except writing. But this "great inclination for mechanics," as Héroard wrote,[79] was considered even less appropriate than musical performance for the son of a king. When, for example, he played at being a carpenter as a three-year-old, his governess warned him that this was not a suitable occupation: "'What, Sir, will they say that you'll turn into a carpen-

Figure 2. Six-year-old Louis's sketch of a bird and his nurse, Doundoun. (BN, fr. 4022, fol. 462.) Photo courtesy of the Bibliothèque Nationale, Paris.

ter rather than a prince?' He throws down the drill, and shaking his head and raising his hand: 'Oh, no, I'm no carpenter! I don't want to be a carpenter. . . . It was my valet who made me hold it!'"[80] Vauquelin was later to advise the mother of Louis's successor against encouraging in Louis XIV his father's taste for "things that depend on the hand."[81]

Louis XIII enjoyed not only the intricate manual activities of artisans but also cooking, cleaning, and other housekeeping chores, which were even less approved by those grooming him to be king.

According to Héroard, Louis also excelled at gross motor activities: marching, manipulating weapons, horseback riding, playing games such as tennis and *palemail* (a game like croquet in which the ball is propelled with a mallet). The doctor admires Louis's skill in military exercises, in which he began to be schooled regularly in 1609. The prince seems finally to have become an able enough dancer as well; this was the one performing art that his father greatly appreciated. But although Louis often took part in dances and was still more often urged to do so, Héroard frequently comments that the child did not enjoy such performances and disliked dancing.[82] It may be that, despite Louis's good muscular coordination and rhythmic sense, he felt uncomfortable in an exercise typically performed without props.

FORMAL INSTRUCTION: BODY AND MIND

When, on January 24, 1609, Louis left Saint-Germain for Paris to begin formal training under Souvré's governorship, the change was, in some respects, minor. Although he was now to receive regular instruction in equestrian and martial arts as well as in history, geography, French composition, Latin, and religion, the child was not a stranger to the rather loose discipline this regimen entailed. He had already learned to read and write, had committed proverbs and aphorisms to memory, and knew the basic concepts of his faith.

Soon after the dauphin's transfer to the hands of men, his new tutor wrote a description of his pupil to a correspondent in the provinces. Vauquelin's remarks are valuable as corroboration of Héroard's testimony, for he was the first intellectual besides the doctor to enter Louis's intimate circle. A few weeks after giving his first lesson, on March 6, 1609, he writes: "What I can report for certain on Monseigneur le Dauphin is his health. . . . He has a very strong body and an equally vigorous mind." Although he judges Louis "sufficiently inclined to knowledge of letters," he finds him slow to learn and slow to relinquish impressions he has already formed. The prince, is, however, persistent in those matters to which he applies himself, "so much so that one must, perforce, wait upon his own volition" to pursue desired aims. Vauquelin has hit upon a euphemistic way to describe his pupil's stubbornness. Louis's tenacity is such, he continues, that once his attention has been won he is capable of devoting himself to a problem for an hour at a time, "of his own accord."[83]

Héroard had long since presented a picture of a little boy with an "admirable memory" for the "least little things," an impression confirmed in part by this new witness, who describes, somewhat less sympathetically, a child slow to admit new information but tenacious in retaining it, slow in sharing it, and capable of storing up far more than he lets on. Louis was as cautious about ingesting knowledge as Héroard had taught him to be about food and drink, and the methods the doctor had used to control the child's evacuation doubtless contributed to Louis's unwillingness to let go of what he had learned.

In the next two years Louis seems to equate taking in medicines with taking in learning. For example, Héroard tells us that at eight o'clock one evening Louis took an enema "on the strength of the promise Monsieur de Souvré made him that he would not have to study." The taking in of one kind of substance can also be made acceptable by giving out another: "takes medicine, on Monsieur de Souvré's promise that he may fire four rounds of the harquebus."[84]

Though Vauquelin does not mention Louis's severe stutter until years later, this handicap surely reinforced the child's inclination to keep his thoughts to himself. As a foreign visitor who saw him as a young adult wrote, "His words were never many," on account of this "extreme" impediment.[85] Once, when Louis was reproached by his governor for a lack of enthusiasm for the sights they saw during a trip, he remarked, "But, Monsieur de Souvré, don't you know that I'm not a great talker?"[86]

Louis's difficulty in speaking and writing impeded his learning of foreign tongues. No systematic attempt seems to have been made to teach him Italian, his mother's native language and the foreign tongue most frequently used in France at the time. Although he was tutored in Spanish, at least after his marriage had been arranged,[87] the claim that he announced Philip III's death to Anne of Austria in Spanish is not confirmed by Héroard's diary. He certainly did not "speak Spanish and Italian well," as Louis Vaunois maintains.[88]

At the same time, the dauphin was a fastidious critic of faulty speech in those around him. His ear for the sounds and rhythmic properties of words was acute from his earliest years. Before he was three he was aware of his mother's deficiencies in French pronunciation and called attention to a mistake—*soucre* in place of *sucre*—that she made in conversation.[89] A few months later, Héroard notes, he "reproves those who don't speak well," correcting his nurse's diction. He would burst out laughing when one of his suite misspoke a single word.[90] He may have suppressed his own speech to contain rage, some of which he could release when others misspoke. He did sometimes express his rage verbally when he could disguise the aggressive purpose of his words, as in witticisms. Thus, when not yet four, he gaily articulated in the guise of an amusing rhyme a murderous thought about his lackey, who had sat in his master's chair without permission:

Ha!
I'll chop off your head. . . .
I'll stick it in a hole!

[*Ha! Je vou' couperai le cou.* . . .
Je le mettrai dans un trou!][91]

ON STAGE

After 1608 the scope of the dauphin's actions expanded, and he was now nominally master in his own miniature court. His establishment was enlarged, separated from that of his brothers and sisters, and given an independent status. He had about thirty young boys as well as many other servants assigned to him and was expected to administer justice among his followers, issue orders to his attendants, and dispatch the daily password to his guards.

This independence was of course largely fictitious. Louis realized this, as he showed on one occasion when Madame de Montglat and Monsieur de Souvré jokingly wrangled over who had possession of the dauphin. Louis remarked ("without raising his voice or looking away from the task he was engaged in," according to Héroard), "I hope that one day I shall belong to myself."[92] The child was no doubt unaware that what others had made of his personality rendered this objective problematical.

A second, more significant effect of Louis's graduation into the hands of men was his increased visibility to the Paris public since the normal site of his activity was now the Louvre rather than suburban Saint-Germain. His comings and goings were viewed and discussed by larger groups, and accounts of them appeared more frequently in print.

An early press notice shows that his preparation was certainly considered successful in terms of bravery; within a year of Louis's arrival in the capital Malherbe reports:

> There is in the queen's great office a portrait in which the Spanish infanta is painted full length. . . . The other evening Monsieur le Dauphin was pointing it out to some of the little ones being raised with him and said to them, "There's my wife!" Monsieur de Souvré says to him that perhaps the Spaniards will be unwilling to hand her over to him, and he replies promptly, "Ah, then it will be necessary to go and seize her!"

The poet exults:

> Truly, this prince will set the measure for the youth of his generation![93]

In the matter of the first attribute of kings, Louis had met the expectations of his public.

CHAPTER SIX

Henri's Legacy

He was born to be king; he bears the name of a holy king; and has had for a father a very glorious king. All these attributes are indications that he, too, will be a very great prince.[1]

As Louis was preparing to leave the nursery on New Year's Day, 1609, Jean Héroard presented him with a copy of his newly published book, *L'institution du prince*—a work "done for him," as the doctor told the dauphin, both in person and in a letter of dedication.[2]

That Louis be encouraged to emulate his father was a prime tenet of Héroard's treatise, one from which no courtier would have dissented openly. "You will always have before your eyes, as the model for your life," the doctor wrote, "the virtuous actions and illustrious deeds of His Majesty."[3]

Henri was manifestly the primary model for his son and successor. The growing Louis consciously saw him as the all-powerful, all-knowing monarch of early childhood. When as a four-year-old the dauphin announced "I'll go down to the river and I'll swim," Héroard asked, "Sir, how would you do that?" Louis replied "'I'll throw myself in the water, then I'll go like that' [moving his arms]. . . . 'Papa knows how to swim well—when he is down by the big river he swims.'"[4] This was but one of Henri's many deeds of skill or valor of which Louis had heard tell since infancy.

At the age of eight the dauphin saw his father not only as the powerful, knowing figure of childhood but also as the protector of all France. When told of the seizure of Portugal by Spain in 1578 during the absence of King Sebastian, he asked: "If my father, the king, went to Flanders"—a project that was being discussed—"would the king of Spain take possession of France?"[5]

Avowedly, the little boy had no will independent of Henri's: his duty was to serve the king at his pleasure. Asked if he would rather go to Fontainebleau or remain in Saint-Maur, near Paris, he replied according to the correct formula: "If Papa goes to Fontainebleau, I'd rather go there; if he stays in Paris, I'd rather be here."[6]

But in reality, as we have seen, Louis's feelings toward this great father were a compound of passionate admiration and distaste, love and hate, longing and fear. And his negative emotions were often covertly seconded by others at court.

INCONGRUOUS MODELS

"People wouldn't recognize you for the son of a king," was a favorite remonstrance of Louis's governess when the child misbehaved. But the fact is that Henri's rude manners were often a source of embarrassment to those charged with the task of civilizing his recalcitrant son. There was a discrepancy between the king's practice and the precepts of gentility taught in the nursery, as Louis realized: "At supper he asked for his jellied dessert. Madame de Montglat tells him, 'Say "please!"' He answers, 'Papa doesn't say "please"' — because she often told him that he should do everything as Papa did."[7]

Many at court were aware that the king was less than scrupulous in practicing what he preached. Héroard records this exchange between a courtier and the five-year-old Louis:

Courtier: Sir, didn't you hear Papa tell you that he wanted you to learn to wash your hands by yourself and wipe your own back end?
Louis: Yes.
C.: Then why didn't you tell him that he didn't wipe his own himself?
L.: I wouldn't have dared. He would have whipped me.[8]

It may not be merely fortuitous that Héroard recounts these exchanges; the pages of his journal frequently contain implicit criticisms of Henri as a model for the dauphin. Temperamentally, the king and the doctor were in striking contrast and thus were often rival influences on Louis during his boyhood.

The doctor could not, of course, present himself as a model to the young prince. But he could, and did, point to figures in the royal past who were suitable alternatives to Louis's father — such as the dauphin's namesake, the holy Louis IX, whom Héroard used to console Louis at bedtime when he complained about not having been named Henri: "I take the opportunity to tell him that his name was much more beautiful and to speak to him of the king, Saint Louis, of his piety, his fairness, and how he made war on the Turks, how he pierced the tongue of blasphemers with a hot iron, died in Egypt making war against the Turks, and then rose to heaven, where he was a saint. He listened attentively."[9] To present Saint Louis as receiving his heavenly reward for merciless aggression against the the Turks—indeed, for damaging their tongues!—is to depict him in a particularly attractive form to the young boy whose own murderous feelings may have been connected with damage to his tongue, feelings that were later reinforced by his fears of giving in to the wish to be damaged. And in suggesting that the name Louis was "more beautiful" than Henri, Héroard was making a daring challenge to the model that the king set his son. The contrast between the chaste Louis IX and the promiscuous Henri IV was striking. The incongruity of the two examples had impressed more than one observer, including the papal nuncio.[10]

Henri and Héroard differed not only on whose conduct the dauphin should emulate but also on what precepts he should follow. The doctor's journal frequently bears witness to these points of conflict. He often seems to be trying to prevent the son from developing certain personality traits of the father and to encourage in Louis moral principles that Henri lacked.

Héroard, for example, perceived an orderly, considered temperament to be a most desirable characteristic of his young patient. In this he was encouraging in Louis traits that he himself possessed; no one could have been more methodical than the doctor. We have noted how he also reinforced the prince's tendency to be neat and meticulous. "He will never be heedless," Héroard observes of Louis, "[he] has never given a single sign of it."[11]

Henri, by contrast, was often heedless, especially in pursuit of personal pleasure. As a worried observer from the Tuscan court writes, "He exhausts himself in violent exercise, eats and drinks without discretion." Most disturbing of all was the king's sexual recklessness, which made his life seem increasingly unregulated and his behavior "scandalous," even to such a sympathetic onlooker.[12]

In view of this, it seems remarkably bold of Héroard to include this advice for the dauphin in a work published during Henri's lifetime: "And since there is nothing in men's deeds more brutal and odious to God than seeing them prostitute themselves, as though to spite reason, and give themselves as hostages to appetites of the senses, to the pleasures of the flesh, may our young prince, in order to avoid these deceptive delights, follow chastity as one of the guides to bodily health."[13] Héroard evidently attempted to reinforce all Louis's early signs of rejecting sexual promiscuity. There is no doubt that Héroard attributes to to the dauphin understanding he does not possess when he represents him, at the age of less than three, as giving a firm "No!" in reply to the joking question of a courtier, "When you grow up, are you going to be as bawdy as your father?" The doctor's motives also seem transparent when in the following year he notes that of the several proverbs of Solomon his little patient recited, "he found this one the most beautiful: 'That man is happy who has found a virtuous woman.'" When Louis recites some proverbs of Solomon and three quatrains of Pibrac two months later, it is again the one that the prince says "I love so much" that Héroard chooses to recopy: "That man is happy who meets a virtuous woman."[14] These were months during which there was once more strife between Marie de Medici and her husband over his renewed attentions to the Marquise de Verneuil,[15] and it is likely that Louis's preference for this motto was not so much spontaneous as prodded by those around him who were most closely associated with the queen's interest—Héroard among them.

Héroard also disapproved of Henri's tactics in disciplining the dauphin, preferring manipulative forms of controlling children. Rather than use physical punishment, he writes, mentors should make children feel sorry for having done wrong by "punishing bad conduct in such a way that one gives them a little honest shame at having done it, rather than too much fear of punishment." The person in charge of Louis should have a "mild sternness" and be "willing and able to take the time to reprimand the young prince without scolding him . . . to make himself loved and respected by him out of respect for his good morals and virtuous life."[16] Once again a contrast is implied with the impulsive, frequently punitive Henri, who firmly believed that to spare the rod was to spoil the child. The king's methods of discipline were a long way from Héroard's policy of building controls from within by gentle but persistent nudging. In his diary the doctor makes clear in both marginal notes and text that he disapproves of Henri's views and practices. He calls his abuse of Louis "bullying" or "manhandling" (*malmener*) and deprecates the impetuous violence or baiting that provokes distress in his son.

Henri and Héroard were opposed on still other matters related to Louis's upbringing. The king held to medical principles exactly contrary to the doctor's: he was a believer in frequent enemas, bloodletting, and powerful purgatives,[17] which were considered violent measures by Héroard. The doctor was noted for a different strategy, as a contemporary colleague observed: "He practiced medicine a bit differently than others; he bled less and employed tonics and specifics,"[18] Despite his early and constant use of suppositories to treat Louis, Héroard was slow, by the standards of his day, to administer enemas, and the laxative medicines he chose were considered mild and benign. He seems to have rejected bleeding as a therapy until it was forced on him. In this, as in other fields, his intrusions were "gentle"; he strove to control by insinuating, whereas Henri would crash head-on toward his objectives.

Nor were these the only health matters on which Louis's doctor and father disagreed. The king frequently offered Louis food and drink that Héroard thought unsuitable for him. The doctor did not share Henri's belief in the salubrious effects of raw garlic and especially disapproved of giving young children wine, which Henri apparently thought would help make a

man of his son. Recording the taste for wine Louis demonstrates while dining with the king Héroard notes in the margin, "For health, beware."[19]
Henri, however, was not in the least inclined to consult the doctor when
making decisions about the child's care.

As a man who regarded his own cultivation with complacency, the dauphin's first physician thought that the king failed to appreciate qualities the
child owed to his mother. Louis's musical sensibilities and his artistic ability, always attributed to the Medici side of his family, were lost on the king,
whereas Héroard considered himself a connoisseur, noting the virtuosity of
artists assigned to the court with the air of a practiced appraiser: "Excellent
painter" or "sculptor" or "musican."

The dauphin took after his mother in other ways as well. Contemporary
portraiture reveals that the dauphin physically resembled the Habsburgs on
Marie's side of the family far more than he did the Gascon king. "By his solemnity, he recalls absolutely the house of Medici; he looks exactly like his
mother," wrote the nuncio.[20] The fact that Louis was so like Marie did
not help to endear him to the *vert galant*, who was not gratified when she
pointed out this resemblance.[21]

In contrast to Héroard's opinion of Henri, his admiration for Marie is
obvious from the day of Louis's birth. During her labor he remarks, "The
constancy and firmness of the queen was marvelous and incredible." Nevertheless, that Héroard appreciated her talents and character and nurtured
some of her attributes in Louis accentuated a dilemma: despite her fortitude
in adversity and even danger, Marie could not be a model for her son. Only
males could serve to exemplify the qualities the prince required to fulfill the
norms for kingly conduct in love, statecraft, and war. Even Héroard had to
acknowledge to Souvré, "It will be for you, sir, to make a man out of the
child, and of that man—a prince—to fashion a king."[22]

COMPETING FACTIONS

Marie's inability to serve as a model for Louis and her need to work through
the men surrounding him did not mean that she lacked power at court.
Prominent among the queen's supporters in her recurrent struggles with the
king was Héroard, whose overriding passion for assuring the dauphin's future had allied him with the one on whose status the prince's legitimacy
depended—his mother. Marie complained of Henri to the Tuscan emissary
in terms that must also have expressed Héroard's view: "The queen can't
understand how . . . the king . . . can give more caresses to the bastards than
to the legitimate children . . . [and fears that] all the world will think that
they are more loved by their father than the queen's children."[23]

Marie apparently recognized an ally in the physician very early, perhaps
valuing his facility in Italian. She soon made him an eager party to her ef-

forts to protect Louis from the king's discrimination in favor of his bas-tards. Héroard's journal reveals throughout how his competitive feelings were aroused at the signs Henri frequently gave of preference for Louis's half siblings and for women other than the queen.

Marie called upon the doctor to second her in opposing Henri's instruc-tions to whip the child. To circumvent Madame de Montglat, who was the king's personal representative and nominally in charge of the nursery, the queen communicated with Héroard via her secretary, Phélypeaux.[24] That Héroard was a willing accomplice in the conspiracy is suggested by the scat-tered passages in his journal depicting the impudent and vulgar behavior of Montglat and her husband and exposing her lack of cultural qualifications for her post, her self-centeredness, and her cupidity. The doctor is, of course, too astute a courtier to allow this opinion to appear in his *Institution*, which gives Madame de Montglat credit for having produced a "well-bred child in the current style [*un enfant poli en la façon*]." Only those who knew him well would be aware of the contempt this implied. In Héroard's opin-ion, Louis's *natural* endowment made him "even better" than this.[25]

The doctor seems to take satisfaction in the dauphin's lack of affection for Madame de Montglat, judging from the care with which he reports every indication of it. When he describes her distress at Louis's final graduation from her care he remarks that the child himself took leave of her "with a dry eye."[26]

In view of Héroard's sympathies and his position at court, it is not sur-prising that he was not very popular with Henri. Indeed, it appears that, had it not been for Marie's insistence, the king would have terminated Hé-roard's appointment, putting an end to his life's work, when Louis left the nursery. In the summer of 1608, the doctor reports, he thanked the queen "for having done me the honor to make the king decide that I would remain the first physician of Monseigneur le Dauphin."[27] It cannot be determined whether Henri recognized the temperamental differences between himself and the physician and the incompatibility of their aims. It seems likely that, at the very least, he regarded Héroard as stuffy, pretentious, and excessively cerebral.

Héroard was fortunate that the queen intervened successfully to include him in the dauphin's new household, for selection of the other personnel was probably entirely Henri's choice. According to one observer, the king's appointments were motivated by the wish to keep control over Louis in his own hands. Vauquelin remembers:

The late King Henry the Great, who thought he would live forever, believed he need not take so much care and thought when he gave a governor to Monsieur le Dauphin, having often heard His Majesty say that he himself was the first governor of his son, and those who held the appointment were only for taking him to mass and having him learn fancy manners [*habitudes tortueuses*] and exercises good for his health.[28]

Vauquelin was chosen as Louis's first tutor for the same reasons that he describes here, according to L'Estoile. It was said that, since everyone was banded against him, "the king resolved to appoint him" so that the tutor "might hold this benefice from him alone and not from another" and thus would be entirely subject to Henri's control.

While Marie, like Héroard, felt that Souvré was at least innocuous, she was antagonistic toward the young prince's new tutor. L'Estoile reports that the queen, on learning of the appointment, "showed herself to be so unhappy about it, they say, as to have cried." The anonymous witnesses may well have included L'Estoile's coreligionist Héroard. A Protestant, L'Estoile thought Vauquelin "corrupt . . . a true . . . courtier of our day."[29] Héroard's diary shows that he, too, was inimical to the new tutor.

The fact that Vauquelin had previously been tutor to Louis's half brother, César de Vendôme, probably contributed to Héroard's disapproval of him.[30] Whatever the reasons, the doctor's journal dismisses Vauquelin's competence and learning at almost every opportunity. For example, since the tutor's first lecture to Louis included, according to Héroard, the maxim that one must love and fear God, it can hardly have been more than a slip of the tongue when Vauquelin later mistranslates a Latin sentence as "Learn to render justice and not fear God." Héroard, however, makes much of the alleged slip and comments darkly, "I would like to believe that it was inadvertent." He further implies that Vauquelin shirked his duties when he tells us that the dauphin "studies a card that his preceptor left from Saturday in order to go off to have a good time in Paris." Shortly after Louis has become king, Héroard's daily record reveals his hostility to Vauquelin still more plainly: "His preceptor had instructed him a few days before that one of the things princes most detest is an old servant poorly regarded. He asks him, 'Sire, what is it that princes detest the most?' The king, reflecting, says suddenly, 'It is vice!'" After Héroard's marginal "*Nota*" is the comment: "More learned than his tutor!"[31]

When Vauquelin was named Louis's tutor, the queen is said to have told him not to thank her for the appointment but the king, "who was the only one to have desired it." "Had she been believed," she said, Vauquelin "would never have had it."[32] If this is accurate, Marie had her wish soon after Henri's death. On the basis of a report of the clergy attacking Vauquelin as ignorant and representing Louis as being in need of a teacher "raised in knowledge of God who might instill this in him in fear of Him,"[33] the queen dismissed the tutor in July of 1611, to the evident satisfaction of Héroard[34] and, no doubt, of Père Coton, Marie's Jesuit confessor; the Jesuits were inimical to Vauquelin and had their own candidate.[35] Indeed, it is plausible that the doctor had a hand in drafting the complaint against the tutor—his journal notation of two years before impugning Vauquelin's God-fearing disposition suggests that Héroard had been building a case for some time.

THE KING AND HIS SON

As the dauphin began his eighth year, his hot-and-cold relationship with his father continued. Héroard describes the child as looking forward to a visit from Henri, full of "passionate love for the king,"[36] whose arrival then evoked the usual mixed feelings in his son. A few months later Henri ordered the child to take his turn at running jumps across a ditch at Fontaine-bleau. Louis refused, afraid of failing in front of the others. The king insisted, making the jump himself "to encourage him" and commanding several others to do the same: "Monsieur de Souvré threatens him with the whip. He answers he'd rather have it than jump. That offended the king, who ordered that he be whipped. . . . Whipped with three strokes of the lash—it was the first time. He says, 'It's nothing; it didn't hurt.'"[37] Welcoming punishment from others was by now a familiar mode of coping with his father's demands.

Later in this same year Souvré scolded him for not having learned a compliment with which he was supposed to have greeted a visiting Florentine dignitary. "Monsieur de Souvré threatens him with the lash, then with telling the king. Thereupon come tears and entreaties: 'I'd rather be whipped and not tell . . . my father,' and starts unfastening himself." Héroard comments in the margin, "love for and fear of the king."[38]

Sometimes, however, rather than seeking punishment from without, Louis imposed the punishment upon himself. Symptoms appeared, usually gastro-intestinal. Héroard reports him simulating a stomachache in order to escape the company of the king, "merely an excuse because the king had scolded him two or three times . . . and he feared worse."[39] If this time Louis's gastric symptoms were only a pretense, by the next month Héroard was convinced of the involuntary character of his patient's digestive disorder. Louis had been ill for several days when the king arrived and awakened him: "He throws himself into his arms, is entirely delighted. The king says, 'Stick up your fanny so I can see it.' He plants himself on his two elbows and shows his whole back side." This posture, as we shall see, was to be assumed by Louis in the course of dreams several years later.

Whatever the king's observations were when he inspected Louis in this way, he issued orders that an enema be administered to his son, a new experience for the dauphin, who was at first alarmed and resistant: "Taking an enema is spoken of to him. This does not please him at all. . . . He asks to defecate but brings forth nothing but water. He is pressed; he storms, 'I'd rather die!' He is threatened by the reminder that the king is coming back. He stops: 'Let me see what's in it. Give it to me standing up.'" If this position was agreed to (a question Héroard leaves unanswered), Louis avoids at least to that extent the surrender commanded by Henri and certainly does not give in immediately: "Finally, a quarter of an hour after all the argument, Monsieur d'Epernon comes and says, 'Monsieur, here is the king.' He suddenly turns around: 'Hey, give it to me!' and takes it all. Thereupon the king came in and stayed until five-thirty." Louis was in bed during this visit, for "shortly afterward he has himself got up and gives back a part of it."[40] Father's good little boy had accepted the anal intrusion, later converting passive reception into expulsive retaliation. In a few years it would be Louis himself who requested the enema.

Although the dauphin's submission to his father's aggression had pleasurable aspects, we recall that it also evoked its opposite—hyperactivity. This same summer Héroard depicts him as restlessly energetic: "Goes here, goes there, can't stay still," adding in the margin, "Always moving."[41]

Louis's incessant motion suggests that inactivity inspires panic. On the first day of the following year he began to express anxiety about oversleeping and being thought lazy: Arising at 8:15 he complained that he hadn't been awakened early enough, "for someone had told him that if he rose late, he would be lazy all year." When a week later he was presented with an etching of Jupiter, he was told that this was a mighty ruler who did nothing but have music played for him all day long. A courtier remarked that one day the dauphin would be able to do the same. Louis was indignant: "'What!' he says, 'That king does nothing? I don't want to be like that! Here, take it—I want nothing to do with it!' and gives it back."[42]

Sometimes it was Henri himself who set the example of the *fainéant* king, lapsing into passivity and insisting that Louis take the active part.[43] He required the dauphin to stand in for him at such ceremonies as washing the feet of the poor on special holidays. It may have been obvious to Louis, as it is to the reader of Héroard's journal, that the king tried to avoid these duties, passing them off on the person who was expected to inherit the thaumaturgic gift, his eldest legitimate son.

After Louis's baptism at the age of five, Henri frequently excused himself on these ceremonial days, pleading gout or other indispositions. The first such occasion was on the eve of Holy Thursday in 1607, when the king was in bed with a "feverish cold." "Not being able to go himself," he ordered Louis to wash the feet of the poor, an idea the fastidious child found repugnant: "I don't want to," he cried, "They stink!" But of course the king's command was law, and Louis was dragged through the ceremony "pulling back and crying," though in the end others were forced to perform the distasteful task for him. Two years later the king, "finding himself slightly ill," as Héroard writes, perhaps disingenuously, again "commanded him to go wash the little children's feet." This time the child carried out the task "very well," according to the doctor, "just as though he had been the king."[44]

At other ceremonies, however, Henri genuinely tried to prepare Louis for kingship. Not long after the child was established in the Louvre his father took him to a meeting of the royal council, standing him between his legs during the proceedings. Héroard learned, perhaps from the dauphin himself, that the topic of discussion on this occasion was coinage and monetary equivalences, a subject that probably had interest for the young boy.[45]

At the same time, the king continued in his seductive ways, and Louis continued to respond to his advances with conflicted feelings. In January 1610, after they dined together at the Frontenacs', the king took him to bed with him, where "he gamboled all night, putting his feet on his [the king's] breast and under his throat. The king kept tickling him. [Later] they took him away without waking him up."[46] As I have suggested, while such play with his father was no doubt pleasurably exciting, it probably also aroused anxiety. In any case, Louis did not admit enjoyment. Once, for example, allowing himself to be tickled by attendants while he was in bed, he said, "The greatest displeasure anyone could give me is to tickle me." Héroard notes, however, that the remark was made "without his getting annoyed."[47]

The hot-and-cold relationship with Henri continued into Louis's ninth year. On the dauphin's eighth birthday there was a celebration at the house of Monsieur Zamet, an old family friend.

> The king drinks to the dauphin saying, "I pray God that I may be whipping you twenty years hence." The dauphin replies, "Not, if you please."
>
> "What? You don't want me to be able to whip you?"
>
> "Not, please."[48]

Within eight months of this toast Henri was murdered. The day after the assassination the grieving L'Estoile expressed the shock of many when he wrote that, in the autopsy, all the "noble parts" of the dead king's body "were found so healthy and intact . . . that the doctors said that in the natural course of things, he could have lived another twenty years, which would have been a great good for France, had it pleased God to permit it."[49]

For Louis, the circumstances of his father's death provided a shock that, for the moment at least, renewed his need to suppress both amorous and angry feelings toward Henri.

AFTERMATH OF MURDER

On May 4, 1610, Henri IV was mortally stabbed in his carriage en route to the Arsenal. The bloody circumstances of his death were not concealed from the new king: Louis XIII saw his dead father brought in and put on the bed in the great chamber of the Louvre.

Such a sight cannot fail to arouse fears in a boy of eight-and-a-half. Louis's immediate response was consistent with his usual pattern of conquering fears; contemplating murder, he responded murderously: "Ah, if I had been there with my sword I would have killed him!"—presumably the assassin Ravaillac.

This intrepid display was followed by anxiety. That night Louis asked to sleep with his governor, "on account of the dreams that I have." Two days later his nurse, who had slept beside his bed, asked him what he had dreamed about. "I was dreaming," he said, "that I really wish that the king, my father, had lived another twenty years,"[50] the same span of time Henri had wanted to continue whipping his son.

Louis's fears of being damaged while he sleeps increased. They were also in conflict with the old desire to be whipped or tickled by his father. "I'm dreaming," he reported to Souvré a few days later, "that I'm being tickled, that someone goes like that," and tickled himself. Several weeks after this he had a tearful session with his half brother César de Vendôme, during which the two grieved for their departed father. That night Louis dreamt fearfully of returning spirits, of which there had been talk during the evening. Several months later he reported that he dreamt Souvré was whipping him.[51]

But during this period his sleep was, for the most part, undisturbed. On the night before his tenth birthday, however, the old conflicts reemerged. He awoke full of anxiety; "having heard talk of ghosts at his bedtime, he feared them," Héroard tells us.[52] It seems to be his father's return that he feared. He had previously refused to sleep in the bedchamber where he had seen him lying dead; now, however, he was persuaded to do so. That night at bedtime he complained to Héroard of pain "at the base of his penis on the left side," which the doctor thought might be "a little larger than the other." During the night Louis had the following dream: "We were going hunting. . . . I went astray. . . . I came to a farm where I found a man; I asked him if he wanted to lodge me in his house—it was a little house. I went in and there I saw in the kitchen some ghosts who were turning the spit. I laughed so much! I laughed so much!"[53] The house Louis is invited to enter is a little one—the very opposite of his father's "great hall of the Louvre." Nevertheless, the *songes* turning the spit, like the *sot* dressed in white of Louis's earlier dream,[54] seem to represent his father (now a *songe*—a dream or ghost) who has impaled him on a spit. The boy laughs instead of screaming, as no doubt he used to laugh while being tickled by Henri.[55] He awakens, "afraid," as Héroard says, "as he has been since the death of his father, the king, whom he saw in bed," and has a valet look underneath each side of his bed "to reassure himself."[56] The next night, however, the pleasurable side of submitting to his father was once again tempting. He let his attendant, Birat, tickle him as he lay in bed.[57]

In spite of these mixed feelings and occasional expressions of nostalgia or grief at the loss of his father, the months after Henri's death were singularly gay and carefree for the young boy. It seems that with the removal of his father a weight had been lifted from him. The day after the murder Héroard felt the need to explain that "the innocence of his age made him somewhat cheerful from time to time." Particularly notable is an unwonted increase in his sociability. At bedtime a few days after the assassination, for example, "he has his ladies-in-waiting come to him and gaily plays with them, chatting."[58] This was the eve of the day on which Henri's murderer was drawn and quartered in public.

Louis's sadness was never more than intermittent, and for most of that year and the next his fears were usually untroublesome, his sleep mostly undisturbed. It was, as we have seen, a time of rapidly growing skills and pleasure in mastering them.

IN FATHER'S FOOTSTEPS?

Alive, Henri IV had been a most popular king. Dead, he became a hero, and in his place there stood only a boy of eight-and-a-half with a speech impediment. The public was "desolate and downcast"[59] at the loss of Henri "Le Grand," as he was soon officially named, and it was not surprising that Héroard was most concerned that Louis appear the true son of his beloved sire. In the doctor's journal as, no doubt, in his encouragements to the new king, no opportunity is lost to note the resemblance of son to father. When Louis went out on horseback and was expansive, in Henri's style, with subjects he met along the way, Héroard notes, "There never was a child who had as many of his father's traits [*actions*] as he did of the late king." When Louis's musicians stop momentarily while singing at his command, he cried, "Sing! Sing!" Héroard tells us, "just as his father used to do, all of whose traits he possesses."[60] Naturally, the doctor was delighted when Louis appeared to good advantage before an expert audience, as when he displayed his knowledge of martial matters and was able to entertain the Spanish ambassador with details of the siege of Juliers. "Admirable," Héroard notes in his margin,[61] an opinion shared by the duke of Feria, who was impressed that the new king could name the captains on both sides, "the fortifications, state of the site, its shortcomings and defects, and what was possible and what not, and illustrate visually on the map everything he said."[62]

The Tuscan emissary, also a sympathetic witness at court, found that Louis resembled his mother physically but was like his father in other respects, as in his love of the poor, a temperament that was "proud" and "ardent," and a physique that was "very agile." The diplomat thought that Louis showed the capacities of a youth of fifteen or sixteen rather than the boy of nine that he was.[63]

Héroard claims a resemblance between father and son not only in those skills Louis excelled at, such as horsemanship and martial arts, but also in those in which he was formerly deficient, such as dancing, that art Henri so admired but which we have been told Louis disliked: "He performs miracles in dancing. . . . He makes himself admired by everyone in all his actions."[64]

Many others, however, did not detect in the little boy the great resemblance to Henri that Louis's physician claimed to see without difficulty. One skeptic, spying the child king on his way to mass on the second day of his reign, cried out disdainfully, according to L'Estoile, "There's a hot king for you!" and burst out laughing (for which he was promptly seized and carried off). L'Estoile's own observation is more circumspect: "As for our king, they don't consider him to be such a great mind as the other, although generous and warlike, but very choleric, stubborn, and difficult to divert from what he wants."[65]

Expressions of the pain this journalist felt at the contrast between his present monarch and the one just murdered echoed from all over the realm and beyond. Typical of the condolence letters Louis received was one from the French emissary to a German court, who reported his own inability to stop weeping and predicted that "all your subjects will . . . groan and weep the rest of their lives" over the loss of their beloved monarch. He urged the new young king to keep in mind all his father's deeds and virtues in order to form himself "on the example of the most excellent and accomplished king that ever was."[66] Henri's reign was not easy to follow.

Yet, in many traits—mannerisms, tastes, and skills—Louis did in fact resemble his father, showing his kinship with the beloved Henri IV in his unpretentious ways with ordinary citizens, his love of outdoor life and sports, and his keen intelligence. But temperamentally there were great differences between the secretive, stuttering, charmless boy and the open, eloquent, lovable father. For Louis to succeed in his new role it was necessary to invoke standards other than those set by the *vert galant* in addition to some that Henri had exemplified. Fortunately the family history was a long one, and there were varying traditions to choose from.

Henri IV (*top*) painted about 1602, and Marie de Medici (*bottom*). Photos courtesy of the Gabinetto Fotografico, Soprintendenza Beni Artistici e Storici di Firenze.

Louis at twenty-seven months with Marie de Medici, who almost certainly did not pose with her son for the portrait. On Monday, November 3, 1603, Louis was sketched full-length (two feet, nine inches, Héroard tells us), probably by the court painter Charles Martin, who signed this work two months later. Photo courtesy of Photographie Bulloz/Arch. Phot. SPADEM, Paris/V.A.G.A., New York, 1986.

A sketch by a court painter of Louis at Fontainebleau on his third birthday, September 27, 1604. Héroard records that the child was three feet and one-half inch tall. Photo courtesy of the Bibliothèque Nationale.

Louis XIII (*above*) and his sister Elisabeth (*opposite*) in 1611, painted by Frans Pourbus. The king is nine years old and "Madame" eight. Photos courtesy of the Gabinetto Fotografico, Soprintendenza Beni Artistici e Storici di Firenze.

Jean Héroard (*top*) in a medallion probably by the sculptor Guillaume Dupré. Charles d'Albert de Luynes (*bottom*), born in 1578, entered the dauphin's household in about 1610 and soon became Louis's beloved confidant. Photos courtesy of the Bibliothèque Nationale.

N. de mantonniere excud.   M. Lasne f.

La Maieste' Royale et la libre nature
Ce chef dœuure ont pare' de leurs plus beaux tresors,
Et lame qui lanime est si parfaicte et pure
Quil nia rien de manque et dedans et dehors

Anne of Austria, in an engraving by Michel Lasne from a portrait probably done
soon after her marriage to Louis, when she was fourteen. Cabinet des Estampes,
Bibliothèque Nationale, Paris. Photo courtesy of the Bibliothèque Nationale.

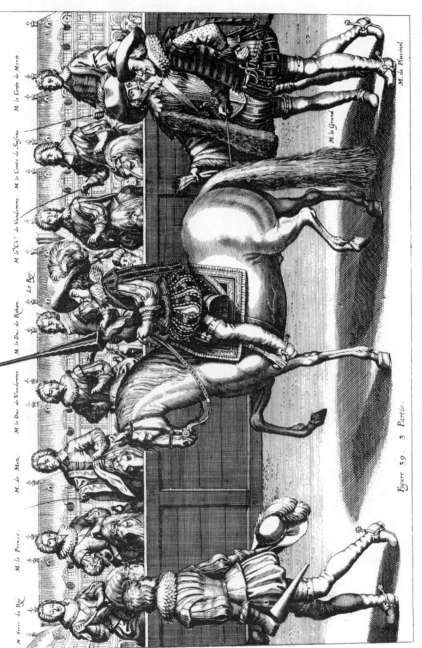

M. Ferro du Roy. M. le Prince. M. de Mer. M. le Duc de Vandosme. Le Roy. M. le Duc de Rohan. M. le Ch.ͬ de Vandosme. M.ͬ le Comte de Soissons. M. le Comte de Moret.

M. le Grand.

M. de Pluvinel.

Figure 39. 3 *Partie.*

Louis at a favorite sport. The spectators are (*from left*) his brother Gaston; his father's cousin the prince de Condé; his half brothers Henri de Verneuil (bishop of Metz) and César de Vendôme; the duc de Rohan; his half brother the chevalier de Vendôme ("Alexandre Monsieur"); his cousin the comte de Soissons; and finally his half brother Antoine de Moret, whom Louis had declared as a child to represent the least of the many breeds engendered by his father. Engraving by Crispin de Passe. Anne S. K. Brown Military Collection, Brown University Library.

CHAPTER SEVEN

Royal Norms and Louis's Temperament

*All his deeds will tend toward what is good and glorious, though perhaps
by methods tinged with extremely autocratic authority
and a rather violent temper.[1]*

In the dedication of his treatise on the prince's education, Héroard professes
to see in the seven-year-old boy all the qualities needed in an ideal ruler.
Characteristically, he mentions intellectual traits first. Addressing Louis, he
commends the curiosity that makes him eager to learn and his sound apprehension of facts—"this desire to know everything, which is native in you,
your good judgment and firm understanding"—attributes that Héroard
claims are "perceived by everyone."[2] The next task, as the child leaves babyhood, is to enlist these capacities in developing the moral virtues of
royalty, "the seeds of which nature has sown with a liberal hand in your
soul." These, according to the diarist, are piety, equity, prudence, valor,
and humaneness.[3]

Louis had not been long under the tutelage of those entrusted to develop
these virtues in him when, at the age of eight-and-a-half, the death of his father called upon him to exhibit them.

The Bourbon royal tradition was supposed to contain examples of all the
qualities demanded in a ruler. Some time after the child succeeded his father
as king, he described in a letter to his governess his ambition to exemplify
the virtues of his ancestors:

For piety, Saint Louis,
For clemency, Henri IV,
For justice, Louis XII,
For the love of virtue, Pharamond,
For valiance, Charlemagne,
and for temperance Charles V.
And Louis XIII will surpass all those kings.[4]

Procreativity, that indispensable condition of dynastic survival, is omitted from the list. Also missing are the qualities of curiosity, judgment, and understanding that Héroard considered prerequisites for all the rest. Most other contemporary lists of the traits desired in a monarch included not only "judgment" but also "prudence" or "wisdom."[5] The best-selling moralist Père François Garasse, for example, listed "vigilance" after clemency and piety (though before justice, valiance, and immortality), implying that mental alertness was essential in a good king.[6] In addition to the "general" virtues of piety, probity, and moderation, Pierre Le Moyne identified the moral virtues needed for achieving royal aims as prudence, justice, authority, fidelity, clemency, kindness *(bonté)*, and liberality.[7] Another Jesuit celebration of Louis XIII called "strength, prudence, justice, and clemency" the "stout columns that support crowns."[8]

The solemn oath to the realm that Louis, like his predecessors, took at his coronation, on October 17, 1610, promised peace, justice, and mercy (as well as the banishment of heretics);[9] the inclusion of peace sprung from the demand that the monarch have consideration for his subjects. If we consolidate the various lists, we may plausibly conclude that leading public hopes for a monarch were that he would be pious, fair, realistic, moderate, brave, and compassionate toward his subjects.

We have already discussed at some length Louis's struggles to become the brave man that his destiny required.[10] The remaining goals are open to varying interpretations. Of concern here is what meanings they had for Louis himself, and how his own resources set limits on his capacity to achieve them.

LOUIS'S RELIGION

Almost from his first public appearance, all evaluations of Louis XIII's performance as an adult agree that he was one of the most pious of kings. The attribution was far from trivial: piety was generally deemed a prerequisite for rule, religion "the first bridle of the king." A monarch who was not God-fearing would jeopardize his kingdom and all its subjects; hence "kings must live . . . as good Christians in order to have the . . . obedience of the people."[11] The justification for tyrannicide, propounded by the outlawed but well-known work of Juan de Mariana, rested on the widely accepted tenet that a godless king had the power to lead his people to eternal perdition. Because the state was organized for the salvation of its members and divine election was the ultimate basis of royal authority, no legal order could protect an impious ruler.

Religious training was the only area of the dauphin's instruction in which neither Henri nor Héroard habitually intervened. Evidently the formal task of instilling piety in Louis was confined to those raised in the Roman church, a count on which neither his father nor his doctor qualified. Decisions concerning the prince's religious practices were made by professional clerics and relayed to him at first by his governess and later by Souvré. His religious observances were handled in the same manner as his state performances: those charged with carrying out the decisions mediated between ecclesiastical authorities and the young boy himself, and the orders were adapted to Louis's changing capacities and special handicaps.

When the time came for Louis to be formally baptized, for example, Madame de Montglat bargained with the presiding archbishop over what responses Louis would have to make at the ceremony. She succeeded in persuading Cardinal de Joyeuse to require only "*Abrenuntio*" and "*Credo*" from the five-year-old, "which will be very easy because there are only two words . . . little different from the French."[12]

As dauphin and as young king, Louis needed religious personnel in his household to provide advice on religious matters and to conduct services. He was assigned a full-time almoner as a child to conduct him in prayers and, after his baptism, to hear his confessions.[13] Later, just before Louis's coronation in 1610, the Jesuit priest Père Coton became his confessor as he had been Henri's. Louis had been carried to hear his sermons before he was two years old.[14]

Louis learned without difficulty the principal religious beliefs and the practices affirming them. It was necessary to love and to fear God, he was told. But the quality of the love required was not specified, and reasons for fear could be warded off by mastering one's lessons with exactitude — indeed, by "swallowing" the required antidote like a good boy taking medicine. Thus Louis once suggested to a Protestant officer of his guard that he eat some of Louis's own rose ointment: "Take it! Eat! Here's something that will make a Catholic out of you!"[15]

The child was taught that God was a powerful invisible spirit who had to be reckoned with when making human plans, much like many other foreign powers whom Louis had to take into account over the years, though he might never encounter them personally. Such correspondences between the divine and the temporal surface in an exchange on hierarchy between Vauquelin and the new king. The tutor tells him that, according to Plato, the gods are above kings, just as kings are above men and captains. Héroard is pleased that the impiety of Vauquelin's analogy is immediately perceived by Louis: "He responds at once," the doctor writes, "Yes, but there is only one God; there are many kings!'" Except for this, apparently, the comparison is apt.[16]

Silent prayer and self-searching were neither encouraged in Louis nor cultivated by him. The necessity for a private relationship with God was obviated by the presence of so many around him whose job it was to keep in direct contact with the Almighty and to mediate between Him and one of his earthly anointed, the king of France. Ambiguities could always be resolved by appeals to these authorities, whom the prince does not seem to have doubted.

The application of morality in everyday life was more problematical, however, and the child may well have felt conflict over demands made upon him to be both aggressive and passive. The moral questions concerning inflicting and suffering pain were particularly difficult to resolve. At three-and-a-half Louis looked at the crucifix and asked, "Where did they put the nails?"[17] Later in the same year he noticed his father beating his breast during a sermon because, as an attendant told him, the king was "incensed" with himself for having struck someone and thus offended God.[18] The dauphin struck his own breast in imitation and asked God's pardon for the same offense. Héroard comments in the margin, "His nature: understanding PIETY."[19]

A few years later Louis again showed that he had taken literally the self-damaging message of Christianity. Père Coton had devised an abridged catechism for his use, in which the response to the question "What are our enemies?" was "The world, Satan, and the flesh." Héroard recounts:

> "The flesh!" says the dauphin, picking up that word.
> "Yes, Sir, the flesh," says Madame de Montglat.
> "*My* flesh, Mamanga?" he asks, feeling it.
> "Yes, Sir, your flesh."
> "Ho! Ho! Then I'll kill it," he says, hitting it. "Ha! Ha! I'll kill you!"[20]

A monarch was supposed to be fierce and brave—a demand that could be interpreted as flying in the face of self-abnegation. Yet, as we have seen, from Louis's earliest years *opiniâtreté*, or willfulness, was discouraged in him. Marie de Medici frequently visited a leading member of the Ursuline order at the time, Anne de Saint-Benoist, whose saintly reputation was based in part on her observance of the vow "never to follow her own judgment." The seven-year-old dauphin, who often accompanied his mother, is said to have watched as Anne catechized the little girls who were her pupils.[21] It may well have seemed to him that to comply with the ban on self-will was to behave in a feminine way. Yet Père Coton took counsel from Françoise de Bermond, a founder of this Order, as he was about to begin his religious duties with the young dauphin.[22]

While Louis was being taught a *credo* by Madame de Montglat, the intent of the Christian message, like that of other means used to discipline him, seemed to him to stress the personal dangers of a lack of docility. What he heard from his governess and in sermons intensified his already severe fears of damage to himself. When Mamanga taught him "God is a spirit," he added on his own, "I bet He is not the one in the red gallery!" This was a ghost he had heard others speak of, no doubt in an attempt to control him by menacing him.[23]

Héroard records only a few of the governess's remarks and tells us little about the sermons the child heard or confidential warnings his almoner or others may have given him. But it seems that one message received by the little boy was that God posed still another threat to his beleaguered *guillery*: "After dinner he makes caca . . . climbs up on his chair, preaches, says some mixed-up words. Gets down, [saying,] 'I'll cut off your cock!' "[24] While such fears may have been fed by sermons or whispered words from the clerics around him, Louis's mastery of the formulae necessary to ward them off was apparently adequate to keep them from appearing in religious form, even in his dreams.

The moral meaning of the demand to turn aggression inward was lost on Louis, and he did not develop a consciousness of sinfulness. Instead, he seems to have viewed God as a punitive figure who could be appeased by offerings and liturgical requirements. Beyond performing appropriate religious actions when called upon to do so, Louis was, in Héroard's term, "inventive" in devising stratagems of piety. Thus on Holy Thursday of 1609, after the prince had performed a foot-washing ceremony for Henri and afterward dined with his parents, he stopped "of his own accord" at a prayer station in the room. "Pious," noted Héroard in the margin.[25] It seems likely that Louis used this ritual of his own devising to ward off the dangers threatened by his angry feelings toward his father, who had forced him to carry out a ceremony he detested, and to reduce the tension aroused by an evening with the royal couple.

The young prince's practice shows that in his mind prayer had propitiatory value, forestalling punishment by striking bargains with supernatural figures. Fears stimulated by his father's earlier demands for submission could be allayed by making appropriate pleas to God or to the Virgin. When he was to be given an enema, he prayed to God "that it may do me no harm"; put to bed the night before a public ceremony at which he was obliged to speak, "he makes a vow to Notre-Dame-des-Vertus if he can, the next day, pronounce all his words without a mistake."[26] And this is exactly how he prepared, as an adult, for the dangerous act of intercourse with his wife. Before the consummation of his marriage, according to a confidant, he knelt beside the bed with his wife of three-and-a-half years and prayed to God,[27] no doubt to keep him from harm.

A few days after noting the three-and-a-half-year-old Louis's "PIETY," Héroard records that he "knows his *credo*," and thereafter the doctor traces, with the same pride he shows in his patient's other accomplishments, the child's progressive mastery of Catholic credenda. Before the dauphin is four he is able to repeat "by heart" all the articles of belief.[28]

As Louis grew older, his reputation for piety increased, enhanced perhaps by the contrast between him and his flamboyantly sinful father, reared by heretics. Yet despite the highly colored religious setting of Louis's early years, his first tutor was aware that sacred values were unimportant in his mental life. Recalling the king as a child, Vauquelin hoped for a deeper apprehension of religious morality in his successor, wishing for Louis XIV "a different kind of devotion than that of . . . his father, who had adopted it more by habit than otherwise, as he did everything else, without spontaneous initiative and without practicing the virtuous deeds that a true devotion usually produces. For his kind, albeit very great and visible in appearances, was really very sterile and quite imperceptible in its effects." Indeed, so strange did this contrast seem in Louis, Vauquelin continues, that "some called him *'l'incompréhensible.'*" This was the nickname given to his distant predecessor, Louis XI, who was beset by such panic in his last illness that he failed even to simulate the beliefs of Christian orthodoxy.[29] In a time of revival of inspirational religion, the tutor felt that Louis's religious observance represented an archaic Catholic outlook in which practices counted for much, feelings for little.

JUSTICE AND CLEMENCY

In Héroard's eyes Louis gave as much promise of being a just monarch as he did of being a pious one. The dauphin was born under the sign of Libra, the scales, and the doctor writes of him as "armed with justice and holding in his hand that balance which he had borne from heaven since the day of his birth."

Héroard had no difficulty in finding signs of the expected passion for justice in his young patient. An observation was made on Louis's very first day of life that seemed to the doctor an augury both of the prince's future piety and of his equity: "Being wiped off and ready for swaddling, as he was lying on his back in his diaper, he raised his two arms high, hands open and the fingers wide apart, joining the two together squarely, putting the fingers of one within those of the other . . . three times, each time bringing them clasped to his mouth as if to kiss them, and after the last time . . . to his eyes, one after the other."[30] The significance of this portent for Héroard was reiterated in his prediction about his seven-year-old patient in *L'institution du prince*: "He will rule his people, holding them to their duty by a just equity; will unflinchingly render and have rendered to each his own: 'rewarding the good, punishing the guilty.'"[31]

Louis's hesitant speech contributed to his reputation for judiciousness. "Since from his earliest years he had had rather great difficulty in speech," an official historiographer writes, "he listened and meditated much."[32] Héroard shows us that Louis's responses were often delayed, which may also be the reason his first tutor found him slow to learn.[33] When words did come, they were, if not always stuttered, often studied, sometimes whis-

pered. This hesitancy is often presented by Héroard as seriousness, reflec-
tiveness, or another similar virtue.[34]

The prince's deeds of "justice" from babyhood to adulthood are a regular
feature of Héroard's journal. Before Louis was three, the doctor observed
him conducting a trial of a valet who had stepped on a baby frog while the
company was taking a walk. "Pardons him," he notes significantly. When
the five-year-old dauphin ordered one of his servants put in "p'ison" (under
the table), Héroard makes another marginal note: "Administrator of justice;
hates to see wrong done." Watching the child playing with toy scales,
"making the weights balance," the doctor comments, "Loves equity."[35]

When Louis XIII was not yet nine, Vauquelin asked him what the duty of
a good prince was. The child's initial answer to his tutor was, in Héroard's
view, letter perfect: "It is first the fear of God." But then, "as he thought
about the rest," his preceptor added: "And to love justice." Louis responded
immediately, the doctor reports: "No! One must say, 'And *to give [faire]*
justice.'"[36] At this age, apparently, Louis thought it right to plan on taking
an active part in having "justice" done. His response here suggests that, like
his piety, his sense of justice did not emphasize internal monitors; rather, it
was a matter of performance—equitable administration of rewards and
punishments.

One aspect of Louis's demand for equity that Héroard admired was the
"wonderful care" he took to pay those from whom he received merchandise. "*Juste,*" the doctor notes in the margin of one such example.[37] The
prince's fairness was similarly commended when he yearned for a mechanical
toy possessed by a poor Marseillais but was apprehensive that Henri, who
wanted to bargain for a lower price, would not pay enough for it.[38] An or-
dinance published in 1612 already seems to bear signs of the young monarch's personal intervention to make sure that peasants whose chickens were
taken for his hunting hawks would be paid.[39]

As Louis prepared to enter his male ménage at the beginning of 1609, the
doctor was a good sounding board for the changed behavior that would be
expected of him when formal studies began. The dauphin had been memo-
rizing sayings of Solomon and called Héroard over: "I've invented a sentence; would you like me to tell it to you?" The doctor, assenting, was told:
"Children who are not good are punished by God." Apparently Louis knew
balance is expected since he soon added the sentence, "Children who are
really afraid of God will be helped by Him." Héroard was approving; his
marginal note is, "Invents sentences like a second Solomon." Only a few
minutes later, however, Louis again weighted the scales on the side of retri-
bution with yet another imaginary sentence of Solomon, this time commenting on a servant who was discovered fighting another: "Those who
fight must be put in prison." To the doctor, this showed that Louis was
"justiciary."[40]

Héroard included humaneness [*humanité*] in his catalogue of the virtues that Louis promised to exemplify. The young king himself, however, did not list this quality in the letter to his governess cited earlier. The doctor rarely recorded the prince demonstrating humaneness toward boys or men under his authority, though he did note Louis's sympathy for animals that had been harmed, like the little birds on his dining table.[41] When the four-year-old prince saw a dead squirrel while hunting, Héroard writes, "he was very humane and sympathetic [*pitoiable*]."[42] He was again described as "humane" when he became furious on seeing someone throw a dog to a lion chained up in the Tuileries garden.[43] But such concern over suffering—even in animals—was unusual, and Héroard gives few examples of it.

An exception to Louis's general failure to demonstrate sympathy for others is his frequently expressed solicitude for his nurse. The feeling that she was like a part of himself may explain his unusual intervention on behalf of a poor woman who had appealed to him in person to reverse her sentence of death for having aborted her child. Héroard notes the "clemency of his nature" as Louis "passionately, with fear and anxiety lest this woman die," marshaled the extenuating circumstances she had explained to him—the miscarriage was spontaneous, the child was dead in the womb. "He remains thoughtful. Suddenly he exclaims to M. de Souvré, 'This troubles me,' almost tearfully." The next morning his plea for the condemned woman was renewed. Once more the doctor notes, "Clemency."[44]

To Héroard, justice was a matter of balance, "rewarding the good" as well as "punishing the guilty," and he was not unaware that Louis inclined to the punitive side. When as a three-year-old the dauphin exclaimed of a miscreant companion, "Ha! Put him in prison!" his diarist noted that "he often gave similar commands."[45] When Louis moved into the Louvre with his own household, his opportunity for "administering justice" was considerably enlarged. Héroard was concerned that the child—now performing before a wider public—should appear to intervene with mercy as well as chastisement. On one occasion the doctor told Souvré sotto voce that he expected "Monsieur le Dauphin would not be long in asking for pardon" on behalf of a lackey whom Souvré was punishing by confinement. This time Louis accepted the cue and asked for the servant's release. But left to his own initiative a few days earlier, he had favored punishment rather than clemency: "Young Monsieur de La Boissière told a lie to Monsieur le comte de Torigny. He overhears it and denounces him to Monsieur de Souvré, commands that he be whipped. It was the first justice administered in his chamber."[46]

Louis soon discovered that clemency, potentially in conflict with justice, was a virtue for which his father was particularly noted. In fact, Henri's displays of clemency were thought to be excessive even by ardent supporters like L'Estoile, who criticized the king for not taking stern measures against several noblemen who had defied his authority: "In the end the king pardoned them all, accounting them on balance his fine cousins and best friends. Upon which it was said at court that the king was like monkeys who are especially nice only to those who attack them."[47]

In one important instance, however—a notorious case of treason—Henri was persuaded to allow a capital sentence to stand. In 1602, the maréchal de Biron, one of several conspirators, went to his death on the scaffold. The flagrant nature of the crimes that occasioned this exceptional obduracy in the king is recorded in an anonymous funeral discourse: "In him justice always ceded to mercy . . . until, crime and obstinacy having overcome both, he was constrained to allow to be lost him whom he could not amend."[48] Louis was not yet a year old at the time of this execution, but as he grew older the sentence was sometimes discussed within his hearing. When at the age of seven he was angry with his young gentlemen attendants, he "wants them to be whipped. Madame de Montglat tells him that they had to be pardoned and that the king pardoned everyone. 'Everyone!' says he. 'He didn't pardon Maréchal de Biron!' "[49]

As time passed Héroard seems to have become aware that Louis leaned toward sternness rather than mercy on most justiciable issues. In this penchant, as in every other, the doctor allied himself with his patient. For example, he made two marginal notes of Louis's "serious" response in an episode concerning a provincial nobleman, Vatan, who had held a tax collector's son hostage in reprisal for state trespasses on his property. The crown's forces, in turn, seized the proprietor and transported him to Paris, where he was awaiting execution. Héroard reports:

> On his text, which was, "*Justus princeps debet semper in promptu clementiam pro delinquentibus*," Monsieur Le Fèvre, his tutor, exaggerates this virtue and lauds it above all others, saying that a prince must always pardon. [Louis] replies, "And Monsieur de Vatan?" . . . Monsieur Le Fèvre says to him, "Sire, the prince must always pardon, but he must leave to the magistrates the judgment of crimes."

Héroard depicts Louis as considering the tutor's words "judiciously":

> He reflects, and to show that he didn't hold with the idea of the sieur de Vatan obtaining pardon, he calls, "Monsieur de Souvré, let me say a word in your ear," and says to him, "My mother says that if he were pardoned there would be lots of others like him who would want to do the same thing."
>
> "Truly, Sire," says Monsieur de Souvré to him, "that is a very noteworthy remark."
>
> I ask M. de Souvré out loud if the king would be willing that I write it in my journal. He says, "Monsieur de Souvré, whisper it in his ear." He shows his discernment secretly.[50]

By judging the prince's unforgiving position worthy of mention in his journal, Héroard in effect supported Louis's disposition to severity against the tutor's counsel for mercy. The doctor's own mixed feelings toward Henri IV may have prompted him to reinforce this side of Louis, in which he scarcely resembled that popular king renowned for clemency.

JUDGMENT: REALISM AND THE SEARCH FOR TRUTH

As a child, Louis's thirst for truth seemed unquenchable. At the same time, he was anxious about failing to learn what he wished to know. "He was always asking for reasons," says Héroard of the three-year-old: "What is this? What is that? When? Why? Where from?'"[51] Again, a few months later: "He asks the why of everything. . . . 'Why did the Jews crucify God? Why is He the son of the Virgin Mary?'"[52]

Louis's pessimism about satisfying his curiosity was probably heightened by evidence that those around him wished to put him off with deception. As a seven-year-old he asked Souvré, "What country is *Querouage?*" The governor lied, "I don't know—what is it?" The dauphin retorted mockingly, "'I don't know!' Oh, but yes, I know very well what it is. Since you don't want to tell me I'll go ask the ladies." Apparently his research proved successful: "Finally he says that *querouage* means to go make love. . . . I had told him that it meant to go in the evening mist by moonlight, to which he answered, 'Ho! That's not what it is!'"[53]

In this exchange the sexual inspiration of Louis's curiosity is evident. As he grew older his belief strengthened that others wished to conceal the truth from him about such matters and many others, and his skepticism about the answers he received increased. Offered yet another tall story, the child would occasionally ask, "Really and truly [*tout à bon*]?"[54]

Louis's frequent infantile disappointments no doubt played a part in convincing him that others were likely to deceive him, expectations that were continually confirmed by daily experience. His suspicions were stimulated by the diffuseness of the dangers he was told were menacing him. As these multiplied they became more fantastic and less credible.

Louis's servants deceived him in both small and important matters, threatening or pacifying him to suit momentary needs. When an attendant said to the three-year-old's steward, "Warm Monsieur's wine," Louis, shaking his head smilingly, said, "Ho! It's tea—it's not wine—you're fooling me!" Again, when Madame de Montglat pretended the breadcrumbs he sprinkled on his stewed pear were grains of salt and a playmate asked if this was really the case, Louis replied, "Ho! No, but that's what they try to make me believe."[55] To forestall his anger at finding that a wing of his boiled chicken had been given to his sister, his nurse told him that it was amputated by the shot that killed the bird. Longing to accompany his father to Paris after a stimulating day with him, he is told that someone has gone to find a carriage for him, although Henri has long since departed.[56]

Deception was sometimes associated with tempting pleasures, which Louis tried to learn to resist. When someone proposed to rig the Twelfth Night allocation of slices of the *galette des rois* so that the bean (conferring the crown) would fall to him, he said: "No! I don't want that! Let it fall as it will!" Héroard notes, "Doesn't like fakery [*tromperie.*]"[57]

The prince's increasing reluctance to swallow stories resembled his hesitation to ingest new substances. Héroard supported his caution in both cases, encouraging him to seek good authority for statements of fact. The doctor was contemptuous of the fairy tales told by Louis's nurse and other servants and encouraged Louis to reject them. Once, at bedtime, Héroard records, "they were telling him stories of Mélusine. I tell him those were fables . . . and . . . not true stories." Madame de Montglat then told a bible story, and Héroard recounted the episode of David and Goliath. Louis asked many questions concerning details and wondered about the truth of these stories:

"Are they true?"
"Yes Sir," I say, "they are in the Bible."
"Then I want to learn them. I'll tell them to Papa because they're true—they're in the Bible. . . . My sister will go on telling stories of the horsefly that stung the goat on the ass, which are not true, but I'll tell the true ones. . . ." He couldn't leave off.

For such myths, as for foods, Louis developed a very sensitive stomach. In Héroard's words, "He noticed the slightest things,"[58] a critical faculty the doctor considered admirable.

Once Louis became king, servitors were more afraid than ever to let facts of their service appear in their true light. "Ah, Marsilly," he said with wry skepticism to one of his household officers who he believed had deceived him, "the Scriptures say that *omnis homo mendax,* and I assure you, you are a great one!"[59]

Louis generalized this observation beyond his immediate circle. Arriving unexpectedly to inspect the Royal College of Navarre, he warned loudly, "Don't let them hide anything!"[60] When courtiers returned from Spain with glowing reports of the beauty of his future wife, the infanta Ana, Louis was doubtful. A rather impudent gallant at court, whom he liked, remarked, "If I'd seen her I'd certainly tell you the truth of the matter [*je vous en dirois ce qui en est*]." Louis immediately "had him given the money and wanted him to make the trip [saying,] 'I know very well that he'll report the truth and won't lie to me.' "[61]

In spite of Héroard efforts to produce a balance between Louis's physical inputs and outputs and his incessant struggle against the boy's tenacious toilet habits, he was highly admiring of the child's capacity to retain what was on his mind. Before the dauphin was two years old Héroard noted his ability to register impressions "without saying a word."[62] The journal comments on his "admirable memory" at an early age, observing that "he retained the proper names of things extremely well." Héroard's description of Louis absorbing the tenets of his faith uses words like those that describe the child's reception of his first enema: "Madame de Montglat teaches him, 'I believe in God the almighty father, etc.,' which he retains very well."[63]

Although Henri had fewer occasions than Héroard to observe this capacity of his four-year-old son, he also noticed it and wrote to James I of England that "the signs he already gives of judgment and of memory" offered great hopes for the future.[64]

According to Héroard, Louis's judgment was acute, even though he might say nothing about the decisions he had reached: "He had an eye and an ear open to everything, without letting on; retained everything, recalled it, and compared past things to those he saw or of which he had heard spoken."[65]

Héroard also obviously approved of his patient's ability to dissimulate: though it might be a sin to tell a lie, it is not obligatory to tell all one knows. Louis might perceive a situation realistically but fail to give others his full view of it. Frequently, the doctor notes, the dauphin responded coolly (*froidement*) or with silence when Héroard knew him to be filled with rage or chagrin.

As a child, the prince could utter threats with a *froideur* that belied their destructive content, and he was so well able to conceal the anger the duc de Sully, his father's powerful finance minister, aroused in him that perhaps no one but Héroard was aware of it.[66]

By the time Louis became king, the utility of dissimulating was apparent. When Condé, first prince of the realm after Louis and his brothers, failed to rise in the nine-year-old's presence, Louis's expression of anger was confined to the ears of Souvré and Héroard.[67] When, about a year later, Condé took Louis aside to assure him of his loyalty, the young king responded nonchalantly, "I'm not worried about it." It seemed remarkable to Héroard that one so young "kept this from Monsieur de Souvré" while a large company was still present, "until the evening at bedtime, when he told it to him of his own accord."[68]

As he grew older, Louis showed a burgeoning capacity for accurately appraising others. He was less objective, however, when it came to his own performance—though he was, it is true, realistic about his failings: "He always admitted," Héroard notes, "when he did not know something." He did not deceive himself when he had not done well. In a shuffleboard game, for example, "if he had hit poorly he would say, 'I've not played well.'" Flattery could not dissuade him: "If one tried to tell him otherwise he got annoyed and said, 'No, I've not played well.'"[69]

Louis's realistic assessment of his performance did not, however, extend to taking responsibility for it. In cases of personal deficiency he turned his anger outward, as though it were not he but others who were to blame. Regret or guilt—possible reactions to shortcomings in himself—was rarely apparent. Thus, when he almost fell while playing with a toy, he got red in the face and shouted, "It's because my valet wasn't holding on to me." Héroard comments: "He tries to excuse himself by [blaming] others . . . is happy if one furnishes him some excuse." This, the doctor notes in the margin, is his "nature."[70]

Information that Louis received critically or with suspicion he might store up for a long time, reflecting on it in silence. But there was always the danger that he would react explosively to news. Cautious ingestion, slow and finicky digestion, and prolonged retention, followed by sudden and violent expulsion, formed a pattern that others were to recognize as characteristic of the way in which Louis dealt with communications. The target of his outbursts was often a scapegoat, however implausible, for his own fault—such as "my little brother of wax," a model of Louis made by a visiting Flemish sculptor. When the dauphin was reproached for speaking rudely to his half brother César, he replied, "It's not I, it's my little wax brother who said it."[71]

If the prince committed an act of which others disapproved, it was not his habit to try to make amends or to show remorse. Rather, neither accepting nor denying blame, he would pass on to others the problem of both discerning it and excusing it as best they could. Thus, one morning, having been taken forcibly to mass, he lay down on the sub-governess's dress:

> [She] . . . reproaches him, saying that he was lying down like her little dog. He calls her an old bitch, and Madame de Montglat too, telling her, "Ho! The ugly one, she's a stinking fart!" He recognizes his fault and, seeing that every last person present finds it a poor show, comes to me to ask pardon. I ask him what he has done. [He] doesn't want to tell me the truth. "It's that I didn't want to go to mass, I didn't want to do writing exercises, and she wants to have me whipped."
> "Sir, there's something more."
> "Go on, go away—she'll tell you what it is."[72]

In turning to Héroard to pardon a fault committed against Madame de Montglat and her assistant, Louis had chosen the servitor who was most likely to forgive.

TEMPERANCE

In being pious, fair, humane, and realistic, a prince demonstrates his public virtues. Temperance is a more personal quality, of less obvious public import. The claim that possessing temperance entitles a sovereign to control others seems to derive in part from the respect his self-control arouses among his subjects. Excessive self-indulgence lessens the esteem of the public for its monarch, even if it may at times contribute to his popularity—as it seems to have done for Henri—by showing him to have the all-too-human failings of ordinary mortals and, perhaps, by providing entertaining spectacles and vicarious gratification.

Henri's weaknesses were notorious at court. We recall that even as a boy Louis detested the evidence, constantly thrust upon him, of his father's adulterous behavior.[73] His own restrained behavior with women as an adult and his lifelong conjugal fidelity justified the doctor's pride in the prince's moral integrity in this respect. Nor was Louis gluttonous like his father. Héroard finds it notable that the prince at three-and-a-half "was not at all greedy for food." Much later the diarist writes, "Very restrained in eating."[74] Furthermore, he never found alcohol a compelling temptation, though Héroard had feared the seductive powers of wine and noted the need to guard against Louis's developing too strong a taste for it.[75] But once Louis joined the company of men and was regularly served wine at table, he habitually diluted it with water. By the time he was expected, as a nine-year-old king, to be convivial with companions, his physician had already relaxed his vigilance. Observing the child dilute wine at table, the doctor commented: "Sometimes he takes less than one might wish," adding in the margin, "Discretion, PRUDENCE."[76]

Louis then, had, little difficulty in controlling his appetites. But it was otherwise with his anger: he frequently gave way to outbursts of rage. We have seen how, as a baby, his fury at his siblings produced murderous attacks on them. Héroard, however, often presents him as striving to govern his violent temper. During that agitated summer of 1604, when the child's struggles with his father reached a climax, the doctor thought he saw Louis making progress in self-control. After a particularly stormy day with Henri, the three-year-old confronts the chef who threatens him with punishment unless he eats his supper, "rises to his full height on the step, raises his hand and his finger, saying in a menacing voice, 'And I'll beat you up, I will,' and then falls silent. Several times, threatened with the whip, he bridles and suppresses his rage, as though wishing to subdue it: 'Ou! Ou!' Finally, eats supper."[77]

It was painful to Héroard when Louis gave in to fury. The doctor loved to see the child in command, both of himself and of others. Thus he was in Louis's corner in a day-long contest with Henri during which the dauphin was whipped by his father and by Madame de Montglat. " 'Hey! My God! My God! Hand over the switches to me! Get out of here! Go away! You get me too heated up,' said he to the king. 'You're hurting me too much. Give me the switches. Hey! That's enough!' . . . As he calmed down he remained the master in his mood and they had to allow him to sit down of his own accord."[78]

As time passed, the doctor became increasingly aware of Louis's propensity to lose control of his temper. Defiance of his authority was a context in which this was likely to occur. In one case, for example, an ensign wounded a soldier with a sword; at Héroard's suggestion, the bleeding soldier was ordered by Louis to withdraw and have the wound dressed, but the officer ignored the command and continued to berate the soldier threatening him with prison.

> The dauphin was holding some little scissors; he turns on him in anger, cold, flushing, restraining himself, widening his eyes with the appearance of a man ardent with fury. He says to him [the officer], "Look here, I'll kill you with my scissors!" Then, regretting the word "kill," for which he was reproved, "You'd better watch out—I'll give it to you in the eyes!"—swollen with rage. I had never seen him do such a thing to show his anger—he was totally enraged.[79]

Louis's fury at the officer's insubordination was probably aggravated by the fact that one of his dearest possessions—a soldier—had been damaged.

This episode was only the first of many that elicited the three-and-a-half-year-old's rage. Though Héroard considered Louis's constitutional make-up to be the ideal one of *sang* (fullbloodedness or robustness), he did acknowledge that Louis was inclined to be "choleric" and quick to anger, "even though *sang* serves as a brake and bridle to restrain . . . his unruly outbursts of fury."[80] The bridle often proved ineffective.

Soon after Louis was settled in at the Louvre, the poet Malherbe, normally an obsequious courtier, reported to a friend a scene in which the prince lost control of his temper: "Last Friday, playing chess with . . . one of his children of honor, La Luzerne gave him check, and mate. Monsieur le Dauphin was so piqued by this that he threw the chessmen at his head." Malherbe managed to see in this a legitimate striving for authority on the young prince's part: "The dauphin will stand for nothing that does not give in to him," and, although he is by nature "extremely good," he nevertheless "insists on being respected, as is reasonable."[81]

Legitimate or not, Louis's preference was for domination over manipulation, for commanding over inducing consent. As the passage at the head of this chapter shows, this was noticed not only by Héroard but also by Vauquelin. On one occasion the tutor drew the young king out on the subject, saying, perhaps disingenuously, that "there was good reason to believe" (as did the faculty of the Sorbonne in deliberations taking place at the time) "that the Council stood above the pope." Vauquelin knew that the pope was not a popular figure in the prince's household. Yet Louis responded, apparently spontaneously, on the side of papal supremacy: " 'And I, not,' replies the king. 'I believe that the pope is superior to the Council.' "[82]

Héroard interpreted everyday instances of Louis's impatience or rage as evidence of his aptitude for royal performance. Thus, when the boy cried over losing at tennis, "it's because he does not like to be vanquished." When at dinner he vituperated the *pâtissier* for having produced a bitter marzipan, Héroard notes that he is "imperious."[83]

But a less indulgent portrayal was conveyed by L'Estoile. On one of his first public appearances in Paris in March of 1609, Louis was observed by the diarist playing *la Blanque*, a popular local gambling game: "Monsieur le Dauphin, having ventured a few *pistoles* without winning anything, called them all, enraged, thieves, and said they must be hanged."[84]

Louis's destructive impulses were released with increasingly deadly menace as the years passed. And to control himself he was more likely to call for outside support than to draw upon inner resources.

CHAPTER EIGHT

Widening Perspectives:
The Boy King and Others

*Louis XIII always loved dead arms more than living ones—that is, than
men, who are the right and proper instruments of princes.*[1]

While Nicolas Vauquelin, Louis's first tutor, found his pupil lacking in love
for those who helped him in the performance of his duties, he could not
have found him disinclined to use men as instruments. Louis's upbringing
had prepared him to make use of *les siens*—those who belonged to him—to
accomplish the tasks assigned to him. As his character developed, so did his
techniques for using others to do what was required of him—and to help
him derive pleasure from the performance.

KING IN NAME

The nine-year-old king's coronation in October 1610 exemplifies some of
the pleasures and problems entailed in playing his new role. The ceremony
itself was the climax of an enjoyable break from schoolroom routine for
Louis. The short journey to Rheims, the traditional site for crowning
French kings, took three weeks, interrupted as it was by hunts and picnics,
sightseeing visits to towns and châteaux, and a stopover at the royal palace
of Monceaux.

The cathedral service was free of dangers for Louis; no apprehension disturbed his sleep in the nights before. No speech was required of him, and
the elaborate ritual was easy for him to learn. The *sacre des rois* was one of
the most ancient ceremonies in French tradition; almost every feature of it
was prescribed. A cast of hundreds supported the child star whose divine
powers were to be confirmed by a formal anointing.

The day before the convocation Louis gaily rehearsed by harnessing his
"little gentlemen" to one another and driving them before him, "flicking

them with his whip."[2] His actual performance was in the same spirit. After receiving the holy unction, the king embraced the peers of the realm, who gave him kisses of allegiance as they passed before him. A chronicler relates that "when the duc d'Elbeuf (who was about the same size as His Majesty) came to kiss him, out of love he kissed him and at the same time gave him a little slap."[3] This playful incident is also reported by Louis's physician, who notes further that his young patient "wipes his cheek" clean of the little duke's kiss. Afterward, Héroard continues, as the comte de La Châtre led the newly crowned king to the altar, Louis tried—unsuccessfully—to catch the count's long train with his foot.[4] The solemnity of the occasion contrasted pleasantly with the mischievousness of the little boy: "During almost all the seven hours this ceremony lasted, one never saw anything so gay."[5]

The following Thursday Louis offered the royal touch to the sick, paled only slightly with the effort (but "never wished to let it show"), and chatted cordially with some of the more than nine hundred afflicted persons who had come to the ceremony.[6]

The happy conclusion of this initiation into royal duties must have been a relief to the attendants who had helped Louis prepare for it. In earlier ceremonies their efforts had not always been successful. During his first public appearance in Paris, at the age of three, he had made audible and visible complaints about the urban stench and had to be prevented by Madame de Montglat from crying out as the Parisians shouted their greeting.[7] At his baptism the five-year-old Louis improvised on the script provided for him. As the duc de Montpensier pulled down his collar to apply the consecrated oil to his shoulders, Louis smiled and said: "There's something cold!" Swallowing the salt, he commented: "That's good!"[8] (We are not told whether or not he stuttered.) This was one of many solemn occasions on which he sought private gratification amid the tedium of public ceremony. At the age of six he obliged others to wash and kiss the feet of the poor for him on Holy Thursday. Dragged to the scene of the ceremony by force, he was "confirmed in his humor" to resist by the sight of his own basin, which had been brought for use in the ritual lavement.[9] With the death of his father, Louis no longer merely stood in for him sporadically; the son had been pushed to center stage for good.

Louis lacked certain qualities required by his new role. Henri had easily produced and delivered the right words for each occasion; his son, with little verbal facility and a crippling stutter, had to have communications drawn up and pronounced by others. This deficiency was accentuated by the absence of the charm and ease that had made his father's impulsiveness endearing and by Louis's need to have his quick temper, impatience, and stubbornness concealed or put in a good light by others. Furthermore, in order to feel complete, he had to keep those persons and objects that belonged to him within easy reach. He relied on his helpers not only as extensions of himself in his official duties but also as instruments for maintaining his self-control and sense of wholeness and for gratifying his drives.

Thus, while Louis was now possessor of sovereign temporal power, he was no more his "own man" than before.

A DIFFICULT TASKMASTER

So long as the newly anointed king remained a child, political decision making lay far in the future for him. Most of his royal obligations consisted of making appearances—before the court, other notables, and the public—according to scripts and stage directions drawn up by others and learned in advance. Within his household alone a host of helpers—from his governor and physician down through tutors, cooks, tailors, portraitists, musicians, guards, pages, lackeys, and valets—had the assignment of making the king *paraître*, look good.

Louis himself, of course, did not care how he appeared in his intimate surroundings: it was not his ambition to be a hero to his valet. His private aims were to extract what gratification—or consolation—he could. Others, more sensitive to court gossip, were left to put the best possible construction on Louis's private conduct. In his public role as king, on the other hand, he was deeply concerned to perform well. But this did not mean that he took responsibility when he failed to do so, since he considered it the task of others to compensate for whatever shortcomings he might have.

Among those whose function included making Louis appear in the most favorable light possible, Héroard was of longest standing. His help in making Louis *paraître* began with covering a rash on the head of the infant dauphin with a bonnet when the child was about to be displayed.[10] What Héroard was unable to cure he continued to present as best he could in the years that followed. Thus his diary sometimes omits accounts of Louis's bad behavior reported by others, sometimes he glosses over Louis's shortcomings by a sympathetic construction, scattering in the margins of his daily entries adjectives such as "judicious," "generous," "clever," "thoughtful," "graceful," "charitable," "serious," "prudent," "discreet," and "inventive."

When Louis, perhaps with Héroard's help, is able to improve conduct that might make a poor impression, the doctor reports it in detail. On one such occasion the adolescent king has been playing a war game, using dogs as drayhorses. One of the animals balks when it is supposed to help pull a cannon up an inclined plank. "He beats it roughly, in a rage. Then he tries it again. The dog goes over without trouble, whereupon he says, sternly and coldly, 'That's how stubborn, bad people have to be treated,' and, giving it a biscuit, 'and the good recompensed . . . men as well as dogs.' " Héroard concludes with the comment, "And thus, the excess to which his anger had brought him in front of everyone present was concealed."[11]

In this scene Louis draws a parallel between the treatment of dogs and persons—an analogy his behavior with courtiers seems to reflect. Soon after he became king, he ordered a valet to remove attendants from his audience room, provoking their complaints and comment from Vauquelin. Louis remarked "coldly," according to Héroard, "Dauzère spoke a little roughly to them, but one must get them used to it early on." Two years later, when told that under his father his guards captains were accustomed to taking a place in the carriage beside the king, he replied: "They became used to it little by little; I will make them lose the habit little by little."[12] On another occasion Louis had a guards captain warned of his own outbursts of temper so that the officer would not "become annoyed," explaining that he had already accustomed his companion, the duc de La Force, to these rages.[13] Thus warned, his attendants would have no reason to complain of his abuse.

In other matters, too, Louis expected his servitors to take responsibility for his bad conduct when he could not control himself. When his governor reproached him for persisting in childish games unworthy of his position, he passed responsibility back. "You will always be in childhood," exclaimed Souvré. "But it is you who keep me there!" responded the prince. Once the child had become king Souvré again prodded him, "Sire, don't you want to give up these children's games?" He answered: "Monsieur de Souvré, I am willing, but I have to do *something*! Tell me what, and I'll do it." It is Souvré's job to provide him with appropriate activities.[14]

Louis often pictured himself as the helpless victim of malevolent adults. Yet those who controlled him were remarkably yielding, rarely failing to comply with his wishes when he resisted strongly.

No sooner had the child become king than rumors began to circulate that some in his entourage were to be dismissed. The Florentine emissary claimed in a letter home that young children were to be removed from his retinue: "They"—perhaps Souvré or the queen—"want to make a man of him." Since Ammirato cited the displeasure that losing some of his companions would cause the young king, it is plausible that he was reporting suspicions Louis himself had voiced. In the event, no such removal occurred, and it may never have been intended.

Louis's mistrust of the good will of those around him was general. When he took a fancy to go swimming on a rainy summer's day twelve weeks after his father's murder, he was told by all, "even by his *premier médecin*," according to L'Estoile, "that the weather was not suitable." Louis replied, "I see very well that everybody is against me."[15] He complained of being victimized again when his half brother Alexandre de Vendôme, a chevalier of the Order of Malta, was assigned to service on the high seas. This was the year after he was supposed to have accompanied his brother César to Bretagne on the trip that Louis's tears successfully forestalled.[16] Now, recording the last encounter between Louis and Alexandre before the exile to Malta, Héroard laments: "It was pitiful to hear his complaints and tears on account of the friendship he bore him." "They want to take him away because I love him," Louis cried, accusing those with authority over him of deliberate cruelty.[17] This is the "Alexandre Monsieur" described by the doctor as being detested by the dauphin in previous years, whose fate now helped Louis to vent his animosity.

Since early childhood Louis had learned by heart the details of each servitor's role, from that of councillor and cardinal down to the lowliest *pannetier*. He often, in fact, enacted their functions himself. Those who performed them were *les siens*, treasured and jealously guarded as though they were a part of himself. Yet, as we have seen, Louis's attachment to them was usually mixed with revulsion. As a small child he had often demanded peremptorily that a sister, brother, or servant be taken away. "*Otez-le! Otez! Otez!*" As he grew older, fury at some felt betrayal or mere shortcoming on the part of a servitor could lead to a ruthless casting out of the formerly treasured possession. Once he suddenly wished to expel his kennel keeper Haran, a favorite servant whose intimacy he had valued, merely because of a "slight error."[18] Only with great difficulty did Souvré manage to induce the ten-year-old to relent.[19] For Louis, loving and loathing were always close.

Once he had become king, such mixed feelings took on political significance, as in the case of his behavior toward the duc de Sully, Henri IV's councillor and right-hand man. Friction between the Huguenot minister and the queen increased after Henri's death until, at the beginning of 1611, Marie accepted his resignation. Héroard reports that Louis, asked by Souvré whether this displeased him, replied with an unequivocal "Yes!"[20] Because of his long association with Henri, Sully was a popular favorite, and his removal increased public mistrust of the queen, particularly among Protestants. This is perhaps why one historian has made much of Louis's displeasure at Marie's action: "France spoke," writes Zeller, "through the mouth of her little king."[21]

Yet Louis's emphatic regret also expresses his "contrariness," for, according to other reports of the doctor, the child had disliked the duke.[22] Just prior to assuming the throne he had been given a great welcome by Sully at the Arsenal, to which he had responded with an open snub.[23] His annoyance at Sully's departure, therefore, may have stemmed primarily from his feeling that *les siens* were slipping from his purview.[24] That Louis's earlier distaste for Sully persisted, regardless of his supposed regret at the duke's dismissal, is indicated by the fact that when Louis recalled some of his father's former ministers to his council in 1617, Sully was not among them.

Indeed, the new king never employed him during his reign, despite the old duke's persistent solicitations.[25]

Louis showed a like contrariness—but in reverse—with Vauquelin. As we have noted, the tutor was disliked by Héroard and opposed by the Jesuit faction at court as well as by the queen, who dismissed him at an early opportunity. Her son had given signs of liking him, however, and took pleasure in planning practical jokes with him.[26] According to L'Estoile, Louis was sorry when Vauquelin was dismissed. Héroard also bears witness to his displeasure. The pupil took his revenge by making life miserable for Vauquelin's successors and by maintaining good relations with the ousted scholar long after his schoolboy days had passed.[27] After Louis's death, Vauquelin wrote of the "raillery with which the king habitually did me the honor to converse with me . . . concerning an intimate of the king."[28] This suggests that Louis used Vauquelin, after his dismissal, as a confidant for his "bad thoughts" about others in his entourage.

Vauquelin, of course, had also had his difficulties with Louis, and the fate of subsequent preceptors was less enviable still. The first tutor's successor, the elderly Nicolas Le Fèvre, found Louis an unwilling student and frequently used threats and bribes to get the child to do his lessons. Once, when Louis believed that a bargain had been struck with his governor to let him out of a session, he was obliged to study "contrary to his intention" and was "angry with Monsieur de Souvré for it." In spite of Le Fèvre's initial circumspection, he soon fell victim to the child's recalcitrance and ridicule when he "pressed him a little" in a lesson: "The king says to him, 'What! And at the beginning you were so mild that you were trembling all over, and now you're so rough!' "[29]

During his short term as tutor, Le Fèvre was often absent on account of illness. Within less than a year, while Louis was suffering from an ailment that made him particularly cross, his teacher was suddenly seized by a "chill" during a lesson and died only a few hours later.[30] During this period of "bad humor," as the doctor calls it, the boy had slapped Fleurance, the underpreceptor, who was to succeed Le Fèvre in only a few days.[31] Perhaps "poor Monsieur Le Febvre," as Malherbe calls him,[32] had also suffered from even more severe mistreatment by Louis than the ridicule of which Héroard tells us.

The tenure of David de Rivault de Fleurance was longer than Vauquelin's or Le Fèvre's, but it was probably no happier, even though, as a mathematician, he was able to entertain the king by discussing military strategy.[33] According to Vauquelin, Fleurance was once bitten by one of Louis's dogs while he was giving a lesson. In return, the teacher kicked the animal—whereupon his pupil, "extremely angry . . . came over to him, enraged, and gave him several blows of the fist." This "affected Fleurance so much that he took to his bed . . . and . . . died soon after."[34]

Louis continued to attack his tutors even after their deaths. The memoir-ist Saint-Simon records that his father, who was intimate with the adult Louis, claimed that the king, "speaking of his education," often complained to him "that they had not even taught him to read."[35] In fact, of course, Louis's rudimentary education had been adequate. Unlike most of his com-patriots, he had learned to read and write before leaving the nursery. Nev-ertheless, his calumny was remembered and compromised the guardians re-sponsible for his upbringing. It was especially damaging to the reputation of the good-humored Souvré, who was a frequent object of his ward's tricks, ridicule, and defiance.[36]

Héroard, though still necessary to Louis, was also a target. Just as the king had confided his bad thoughts about his half brothers to him, so he ex-pressed his distaste for his doctor to Vauquelin and, apparently, to others. After his death the physician suffered the ultimate deprecation by his mas-ter: Héroard's successor as Louis's physician claimed that the king had called his first doctor a charlatan.[37]

By thus depicting himself as badly served, Louis could enjoy the pleasure of taking revenge. For this purpose, he could cast any of his servitors as the whipping boy who had been a feature of his early childhood.[38]

DISTANT OBJECTS AND SCHOOLROOM POLITICS

Though the dauphin rarely ventured beyond his country's borders or be-yond his own circle within France, he had nevertheless to learn his relation-ship to countless others who were far distant. This he was taught mostly by his intimates. Louis XIII's perspectives on the political world and his strate-gies for coping with it were crucially shaped in the nursery and later in his bedchamber. The young boy was courted by many who sought to influ-ence him politically.

While Henri IV was alive, the direction of political influence in the royal nursery was largely controlled by his active intelligence; after his death, his son was exposed to a wider array of competing forces. To this charged situ-ation the child king brought the set of dispositions that he had formed under the aegis of his father and his father's functionaries. Reinforcing these were the obvious love and reverence that Henri's memory continued to inspire in his subjects, as well as the general belief that his reign had been an outstand-ing success.

In Henri's lifetime his policies of advancing the temporal autonomy of France and the authority of its ruler were reflected in his children's entou-rage. Héroard, for example, though allied with and sympathetic to Marie, was nevertheless an unqualified partisan of her husband's politics. Henri fostered opposition to Spain and the Austrian Empire, alliance with Protes-tant states, respect for Huguenot religious autonomy, and deference to those *grands* (including Huguenots) who were loyal to the new dynasty. The Holy See, though not numbered among "Papa's enemies," was by no means on France's team, and Henri's resistance to Ultramontanist factions was approved of by the nursery personnel he appointed.

Héroard's diary reveals several of these political dispositions taking shape in Louis's mind as he expresses himself over the years.

In the nursery, Spain was a frequent topic; the menace of the Escorial was something the future king learned early and well. A royal historian would later recall how Louis, "still scarcely able to walk alone," exclaimed when told that some visiting Spaniards awaited an audience with him, "Spaniards! Then let me have my sword!"[39] While playing war a few years later he cried, "getting animated and stuttering," that he had "killed a Spaniard" and that his companion, Alexandre de Vendôme, had "dealt him a big sword's blow in the stomach."[40] Héroard seems to encourage hostility to Spain in his little patient. When Henri went to Paris in 1605, the doctor asked the child, "To whom will he give battle?" Louis replied, "To his enemies." Héroard pursued, "Who are these enemies?" The boy "was in the act of naming the Spaniards, and had pronounced the first syllable of the word— 'Against the Span . . .'—then, catching himself, he said coolly, 'Turks,'" As heretics, the Turks were acceptable substitutes for the Spanish threat, which one did not mention too publicly.[41] Nevertheless, Héroard's influence may have brought Spain into the picture in this instance, since Courtaud records the dauphin speaking only of Turks a few weeks before.[42]

Although most courtiers supported Henri's anti-Spanish policy, opposition to it, particularly from representatives of the clergy, sometimes made itself felt at court sub rosa, as in a conversation Héroard recounts between Louis and his almoner. The cleric was having the five-year-old dauphin recite the Ten Commandments:

> When it came to saying, "Thou shalt not kill," he says, "Not Spaniards? Ho! Ho! I'll kill the Spaniards who are Papa's enemies! I'll skin them good!"
>
> The almoner says, "Sir, one must not kill Spaniards. They are Christians."
>
> "But they're Papa's enemies!"
>
> "But they're Christians!"
>
> "Oh well, then, I'll go kill the Turks."[43]

The almoner's influence was temporary, however, and Henri's enemies continued to be Louis's enemies.

On the international canvas Henri's friends, too, were Louis's—and Héroard's. When a group of emissaries arrived from allied German Protestant states, the Huguenot doctor sedulously recorded the names and titles in his register, and Louis was schooled to welcome them with the utmost respect.[44]

As the years passed, Louis's remarks concerning enemies became more sophisticated. There was often playful talk in his entourage of his possible marriage to a Spanish infanta. Although Henri sometimes took part in this play, he had apparently decided against such an alliance. When Louis gave an emphatic "*Non!*" to the question whether he would be married to the infanta, Héroard asked: "Sir, do you like the Spanish?" He replied, "No, but I like the Spanish girl [*l'espagnole*] a lot."[45]

Similarly, Louis's discrimination concerning the German allies increased: "Monsieur de Souvré tells him that the duke of Wittemberg's son is coming to see him. He asks, 'Is he more than I?' . . . Madame de Montglat replies, 'Sir, he is a prince, like you.' The dauphin, eating a cherry, and having reflected, says, 'I am more than he in France, and he is more than I in Germany.' In the margin Héroard remarks, "Handsome [*généreux*] response."[46]

Vigilant at Louis's side, Héroard's aim was to reinforce the model set by Henri, which sought the independence of France and its primacy in Europe. When Louis examined a book printed at Antwerp, with a privilege "from the pope, the king of Spain, and the king of France," the doctor records— with a marginal "*Nota: Serius*"—that Louis took up his pen and advanced "the king of France" to first place, after the pope.[47]

In Henri's lifetime there were too few Spanish or Austrian representatives at court to make the dauphin's indiscretions concerning them very worrisome. It was otherwise, however, with papal emissaries and various clerical personnel, who were highly visible (though not correspondingly influential) in French governing circles. Overtly, Henri's policy toward the Holy See was conciliatory. He had implemented this policy by converting to Roman Catholicism, by inviting the Jesuits in 1603 to resume their activities in France, and by taking Père Coton, a Jesuit, as his confessor. Though the king made a show of his new Catholic piety, one may speculate on how much his private attitudes had changed. Certainly, among those whom he assigned to care for his son were some who were less than assiduous in instilling in the heir to the throne respect for the head of the Roman church and the Catholic clergy.

Héroard rarely reports what is said to Louis unless it is necessary to explain the remarks of the child himself. Even so, an antipapal bias among those around him can often be inferred: "They were talking about the pope. He asks, 'Is the pope richer than Papa?' Someone answers, 'Yes.' 'Then I don't like him at all.'"[48]

From other conversations one may surmise that some of Louis's servitors encouraged him to direct toward Rome fears that were more naturally focused on objects nearer home. For example, at the age of seven he confided to Héroard that he was afraid to go to Rome because "they would gouge out my eyes [the way] they gouged out those of [a certain priest.]" The doctor's marginal note is, "Doesn't want to go to Rome, and why."[49] A few days later, during the child's lesson, Madame de Montglat asked him (perhaps disingenuously) whether he wished to send a message to the pope:

> Louis: What kind?
> Montglat: That you kiss his feet.
> L.: Yech! Yech! I won't do it!
> M.: All right, then, his carpet slipper.
> L.: No! No! I don't have to![50]

The emotional quality of Louis's rather narrow conception of his religious duties was probably influenced in part by his contacts with the many clerics at court. A number of priests and almoners had been members of his staff since infancy. And since infancy they had been occasional targets of his hostility, ridicule, and wit. Louis's Protestant-reared physician faithfully records his royal patient's signs of irreverence. Thus he observes of the three-year-old playing with his almoner: "He gets angry suddenly, scratching at his hands, trying to bite them. 'I don't want you to play with me,' he says." A few weeks later the child imitates a priest giving a sermon. First he "coughs, spits, makes the sign of the cross," Héroard relates. "Then he says, '*In nomine pat'i*, etc.,' and then some gibberish."[51] During these months the dauphin's aggression toward clerics seems to have mounted. This may be related to his greatly increased difficulty with his father at the time—Henri was not so safe a target.

Even a prince of the church, on the other hand, could become the object of Louis's anger. Guérin, standing in for Héroard, records the drama when Henri de Sourdis, cardinal of Bordeaux, arrived as the dauphin was being served his afternoon collation. The cardinal sat down and put his elbows on the child's table. Louis, "having considered him, said brusquely" and repeatedly: "'Get away from there! Get away from there! Get away from there!' raising his voice continuously until [the cardinal] got up and withdrew."[52]

The background of many members of the clergy left them particularly vulnerable to the young prince's attacks. While the First Estate claimed primacy among the three estates of the realm, and cardinals sought precedence over dukes and even princes of the blood in official ceremonies, the origins of many of the priests and monks at court made them socially inferior to the nobility. Louis was encouraged to be sensitive to such gradations and soon became knowledgeable about them. When he was not quite four, Madame de Montglat asked him to make a request of Père Coton using the polite term "I pray you." He firmly refused and decided instead on the more peremptory "Do something for Tétai, Père Coton, if you please." Héroard observes: "This kind of discrimination in speaking and in commanding everyone according to his status came naturally to him." Despite his divine office, the "good Father Coton," as he was often called, was little better than a lackey in Louis's view. A like "discrimination" (bordering on contempt) seems implied by the dauphin's facetious suggestion that Cardinal Du Perron, having no stablemen of his own, use his almoners for that function.[53]

Louis's usual childhood reaction to priestly performances, however, was boredom. Héroard may have derived some satisfaction from his young patient's complaints, recording that on one occasion the dauphin, not yet four, listened to Père Coton for three-quarters of an hour without protesting: "He was bored without saying a word." A year later it was exceptional when he was "patient for a quarter of an hour" at a sermon—though he did refuse to hear mass. By the age of six he was yet more obdurate, leaving a mass conducted by the Cordeliers at Noisy because, he said, the service was too long. He was threatened with punishment, but, Héroard reports, "that doesn't budge him at all. He is whipped in front of the gardener's lodge, Descluseaux holding him. He goes back, forced."[54]

As he grew older, Louis's wit at the expense of the clergy continued to express the impatience of an active young boy. When he was nine he bargained with his almoner, the bishop of Bayonne, who tried to persuade him to hear a certain young doctor of theology preach at Saint-Paul's. "But those doctors are so long-winded," he objected. The prelate persuaded him by promising that this particular sermon would take only half the time of one of Père Coton's, and Louis vowed to hold him to his promise. When told months later that Père Coton might be insufficiently prepared to deliver a sermon in place of the absent bishop of Luçon, he remarked: "I'm delighted! . . . Then it won't be as long!"[55]

Clerical preoccupations came in for their share of ridicule from the martially minded young prince. Thus, "muttering and shaking his head," Louis complained: "My almoner talks of nothing but canons and monks." The distinctive dress of some Carmelites whom he espied below his window inspired the facetious inquiry (reported by Héroard), "What sort of beasts are those?" He jokingly attributed a want of manly courage to Du Perron, pretending that the cardinal was unwilling to go outside in the evening because he feared the *serain*—"like a girl!"[56]

Louis was encouraged by some around him to make critical assessments of the clerics who were presented to him. Once, at the mischievous instigation of Vauquelin, he played a trick on the bishop of Soissons, who, he was told, was weak in scholarship: "The king's preceptor whispers in his ear and induces him to take a Latin book and, presenting it to [the bishop], . . . ask for an interpretation of it. He goes along with this."[57] We are not told whether the practical joke proved embarrassing for the prelate.

While Louis's father lived, his firm hand made it clear to both secular and regular clergy that their welcome at court was dependent on good behavior, and the dauphin was sometimes made aware of the conditional nature of this tolerance. When he was visited by two Minims, for example, he learned that an extra contingent of guards had been ordered for his protection by Henri because "the late king [Henri III] was killed by a monk."[58]

Once his father was dead, Louis's behavior toward the clergy became more interesting for what it portended of things to come, as rival political currents in the child king's entourage became more energetic. Thus, it is doubtless with some glee that the Huguenot L'Estoile reports, soon after Henri's murder, the following anecdote about Louis: "Coton, seeing our little king lost in thought, asked him what was wrong. 'I'm afraid to tell you . . . because you'll write off to Spain about it right away.'" This remark made the clerical faction at court suspect the child's servitors of subversive influence. According to L'Estoile, Coton complained to Marie de Medici, apparently identifying the probable culprit as Doundoun. As a result, "the nurse was worried and feared her dismissal."[59] Antoinette Joron's good standing at court survived this incident, but Vauquelin's tenure continued only a few months into the new reign. He had always been suspect to the court clerics, and we have seen that he found no ally in Héroard, perhaps because the doctor viewed him as his first effective competitor for moral influence on Louis.

Héroard's diary shows Vauquelin trying to introduce political controversy into the schoolroom. Thus he reports that Louis's first written assignment was on whether ecclesiastics ought to be named to the councils of princes. (Cardinal Du Perron contended that they should, and he had been pressing on Henri the special qualifications of the clergy to advise the king on state affairs.) Not surprisingly, Louis answered orally: "I don't know."[60] The doctor repeatedly disapproved of the tutor's raising inappropriate issues "without justification [*sans sujet*]"[61] during lessons.

Without Henri to preside, various factions within Louis's official family overtly carried on a competition of religious-political views. Apparently Le Fèvre was approved as Vauquelin's successor by Villeroy, the secretary of state.[62] The choice of Le Fèvre's successor, Fleurance, was a much happier one from the point of view of the Ultramontanists at court. Unlike either of his predecessors, he was the "creature" of Marie, sponsored also by Père Coton.[63] The papal nuncio, Ubaldini—a Spanish sympathizer close to the Jesuits—was delighted with Fleurance's appointment. And the new under preceptor, Chaumont, was even more agreeable to Ubaldini, who considered him his "intimate friend," a "good Catholic," and "devoted to Père Coton and all the Company [of Jesus]." The nuncio continues: "Furthermore, Père Coton is present at all the lessons given to His Majesty, and he will not suffer him to be taught anything except what is proper for the eldest son of the Holy Church."[64] This supervision, unimaginable in Henri's time, was authorized by Souvré, who seems to have moved closer to the clerical faction at court after his benefactor's death.[65]

Louis resisted these newly powerful influences at least some of the time.

The support of Héroard and others in his entourage probably fortified him against them, if only silently. Whether or not the doctor had converted to Catholicism by this time, and despite the fact that his alliance with Marie de Medici remained unbroken, his Gallican sympathies were persistent and unmistakable.[66] The Gallican Edmond Richer provides independent evidence that the doctor tried to counteract Ultramontanist influences around Louis:

> As the king was going to bed and was with his favorites, he asked what the *"Richeristes"* were. He was told that the sieur Héroard, his doctor, attested that they were the most faithful and the best subjects of the king, the best servitors he could have, who were detested and mistreated for no other reason than that they defended and courageously supported the ancient maxims of the Gallican church, the independence of the crown, and the sovereign royal authority.[67]

The conversation Richer reports allegedly took place in 1621, during the siege of Montpellier, where Héroard had indeed accompanied Louis (and where he may have gained in authority because he was a native of the city). If the account is accurate, it throws light on what motives this most jealous protector of the king's authority may have had for his own conversion.

Louis's contrariness and his desire to emulate his father may also have contributed to making him impervious to pressure from the Jesuits and their allies. Such predispositions help explain this scene between Souvré and his eleven-year-old charge: "Monsieur de Souvré talks to him of a preacher called Valadier, who formerly was a Jesuit. He reflects on this a bit and says firmly, 'No, Monsieur de Souvré, I don't at all want to go hear Valadier. He does nothing but declaim against 'Pouillan and Beringhen and the Huguenots.'" Héroard's marginal note indicates his satisfaction: "Facetious and serious."[68]

By the age of fourteen Louis's critical posture toward the illustrious Company was highly discriminating. He refused to attend a morality play staged by the Jesuits. When asked later by a courtier if he had seen the play, he replied, "No, I like their performance well enough when they do good preaching, but I don't like these little games."[69]

With Henri's death, conditions for competing for power at the top had changed drastically. From the point of view of most factions, however, the young king was still an insignificant player in the political arena. Some, indeed, overlooked him entirely, taking into consideration only those who spoke for him or acted in his name.

CHAPTER NINE

Queen Marie's Court: 1610–1614

They showed him a map of Spain and the approaches to the frontier. . . .
Monsieur Le Fèvre having told him that France was a much bigger, more
beautiful, and richer realm, the king says: "I only wish it were mine."[1]

The contrast between Louis's august status and his powerlessness no doubt exacerbated his resentment of those who continued to hold him in tutelage after his coronation. Yet his suspicions about them had some basis in reality: particularly after his father's death, many of his nominal servitors responded to pressures from beyond the boy king's purview and acted on behalf of interests separate from his.

THE RULING QUEEN

In law, Marie de Medici was the chief of her eldest son's servitors: as regent she was his surrogate. The success of her regency, her apologists claimed, depended on preserving intact the authority of the crown that would pass to Louis when he reached an age of judgment.[2] She often insisted that her interests were identical with his, but in reality elements in the characters of mother and son made this doubtful.

Looking back in 1617, the queen mother confided that "she had never had any peace in France, no more in the time of her husband than afterward."[3] The ill treatment she felt she had suffered at Henri's hands certainly contributed to her resentment; she was in any case given to self-pity. During the years of her regency she would frequently inveigh against her subjects for not fully appreciating her efforts on their behalf. To petitioners from the court of Parlement she complained that "instead of being grateful . . . and thanking . . . Louis for his good government she saw that they were attacking her regency, which had been praised by all the orders of the realm assembled. . . . There had never been a happier regency than hers. . . . Anger prevented her from saying more."[4]

When, as in this instance, she felt herself at bay, Henri's widow would often compare her lot with that of her embattled compatriot, relative, and
predecessor as regent of France, Catherine de Medici. Catherine's private
correspondence was available at court and was read with pleasure by Marie,
who often seems to have taken the conduct of Henri II's widow as the
model for her own.[5]

Even before Henri's death Marie had given signs of ambition—ambition
that was perhaps intensified by the public humiliation she had endured as a
consequence of her husband's conspicuous infidelities. Just the day before
his murder she had had herself crowned queen, in a lavish and stately ceremony, so she could act in his name during the military campaign he was
about to lead. Henri, by most reports, had agreed to this formality reluctantly, and only at her insistence. Marie's importunity seems to have been
supported by illusions of self-importance and by overconfidence in her
abilities.[6]

In a letter to her sister in Mantua three months after Henri's murder,
Marie reveals considerable satisfaction in her new role. In spite of her great
loss, she reports, "I can call myself very fortunate and quite consoled because of the good order and great tranquillity that begin to be seen in the affairs of this realm."[7] Her optimism, if genuine, was premature. Many astute observers felt she had few of the qualities needed to match the respect
and authority her husband had won for the Crown. As an Italian princess of
doubtful French patriotism, limited intellect, volatile temperament, and little experience of great affairs, she seemed ill suited to represent the young
king. In addition, the fact that her coronation virtually coincided with her
husband's murder intensified suspicions (albeit unvoiceable ones) among
those who would have been mistrustful of the queen in any case. Louis's
usually mixed feelings toward his mother could not have been improved by
his likely knowledge of Catherine de Medici's history, since he would have
been aware that three of her four sons became king before she died, and that
the third, Henri III, was overwhelmingly her favorite. The suggested
analogy between the queens would not have escaped him; his brother
Gaston, born on April 25, 1608, was reported to be Marie's favorite child.

We have seen how the emotions that usually bond a mother to her infant
had little chance to form in the case of Marie and Louis. The life-or-death
demands made on the queen by her aims and interests outside the nursery
were cause enough for her to leave the daily nurture of Louis to others. But
there were further reasons, particular to her character, that the new regent,
more than most mothers who are separated early from their offspring, was
deficient in warm feelings for her child.

Marie's history indicates that she herself had suffered maternal depri-
vation in infancy—a poor augury for motherly qualities. The closest attachment of her life was to the somewhat older Leonora Galigai, who had

been in her household since her childhood, apparently as a *soeur de lait,* a daughter of her own wet nurse.[8] During their long intimacy Marie demonstrated all manner of loving solicitude toward Leonora. This "most extraordinary" friendship of the queen for her lady-in-waiting, which one contemporary described as her being "in love" with Leonora,[9] suggests that Marie yearned for a mother's physical care, her moods depending on the other's cheerful presence. In order to obtain this presence she courted Leonora with gifts and favors, all the while plying her with constant demands.[10] Marie's coldness toward everyone else was frequently remarked on. She could no more express warm feelings toward her children than she could toward the courtiers and foreign emissaries who sought her favor.[11]

Considerations of state, however, take little account of feelings. Immediately after Henri's assassination, new reasons emerged to reinforce those that already existed for Marie and Louis to maintain an alliance despite the absence of much affection between them.

MOTHER AND SON

Henri's murder produced in Marie an anxious concern for Louis's safety. She gave orders that he was to sleep in her quarters for the first few weeks, and her chambermaids watched over him at night. Captain de Vitry, long in Louis's service, was put in charge of a more assiduous regimen of guarding the young king.[12] These fears for Louis's physical well-being were intensified when in November 1611 Marie's second son, then Duc d'Orléans, finally died of what appears to have been a congenital malady.[13]

The queen's apprehensions for Louis took the form of lessening demands upon him and increasing leniency in his discipline. Thus, when Louis had a sore throat during the last illness of Orléans, Marie kept him from the traditional Paris ceremony of thaumaturgic touching of the scrofulous on All Saints' Day, "for fear that the cold and fatigue might aggravate" his condition. A witness noted after the death of his brother the queen "commanded that they press him even less, for fear of bad occurrences," and he judged that Souvré and his subordinates were "too indulgent of his obstinacy."[14]

Despite this evidence of Marie's leniency with Louis, Héroard shows that he was fearful of her. He describes, for example, how Louis got down on his knees before Souvré to beg him not to report to Marie an insult he had just given him, which shows his "fear of the queen."[15] He was not whipped on this occasion, or almost any other after his father's death. Héroard reports only two exceptions. The first, on May 29, 1610, was apparently before Marie had ordered leniency. The second, at the end of 1612, took place "after hours of threats and arguments," when Louis *chose* to "endure the whip" rather than take medicine prescribed for his earache.[16] Louis's anxiety at the prospect of Marie's discipline seems to be exaggerated. A year later Héroard recorded the young king trembling when he awoke one day, "from apprehension of the whip." Louis had been too free with his mother: "The preceding day he had answered back to the queen that he would not go to see her for two days because she had not permitted him to watch the rut [of deer]." Though Marie had already pardoned his impertinence, Louis continued to tremble, "not being reassured," and asked for pardon once more.[17] His trembling and repeated requests for a forgiveness already given seem to mean something other than fear of the queen's rigor. A likely explanation is that he again invited punishment to gratify wishes partly concealed from himself. Consistent with this is the probability that during the years following his father's murder Louis felt that Marie was taking her husband's place in some respects.

Another result of Henri's murder was the introduction of rules that entailed frequent and regular contact between the young king and his mother. Whenever they were in residence together, it was usual for them to visit each other several times each day. This familiarity brought to light both temperamental similarities and differences between the two that account for some of the effects of Marie's regency.

Louis and the queen mother shared, in the first instance, a common dislike of governmental work. This is hardly surprising in a child of less than fourteen, and during the regency years Louis often sought to escape public duties to pursue private pleasures. Marie had never acquired a long attention span for affairs of state, and she too was easily diverted—which was deplored even by her friends,[18] not to mention partisans of her son. The recreations she enjoyed, however, were different from those that appealed to Louis—personal and household adornment, for example, rather than sports and crafts.

The fact that they were both temperamentally volatile did not contribute to Marie's usefulness as Louis's representative. The queen was quick to anger and, like her son, often allowed her temper to prevail over self-restraint. She, too, was likely to express her moods in visible physical changes. During an interview in 1615, a delegation from Parlement first "recognized . . . indignation in the king's face" on making their plea and then, when it was repeated, saw "anger rise to the face of the queen."[19]

Marie was also like her son in her jealousy over possessions. Louis had to reproach her on several occasions for refusing to relinquish objects he believed were rightfully his—such as a prayer book that had belonged to his father[20] and a dog that was the mate of one of his.[21] The deeper reproach that she was careless of his prized possessions went unspoken during these years, but it will later be seen to have had momentous consequences.

The artistic interest they shared showed itself in divergent tastes, and Héroard regretted that Marie did not have more empathy with her son's preferences. There was a difference in the objects each valued most, and this, too, stood in the way of good rapport. When she offered him a dia-mond-studded trinket, "he refused, rather brusquely"—mere show did not interest him. At the annual fair she gave him a princely chain of diamonds, but "he wants none of it," as Héroard reported understandingly, and "says he would rather have paintings." And when she presented him on New Year's Day with jewels enough for a king's ransom—"a great quantity of various kinds of rings, of diamonds and of very beautiful pieces," he ex-claimed over and over again as he opened the cases, "Ah, Madame, this is too much for us!" According to Héroard, this was because "he would have preferred to find rings of less value . . . [or] some kind of picture [*figure*]." [22]

Marie's feelings of being ill treated propelled her toward a policy quite different from that of her late husband. They tended, in fact, to drive her into the arms of those whom Louis had often described as "the enemies of Papa." Her isolation as a foreign princess and her lack of charm prevented her from winning popularity in France. This difficult position no doubt re-inforced her sympathy with the most distinguished Italian representatives at court, many of whom were clerics of Ultramontanist allegiance. Indeed, Marie's rearing predisposed her to feel an affinity with this party. Her child-hood had been spent in an exclusively Catholic milieu, and her kinship con-nections with the papacy and the Italian clerical elite probably helped instill in her a horror of Protestantism.

All these influences help explain why Marie looked to foreign powers—the Holy See, the Habsburgs—for support and sympathy in the face of do-mestic criticism. Her resentment at what she felt was public ingratitude for her sacrifices on behalf of her son and her adopted country intensified her feeling of kinship with her "good brother" (as she called him)—the king of Spain. [23]

Marie's mother, a Habsburg princess, had held a social position superior to that of her husband, who was a descendant of Tuscan merchants. This background may help explain her daughter's obvious belief that affiliation with the Spanish royal house was the peak of achievement. [24] Marie's lean-ings toward Spain were also fueled by her antipathy to Protestantism, a sen-timent it was impolitic to express publicly after Henri's death, because of Huguenot suspicions. She assured Ubaldini, when the pro-Spanish papal delegate warned her against arranging a marriage for Elisabeth in England, that she "would rather see her daughter dead than a heretic." [25] She brought to her aspirations for a closer affiliation with the house of Spain a liking for marriage politics, the only kind of political matter that sustained her atten-tion. Her interest in high-level matchmaking, indeed, made her seem to have a "mania for marriages." [26]

Thus, little more than a year after the death of her husband, who had de-cided against such alliances, Marie began actively to negotiate marriage with the Spanish infants for Louis and Elisabeth, breaking a promise made by Henri to the duke of Savoy. The project was afoot by 1611, and the following summer the contracts were ratified in a formal ceremony at the Louvre. As Elisabeth signed the papers for her marriage to the heir to the Spanish throne, Louis mischievously nudged her with his elbow — "to cause her to make a mistake," he claimed. Perhaps Héroard, in patriotic zeal, saw this as an augury, describing the horseplay as "*facetum*" in the margin.

Whatever the young king's suspicions of Marie were at the time, it would be unwarranted to believe that he was clearly opposed to the direction his mother's government was taking. Indeed, he himself preferred the Spanish marriage alliance to an English one when Marie pretended to give him a choice. Héroard explained, "It is because he thinks there is more grandeur in it."[27] Nevertheless, a year later, greeting the Spanish emissary who had come to sign the marriage contracts, Louis revised a pronouncement, certainly drafted with his mother's approval, in a way that Héroard thinks significant. Though he promised to honor the king of Spain as his father and to love him as his brother, he omitted the phrase "I shall make use of his good advice." This, Héroard reports, "he does not say at all, whether by design or forgetfulness." The doctor emphasizes the omission with a marginal "*Responsum.*"[28] Such reservations suggest that those around Louis, and on occasion Louis himself, felt that the direction taken by the queen regent was wrong. Yet the importance of these reservations at this point should not be overstressed: the alliance of Marie and Louis remained paramount.

THE CONCINIS

The difficulties that Marie faced when she assumed the regency were aggravated by the fact that most of Henri's cronies and counselors were not her friends, and she soon became more and more dependent on Italian courtiers for advice and support. Some of these were secular emissaries from her home state of Tuscany. Others were clerics deputized from the Holy See to the French court. Still others, often also church officials, were connected to Italian families, like the Zamets and the Gondis, that had long dwelt in France. The Italian connection she relied on most, however, was with her intimate friend Leonora Galigai. And Leonora, by this time, was no longer alone.

Both Leonora Galigai and Concino Concini (later the Marquis d'Ancre) had come to France in 1600 as members of Marie de Medici's Florentine retinue. They had married in 1601, before Louis was born. Although as an infant the dauphin was only seldom and briefly in his mother's company, Leonora was often present on these occasions. The queen's need for the constant companionship of her *soeur de lait* was the subject of much unfavorable comment at court while Louis was still a baby. Particularly scandalized were the noble ladies who were expected to share the places of honor near Marie with the low-born signora, and the queen had to explain that the services Leonora performed required a place for her in the royal carriage to which she was admittedly not entitled by rank. Henri was not hospitable to this idea, since he hoped to control appointments to his wife's entourage—as he did those to his children's—for his own purposes.[29]

The dispute over precedence for Leonora seems to have reached Louis in the nursery. Once, when less than two years old, the dauphin was playing with a carriage and dolls, to which he assigned the names of the countess and duchesses who were Marie's maids of honor. Concino went over to ask him what place was to be given his wife in the carriage. Louis, Héroard relates, "shows him a perch that was on the outside, at the tail end of the carriage."[30] Such relegation could only have been suggested to a baby by scornful gossip—if not actual incitement—from courtiers in his entourage.

As Louis grew older, however, his relations with Leonora seem to have become, if not affectionate, at least familiar and amiable. Since the queen lacked talent for dealing with children, her favorite's mediation might have made access to his mother easier for Louis. For example, when at the age of ten the young king was annoyed that his governor, chatting with Marie, had turned a deaf ear to his requests to be allowed to leave, it was Leonora to whom he complained—"facetiously," as Héroard notes—"There's Monsieur de Souvré, who takes care of his own affairs first; afterward he'll think about mine."[31]

Just as Louis's feelings for his mother were less highly charged than those he had felt for his father, he did not feel toward Leonora that mixture of love and desire, rage and fear that he felt for Concini—the same emotions that Henri had inspired in him. In the early years of Louis's life, the Italian was officially attached to Henri's suite. As an efficient servitor he was able to facilitate some of the king's amorous adventures and, no doubt with his wife's help, to smooth over some of the royal marital difficulties to which these adventures gave rise.[32] An able courtier, Concini did not neglect the nursery, and Madame de Montglat, Louis's governess, was cordial to his overtures there. When he gained permission to watch the dauphin being dressed, he took advantage of the opportunity: leaning over the infant, Héroard tells us, "he measures his length, the circumference of his arm, and the length of his shoe."[33] So he became yet another who took it upon himself to handle the child's body.

Héroard depicts Louis as resisting Concini's advances from the beginning, possibly because Mamanga's sponsorship of the man made him suspect to the child. Thus he refused candy that his governess had given the Italian to offer him: "Draws back, looking at him as though importuned," reports the doctor. Seemingly more cordial to Leonora than to her husband, Louis is induced to kiss the signora's hand when she comes to dine with Madame de Montglat a few months later. The following year he "gets into a bad humor with Madame de Montglat; does the same to Monsieur Concino."[34]

The Concinis at first fused their family interests with those of the French royal family. Their son, born in 1603, had Marie as godmother and Henri as namesake. Five years later the king stood as godfather for their daughter, named after the queen. Leonora sometimes acted as a surrogate for Marie in matters concerning the royal princesses. For example, she assured Madame de Montglat that she would take responsibility for any consequences to the health of one of Marie's daughters should there be any ill effects from moving her from Saint-Germain to the queen's Luxembourg palace: "Promising you that if some misfortune occurs, I will be responsible to the queen, making Her Majesty understand that it was by my advice and that you didn't want to do it . . . and I myself will have an eye out to make sure that she wants for nothing."[35]

Concini was a devoted father, and his behavior with Louis revealed a sensitivity to children's tastes. When the dauphin was seven he brought him a present of miniature harnesses so that the child could attach his two favorite dogs to his little carriage. At the age of nine, sleepy after a day of hunting, Louis "goes to the library to play with the little men that Monsieur le marquis d'Ancre had given him, but he forbids us to say it was for that."[36] His discretion here suggests that he did not want it known that he had yielded to blandishments offered by the marquis in the form of these tempting toys. Yet many of Concini's personal qualities must have appealed to the young boy. By all reports he was an able military strategist and "adept at arms."[37] According to another contemporary, the Italian was "tall and straight," with a feminine quality that enabled him to play the "woman among men."[38]

With the change brought about in the Concinis' position by Henri's death, there was reason for negative feelings toward the Italians to predominate in Louis's mind. Marie's increasing reliance on her favorite, Leonora, made Concini the beneficiary of many of the prerogatives and powers Henri had enjoyed. To Louis it may well have seemed that the Italian parvenu was usurping his father's place.[39]

On a more intimate level, too, Marie allowed Concini to play a fatherlike role in her son's life, sometimes using him as her emissary to transmit her commands and demands to Louis. For example, when the ten-year-old monarch refused to do his lessons after lunch, Marie was notified, and "Monsieur le marquis d'Ancre comes on behalf of the queen." The messenger was effective: Louis studied until four o'clock.[40]

Cast as Marie's menacing arm, Concini not only ran the risk of incurring the kind of wrath that Louis already showed Madame de Montglat; he was now also the bearer of threats of punishments to which, when they had been administered by Henri, it had been Louis's duty, and sometimes his pleasure, to submit. The child felt no duty toward the Italian, however, so that he would have rejected any possible thought of pleasure with less severe conflict than Henri had aroused.

The queen further unwittingly encouraged Louis's aversion to Concini by official acts that gave the marquis more intimate access to the young king. Having first made it possible for her compatriot to buy the title of Marquis d'Ancre, she appointed him, four months after Henri's murder, first gentleman of the king's bedchamber.[41] In this position he could claim a place in Louis's intimate circle. He tried to do so at the beginning of 1611, asserting his right to begin his attendance for the ensuing quarter in alternation with Souvré. Another *premier gentilhomme de la chambre* at the time was Roger des Termes, duc de Bellegarde, one of Henri's courtiers and a particular favorite of Louis. As *grand écuyer de France*, he had the title of *Monsieur le Grand,* the most honored in the king's household. On January 2 Ancre averred to the old duke that he now had the right to take over the room of the *grand écuyer* at the Louvre. This precipitated a quarrel—of which Louis was doubtless aware—so serious that Marie's mediation was required to forestall violence.[42]

Louis certainly resented the newcomer's claims. If Concini was aware of this, he did not react but instead pressed on with his aims. Berthold Zeller, summarizing the Italian emissaries' reports of the quarrel, suggests the nature of these aims: "The . . . Florentine hoped to improve his prospects through the intimate access to the king assured him by the duties of his office, and he counted on winning the mind of his master by a kind of seduction that a child who is becoming a man rarely resists, that of light words, and perhaps even bad examples."[43] Louis had been deeply tempted in this way by his father. With Ancre, however, he resisted the seduction fiercely.

Héroard recounts a scene that reveals how Louis responded to the Italian's sallies with revulsion (perhaps connected with unacknowledged desire), a reaction that may have been strengthened by the impudicity of his father. The young king, in bed after a hard day's hunting, was conversing with courtiers. The duc d'Aiguillon was there, Héroard relates, as well as the Marquis d'Ancre and "Madame his nurse, too." Relaxing his tongue and giving free rein to his fantasy, as he often did in such convivial sessions, Louis remarked of a group of Gypsies he had seen in the forest, "If one hunted for Gypsy, the grand provost would be a good falcon." Concini fell in with what he thought to be the spirit of the exchange: "Monsieur le Marquis d'Ancre says to him, putting his hand on Madame la Nourrice, 'Sire, women who are at your *coucher* must sleep with M. d'Aiguillon, who is grand chamberlain, and with me, who am first gentleman of your chamber.'"[44] Louis was furious: "Looking at him in rage, [he] turns his back on him saying these words: 'Listen to the obscenities.'"[45] By just such claims to *les siens* Henri had threatened Louis's possession of his beloved nurse.

To the young king, Concini's depredations on the public treasury may have seemed as serious as his predatory behavior toward Doundoun. Marie was lavish in bestowing goods and honors on Leonora and her husband. Louis was sometimes taken along on trips to the Bastille, where treasure that Henri's frugality had amassed was disbursed to the queen. Even in these first years of the regency the child may have thought that royal possessions were being dispensed that were rightfully his alone to give or, as important, to withhold.

Louis's jealousy of *les siens*, whether persons or things, by no means diminished with time. But he did become more sophisticated about techniques of granting and retaining what it was in his power to give. Once, not yet ten, Louis was unwilling to give a ring to one of his favorite attendants when Souvré suggested he do so. Instead, he listened silently to his governor's proposal and, "a long time afterward," called: "Beringhen, I give it to you. If I had done it when Monsieur de Souvré had said, you would have been obliged to him for it, and not to me."

The ring in question here was merely one of copper.[46] Even before Louis reached the age of majority, however, subjects would approach him for benefits that could mean life or death to them — as in the case of the woman who had been condemned for killing her unborn child. As the young king came home from hunting she threw herself at his feet, begging for clemency. He was touched by the appeal and convinced by the woman's claim of innocence. But he was also aware of the power of others. He asked Souvré to speak to the queen and to a certain courtier whom she esteemed. Then he said to his nurse, "Doundoun, tell the Marquise d'Ancre to dispose my mother to grant her pardon."[47] He was realistic both about the weakness of his own position and about the dependency and lack of resolve of the one who still held the legal right to act on his behalf. And, if we are right in drawing this conclusion from suggestive evidence, the Marquise d'Ancre was realistic too, not only about Marie's vulnerability but also about the character of her elder son. Soon after a conversation with Leonora, the Tuscan emissary dispatched this report to Florence:

> Speculative persons, who know the nature and temperament of this king, maintain that, in four or five years, the queen will be left without any authority with her son, and for this reason: The king is lively [*vif*], wrathful [*emporté*], and willful [*volontaire*], and it is not impossible that, prodded by the princes who might be found around him and who are displeasing to the queen, he may want to govern by himself.[48]

If, as seems likely, Marie's cherished Leonora was the source of these speculations, it is not surprising that they were proved correct. The Marquise d'Ancre was an astute observer, and since Louis's early childhood she had visited his household frequently and had occasionally dined below stairs with his nurse and governess. More than most, she was in a position to be aware of elements in Louis's temperament that would one day lead him to free himself from his mother's tutelage. The accuracy of the predicted time lapse before Louis came into his own could well be based on solid judgment rather than the uncanny powers of foresight later attributed to Leonora. For, in the autumn of 1612, the conditions for Louis's emancipation were just beginning to be set.

CHAPTER TEN

Interregnum: Pleasures and Pains

*In three or four years this prince will no longer be subject to shaping; he
will command rather than obey.*[1]

One summer afternoon in 1611 Louis asked his mother for leave to visit
Saint-Germain en Laye the next day. The queen demurred, on the grounds
that he had to remain with her to receive the list of complaints drawn up by
the recent Protestant assembly. He responded, "Madame, you will do it
well without me; besides—I am too young."[2] The trip to his little stable
that followed this exchange, like trips to the childhood home where his sisters and brothers were ready to gratify his every wish, gave Louis much
pleasure; by comparison, politics was at best a dry occupation. Although
the nine-year-old had attended council meetings fairly regularly since as-
cending the throne, he still showed little desire to take a larger part in state
affairs.

When matters of policy were discussed before the new king, he was usually a silent auditor. As Héroard describes him during one such discussion,
"He listens to everything, retains everything, knows everything, doesn't let
on."[3] However strong his resentment of those who acted for him may have
been, at this stage he had no active drive to assume public responsibilities.

PROVIDERS OF PLEASURES

For the most part, the first months of 1611 were filled with activities that
Louis enjoyed. His favorite pastime was hunting—birds, wolves, hare,
deer, and other animals—in the woods and parks surrounding Paris. When
he returned to Saint-Germain for the first time after Henri's death, he was
full of excitement at the pleasures ahead: "We'll go to the park where I'll do
lots of things—I'll do jumps [on horseback]."[4] A holiday at Fontainebleau
later in the spring was just as full of delights; despite the late hour of his ar-

rival, a visit to the *volerie* there could not wait until the next day.[5] In between these trips there were other excursions—to Saint-Germain des Prés,
for example—to attend fairs and other entertainments. Even in the Louvre,
where certain diversions were excluded during the year of mourning for his
father, there was still a wide variety of games and amusements. Almost
every day a list of elaborate pastimes was arranged for the young head of
state. His recreation schedule demanded constant attention; arranging and
facilitating it was a full-time occupation for many attendants. Those who
supplied these pleasures were often the object of the king's special attention
and favor—sometimes also of his love.

Boon Companions

Soon after Henri died, a group of courtiers who provided the prince with
easy camaraderie, facilitating his enjoyment of everyday life, became noticeable in his public appearances. Part of Louis's duties required him to eat,
drink, talk, and be merry with the *bons compagnons* around him, as his father
had done.[6] Because Louis is the star of Héroard's drama, the diarist rarely
gives us a *mise en scène* that fully identifies the supporting cast. Thus it is
possible to overlook the fact that the young king's waking hours were almost all spent in the company of a group. Gentlemen attendants, often numerous, accompanied him everywhere. On one occasion Héroard does
identify them: when the royal carriage overturned at Brie-Comte-Robert
during a fierce thunderstorm and Louis and his attendants had to be transferred to another coach, Héroard lists "all those who were inside"—both
Vendôme brothers, Henri de Verneuil, the Chevalier de Guise, the Marquis
de La Valette, Baron de Vitry, the guards captain, and Souvré.[7]

Those who gathered at Louis's bedside in the evenings of his first months
as king included a group of older servitors, many of them great noblemen
of the realm, who shared the boy's interest in sports, especially falconry.
Their political records and inclinations seem to have held little interest for
their young master. Consequently, the group included the chevalier and the
duc de Guise, experts in falconry and its lore. Though the Guises had not
been friends of the most recent kings of France, they were now in new favor
with the queen mother. The fact that they had been kept at arm's length by
Henri was no barrier to Louis's friendship with them. He would later
mourn the slain chevalier de Guise with the words, "He was always with
me; I never went hunting except that he came with me."[8]

Another prominent *grand* who was popular with Louis was the duc
d'Epernon. Though an old *mignon* of Henri III, he had not been a favorite of
Henri IV. Now newly admitted to Marie's inner circle, however, he also
made himself very welcome with Louis, as Héroard reports: "After supper
he went into his bedroom with Monsieur d'Epernon, who had entertained
him all during his supper." A few days later, "Monsieur d'Epernon takes

leave of him to go to Angoumois; he embraces him and kisses him several times,"[9] unusual effusiveness for the nine-year-old.

Like Epernon, the duc de Bellegarde, *grand écuyer* of France, had been a favorite of Henri III. His sweetness of manner is said to have been the characteristic that caused Henri IV to maintain him in favor,[10] and his company was now particularly congenial to Louis.[11] As First Gentleman of the King's Bedchamber he was frequently in intimate contact with the young king. Bellegarde had been persona grata to Louis since early in his childhood, when the duke used to intervene to moderate Henri's provocation of his son. The older man often played with the little boy at the sports, games, and practical jokes that they both enjoyed.[12] Receiving Bellegarde among the chevaliers of the Saint Esprit soon after Henri's death, Louis seized the beard of "*Monsieur le Grand*" and said, laughing, "There's a fine man!" More significant still was Louis's reception of him after an absence: "The king welcomes him warmly, transported." And again, after another, longer, absence: "He receives him with unparalleled delight. 'I've been waiting for you for ages,' he tells him, having embraced him over and over."[13] The *grand écuyer* seems to have played a fatherly role for Louis, bringing joy unalloyed by the pain that his own father had often caused.

Another popular member of Louis's circle of favored older men was François de Bassompierre—formerly a sexual rival of Henri's though his political supporter as well. Comparably amiable, jocose relationships also existed between the young king and his longtime favorite, Courtenvaux, Souvré's son,[14] and the young baron de Montglat, son of the formidable Mamanga. As these two attended him one evening at bedtime, he made plasters of his ointment and applied it to their faces.[15] Louis derived pleasure from these exuberant sessions with his gentlemen supporters. Under these conditions, reports one who used to read aloud at the royal *coucher*, the constraints that normally inhibited his speech were relaxed, and he "entertained . . . company with good stories which he could tell as easily and fluently as anyone else."[16]

A different kind of adjunct to Louis's pleasures was not a high personage or even a gentleman. This was Haran—never referred to by more than one name—the young king's kennel master and chamber boy. In addition to caring for his beloved dog-family, Haran provided various other domestic pleasures to Louis, who frequently visited him at his dwelling, eating food prepared by him or cooking himself. This playing house eventually became enduring: Louis bought Haran a house in a suburb of Paris, where he continued to visit him.[17]

The winter of 1610–1611 was unusually cold, and when weather prevented the outdoor sports Louis preferred, he played indoors at games and crafts or, taking aim from his windows, brought down birds with bows and arrows or guns. Little hunts were even staged within the palace: small dogs chased a hare in his bedroom, his yellow parrot was sent after a sparrow in the Louvre gallery. Few waking moments passed without an arranged activity. Noble supporters stood behind Louis to converse with him at mealtimes, and bedtime, their efforts supplemented with marionettes, musicians, and other performers. Soon after Henri's death the Venetian ambassador wrote home: "The king begins to have a larger cortège than before. Sunday . . . he had more than three hundred gentlemen with him."[18]

The fact that his life was conducted in the midst of a host of others was a great satisfaction to Louis. His dependence, as a minor king, on those around him was reinforced by his need to retain and defend *les siens* as a part of himself. His desire for support probably made it significant that one of the crowd, Charles de Luynes, entered Louis's service as the eldest of a trio of brothers.

Luynes

Born in 1578, Charles d'Albert, sieur de Luynes, was past his first youth when he came into Louis's ken. Described by one who knew him as only one-sixteenth noble, his origins could not have been more modest for one admitted to the service of the great as a gentleman. The Luynes family seat was near Mornas in Languedoc, where many years later the sight of their dwelling betrayed a "very mediocre nobility" to the court, which was on a military campaign with Louis in the neighborhood.[19] One disparaging description of this estate, the property of Luynes's father, seems to be based on a firsthand view: "To a tiny house [of Luynes] . . . between Aix and Ardaillon he added a tacky outhouse called Brante, situated on a rock where he had a vine planted . . . and an island that the Rhone engulfed more often than it exposed, called Cadenet." These were the family properties from which the three brothers—Luynes, Cadenet, and Brantes—took their names.[20]

Their father had been a soldier of fortune who lent himself to Henri IV's interests; an uncle had been a physician in the service of Henri's mother. This record of loyal service accounts for the king's favors to Charles: Henri acted as his godfather and later brought him to his court as a page.[21] Having reached young adulthood, Charles entered the service of the comte Du Lude, along with his brother Brantes. Henri recalled Charles to court in 1606 and his brother in 1608; perhaps it was at this time that they were installed in the dauphin's service.[22]

Despite the Luynes brothers' modest upbringing, they were conversant with the techniques of falconry, a sport that had become fairly arcane by 1600, and they were able to aid Louis's passion for it. As the sieur d'Esparron, royal falconer, attested: "Monsieur de Luynes . . . is always near him, as are also the sieurs de Cadenet and La Brandes [*sic*], his brothers . . . being particularly capable in this science."[23] By 1611 Luynes was caretaker of the larks and other small birds that Louis kept in his chambers and to which he was so devoted that he rose at all hours to tend them. The assignment gave Luynes intimate access to the young king, and it seems to have been at about this time, when Henri had been dead for more or less a year, that a transformation took place in Louis's feelings. From being simply one who arranged pleasures for His Majesty, Luynes became one whom Louis loved.

By the end of 1611 the young king had recently lost several other members of his family. This may have made him more open to the Luynes brothers' assiduous attentions. César de Vendôme had married and established a separate household in 1609, to be replaced in Louis's affections by his brother Alexandre. (When asked by an ambassador which of the two he preferred, Louis is said to have replied, "Alexander before Caesar.")[24] Alexandre was then removed from the young king's entourage in August 1611. Despite Louis's mixed feelings toward these half brothers, he did have strong desires to keep them near him. His first full brother died the following November, a death that most likely made him feel diminished; his sense of solidarity with his full brothers is expressed by his reaction to the birth of Gaston, the second one, in 1608: "It's a brother! I'm so happy!" It was then that he added, as we noted before, "Now we are three!"[25] It was at just about this time that the second, and perhaps also the third, of the Luynes brothers took up a post at court.

An indication that Charles de Luynes had become important in Louis's thoughts appeared in a dream in the autumn of 1611. The young king had been ill with an infection causing swollen glands—a condition in which old fantasies tend to surface. A few days before he had dreamed of the *songes* that were roasting him on the spit.[26] Now he recounted to Héroard (commanding him to write it down) that in this new dream "Courtenvaux had a daughter that his wife had delivered and Haran had been its godfather." The dream evidently gave him pleasure, for after he had finished telling it, "he bursts out laughing."[27] In the earlier dream with the *songes* where it might be expected that he would have felt pain, he related instead, as though he were being tickled, "I laughed so much; I laughed so much!"[28]

Courtenvaux, a childhood favorite, was still in close attendance on the young king. The second dream suggests that Souvré's son was linked in Louis's mind with the newer arrival, Luynes. Haran, whose name resembled Henri (and who took the role of father to Louis's role of mother when they played house together), was godfather in the dream to Courtenvaux's daughter, as Henri was in fact godfather to Charles de Luynes. As I shall argue later, it is wholly plausible for Luynes to be represented as a girl in this dream.

A sure indication that Luynes had begun to play a significant role in Louis's unconscious was an incident that occurred a month later. This time the young king identified the falconer in a dream that caused him to call out in his sleep: "Oh, how beautiful it is! How beautiful it is, the lure, the lure. Luynes! Luynes!" The lure was no doubt one of those Louis and Charles fashioned out of string and leather to entrap little birds. Héroard, who had just returned from a two-day absence, identifies Luynes as a "gentleman who took care of his larks."[29] Luynes probably had access to Louis's bedchamber in those late hours of easy companionship—from which Héroard was apparently excluded.

I mentioned earlier that Louis saw his older half brothers, particularly César de Vendôme, as possessing both enviable and detestable attributes. Their association with him and their relationship to his father made them, in his imagination, stand-ins, or proxies,[30] for himself, gratifying him by possessing qualities he lacked or indulging appetites he restrained. Luynes's status as Henri's godson, together with his ability to further one of Louis's principal delights, may have put him, too, in a position where Louis felt him to be another self. His name, pronounced so distinctly in the dream, was even more like Louis's own than appears in modern spelling. The king sometimes signed himself Louys, or Loys; Héroard spells Louis's nighttime voicing of Luynes's name as "Loïnes," indicating by the dipthong a similar sound.

Luynes also played the obvious role of father substitute (as in some manner did all the older *bons compagnons* of the young king's suite). Luynes was easily old enough to be Louis's father, although much younger than Bellegarde and some other courtiers. He had a notable attribute in common with the *vert galant*—the reputation of being a lady killer. When he entered Louis's service the young attendant already was known to have had several rather scandalous conquests.[31]

Like the *grand écuyer*, Luynes protected and facilitated Louis's pleasures. He was the good companion that Henri could sometimes be, but, unlike Henri, he held no terrors for his child partner. Indeed, the very pleasures he provided at court were not the big-game hunting and martial exercises that inspire fantasies of blood and danger (though Louis also loved these sports) but the more delicate art of falconry. As described by an English observer of the time, this sport, under Luynes's guidance, evoked a rather precious image: "His favorite" wrote Lord Herbert of Cherbury, "was one Monsieur de Luynes, who in his nonage gained much upon the king by making hawks fly at all little birds in his gardens, and by making some of those little birds again catch butterflies."[32]

Though it did not employ the brute force of other blood sports, falconry had its sadistic gratifications. One of the *vols* invented by Charles and Louis is described by Esparron: "The sieur de Luynes has plucked pigeons in quantity and male hawks whose claws have been pulled so that they can strike down the pigeons without being able to kill them."

Deprived of their tail feathers, the pigeons were unable to soar away, allowing the game to be replayed repeatedly. "This *volerie* gives much pleasure to His Majesty."[33]

Luynes gave no one the impression of menace. The best contemporary portrayal of him shows a middle-aged man with boyish—even babyish—rounded features, a turned-up nose (sometimes the object of Louis's wit),[34] and an agreeable expression. The image contrasts with those portraits of Henri that depict a lean and wiry body and aquiline features.

Strong as the physical differences between Luynes and Louis's father were, their characters contrasted even more. In addition to a "pleasant physiognomy," as Griffet puts it, Luynes had a manner that was "*doux*"—gentle or sweet.[35] Another English observer who knew him describes him as a man of "mild comportment, humble and debonair to all suitors."[36] This was in clear contrast with the selfish and masterful Henri IV.

Luynes's charm and easy good nature were qualities that could give Louis both vicarious and direct pleasure. The appeal for women, for example, so threatening in his father, appeared harmless or even attractive to Louis in the falconer. Luynes's courtliness could be exercised on his young master's behalf.

Luynes's failings, too, served to gratify Louis. He had weaknesses that the young king did not allow himself. Luynes's gentleness was perceived by some as cowardice.[37] The nuncio Bentivoglio found him inclined to "diffidence."[38] The demand that Louis made upon himself to show fortitude in all circumstances could be relaxed in the case of his favorite, whose lack of bravery may have served not only to display the king to advantage but also to indulge, by proxy, his impulses toward surrender. In contrast to his young master, who was likely to appear peremptory and stubborn, Luynes was indecisive and seemed malleable, given to changing his mind.[39] Fontenay-Mareuil described him as careless and disorganized, whereas Louis gave sedulous attention to order and detail.[40] And again, unlike the young king, Luynes was "open." The older man was incapable of keeping a secret,[41] while Louis's ability to hold his tongue was already obvious.

Over the years Luynes was to receive from Louis ever-greater distinctions in wealth, rank, and responsibility. As honors multiplied, however, the contrast between his high status and his low origins became increasingly conspicuous. Louis's pleasure in the company of his favorite seems to have been enhanced by this disparity. Since Luynes was completely dependent on the king for his good fortune, he was in a sense a lackey, like Bompar, the page, and Haran, the kennel master. Perhaps this was a condition of Louis's love for him, a love which mixed with opposite feelings as time passed. When, after Luynes's premature death in 1621, the king tried to account for his feelings, he could only say: "I loved him, despite his faults, because he loved me.["]42 It was probably as much because of his faults as despite them that Luynes inspired love in Louis. He had been to the young king the valet that Louis had tried to be for his father.

Illuminating the varied roles that Luynes came to play in Louis's mental life is a dream the king reported to Héroard toward the end of 1614, after Luynes had been at court for about eight years:

> He says he dreamed that the sieur de Luynes, a gentleman he loved, was dressed as a Swiss guard with yellow cut-off knickers, a fat green codpiece [*brayette*], and a high ruff [*fraise*] like that of women, and that he played on a fife, and that his mistress also was dressed as a Swiss and played the tambourine, and that she knew well how to play the *abattis* [sounded after a successful hunt] but not the trill [*fredon*].

In this dream the identity of Luynes with Louis's father, the *vert galant*, is signified by his role as a gallant, by his large green *brayette*, that ornate protector of the male genitals, and by his fife, another symbol of the organ on which Henri so prided himself. The mistress is Louis—a tambourine player, as was Louis in waking life.[43] The significance of other parts of the dream is obscure. *Fredon* has a possible sexual implication, as does *fredaine*, from which it is said to be derived.[44] Louis's wish to be mistress to Luynes (as he also imagined himself to his father) is masked by the femininity of Luynes in the dream. (Luynes's "softness" facilitated this representation.) The ruffs that both dream personages wear link them to the birds that Luynes and Louis raised and pursued in waking life. These disguised meanings explain why this dream, like earlier ones, aroused no anxiety in the thirteen-year-old-boy. Héroard tells us, "He told it to everybody and commanded me to write it down."[45]

In his relations with Luynes Louis could be the able, energetic, and confident boy that his father had wished him to be. But another side of his temperament persisted as well. In his waking behavior and in his dreams, the opposite qualities were occasionally revealed: passivity, lassitude, and anxiety.

MEETING OLD FEARS

In the first winter after Henri's death, Héroard represents the new king as happily absorbed, for the most part, in strenuous recreations. But he also shows Louis struggling against lassitude, a fight he sometimes lost—as when he overslept. Awakening an hour past his normal time one morning in January 1611 he complains, "almost to the point of tears," that "they" have let him sleep so late: "What's this?" he cries. "They'll say I'm an idler. . . . They'll say I'm lazy." Héroard's note here is, "Hates idleness." Perhaps it was to make amends for this transgression that the child insisted on going hunting on horseback that afternoon. Although "it was cold," Héroard tells us, Louis dismounted and "went on foot for a long time."[46]

The next week Louis awakens later still. He is again "near tears" that "they" have allowed him to oversleep, fearing that "everybody will say he is lazy." Héroard, however, believes that these fears show he is "diligent."[47] Nevertheless, such derelictions are repeated. Having fallen asleep one February night while playing with his ivory balls in bed, bumping them together and "saying they are birds attacking a kite," he gives way to tears when he oversleeps in the morning. And in April, waking even later than on the first occasion, he again weeps.[48]

The doctor's reiterated affirmations of his patient's energy arouse the suspicion that he, as well as Louis, was apprehensive about these lapses. Any sign of activity was welcomed by Héroard. When the child planned a strenuous winter's day hunt, the notation is, "Never indolent." Even when Louis, sitting on his toilet seat one evening, had a bird killed in the torches for amusement, Héroard noted approvingly, "Never lazy." When he undertook to mold candied fruits he was commended as "active, industrious." When he had attendants sing and play together at bedtime, Héroard commented: "He must always be doing something," is an "enemy of repose."[49] When Louis went to bed with a stomachache on a hot July afternoon, Héroard was relieved to find him "back in action" after supper. "Idle games don't please him at all," the diarist comments. And when Souvré induced the young king to join in a game of cards on a voyage, the doctor assures us he "becomes bored with it." (Henri had been a passionate card player.) It is a sign of Louis's "active disposition" that he prefers to help with the milking. "He could not remain inactive," Héroard insists.[50]

Martial Fervor

Nowhere did Louis's desire to be active appear more obviously than in his passion for military arts. Barely a week after Henri's death, a commander going off to his post asked the new king for orders. "Give battle," the child replied—a "regal, generous response," in Héroard's estimation.[51]

Soon after this exchange, Marie abrogated Henri's agreement with Savoy to marry Elisabeth to Prince Victor-Amadeus, heir to the dukedom. The duke of Savoy then broke a treaty with France by threatening Geneva. On March 2, 1611, a council meeting, attended by Louis, decided on war. The Florentine resident at court records that afterward the young king showed the company assembled in the queen's office how great his elation at this prospect was, and how extreme his impatience to mount his horse and ride off to battle: "Running to a mirror and having looked at himself he turned toward those present, saying that it seemed to him that he had grown twice as tall since they had started to talk [of war]." The next day Héroard recounts that when during a geography lesson Louis's preceptor

related how Atlas bore the world on his shoulders, "the king responds immediately: 'I would gladly carry it.' And he puts one of the volumes on his
shoulders. . . . 'Look! I bear the world in France!' And then, taking the
other volume, 'I could easily carry another!'" In the margin, the doctor
notes this "*augurium*" of his "courage."[52]

   In the following spring Louis had a similar reason for elation. At a council
meeting that he attended, war against the duke of Savoy was once more decided on, this time in support of the duke of Mantua. "Madame," he said to
his mother, "I'm delighted; we have to make war." Despite his apparent
confidence, however, his sleep was disturbed that night.[53] The prospect of
taking part in a war not only aroused delight but also contributed to the
anxieties evoked by other events in the year just past.

RETURNING GHOSTS

For more than a year after Henri's death, Héroard's emphasis on Louis's
cheerful vigor seems justified by the facts he reports. Only during the weeks
around the anniversary of the murder, when memories were revived by ceremonies marking the event, did the child show some of his old symptoms
and worries. At Fontainebleau, in that fateful second week in May, "he
complains of stomachache, has anxiety [*inquiétude*] about it." Indeed, he
goes so far as to request what would be only the second enema of his life.
The pain persisted, and another enema was administered two days before
the trip to Paris for the rites commemorating Henri's death. On the evening
of the day following the service for repose of his father's soul he again suf-
fers from stomachache. His night fears of ghosts in the Louvre at this time
have already been noted.[54]

   In the autumn of 1611, Louis began to suffer from the swelling in the
groin mentioned earlier. This was the time of those dreams concerning
songes turning the spit and Haran's goddaughter, the child of Courtenvaux
and his wife. During the ensuing winter, as he spent more and more time in
the company of the Luynes brothers, he was very active, especially with
birds and hunting, and his spirits were seemingly untroubled. But toward
the end of February 1612, the king complained of pain in the bowel "on the
left side." The swelling in his groin was again observed. When fomenta-
tions failed to relieve the problem, a truss was applied. Soon thereafter,
Louis had a dream like one he reported earlier in his childhood: "He says he
dreamed he had his head in a hole and couldn't get it out."[55]

   This carnival season, the first to be observed since the end of mourning
for Henri, was marked by many court festivities exciting for a ten-year-old.
An accident during one of them caused the death of an attendant and started
a fire in a tower of the Louvre. Louis, who witnessed some of this, dreamed
the same night of fire and broken lances. During Lent Louis's and Elisa-

beth's marriages were arranged, to be celebrated with elaborately planned recreations. Louis's health continued to be imperfect: toothache disturbed his sleep for several days. To combat this an enema was administered.[56]

Festivities in observance of the marriage agreement came to a climax on April 5–7 with a gigantic carrousel in the Place Royale, followed by other entertainments and by the reception of visiting dignitaries.[57] At the end of the week Héroard noted a conjunctivitis in Louis's eye, which he treated topically. At bedtime two days later, the eruption of smallpox was discovered on the patient's chest, stomach, and back.[58]

During the days that followed Louis was mostly confined to bed. Héroard was relieved that his case was light; the pustules on his face were few, and all discharged by themselves. Three days after detecting the disease, he noted the child's renewed industry in devising amusing pastimes: "Can't remain idle."[59] But the young king was ill-humored during much of this illness, though Héroard reports few details of this. He does set down an account of a scene between Louis and his governor, who reproached his young charge for having failed to converse with some lords who came to dinner. Louis was "angry at this, and as Monsieur de Souvré wants to leave in order to go to dinner," he recalls him:

> "Monsieur de Souvré, you want to go to dinner?"
> "Yes, Sire."
> "You're too good company to go away to dinner," and he holds him
> by his coat. It was in order to take revenge.[60]

All during his illness Louis continued to amuse himself with his birds and harquebuses. Héroard administered medications constantly and, from time to time, enemas. As his patient was recovering from the infection, he prescribed a new therapy: Mademoiselle Bélier, his dresser, bound the king up with a linen bandage, presumably in place of the truss that had been applied earlier. When he was unbound at bedtime after the first day of this treatment, he was found to be twice as swollen as before. The bandage was reapplied the next day, however, and then regularly renewed every few days.[61]

Despite these difficulties Louis was active during an exceptionally hot summer. In August elaborate plans were begun for receiving the duke of Pastrano, who was to represent the Spanish prince and princess in the marriage ceremony to take place in the Louvre. These preparations evoked general excitement. For the first time since February, Héroard describes a dream of Louis's on August 4. In the middle of the night, "he awakens with a start, crying: 'Hey! Come quick! Hey! Come!' . . . [Later] he was asked what made him cry out. 'It's that I was dreaming that there was a man hanged in the courtyard, and that ghosts [*esprits*] wanted to beat me.'" Seemingly, this is another form of the *songes* dream. It is Louis who has his head in the noose. There is a hanging (by his father, the ghost?) and a threat of beating, rather than the "tickling" of being turned on the spit: Louis's anxiety is nearer the surface. In this version, instead of laughing, he screams for help. That evening there is an unusual scene with Souvré at bedtime:

> He calls him to his bedside and asks, 'Well, have you anything to scold me for?'
> 'No, Sire.'
> The king stands up and embraces him saying, 'Ha! Good man! There's the best man in the world! Go! Go! And sleep well.'

It is not Souvré who will beat him. He need have no fear for himself during the night.[62]

The combination of Louis's illness and his forthcoming marriage may have revived his old wish to be loved by his father, along with the fears this entailed. Héroard implies that there had been allusions by adults to future sexual duties for the young king. The day before Pastrano's official entry into Paris, as Louis and his company were returning from Plaisance, they passed the Tour de Brante. The doctor recounts: "He asks what tower it was. . . . [A courtier] answered that it was there that a king of France once kept La Belle Agnès, his mistress." Louis, addressing his half brother Henri de Verneuil, says, "That's like your mother." But Henri reminds him: "'That's like when the infanta will be here.' The King: 'Ho! No! There's quite a difference!'" Louis's betrothed is his mother's candidate to replace herself; Henri's mother had been Marie's dangerously seductive rival.[63]

The next day Louis accompanied Marie, Elisabeth, and Queen Marguerite, Henri IV's first wife, to the bridge of Notre Dame to watch secretly as the duke arrived.[64] The sight of the man who came to bind him to a bride may have stimulated some misgivings. When Souvré told him teasingly some days later that he was to be married the following morning, he responded, "coldly and brusquely, 'Let's not talk of that; let's not talk of that!'"[65]

All this time Louis was regularly being given fresh bindings. A few weeks later Mademoiselle Bélier, who applied them, figured in a new variation on the "caught in a hole" (or noose, or snare) dream that Louis related to Souvré: "I dreamed that you were in a hole with my dresser, and I had so much trouble in pulling you out and I couldn't do it."[66] Imagining his governor entrapped by the female perhaps lessened the danger to himself.

Toward the end of September a rumor of the king's assassination spread rapidly through Paris, with strong effect on a population not yet reconciled to the loss of its beloved Henri IV. The following day Louis was taken in a carriage to Notre Dame to "reassure the people," as Héroard reports. "The rejoicing and loud acclamations were unbelievable." The experience may have revived feelings in Louis that were associated with his father. After tea he seemed exhausted, asked for a chair, and fell asleep in it. When an enema was prescribed the next day, he resisted the idea. To persuade him they cited his sore throat and mentioned that his skin had a yellow cast. "This gave him pause," Héroard relates, for "he feared being ill." Louis asked his doctor whether he had a fever: "I tell him no, but he could get one if he didn't take the enema. On the point of taking it, he asks to pray God. I ask him what he asked of God. 'Ah, that it doesn't hurt me!' He takes the enema.[67]

During the following month Louis suffered from some malady that caused weakness and swollen glands. It may have been mumps: it caused swellings, Héroard tells us, behind the ears where the jaw intersects with the neck. Louis was not one to bear such an affliction in silence, and he sent for Héroard in the middle of the night, complaining of pain "on the other side." His sleep was disturbed on subsequent nights, and one morning he cried: "I haven't slept the past seven hours." He blamed Héroard for the "bad remedy" he had been persuaded to take: "Instead of curing me, I'm burning up! Hey, how hot I am, I'm burning. Let them bring straw to set me on fire! Good Lord, how bad I feel!"[68]

By the beginning of November Louis had resumed his normally strenuous days of hunting and traveling, but he still had "lassitudes." On November 8 he was so resolved to refuse a medicine prescribed for him that neither the queen's repeated appearances nor threats from Souvré availed. He preferred to "endure the whip" and at ten o'clock was "thoroughly whipped, without tears."[69]

During the first months of the new year, his sleep was frequently disturbed by chills, headaches, and toothache. Once he woke with a start, crying out that there were frogs in his bed. Enemas were frequently administered.[70] In June he was still suffering from toothache and disturbed sleep. One night he woke from a dream crying and "speaking Latin." In July a dream caused him to leave his bed. He "jumps upon it, saying, 'I'm 600 years old, Comte de Maure, I'm fifteen—you have to count twelve for each month.'"[71]

Throughout the summer Louis would often wake in the middle of the night with a need to urinate. His dream about a beating kept recurring. According to Héroard, on August 23 he woke from dreaming saying, "Don't beat this dog!" Five days later it was "Hey! Don't hurt him!" The same expressions followed as he woke, "complaining and crying," on August 29 and 31.[72] As well as the terror, the pleasure of his father's punishments seems to have come near the surface.[73] In September Louis's dreams more clearly recreated his early experiences of his father as a seducer. "While dreaming," Héroard reports, "he strips off his shirt, wants to cut it up, is found entirely naked." Two months later, still asleep, "he gets up on his knees and opens his eyes."[74] This was the position he had assumed for

Henri's inspection during an illness years before, after which the king had insisted he be given an enema.

In these months, Louis's physical ailments became chronic. Medication was constantly prescribed for him and he submitted frequently to enemas.[75] The queen willingly administered her son's treatments, many times appearing in his apartments while he was kept in bed. She again became a figure in his dream life, as toward the end of the year he often talked of her in his sleep. When in January 1614 he refused his medicine, she threatened him with the whip, as Henri used to do. He took the potion, Héroard tells us, "for fear of her."[76]

As winter deepened, Louis admitted to lassitude—in contrast to the excitement of his dreams.[77] One night at bedtime he declares to the doctor, who reports it without explanation, that he is "so sad that he cannot enjoy himself."[78]

The incompleteness of Héroard's account often prevents us from guessing what specific events in waking life may have triggered particular dreams. The dream from which Louis woke on his knees occurred the night before Concino Concini took the oath as maréchal of France, kneeling in the queen's chambers in the presence of Louis and Marie. Héroard tells us nothing of the young king's demeanor as Ancre gave a short speech proclaiming undying gratitude to the monarch and the regent for so many benefits bestowed on one who, "as a foreigner, had come to France with nothing."[79] This appointment, which conferred the second-highest military honor in France on the husband of Marie's favorite, was painful to Louis, absorbed as he was in all things martial. The king confirmed this resentment of the promotion when he told a courtier, after Concini's death in 1617, that "he did not wish that he be called Maréchal but only Concino, his intention never having been to make him Maréchal."[80]

Ancre's rise to eminence in the realm was only one of many events that may have seemed to Louis to usurp his possessions or to impinge on his ambitions. At just this time, challenges to the queen's government became more serious as its financial moorings continued to weaken. When, on the night of Epiphany in January 1614, the young king himself drew the symbol of kingship from his serving of Twelfth Night cake, he could anticipate with misgivings the coming year, in which he would be declared an adult— and sovereign of France.

CHAPTER ELEVEN

Coming of Age

May God bless this prince's beginnings! I believe we shall have . . . no regrets for the past.[1]

As Marie de Medici bestowed more and more benefits on those through whom she hoped to strengthen her hand, the restiveness of the *grands* who had no share in the largesse increased apace. French kings reached majority at the age of thirteen. For Louis this would be in the autumn of 1614. Early in that year several great lords were already looking forward to the time when Marie would cease to be regent and political influence in France would owe more to winning favor from the son than from the mother.

DEFECTIONS

At the start of the new year the disaffected *grands* gathered at a long conference, apparently to plan how to put an end to the queen's rule once Louis had been proclaimed an adult.[2] The conference was followed by an exodus of these lords from court. In the past such a move had signaled both protest against the regency's policies and a bid by the *grands* to extract concessions. This time, however, the prospect of Louis's changed status made him a factor in the rebels' strategy. In withdrawing, some of them made a point of showing the young king that their dissatisfaction was with Marie and not with him.

The duc de Nevers was the first to depart, much to the queen's displeasure. He left the pointed message that he would never be anything but a good servitor of the king. He did not say, as Arnauld noted at the time, that he would be the same for Marie.[3]

A few days later Nevers was followed by the prince de Condé. Next to Louis's brothers, Condé was his closest living male relative on his father's side, which caused some tension between the two. A few years before, at

145

the start of the regency, the prince had outraged the child king by failing to show him the prescribed signs of respect: he had seated himself in Louis's presence and failed to remove his hat.[4] It may be that the offender was told of Louis's anger; there is no report that he ever repeated such conduct. Before taking leave following Nevers's departure, the prince had a private conversation with Louis, telling him "quite a few things," according to Malherbe. Since only the two were present, however, we can know nothing of what was said "except what the king tells about it"—and Louis told nothing.[5] Héroard does not report this conversation, unless his notation that Louis was "conversed with [*entretenu*], quietly, gaily," for half an hour at bedtime is an allusion to the event. That Héroard makes a point of Louis's efforts to please the queen during the same day—a rare endeavor on the child's part—may indicate that he was aware that she had been discussed by the two cousins.[6]

If Condé had whispered words to Louis that were critical of Marie, they were not, apparently, disturbing to the child. During the next few days the doctor frequently notes his patient's gaiety—once even his complaint that a stitch in his side prevented him from running and laughing.[7] Louis seldom laughed out loud, and his good humor after the departure of so valuable a member of *les siens* argues that Condé had given Louis strong reassurance of his loyalty.

Further defections followed in short order. With the departures of the ducs de Mayenne, Bouillon, and Longueville, the court was virtually emptied of all *grands* except the Guises, their allies, and the Concinis. One prince alone remained—Louis's half brother, César de Vendôme, who was lodged with his wife in the Louvre. Because the queen suspected him of planning to join forces with the departed lords, she refused his request to be allowed to withdraw to his government seat in Bretagne and had him put under house arrest, with his windows barred.[8]

Shortly after this it was learned that the duc de Nevers had seized the royal citadel at Mézières from the king's forces. The queen, outraged, declared herself ready to set out with her son to retake the fortress. Louis greeted this prospect with enthusiasm and after supper went to his closet to choose equipment for the expedition. Malherbe gives details: "The king shows a strong desire to go to war, and day before yesterday had himself armed with all his pieces, with such satisfaction at seeing himself in this outfit that he didn't want to take off his helmet when he was put to bed and argued for a long time that he would sleep better with the helmet than with his nightcap."[9] Preparation for a military campaign was a protection against night fears. But the next morning he told the doctor that he had not slept well—that he "had had war in his head all night long."[10] This suggests that some anxiety was mixed with Louis's martial zeal.

Events of the following day increased Louis's malaise. At seven in the evening Vendôme, one of the most cherished, envied, and sometimes detested of *les siens* of Louis, escaped from the palace. A general alarm followed, with cries of "*Aux armes!*" from the guards.[11] Héroard omits from his diary any report of this event, but his meticulous reporting of Louis's comings and goings show that the king was with his mother when the distressing news was learned and withdrew to his quarters a half hour later. That night, too, his sleep was disturbed. At midnight he awakened, "had himself got up," and sat by the fire until he complained of the heat.[12]

Although Vendôme did not join the princes gathered at Mézières, he proceeded to fortify his own citadel and spied on royal communications, intercepting, at Angers, official instructions sent from the court to the lieutenant general of Bretagne. A letter from Vendôme justifying his insubordination was received at court in the first week in March. During the night of March 5 Louis had a dream that caused him to speak in his sleep. His words, reported to Héroard by an attendant, in the king's presence, were: "Throw this hat over the wall! Hey! Throw it, throw it over the river that flows to Bayonne! Why didn't they put him in the Bastille?"

Several elements in this dream suggest what the dreamer's deeper feelings may have been. According to the diarist, Louis himself contributed a partial explanation: "The king hears him and says: 'It's that I was asking why they hadn't put my brother Vendôme in the Bastille. He opened my dispatches that I was sending to Monsieur de Montbazon. He opened them!'—showing displeasure [*mécontentement*]."[13] At the time Vendôme was first detained by the queen there had been talk in her circle of consigning him to the Bastille for safekeeping if Their Majesties should leave the city.[14] When on the night of the duke's escape a false rumor of his recapture circulated, Marie vowed that this time it would indeed be the Bastille for the rebellious *grand*.[15] It is little wonder that Louis was resentful of Marie and the guards for allowing this important possession of his to slip away (down the river) rather than shutting him up securely in the Bastille.

Further interpretation of the dream is more speculative. The lieutenant general of Bretagne, whose communication with the king César had interrupted, was Hercule de Rohan, the Protestant duc de Montbazon, an old comrade of Henri's who had played an avuncular role with both César and Louis when they were young. César had then stood between Louis and his father; now he was encroaching on Louis's relationship with this father surrogate by opening private dispatches from his brother to the older man. But the dream anger that is directed at César also seems, less obviously, to be directed at Henri. For the river Loire, where César intercepted the communications, goes toward Nantes, near César's domain. It does not pass near Bayonne, in the kingdom of Navarre, of which Henri was the native ruler.[16] Perhaps throwing the hat across that river in the dream (rather than jumping across it himself, as he had once refused to jump the ditch for

Henri, despite the threat of whipping) has the same meaning of angry retaliation at his father that throwing his own hat at the picture of Henri and
Marie did when he was three years old. That outburst had followed the hat
scene, during which Henri had manhandled and outraged him.

Marie did not keep her promise to combat Nevers's insubordination directly, taking Louis with her. Although a faction among her councillors
was ready to give battle, believing that opposition would melt away before
a firm royal stand, she was more cautious. As Père Griffet writes, "When
the government is weak, the party of gentleness and moderation is always
preferred."[17] Accordingly, Pierre Jeannin and the venerable president de
Thou were sent to negotiate with Condé. As a result of the envoy's efforts,
a peace was negotiated with Condé at Sainte-Menehould. It conceded large
indemnities to the dissident princes, agreed to defer the Spanish marriages
until after the king's majority, and acceded to Condé's demand for conven-
ing the Estates General in an assembly in which he hoped to play a prominent role.

Meanwhile, Louis's everyday life continued, as before, to be occupied
with amusements. He invented pursuits of water fowl "that had never before been attempted," Héroard records, with an approving "*Nota*." He also
played tennis and hunted deer, "always right on the tail of the hounds."[18]
On receiving news of the peace agreement, the doctor writes, Louis "does
not allow any sign of joy or sadness to appear on his face," dissimulating his
awareness of the event until all the company is retired and then remarking
to Héroard and another attendant, "Peace is made; I think it must be the
forty hours of prayer [a special session declared by the bishop of Paris to
ward off public calamity] that are responsible."[19]

STIRRINGS OF MANLINESS

During the weeks of negotiation with Condé, Louis had been preparing
himself for brave and warlike actions with mounting enthusiasm. When the
commander of his personal guard informed him that the queen had ordered
that the guards be armed when accompanying him about the city, Louis
was concerned lest the people of Paris think he feared an attack from the
princes. "I'm not at all afraid—I don't fear them at all!" he said—a "handsome response," according to Héroard. On April 22 he diligently reviewed
his guards regiment, taking "a good two hours, going first to one, then to
another, watching them do their exercises." He himself performed his martial routines "very well" before the queen. Afterward, while seated on his
toilet seat, he amused himself by setting up time bombs—"clocks, which
had springs to set fire to gunpowder."[20]

The peace treaty with Condé turned out to have a secret article: the prince
had been promised by the queen—privately, through the Ancres—that he

could hold the royal citadel of Amboise as security for execution of the three chief terms. Condé brought the matter into the open by arguing before the council that the fortress should be conceded to him.[21] Louis was disturbed by the notion that so valuable a possession was being alienated from the Crown. On May 2, Héroard reports, the king "dreamed that they were drawing blood from him," adding, "It was during this time that Monsieur le Prince de Condé was arguing to have Amboise."[22]

The next day, when the Council discussed the matter in the queen's chambers, Louis entered the room alone, according to the Venetian ambassador, and, "turning to his mother," told her not to give Amboise to the prince:

> "If he wants to come to an agreement, let him agree [without Amboise]."
>
> "Sire, who gives you this advice?" asked the queen. "Such a one desires neither your welfare nor that of the realm."
>
> "Mother," the king replied, "under no circumstances give that place to him; let the prince do what he will!"

Zeller notes the significance of this intervention:

> Such was the first official, considered demonstration of a political will from Louis XIII; the young king wanted obedience without conditions; he was ready to go and impose it.

The ambassador believed that Louis had been influenced by Souvré. It is known, however, that others whom the young king liked or admired, such as the Guises and Epernon, also opposed the concession to the prince. The fact that the Ancres counselled appeasement was probably at least as significant; they had been the main negotiators and advocates of this concession.[23] Héroard looked with approval on all indications that Louis would be vigorous in defense of his rights, and he was no champion of Condé. For the doctor, the significant fact seems to have been that the prince continued to pose a potential challenge to the young king's authority. |

Louis's more confident masculine aspirations at this time are suggested by a dream on the fourth anniversary of his father's death — an occasion always weighted with significance:

> He was in the little gallery, where he encountered the shaggy monk [a phantom bogeyman who was supposed to poke around in the bodies of women with his ironclad fingers] who was holding a little black devil that looked like a monkey by a leash attached to a collar around its neck. He asked the shaggy monk to lend him this little devil to scare Madame de Guise with. . . . The monk commanded him not to come nearer, telling him, "Go to the Devil." He went away . . . to find the

queen . . . and spoke in her ear; she commanded him to go scare Madame de Guise.[24]

In this dream the little black devil-monkey seems to be Louis himself. At the same time it is an organ of the monk (who is probably Louis's father), attached to his body by a leash and able to damage women as are the iron-clad fingers of the bogeyman. The monk refuses to lend his powers to the little boy, but Louis defies him. First he speaks into his mother's ear. (In fables told to Louis in childhood, this was a means of insemination.) His mother validates his aspiration to replace his father by commanding him to go terrify Madame de Guise, presumably with this devil-organ, as he used to imagine himself frightening little girls with his own organ. The young duchesse de Guise, a favorite of Louis, had already been delivered of three babies since her marriage three years earlier. Thus this dream, in which Louis takes a masculine role, contrasts with previous dreams in which he was caught in a hole or kneeling, inviting intrusions into his own body.

For Louis the next few weeks were carefree and active. He did his exercises in arms "marvelously ardently and expertly," played tennis, and hunted passionately. Deer-hunting for the first time in the forest, he rode without changing horses for more than two hours and was in at the kill. Even the accidental death, from a cannon explosion, of a favorite hunting companion, the chevalier de Guise, failed to disturb his sleep or dampen his spirits for long.[25]

ASSERTING AUTHORITY

In these weeks following the signing of the peace treaty some of the *grands* returned to court, among them the duc de Longueville, who had been engaged, in Picardy, in challenging Ancre's attempts to exercise his new powers over the duke's domains. Louis had a private conversation with Longueville—a fact reported by Malherbe but not by Héroard.[26]

But public tranquillity continued to be disturbed by dissatisfied lords. At Blavet, in Bretagne, Vendôme entrenched himself behind strengthened fortifications. Condé now wrote complaining to the queen of efforts by the bishop of Poitiers to prevent him from entering that city with his forces. To palliate these and other discontents, Marie was forced to go several times to the national treasury in the Bastille, on each occasion extracting several hundred thousand livres from the gold stores that had been amassed under the thrifty management of Sully and her late husband. The policy of appeasement was costly.

It was decided to take a stand against insurrection in the realm by making a royal expedition in force to the Breton coast. The Ancres reportedly urged that Marie and Louis not venture outside Paris, but Marie, with the support of most of her cabinet, decided on the bolder course and prepared to lead the excursion westward in order to rally support for the monarchy. The trip was also planned to influence the Estates General Assembly, from which Condé hoped to draw new strength. The royal party planned, instead, to insure that delegate selections, then in progress in the western provinces, would produce a gathering favorable to crown policy.

Louis had always been excited by the prospect of travel. Changes in domicile for political, seasonal, or health reasons had often been ordered for him by his father, and he had always joined eagerly in preparations for the transfer. Since the happy trip to Rheims for his *sacre*, this enthusiasm had continued, as when he was impatient to set off for Fontainebleau at the end of 1611. Now, two years later, he was "all in action" to set off in the opposite direction, going to Souvré's apartments "in order to hurry him up."[27]

On Saturday, July 5, Louis and the queen, with a large retinue, set out on their long itinerary. After two stopovers en route, they made their first ceremonial entry in Orléans, on July 8. The king and his party were received by six companies of armed noblemen, each a hundred strong, all the clergymen of the city, including the archbishop, and all the officers of justice, followed by the royal tax collectors and other officials of the Crown, groups of local merchants, the mayor, and the town councilmen—all in full regalia. A forty-gun salute was fired to honor the royal visitors.[28]

In succeeding days they proceeded by slow stages along the Loire toward Nantes, stopping at frequent intervals for similar, though lesser, receptions and for lodging, dining, and recreation at royal châteaux, courtiers' estates, country inns, and farmhouses. When the court moved, all its amusements moved with it as well as its everyday equipment, from pots and pans to animals and furniture. Louis enjoyed supervising details of the procession, trying out the role of *bon compagnon* by drinking, eating, and carousing (modestly) with his older courtiers, playing tennis, and hunting at every opportunity.

On August 8, the royal party boarded a boat at Saumur and proceeded down the river. The young king had never before traveled on water, and his anticipation of this adventure was not altogether pleasurable.[29] Héroard reports the boy's excitement the night before and then notes that his sleep was disturbed by anxiety (*inquiétude*).[30] Louis's apprehension at the prospect of this kind of travel seems to have been dissimulated by intensified activity while on board: "Along the way he never once sat down, nor was he ever quiet. He has his pistols loaded, fires them, and hands them over to be fired in salvos against others of his suite who were in other boats. He has made and makes himself little fuses which he ignites in the boat and in the water."[31] The frenzy that water transport inspired in Louis contrasts with his calm mastery of movements on land. His taste and training inclined him toward army life rather than navigation.

As a political tactic, however, the boat trip was a success. Héroard reports Louis's popular triumph: "The people were massed in throng after throng on the shores of the river and [hailed the king] with tears and great acclamations of joy and of '*Vive le roi!*' A little below Roziers, fifty or sixty women waded into the water up to their knees to get closer to the boat and see him."[32] Héroard makes no comment on Louis's reaction to this adulation. He had been exposed to examples of it since birth. These new experiences, however, more distant from home, may have confirmed in him the expectation of profuse signs of obeisance.

The return to allegiance of a subject who was important to Louis—his half brother César—was surely especially welcome. César was one of the princes who had defied the queen in the previous spring. His fortification of the Bretagne stronghold he held as governor gave notice of his readiness to join the rebellion. As the royal party progressed triumphantly westward, however, opposition from the *grands* seemed to melt away, and as they drew nearer to Vendôme's fortress he, too, made moves toward capitulation. He sent a courier to Louis, advancing from Poitiers, to give oral assurances of his "attachment and fidelity" and of his "obedience to His Majesty's service." "Ho!" Louis exclaimed in a retort that Héroard characterized as "firm, ingenious, and serious," "Some obedience! He's not yet disarmed!" He refused to receive the letter his half brother had sent him.[33]

When Louis reached Nantes César sought an audience, and the king, no doubt on instructions from his counselors, received him personally but "coldly, and as he would have done a simple gentleman." Vendôme signaled his capitulation, pledging his loyalty and readiness to die for his monarch. Héroard knew the extent of Louis's fury at this prince, in rank one of his first subjects and the "captain" of his childhood, for whom he had felt envy, admiration, love, jealousy, and spite. "The king," records the diarist, "voice trembling and face pale"—a sign of anger in Louis—"replied merely, 'Serve me better in the future than you have done in the past and know that the greatest honor you have in the world is that of being my brother.'" These words were probably assigned to Louis by his elders, but they may have been strong enough to suit him.[34]

Sometimes, however, Louis balked at the propitiatory tone of speeches that were drafted for him. Thus, with the enthusiastic support of Héroard, who wrote in the margin "*mirum judicium,*" he bridled at addressing a group of magistrates from Nantes, complaining to a valet that he did not want to speak the complimentary words that Souvré handed over to him: "I doubt that they have all served me well."[35]

After more than a fortnight in Nantes, during which Louis received a parade of notables, accepted tribute from the Breton Estates, and gave an audience to the Spanish ambassador, the royal party turned back toward the capital on August 30. A ceremonial stop had been arranged at Le Mans on a petition of a deputation of city councilors of that city, which had vied successfully for the honor of receiving the royal train, at tremendous cost to the townsfolk. We are assured by a local patriot, however, that "the presence of the king rekindles the courage of his subjects and dissipates all the winds of sedition and strife." An elaborate *tableau vivant* in a meadow, featuring a dryad "dressed in rustic fashion" who had been rehearsed in a specially composed verse of welcome for the occasion, was ready to greet the king. Unaware of these preparations, however, and in hot pursuit of gamebirds, the royal company entered by another route and did not meet the welcoming party until they were within the city. There Louis was regaled with pageants, harangued by the bishop, and obliged to kneel throughout the mass held in his honor. The verses, addressed to the king and published for him and the "*beaux esprits*" of the court who had missed the "dryad's" delivery, recounted the alarm the people of Le Mans felt when Louis's father had "joined the spirits of the first three kings named Henri" and their joy at now being reassured by the "sunshine cast by your eyes."

As usual, there were some diversions from the tedious chores to which Louis was subjected. After vespers the next day he visited a nearby priory, where he made the obligatory reverence to the ubiquitous portrait of his father displayed in the entry and then proceeded to the garden. There he brought down a bird pointed out to him in a tree with a single shot of a harquebus. The chronicler continues: "As this prince was born to action, [this] made him wish to see if the soldiers who were so well ordered at his entry were as skillful at . . . arms." Twenty of the best were picked to fire at a target from 120 paces. Offered two elaborately engraved firearms, "His Majesty refused to accept them if he could not earn them by his skill." Thereupon Louis took aim and fired, coming within a "finger's width" of the target. "The guardian angel who attends him," we are told, "always guides his hand so skillfully" that, in all the towns of the realm he has entered, he has won the prize "legitimately" from all those who presented themselves. Indeed, some version of this entertaining competition seems to have been staged in several towns where Louis stopped along the way.[36] The stage management necessary for such demonstrations must have been considerable, and we can be sure that they did not always come off without a flaw. Nor could the youthful king have been without peer among the best marksmen in his realm. Nevertheless, such theater seems to have served its purpose. The chronicler of Le Mans affirmed his awe at the precocity of his monarch.[37] An English observer—a Protestant—remarked on the good "order . . . observed through all his progresse in every towne."[38]

That night the heavily scheduled Louis dreamed of flying fishes, threw off his sheets, and cried, "How many do you want? Which ones do you want?" His valet de chambre asked for trout, Héroard reports, and the king was put back to bed without having awakened.[39]

The returning caravan passed through Chartres and, not far from there, Héroard writes, Louis "paid us an honor neither hoped for nor expected— and of his own accord" by coming to Vaugrigneuse, Héroard's charming chateau near Limours, built with income and gifts from Louis himself. It was a high point of the doctor's life, and he provided his master with "whatever happened to be ready" for breakfast: "black grapes, chicken fricassee . . . three charcoal-grilled mutton chops . . . pâté of hare . . . homemade bread." To Héroard's delight, Louis ate unusually heartily, especially of the bread: "He found it so good that he took three [loaves] of it away with him" and later, at dinner, "had himself served the bread from Vaugrigneuse."[40]

The next day, Louis and his party reached Bourg-La-Reine. There he abandoned his carriage for a horse and rode into Paris that afternoon, surrounded "on both sides" for almost all of the two-hour trip by "an incredible multitude of people." Though it was late, it was necessary to proceed to Notre Dame for prayers of thanks. He entered the Louvre at 8:00 P.M. It was the beginning of autumn; he had been away for more than two months.[41]

The conclusion of Louis's journey was soon followed by the end of his thirteenth year. His attainment of his majority was to be marked by a ceremony in the palace of the court of Parlement. Anticipation of the event, as usual, made Louis nervous. At bedtime the night before "he makes a vow to Notre-Dame-des-Vertus if he may, next day at the palace, pronounce without a mistake all his words for his majority." According to the doctor, Louis's prayer was granted; the next day he spoke the following words "loudly, firmly, and without stuttering": "Gentlemen, having arrived at the age of majority . . . I intend to govern my realm by good counsel, with piety and justice. I expect from all my subjects the obedience and respect that are due the sovereign power and royal authority which God has placed in my hands."[42] He concluded the declaration that had been prepared for him by thanking his mother for the trouble she had taken as regent and asking her to continue "to govern and command as you have done heretofore." Marie was now to be head of his council and therefore in effect still ruler of his state. Louis, however, had been formally declared in control of the realm. In the future more and more of its forces would focus on him as the fulcrum of decision-making power.

CHAPTER TWELVE

Rehearsals for Kingship

It is not the king's nature to display himself; if age and love do not change
his temperament he will be interested only in solid matters. It is my opin-
ion that he will be a very great and good king.[1]

In the two-and-a-half years that followed the proclamation of Louis's majority his personal amusements changed little. Only rarely did he permit those
beyond his intimate circle to glimpse his private thoughts about the parts he
was often called upon to play in his public role as head of state. These official
performances, however, sometimes foreshadowed the style and policies of
the adult king.

ROYALTY ON THE ATTACK

Three weeks after Louis was declared of age, he presided over the opening
plenary session of the Estates General Assembly of France, the first such
gathering for more than a quarter century. The last one had been held under
conditions of insurrection and had ended with the royally commanded murder of leaders of the "opposition." That coup, in turn, was followed by the
assassination of the last of the Valois kings, the installation of a new dynasty,
and years of civil war. For many who observed the convocation in 1614, the
events of 1588 were still a living memory.

One of these observers was Charles, duc de Guise, successor to his murdered father. The fact that this nobleman was now an ally of the queen
mother and a supporter of the monarchy demonstrated the extent of the political realignments that had taken place since the earlier assembly. Another
observer was Jean Héroard, who had carefully followed the dramatic events
of 1588. Later he would reveal his interpretation of some of them in a memoir colored by his attachment to Louis XIII.[2] Another who took a prominent
part in the meetings of 1614–1615 was Armand Jean Du Plessis de Richelieu,

bishop of Luçon. Although this prelate had been only three years old at the time of the 1588 sessions, they must have figured importantly in his own family's legends. Richelieu's father, François, as grand provost of France, had been Henri III's personal "enforcer"; having cleared away the corporeal remains of the murdered duc de Guise, François was dispatched to the 1588 Estates meeting to quell any disorders that might follow the assassinations. In the Estates meeting of 1614 the young Richelieu was a clerical representative of his western province, an ambitious courtier, and, like his father, an ardent Gallican partisan of monarchical supremacy.

Whatever misgivings were entertained by some oldtimers, Louis and his mother had few reasons to fear insubordination from the group that convened in October 1614. The First Estate, the clerical order, sought advantages for the Roman church in France, but it was led by prelates who were closely linked to the queen mother. Representatives of the Third Estate, comprised mostly of magistrates, were overwhelmingly Gallican in sympathies. Those representing the nobility, the Second Estate, did not include the factious *grands* who had been temporarily pacified by the treaty negotiated at Sainte-Menehould earlier in the year, but rather were the loyal *noblesse moyenne*—including a substantial Huguenot contingent—that was suffering from the rising prices of government offices, which had put such posts out of reach for many of them. At the same time, they resented their exclusion from a share in the government pensions, payments, and posts so liberally dispensed by the Crown to the great lords.

A "fourth chamber" of the assembly, linked especially to the Third Estate by professional affinity but also to the other two, and to the factious *grands*, by overlapping interests and kinship ties, was the group of magistrates and judges that comprised the Parlement de Paris. Under the great Henri this concentration of administrative, financial, and judicial power, which had formerly supported the Catholic League, had swung over to a fiercely Gallican, pro-monarchical position.

The royal court looked to the Estates for support. For the queen, as chief of the young king's council, this meant endorsement of the yet-to-be-realized Spanish marriages and of the various policies designed to maintain her government in power by controlling centrifugal forces within the realm and menacing incursions from abroad through propitiation, evasion, and temporizing. The queen could count on a few of those "good old councilors" of Henri (as L'Estoile called them), notably Villeroy, the secretary of state, Sillery, the chancellor, his son, Pierre de Puisieux, the *garde des sceaux*, and President Jeannin, the superintendent of finances. Leaders of the clerical party—Gondi, Du Perron, Bérulle, Coton, Michel de Marillac, the Guises, Epernon, and the nuncio—shared their close access to the queen's ear, as did occasional visiting Spanish grandees and Florentine emissaries. More influential still in managing the queen were the Ancres. Their increasing control of state machinery was facilitated by a coterie of able parvenus—Barbin, Mangot, and Dolé—soon to be joined by the young bishop of Luçon, Richelieu. As a group, these new leaders possessed practical administrative experience and legal and financial skills.

Excluded from the meeting of the Estates was a bevy of hostile, suspicious, or unsympathetic princes and lords—Vendôme, Mayenne, Longueville, Bouillon, Rohan. In most of them a weak sense of patriotism was subordinated to a strong sentiment for their own house's glory and possessions. Less out of common interest than by default, Condé, first prince of Bourbon blood, assumed leadership of the dissidents.

Condé's long-term policy objectives, if he had any, are uncertain, but two immediate aims were clear enough: he sought material advantages for himself and a preeminent position in state councils. The second aim called for displacement of the queen mother, or at least of her party of friends and advisors. The strategy he followed, with fluctuating degrees of industry, was to mobilize various groups that might have an interest in this displacement —magistrates, Huguenots, disaffected lords, even foreign powers. Once he had looked to Spain and the Holy See for help in advancing his ambitions; now he encouraged the king of England, the house of Savoy, and Gallicans everywhere to join in his plans. Since he could not participate in the deliberations of the Estates, he tried to muster support from Parliament. He also addressed Louis himself.

The opening sessions of the Estates General Assembly were reassuring to the queen's party. Efforts made during the preceding summer had been effective: no policy for which Marie had been responsible would be challenged. The three lists of complaints that comprised the three orders' agendas called chiefly for measures that would increase the influence each had in the state, either by improving its legal status or by transferring fiscal advantages to it from another group. In this diversity of aims there was protection for the Crown: the three orders would not combine in a common front against the royal party. The Third Estate might go along with the demand of the clergy and the nobility for an end to venality in office, but its support could be no more sincere than the Second Estate's reciprocal agreement to endorse a call for an end to pensions to unqualified nobles. The clerical leaders' efforts to win support for enactment of the Council of Trent might, through a log-rolling process, gain lip service from the other two orders, but the queen's government knew well that the Third Estate, with its Gallican bent, would not repine if the Tridentine reforms, which reduced royal power over the French Catholic church, were not accepted by the king, any more than would the considerable Huguenot minority among the *noblesse* of the second chamber. Thus, as the conference began, prospects seemed good that the court would be able to conciliate an assembly stacked in its favor and neutralize its critics by a policy of divide and conquer.

As the sessions continued into 1615, however, an issue was introduced by the Third Estate that had the power to split the royal council over which Marie presided and to rally public opinion against the clerical party, from which she took considerable counsel. Early in the year, in the famous "First Article," the Third Estate demanded a royal declaration embodying the basic Gallican premise that the French king's temporal sovereignty was complete, acknowledging no superior whatever. It followed, therefore, that no earthly power could absolve subjects from the allegiance they owed their monarch. The magistrates of the Third Estate affirmed, further, that regicide could never be justified, and they condemned the Ultramontanist doctrine advanced by Cardinal Bellarmin, and supported by Du Perron, Bérulle, and the Jesuit faction so close to Marie, that seemed to legitimize the murder of kings who had been excommunicated by the pope.

Introduction of this article immediately excited the ire of the First Estate, whose leaders took the position that the relationship of the French king to the authority of the pope was strictly an ecclesiastical matter. If the Crown endorsed the clergy's position, debate on the article had the potential for arousing antagonism toward Marie and her closest allies, for to seem in any way to support a doctrine that justified regicide was to inspire or renew the suspicion that the Italian contingent at court had been accomplices in Henri's murder.

In the controversy that followed, all parties appealed to the king and his council to resolve the matter. Louis, Marie, and members of the government gave audiences to delegates from the Estates and interested parties from outside that assembly.

Initially, Their Majesties followed the clerical line to the extent of forbidding the Third Estate and Parlement to propose resolutions that concerned royal authority. But this was not enough for the Ultramontanists among the clergy, who insisted that not only the Third Estate and Parlement but the king himself had no right to rule on the temporal powers of the church. Yet, when Condé had appeared to plead for the First Article, Louis reserved to himself all rights to pronounce on the issue. Certainly he took this position on instructions from his council—the young boy was not permitted to make decisions on his own. Yet we may assume that Louis was not averse to declaring the absolute autonomy of French sovereigns, particularly in the context of defending their persons against assassination. There is contemporary evidence that the young king also thought that the prerogative for ruling on such matters should be his alone. After Marie had reproached Parlement's delegates for having published an *arrêt* supporting the Third Estate's position, she went on to prohibit their further discussion of the matter. At this point, a listener writes, Louis joined in with these words: "I forbid you to do it! I forbid you to do it!" If this unknown witness is reliable, this was the first time Louis expressed himself as an official adult on a question of policy. The report of this interjection is to be found among documents that at one time formed part of Richelieu's papers.[3] Perhaps its presence there indicates that the significance of Louis's words for revealing his temperament was not lost on the future prime minister, then an active representative of the Poitevin clergy at the Estates Assembly.

Clerical leaders were not content with the king's prohibition of discussion of the matter by others; they sought a ruling from him that the matter was outside his ken as well as that of all other bodies except the church itself. Emboldened by their awareness of Marie's sympathy with them, they asked the king to deny himself jurisdiction. In other ways also they widened their demands.

The day after Louis had claimed exclusive jurisdiction for the king, a delegation from the First Estate won an audience with Louis and his mother. Héroard's account of this meeting is fragmentary. Relying on hearsay, he seems often to have confused certain of the chief clerical complainants with one another.[4]

Condé was suspected of having participated in the Third Estate's drafting of the First Article for ulterior motives and of having encouraged the Parlement de Paris to publish it, actions that seemed to some clerics to signal a revolt of the magistrates against ecclesiastical primacy. The cynicism of Condé's tactics was not lost on some, for during Henri's last years his cousin had been his bitterest enemy and had not hesitated to seek support from Ultramontanist and Habsburg forces. Guez de Balzac, a writer who depended on the patronage of Epernon, one of the chief pro-Jesuit counselors of the queen, denounced the prince as a hypocrite: "Since when has his heart been so acutely touched by that execrable parricide? . . . You know very well how Monsieur le Prince received the news of that death when the comte de Fuente roused him . . . to congratulate him as though for the luckiest event that ever befell him."[5] Now, by contrast, the prince's strategy called for inflaming the Gallican sympathies of the magistrates and burgers of Paris and of currying favor with Huguenots and their foreign supporters, especially the British monarch. He also sought support for the Third Estate's article within the queen's own government, where some venerable councilors were believed to be inclined to the Gallican contingent. Villeroy and Jeannin, for example, seemed to be uneasy about Marie's alliance with the Jesuit faction against Parlement and also to have misgivings about the influence of the queen's favorites, the Ancres.[6]

The prime target of Condé's efforts, however, was Louis himself. Apparently hoping to increase his own influence, he made the boy king the object of his attentions. It was the first time that Louis had been treated publicly as an autonomous figure; all the queen's councilors, as well as leaders in the Estates and Parlement, had dealt with him as Marie's ward.

How much did Condé perceive of Louis's character? Did he surmise that the boy was becoming increasingly restive in his enforced dependence on his mother and her party? There were signs that could have informed him. On January 5, 1615, for example, Héroard noted a change in the king's behavior during the little ceremony of Twelfth Night. In previous years the doctor had reported Louis's unwillingness to assume the appropriate role when the pellet that identified the ruler fell to his lot. Now, however, he tells us that when the boy has successfully drawn for kings, he "offers the bean to God; then to himself."[7] In this new acceptance of kingship there is an intimation of Louis's growing impatience with his subordinate status.

Three days later Louis had an opportunity to reveal his aspirations. The prince was present at the meeting on January 8 in which Marie and the king were besieged by Du Perron, Sourdis, and Charles Miron, Bishop of Angers, who suggested that those responsible for the resolutions they deplored were in the pay of the king of England, thus virtually accusing Condé of treason. Sourdis went further, demanding that Condé abstain from giving his opinion on matters within the clergy's domain.

According to one account, Louis tried to end the dispute by ordering the complainants to finish their chamber business promptly.[8] Héroard, however, throws more light on Louis's sympathies. According to his detailed report, Louis rose from his chair and, going over to his cousin, took his part in no uncertain terms: "'Sir [he said], I pray you, let us speak no more of this,' and then, turning to the others, said, 'Since they are challenging the competence of Monsieur le Prince [to discuss this matter], they will end up by challenging me.'"[9] Thus, as Héroard tells it, Condé had some success in gaining Louis's favor on this occasion. The *premier médecin*, of course, shared the Gallican position exalting royal authority. And it was indeed the intention of the leaders of the clerical party to challenge the king's power to rule on this important issue. The doctor signals the importance of Louis's reproach to the cardinals by three marginal notes. After this entry he leaves two pages blank, as he will do two years later after another, more momentous assertion of royal authority by his patient.

Later that afternoon, according to Arnauld, Condé happened to meet Louis and his mother. He told them that what he had intended to say, had he been permitted to speak, was that he would run his sword through Sourdis—an intention, and a form of expression, that showed his affinity with the young king's temperament.[10]

The clergy used heavy artillery to combat Condé's tactics. All over Paris the prince's strategy of dividing Louis from his mother was decried from the pulpit. Citizens were warned that their prosperity depended on maintaining the union between Marie and her son. One could not be struck down without endangering the other, the clerics declared.[11] Nevertheless, in the month following the scene between himself and the cardinals, Condé took a further step to win Louis over: he voluntarily surrendered his authority over the château d'Amboise. This was a surprise move, since the previous summer's peace treaty entitled him to hold the fortress until the adjournment of the Estates.

We have seen how Louis had protested the loss of this royal stronghold. His delight at having it returned was apparently as intense as his previous complaints when his mother was agreeing to put it in Condé's hands. He received the papers in Council, "clapping his hands," according to Héroard, and exclaiming, "I am delighted!" For Marie, the unexpected move was a vindication of her earlier policy in surrendering to pressures from the *grands*. Presenting the letters of patent to her son "with an extreme joy," she declared that "of all the acts of her regency there had remained only this one . . . that gave her pain, but that she had been obliged to do it out of prudence."[12] Whether or not Louis accepted her self-justification, Condé probably could have done nothing more effective to renew the young king's good will toward him.

As the days passed, Marie collaborated with Du Perron, Sourdis, Marillac, and other members of the clerical party to exert pressure on the Third Estate to withdraw its article and on Parlement to resist Condé's inducements to support the Gallican resolution in public declarations. A few weeks later the prince precipitated another *brouillerie* in which, seemingly, he again appealed to the king for support against the queen mother. On his instructions, one of his attendants had beaten a courtier of Marie, one Marsillac, who had formerly been in Condé's service and who he believed had betrayed secrets concerning his household.[13] Condé's professed surprise, the next day, on learning that the queen took his act amiss suggests that he felt that some depredation on Bourbon honor had been punished. That evening he declared at a ball, "with execrable oaths," according to Arnauld, that he had not expected the queen to find fault with his action. In a similar vein he expressed righteous outrage at Marie's disapproval in an interview at which both she and Louis were present. He challenged: "How could anyone do anything to me for that?" Marie claimed he showed "great effrontery." Condé replied that "a prince of the blood had never been outraged in this manner. . . . He could see very well that they wished to send him away from the king, but . . . despite his enemies he would remain." Louis wished to speak, Arnauld continues, but the prince restrained him, saying, "'You are my master, but as to the queen I do not say the same.'" Turning to Marie, the prince declared pointedly, "'I am of this House, and hold nothing from you.'"[14]

Soon after Condé returned the papers that entitled him to hold Amboise, Louis had a signal and unaccustomed delight: he was allowed to appoint his beloved Luynes to the governorship of that fortress in the prince's stead. By this time, the king's intimacy with the three Luynes brothers was evident to all the court. A few months earlier, a newly arrived Italian ambassador had reported: "They have been, as it were, raised with him, and the more the king has grown up, the more they have been favored, one of them particularly. They are found assiduously at the king's *lever* and *coucher*, they are present at his meals, and are always with him in the country."[15]

At this time nothing was known in court of any political views or ambitions harbored by Louis's favorite and his brothers. Their activities seemed confined to ministering to their master's recreations. Their intimacy with Louis, however, did not appear innocuous to Gilles de Souvré, Louis's governor since childhood. Souvré complained to the queen that the continual proximity of the Luynes brothers interfered with the king's performance of his duties to entertain princes and other dignitaries. Souvré proposed that the brothers be excluded from Louis's intimate entourage,[16] and the queen gave her consent. Louis somehow learned that the exclusion order had been given at the instigation of his governor, and was so outraged that he went "so far as to ask the queen to remove Monsieur de Souvré, saying that he could no longer endure that man with him." Héroard tries to make light of this rage, calling it only "fleeting anger."[17] The queen, bending, as usual, first under one influence, then another, rescinded her order barring Charles and his brothers. Perhaps it was Ancre's counsel that caused her to change her mind; Luynes is said to have alleged that the maréchal had tried to buy for himself the loyalty of Louis's favorite. Defending him against Souvré might be expected to win his gratitude.[18] Perhaps the Florentine also hoped, by thus influencing Marie, to ingratiate himself with Louis.

The promotion of Charles de Luynes to custodianship of a royal stronghold, a position of splendor, trust, and revenue, was the first great reward for his intimacy with the king. According to Arnauld, Louis had asked Ancre to influence the queen to permit this appointment. Arnauld also tells us that Louis gave "extravagant thanks [*remerciements extrêmes*]" to the queen, not only expressing his own gratitude but bringing Luynes to do likewise. When she told the falconer, "It is the king you must thank," Louis insisted, "On the contrary, Madame, it is you whom one must thank."[19] This graceful expression may have been ironic: in Louis's view, it was Marie who had consented, against his wishes, to the alienation of Amboise in the first place. Moreover, Louis had shown at other times that he felt the anomaly in owing thanks to others for what was legally his. Mixed feelings may account for Héroard's disregard of both Louis's gift to Luynes and his thanks to his mother. Perhaps the doctor shared the belief that Ancre had intervened with Marie in the hope of winning the loyalty of Louis's favorite for himself. Souvré, who had sought to frustrate Luynes's ascension and thus incurred Louis's wrath, had recently been compensated for his own frustration by being appointed maréchal de France. He had shared with the maréchal d'Ancre (and with Bellegarde) the post of Louis's *premier gentil-*

homme de chambre (with seniority over the Italian); now, as maréchal, he was his equal in rank.

His valuable gift to Luynes made it clear that Louis's favor had become worth vying for, although his freedom to exercise it was scarcely greater than before. His few powers, moreover, were further limited by the weakness of a government that itself lacked resolution and authority and attempted to postpone decisions by temporizing and propitiating.

Condé continued his challenge to the queen. While the Estates continued to meet, his strategy remained circumspect. Barred from taking part in their deliberations, he appeared frequently instead before the magistrates of the Parlement de Paris, guiding the form of their remonstrances and influencing the Assembly. When, in March, he was forbidden by the crown to appear before Parlement, he continued to court its members' favor by entertaining them in his lodgings. With his huge suite of armed followers he was conspicuous in Paris, extending his quest for popularity "into the very streets."[20]

Parlement's challenge to the clerical party, like the complaints of the Third Estate, implied a criticism of the queen for lending her ear to foreign councillors at the expense of the interests of France and its king. In response, Marie, acting in Louis's name, dismissed the Estates Assembly, promising to redress the grievances they had exposed. Parlement, however, was a permanent, partly independent body, and it continued to issue complaints against the Crown and claims for higher consideration of the interests of the groups it represented.

Most of the demands on which the Estates had been able to agree were taken under advisement by Louis's government. One, however, was agreed to promptly: abolition of the *paulette*, the annual tax that gave magistrates and other officers of the Crown the right to pass their offices on to their heirs. This form of venality greatly reduced the number of offices that fell vacant, increased the price of those few that did, and gave the magisterial class a virtual monopoly in perpetuity of its important and lucrative functions.

In agreeing to abolish the *paulette*, Louis's government was nominally complying with the unanimous demand of all three orders of the Estates. In reality, however, the Third's chamber, which comprised so many who paid the tax to conserve their positions, had been induced to join the other two orders in condemning the levy only because the trade-off of a royal pronouncement ending high pensions for the nonserving nobility was supported by the clerical order at the concluding session.

Parlement, however, had not been promised a trade-off, and in any case the Crown took no steps to reduce the pensions and benefits it paid to the *grands* to buy their complaisance. With the threatened disappearance of the *paulette*, members of Parlement saw the capital on which their heirs had counted about to evaporate and their power threatened with serious diminution. They feared that Marie and her party were eager to distribute the offices that would be thus vacated to partisans of Ultramontanism and other court favorites. The members of the clerical party exacerbated these suspicions by proposing a scheme to exempt themselves from Parlement's jurisdiction. Toward the end of the Assembly sessions, the First Estate representatives sent an emissary, Michel de Marillac, to request a ruling from the court removing from Parlement's purview those personal affairs of high clerics that might give rise to lawsuits. This precedent-breaking demand for special privilege—Parlement had always had authority in private, temporal litigation of French clerics—further inflamed the magistrates.[21]

The first effect of Louis's declaration that the *paulette* would be abolished was to increase Condé's influence on an already mutinous Paris Parlement. For while abolition of the tax might be popular both among impecunious aristocrats who were excluded from influence by the high price of office and among the much larger groups at the lower rungs of the social ladder, most of the powerful magistrates in the highest court of the realm were beneficiaries of the existing arrangements.

However vulnerable Louis may have been to Condé's blandishments, he was jealous of royal authority and unattracted by schemes for sharing power, whether they were based on claims advanced by Parlement or by any other body. Thus, when he was called upon to express the government's intention to act autonomously and suppress all criticism, denying Parlement any right to meddle in political decision making, he was temperamentally quite ready to comply. Authoritarianism came naturally to this youth. Three years before, when Marie had pressed a recalcitrant Parlement to register a royal command, Louis, not yet eleven, had offered confidently, "Madame, send word to have them assemble, and send me there—they will never refuse me!"[22] Now, just recently, he had supported the queen with enthusiasm, forbidding Parlement to consider matters within an area in which the Crown claimed jurisdiction. Louis's words condemning Parlement's *arrêt*—"I forbid you! I forbid you!"—were recorded, as we have seen, in the papers of a rising young bishop who was to play a leading role in closing the Estates General meeting soon thereafter. When it came time for Armand de Richelieu to deliver a final harangue, on February 23, 1615, his words suggest that he may have recognized Louis's ambition for authority.

INTIMATIONS OF GREATNESS

As a seven-year-old, Louis had been asked, in his first formal lesson, whether it was right for kings to take counsel from clergymen. Young

Bishop Richelieu was acquainted with Vauquelin, the tutor who put this question, and may also have been given an account of the lesson by others. Selections from Héroard's diary circulated at court, and as a member of Louis's entourage Henri de Richelieu, Armand's eldest brother, may have had access to it. Louis's response to the tutor's query was noncommittal. Seven years later, Richelieu, opening the plenary session that concluded the Estates General Assembly, put the same question to the young man who was now the king and answered it himself with a resounding affirmative. Indeed, he not only offered the clergy as the best class of advisors to royalty but proposed himself in particular as an appropriate surrogate for the king.

Whether Richelieu's personal ambition was apparent to Louis in the speech addressed to him on February 23, 1615, is impossible to know. If the king had closely followed the daily business of the Estates, however, he would have seen that the importance of the role played by the bishop of Luçon was disproportionate to his modest rank and low seniority in the church.

Richelieu's eminence at these meetings was due in part to special capacities of mind that were recognized by his older colleagues. In addition he had already won recognition from the queen through personal connections at court and services rendered to the Crown that gave him political influence beyond what his years and formal status seemed to justify.

Members of the Richelieu family had long held posts at court. Armand's father, as grand provost of France, had had important responsibilities in the turbulent years at the end of Henri III's reign and the beginning of Henri IV's. The latter had compensated the provost's widow and children for François's services when Richelieu died in 1590 in pursuance of his duties. Armand's mother had been for a while lady-in-waiting to Queen Louise. Henri de Richelieu, her eldest son, became a member of an inner circle around Henri IV and, as we have seen, was one of those *bons compagnons* who gathered around the dauphin to guard and amuse him.[23] Père Coton, Souvré, Cardinal Du Perron, and many others at court were old acquaintances of the Richelieu family. Henri IV had nominated Armand for his high church post even before Richelieu had reached the age of twenty-one, and the young bishop was later welcomed at court. In 1612 he preached a Sunday sermon before Marie and Louis. From then on he was in increasingly frequent contact with the queen, not only through his family connections, but also through the Ancres and various high government officers for whom he had been able to perform appreciated services.

Now, in the closing session of the Estates, Richelieu had for the first time the opportunity to discourse before Louis, as well as before the queen, the court, and the assembled orders, on matters of political importance. Nothing is known of Louis's reaction to this speech. It certainly gained his attention, however, because it was the first of the three presented that day and, though it was also the longest, its delivery was dramatic, its style popular, and its contents intended to be particularly interesting to the king himself.

Using simple language and secular illustrations, Richelieu gave less attention to the demands of the clerical order, which he was supposed to be representing, than to the opportunities Louis could exploit to increase the authority and glory of his reign. Indeed, some of his words seem specifically designed to stimulate Louis's ambition for grandeur and power; for example, "Glory [is] a spur that piques generous minds." While the speech praised Marie's performance as regent and begged her to continue as chief of her son's council, it flattered her less on her own account than as Louis's representative and guardian. Her merits are lauded because they add "a thousand crowns of glory to the one that crowns your leader"; Louis will reward her by adding to "the glorious title you have of being his mother." After such perfunctory plaudits for Marie, Richelieu addressed most of his remarks to Louis.

The bishop's intention to whet the youth's appetite for power seems unmistakable. He assures the young king that a glorious reign is not only within his grasp but even (with, it is implied, Richelieu's guidance) "as easy as it is just." And to Louis, who already had a fairly grandiose notion of his own capacity to quell opposition with a word, the bishop's explanation of why reform of his realm would be a simple matter may not have seemed farfetched. Richelieu's claim is: "It is easy Sire, because in most good things it is with kings as it is with God, for whom to wish it is to do it."[24] To the thirteen-year-old this assertion of kingly omnipotence may have seemed the simple truth. Yet, if Richelieu's words captured the boy's imagination, he might have reflected that though he could eventually expect to have such glory, he had not yet been permitted to enjoy it often.

One of the main arguments advanced by the bishop of Luçon in favor of abolishing the *paulette* was that once hereditary title to office was ended, Louis would have patronage at his disposal with which to augment and consolidate his authority. Louis had known little of that pleasure either; until now he had been given few chances to reward those whose services he valued. It was not until several weeks later that Louis had his first real taste of such power, when, as has been noted, he gave, with Marie's acquiescence, a great post to his friend and companion Charles de Luynes.

After the Estates adjourned, Parlement, encouraged by Condé, grew increasingly fractious, demanding to be heard in the determination of financial policy. Alone, Louis might have preferred to be obdurate. Nevertheless, the Crown was soon forced to renege: it decided to "postpone" the repeal of the *paulette* until 1618. The suspicion that this retreat was motivated by weakness was well founded. Not only was the government vulnerable to Condé's menace; it also could ill afford to abolish venality and hence forego the important revenues paid to conserve hereditary rights to magistracies and other posts. To give these up also entailed another risk of bankruptcy: government tax collectors and money lenders whose offices were no longer guaranteed by the *annuel* would make formidable difficulties about extending credit. In Roland Mousnier's words, "Money talked."[25]

By rescinding its first order, the government conciliated Parlement and the high officer class and thus made sure that Condé and other dissident *grands* could no longer count on majority support in the high courts of the realm. In response, the princes commenced once again to withdraw from court. Condé began to organize armed opposition to Marie and her counselors. From Coucy he issued an open letter addressed to Louis that seemed aimed not only at encouraging the king's misgivings about his mother's policies and her advisors but also at rallying support among the public at large. Without attacking Marie's integrity, it referred to her "good nature," which, together with a "too great credulity," allowed her to be easily, though innocently, "carried away" by "evil souls" (clearly the Ancres), whose counsels were detested by all "good Frenchmen." These foreigners, the prince averred, cared little for the good of that *patrie* to which he professed himself entirely bound by "natural attachment" or for their duty, felt so strongly by himself, to obey the king.[26]

Much of what Condé said about Marie probably seemed evident to Louis. We have already seen, as well, the reasons the young king had for resenting the Ancres, especially Concino. Nor would it be surprising if his misgivings were stimulated by Condé's complaint, in the same letter, that "they" had "drawn from the Bastille money that the late king had put there to serve as a terror to foreigners." Louis frequently attended council meetings and may have been present at one in January at which Jeannin announced to Marie that there was a deficit of one million écus in gold. Isaac Arnauld had then told her that "her entire authority depended" on making good the shortfall.[27] Yet three weeks before Condé's letter Louis again had to escort Marie to the fortress, where she drew heavily on the treasury—this time in order to finance the coming marriages in the style she thought appropriate. The Chamber of Accounts, the supreme financial court of the realm, had refused to authorize these withdrawals, and the royal council had been obliged to act without its endorsement.

Henri's frugality was legendary, and in this his son resembled him. The dissipation of his patrimony very likely displeased Louis. He may, as Condé suggested he should, have held the policies of Marie and the Concinis responsible for this apparent disregard of his interests.

THE SPANISH MARRIAGES

Meanwhile the queen increasingly centered her thoughts on the benefits to her own position and to "our house," as she called it, that would be secured

by the Spanish marriages. In sharp contrast with the policies of the two preceding monarchs, she looked upon the king of Spain as her ally against domestic dissidence. A dispatch of the Venetian ambassador reports that she
actually conveyed through the Spanish representative in France the hope
that the "Most Catholic King would view with displeasure all these movements [of rebellious princes] and that she could expect aid and support from
him if things went further."[28] There were, of course, cogent political reasons for a weak government to seek to forestall internal insurrection by
conciliating a powerful foreign neighbor. But passionate inclination rather
than rational calculation conditioned Marie's penchant for Spain.

Marie's susceptibility where Spanish royalty was concerned became more
evident as she exhibited the lavish diamond bracelet that was to be the
model for a matching necklace twenty-five times its size, to be sent to Spain
as a gift for her future daughter-in-law, the infanta Ana. The queen promised her own daughter Elisabeth: "This will show that you come from a
good family." Malherbe, who was present, found the scale of the projected
gift so extravagant as to be "incredible."[29] Louis himself expressed misgivings. In Bordeaux, later in the year, he went to view Elisabeth's trousseau,
in the company of Père Coton. The king asked the priest, reports the *Mercure*, if his bride would bring as much from Spain. His confessor replied
"that it was probable, but in any case that it was better for France to surpass
Spain in such matters as well."[30] What Louis thought of one-upmanship
played with the wealth of his realm is not known.

Marie's ardor for his marriage must have been as obvious to the young
king as it was to everyone else: "She speaks of it continually," reported the
Venetian ambassador; "She gives the impression that she has no other purpose in life than to have the princess here at the tenderest possible age."[31]

During the summer of 1615 the planned trip of the court to Bordeaux became the subject of dispute. Although endorsement of the marriages by all
three Estates had quieted much opposition to the alliance, some parliamentary notables argued that it was not necessary for Louis to go almost to the
frontier to meet his bride. Henri IV, indeed, had gone only to Lyons to
meet the arriving Medici princess in 1600, much nearer than Bordeaux was
to Paris. With the new rebellion of the princes, anxiety ran high in Paris at
the prospect of the departure of the royal family for so distant a place, leaving the city undefended. Reports from the provinces expressed dismay and
pessimism at the inability of the government to quell Condé's insubordination.[32] Difficulties such as these caused postponement of the trip from one
week to another.

GROOMING FOR GALLANTRY

While the court waited, the young king found new pleasures. On July 6 he
commenced lessons in equitation with the renowned Antoine de Pluvinel,

who had opened an academy near the Tuileries for instruction in this skill, formerly taught only to young noblemen in Italy.[33] Louis immediately became proficient: every person present admired his first performance, Héroard tells us, adding: "I say this truthfully and without flattery."[34] The new master seems to have been highly gratified; to him is attributed the felicitous compliment to Louis: "On foot . . . the king of his subjects, but on horseback . . . king of other kings."[35]

The day after Louis's initiation into Pluvinel's select company he was allowed to demonstrate his skill in the courtly art of catching the ring. Six years before he had watched his father exhibit proficiency at this game. For Henri it had been an act of gallantry, intended to inspire the admiration of the newly wed young princesse de Condé, his last infatuation.[36] Now Louis gave a similar exhibition, in the Place Royale that his father had created, this time for the benefit of his own first love, his nurse: "The prize was a rosary, given by his nurse, whom he had called Doundoun since his earliest years and still did, even now, when she was very fat."[37] In another week he was winning the prize himself.[38]

While Louis continued to amuse himself by practicing horsemanship every morning, the queen impatiently prepared for the excursion to Guyenne that was to unite her two oldest children with those of Philip III. Toward August she developed a brief illness, which Arnauld attributed to Condé's contumacious letter threatening the security of the royal cortège.[39] After further fruitless struggles with Parlement, the queen, accompanied by Louis, went in person to the Bastille to extract the last 400,000 *écus* from Henri IV's treasure to supply the troops for the voyage.[40]

In March, the Venetian ambassador had detected no enthusiasm on Louis's part for his forthcoming marriage: "He does not speak of his marriage with Spain; he says of it only what the queen wants him to."[41] As the departure date approached, however, he became, as usual, pleasurably excited by the prospect of a trip. The journey finally commenced August 17. Elisabeth soon came down with smallpox, forcing part of the royal train to stop for several weeks at Poitiers, so that progress westward was more leisurely than it had been the preceding summer, and Louis was often able to make side excursions. At Amboise he had the delight of being feted by Luynes.[42]

A Painful Separation

Once the destination was reached, Louis was faced with the painful obligation of acting as his sister's best man in her proxy marriage to the heir to the Spanish throne. At no time in his life would he show less ambivalence than when he expressed grief at the departure of this beloved companion of his childhood. Héroard was touched: "The king goes. . .to say goodbye, not without sighs and tears, even actual outcries."[43] Lest one suspect that Héroard exaggerates Louis's tender feelings in this instance, another witness has confirmed them. According to the king's historian, the leavetaking was accompanied by tears and demonstration of that "deep affection . . . which he has always been known to bear toward those who touch him most closely."[44] When Louis finally dismounted his horse to bid Elisabeth farewell, continues Héroard, "it was then that nature brought into play her strongest forces: sobs, sighs, and cries, mixed with kisses and embraces, such that they could not bring themselves to separate."[45]

All the spectators experienced "compassion," Héroard tells us, "moved by the tears of these young princes," except for the Spanish ambassador, who looked at them with a "dry eye" and tried to break up the scene, crying in a powerful voice, "Come on, let's go, Princess of Spain!" Elisabeth was taken off, and Louis, still crying, returned to Marie (who had left her daughter abruptly, according to Héroard, in order not to give way to tears). Louis and his sister parted at about noon; "he could not restrain his grief or his tears" until two in the afternoon.[46]

It was characteristic of Louis, as it was of his mother, to transform his emotions into physical sensations. Thus, Héroard reports, "he returns at two-thirty, complaining of headache, and tells me 'It's for having cried.'" And although he talked a bit of Madame at bedtime, "saying that he is sad," the next day the evidence of his grief (to Héroard a very serious symptom) is that "he says that he has no appetite." During the next few days he also developed a rash, and the pain in his groin returned.[47] Consequently, Louis was confined to bed for part of this time. Still, he struggled against inactivity: he had a billiard table brought to his room and constructed fly traps out of playing cards.[48]

In exchange for surrendering his thirteen-year-old sister to the ten-year-old Spanish prince, the king was to receive the infanta Ana, Elisabeth's age-mate. In this ceremonial process both kings made use of their favorites. Philip assigned his favorite, the duke of Lerma, as stand-in for Louis XIII at his daughter's marriage by proxy in Burgos.[49] To represent himself in Bayonne, where Ana (now Anne) first stopped in France, Louis, still in bed and "suffering," sent Luynes, "one of my most intimate servitors," with a message to his betrothed. The surrogate Luynes returned with her reply on November 13 while Anne proceeded more slowly to Bordeaux, where she arrived on November 21.[50]

Children at Play

Fifteen years before, when Louis's mother had first arrived in France, she had traveled to Lyons, where she had been espied, supposedly without her knowledge, by the king to whom she was already married by proxy.[51] No doubt Louis had heard the story of his father's first glimpse of his mother; such preliminary informal encounters were a royal tradition at least since the time of Charles IX.[52] Now Louis imitated the *vert galant* by gaily making an incognito appearance to his bride as her carriage approached Bordeaux. Once in the city, Anne was received with enthusiasm by the queen mother and presented by Louis to Souvré (and then, says Héroard, "to me"). The king gave unexpected signs of gallantry in his first contacts with his young bride. Even Héroard was surprised when he proffered a feather from his hat in exchange for a ribbon from her.[53] At this time it was remarked by more than one observer that Anne resembled her new husband far more than she did her own father.[54] The *Mercure* also reported an "unbelievable" resemblance between the two spouses.[55] The two were, of course, distant cousins. No portrait of the time suggests, however, that the resemblance between them was as great as that between Louis and Elisabeth. Nevertheless, his kinship with Anne as well as his earlier ease with his sister no doubt contributed to the relative freedom Louis felt with the girl who supplanted Elisabeth.

The marriage was celebrated with a nuptial mass in the cathedral Saint-André of Bordeaux on November 25, 1615. During the two-hour ceremony, says the *Mercure*, the king often looked at the new queen, smiling. And she, "weighted down with robes and diamonds and pouring sweat [*suant à grosses gouttes*]," could not keep herself from smiling back at him.[56] When the ritual was terminated by the nuptial benediction, the royal party withdrew to their quarters. Consummation of the marriage was now supposed to be effected—an obligatory duty for Louis, even though "he was shy and very fearful." Guise, Grammont, and some other young lords told him off-color stories "to reassure him," Héroard reports, finally succeeding, according to the physician. Donning his robe and slippers, Louis was escorted by his mother to his queen's bedside, and the newlyweds were left alone within the curtains for about two hours.[57]

As Louis's physician it was Héroard's duty to examine the patient and get the important details: "At a quarter past ten he returns, having slept about an hour and done it twice, according to what he tells us. His glans appeared red. Asked how he had made out, the king said, 'I asked her if she was willing; she told me she was willing,' etc." Héroard notes, "He was thirsty"— unusual for Louis. He was given rose julep with water and put to bed.[58]

Whatever happened between the two spouses that night was not to be repeated for three years. Children were not supposed to cohabit. For boys especially, intercourse at too young an age was believed to be detrimental to health.[59] Thus, the historian de Thou thought, "They put the newlyweds to bed . . . only for the form, and without consummation of the marriage," although, formally, consummation had been accomplished.[60]

For the time being, then, Louis's private life went on much as before; he paid little attention to his new wife except when her presence seemed to thwart his desires, at which times his old, hostile attitudes toward Spaniards resurfaced. Such events became frequent in the following spring. Héroard reports his "extreme anger" early one morning in April because "they" had stolen his dark linnet: "Opines that it was some of the queen's Spanish women; rolls his little cannon through the office to make a noise at them and says that if it weren't for fear of waking . . . his mother he would fire it against the bedroom door. Sends out to buy a padlock and attaches it to his door."[61]

A coded message from the observant Venetian ambassador reports the development of negative feelings in Louis toward Anne and her company: "No great inclination toward his wife is shown by him, and he abhors all those close to her who belong to the Spanish nation. . . . While during earlier months they tried to keep him from making himself his wife's slave in everything [Héroard shows us nothing of this except for the initial encounters], now they have to work at preventing him from showing how little he cares about her."[62] Louis cherished everything belonging to his nurse, including her child, Louise. Imagine his rage the next month: "He goes to the . . . queen's [apartments]; locks up the Spanish women for having, the previous evening, taken the keys to the chests from Louise, his nurse's daughter."[63] Anne got little sympathy from her husband when she complained of being deprived of all control over her household.[64] Louis was often to be spiteful toward his queen.

TAKING PART IN A COUP D'ETAT

It was nearly six months after the marriages before the court returned to Paris. The interval was politically eventful. The *grands'* insurrection continued; Condé's troops ravaged the countryside of Poitou. They never actually encountered the king's forces head-on, however, and thus major battles were avoided as the royal party sojourned in various cities of the province and in Anjou and Touraine. Negotiations were opened with Condé, and while they proceeded the court set up headquarters first at Tours, then at Blois.

A truce was signed in February, 1616, whereupon bargaining began at Loudun. As the government showed every sign of desiring peace at any price, demands of the *grands* multiplied apace. The great nobles were less interested in matters of larger policy, however, such as the proclamation of Gallican principles and protection of Protestant rights. This enabled Ubaldini, who, though reassigned to Rome for some time, lingered on as the queen mother's close advisor, to make sure that nothing essential to the Ultramontanist, anti-Huguenot position was given away in the treaty that the king finally signed on May 6. "The treaty of Loudun was, in effect, the triumph of pontifical policy," concludes a historian who relied on the Italian correspondence. The Tuscan emissary believed that the nuncio could take full credit for inspiring the queen mother's decisions: "On all those points where he had guided her resistance she stood firm; on all others she ceded to the *grands*."[65]

The rebels had been even more generously rewarded by secret articles of the Treaty of Loudun than by its public provisions. All together, these gave them new powers over strongholds and localities, and new powers within the state. As their leader, Condé was specially rewarded in charges and benefits and was admitted to a central position in the government as chief of the council on finances.

To further placate the prince, the treaty called for changes in top government personnel. This was an important concession, for in royal politics of this era turnover in such high places was normally slow and occurred most often through natural causes. Thus, Sully's resignation in 1611 had caused popular wonderment and widespread misgivings. During the Estates meetings, the withdrawal of Villeroy, secretary of state, to his country house had a powerful effect, because of his long-standing prestige and influential following, in forcing Marie and her remaining advisors to make conciliatory moves in order to induce him to return. Yet over the summer of 1616 he and the chancellor, Brûlart de Sillery, two of the remaining loyal *barbons* of Henri IV, were dismissed, along with Sillery's son, Puisieux, who was Keeper of the Seals. These concessions had been made with the concurrence of the Ancres, still apparently hoping to co-opt the prince by propitiating him and thus to contain his power.

In this they were unsuccessful. While Condé may have been willing to cooperate with the Ancres—his motives have never been fathomed convincingly—his position as leader of the *grands* was incompatible with such cooperation. The other princes and great lords—notably Vendôme, Longueville, Bouillon, Mayenne, and Nevers—were determined that Condé not separate himself from them in order to seek his own advantage at their expense. They insisted that Ancre's power be terminated and held secret meetings late at night to devise means to rid themselves of the Italian. Condé himself attended these meetings, and, although he warned Ancre of danger, at the same time he also had to warn him that his own earlier promise to support him could no longer be kept. This was sufficient to cause the maréchal to flee Paris for a time.

Of the many provocations from the *grands*, this intimidation of the queen mother's chief deputy seems to have been decisive for her. It showed that the rebels could influence policy and that Condé was of no use in controlling them. Thus, even Marie was finally able to see that propitiation would no longer avail to procure the support of these challengers. She now had a new group of councillors, advanced chiefly by the Ancres, which included most prominently Barbin, Mangot, and Armand de Richelieu.[66] Under their leadership, a plan was formed to arrest the leading fomentors of rebellion, Condé in particular.

At some point, the young king was made a party to the plan. How was his support acquired? Was he persuaded, as his minister was later to claim in public, that Condé was an accomplice in a plot to capture Marie and himself and to end his rule? As we have seen, it was not difficult to arouse suspicions in him that those who seemed to be his friends were his enemies. Louis, who was even ready to turn on Héroard and to claim that "everybody is against me," was certainly ready to believe the worst of Condé. The duc de Vendôme, who had at times been dear to him, was now, once again, among the open rebels. It is likely that the king did believe in a plot against himself and in Condé's treachery. In any case, Louis entered into the scheme to seize the prince with zest and confidence. In the coup he demonstrated a "sangfroid and a capacity for dissimulation" that few outside his intimate circle had known him to possess.[67]

When the prince came to report to the queen mother after a morning meeting of the finance council, it was the king he encountered in her antechamber. Louis made small talk with the caller, inviting Condé to join him in a forthcoming hunting excursion. After Condé had, as expected, declined the invitation, Louis left the room. This was the prearranged signal for Thémines, a guards captain, to enter and arrest the first prince of the blood.

Héroard briefly reports the arrest without recounting Louis's part in it. The king did not go hunting that day. With his usual discretion the doctor indicates the boy's excitement indirectly: he did not want his midday dinner; "commands that they keep some cold meat [for him.]" Instead, he dined with Marie. At bedtime he feigned sleep on the straw pallet that was laid on the floor for the guard on night watch. Playfully, he pretended to be the guard and had his little attendants also play at guards. Soon after, however, he went to sleep on the mat. Descluseaux, his favorite of early years, was commanding the guard that morning. He pulled Louis out by his feet and playfully stationed him *en sentinelle*. But Louis fell asleep again, so the corporal carried him back and put him "in prison." Héroard explains, "It was his bed."[68]

Thus Louis reenacted in play the real-life experience that had been Condé's. It was pleasurable both to be the cause of the arrest and to pretend to be its victim. This was the prelude to a much greater delight.

CHAPTER THIRTEEN

Motives for Murder

*What good may Christianity not expect from this prince when he reaches
the age of majority if, before he is is fourteen, he puts to shame those who
have grown old bearing arms under him?*[1]

The arrest and imprisonment of Condé, at the beginning of September
1616, alarmed lesser lords at court, most of whom promptly decamped.
Among those who slipped away in the week following the move against the
prince were the dukes of Mayenne and Bouillon and Louis's half brother
César de Vendôme. Even the duc de Guise, who had hitherto supported the
regime loyally, felt sufficiently threatened by Condé's arrest to depart, accompanied by his brother, the prince de Joinville.[2] The Guises, as has been
noted, had until then always made themselves agreeable to Louis.

As these important supporters defected, Ancre's power over Marie increased. Not only was Louis's position weakened by the disappearance of so
many of *les siens*; his participation in the coup against the prince made it
seem that he endorsed the ambitions of the Florentine.

RISING ANGER

Condé's arrest proved to be unpopular in Paris. The prince had many followers there; moreover, Concini was the universal scapegoat for whatever
was found wanting in government policy. Soon after the arrest a mob attacked the Ancres' dwelling in the Faubourg Saint-Germain, looting and
destroying with such fury that scarcely a nail remained.

Parlement, where Condé had much support, demanded an explanation of
his arrest from the king and Marie. Ancre, who was generally believed to
have been the instigator of the prince's imprisonment, was at Amiens, "so
that" (as it seemed) "he might not appear to have been involved in so odious
a deed."[3] Louis and his mother were obliged to go in state to the *palais* to
present an explanation for their action against the prince.

The young king's temperament did not dispose him to meet criticism with equanimity. Nor had anything in his experience prepared him to take responsibility for an unpopular policy. Later, after Ancre's death, he disclosed to a delegation how detestable he had found this necessity. Marie, he declared, shared the blame with Concini, who "made me imprison my cousin, the prince de Condé, drove away the other princes, coerced me [*me violenta*] into appearing in my parlement to declare them criminals. The queen . . . forced me to do it."[4] His feeling that his position had become intolerable may well have dated from this first experience of the disagreeable consequences of complying with his mother's strategies.

Symptoms

On October 2 the maréchal d'Ancre returned to court.[5] The next day Louis showed the first symptoms—stomach cramps and upset—of what was to become a serious illness. The Venetian ambassador was not alone in attributing this change in the king's health to his sense of powerlessness and feelings of rage. The queen's secretary also reported that "aggravation and depression [*fâcherie et mélancolie*]" were widely thought to have had this effect on Louis's body.[6]

When the malady struck, the king felt a pressing need to have his old supporter, Héroard, at his bedside. The physician, who had been at his country home for a few days, was urgently recalled. He reports arriving at court at seven in the morning, having traveled all night.[7]

Héroard details his efforts over the following days—with many medications administered orally, rectally, and topically—to combat his patient's affliction. Yet it worsened intermittently throughout the month, frequently incapacitating him with cramps and other gastroenteric disturbances. Louis responded to these attacks with despondency and taciturnity. Héroard tried to provide amusements to cheer and enliven him. Sometimes he would call in the young king's falconers, the Buissons, father and son, so that "he can speak with them of birds." On October 15, 1616, for example, Louis "said not a word" while the company tried to entertain him, but afterward he talked gaily to his falconers. Two days later he complained of colic and was "*taciturne*" but commenced to talk to the young Buisson "as though he had not been ill."[8]

The turbulent state of mind that Louis's quietude only partly concealed is suggested by dreams that Héroard reports. In one, Louis calls his valet, stuttering in his sleep: "'Soupite, tell Loménie to bring me the croquet . . . croquet balls, and bring me . . . cannon balls. Hurry up! I want to knock down this gallery.'" A few weeks later, having fallen asleep while in "an angry mood," he starts, "calling out angrily, asking to urinate." Then, still dreaming: "'What a pleasure to extinguish a faggot. There! Stab it! Now there!'"[9] We may recall a scene of Louis's childhood in which his father used the occasion of urination to point out the powers of his penis—perhaps suggested by the faggot.[10] Usage of the time connected the word "faggot" with "heretic"—loosely, "he smells of the stake"—suggesting another link between Louis's feelings of aggression toward Ancre and toward his father, the former "heretic." The dream ended, " 'Who wants to bet a sou (*sol*)? It's a nice bet, a sou . . . [then suddenly], Now let's sleep.' "

Just a week before this second dream, Louis's illness had reached a climax. On the eve of All Saints' Day his stomach pain—"around the navel"—became acute, and his felt feet swollen and numb. Héroard, summoned, applied a poultice to the painful spot and administered rose water orally. Later he heard his patient "rail and snore very loudly." Dashing in, he found him in bed face down, his mouth against his arm, his teeth clenched. While the doctor and an attendant tried to pry open his mouth with finger and knife handle, respectively, Louis seemed to lose consciousness. This was a "convulsion" according to Héroard's note. The doctor treated it by forcing his patient to walk and administering brandy. The seizure lasted about seven minutes.[11] After this episode, Arnauld tells us, two Paris physicians, Petit and Delorme, were brought in for consultation. The next day Louis was bled, for the very first time, by the queen mother's surgeon.[12] This move may have been made against Héroard's advice, since, as has been seen, he did not favor this kind of therapy. Moreover, according to Arnauld, he called the king's seizure a "mere intestinal vapor," although most courtiers regarded it as a life-threatening "kind of apoplexy."[13]

Although one modern medical historian has attempted to construct, out of this attack, a case for chronic epilepsy in Louis,[14] there was never a recurrence of this particular group of symptoms. The cause of the episode is obscure. Louis had been much medicated over the previous few days, especially with enemas, and this could have occasioned a loss of consciousness. Or his illness, including chronic diarrhea and vomiting, could have caused excessive dehydration. The railing and snoring may have been chronic: Héroard had observed when Louis was four-and-a-half that while sleeping he "snores like a man."[15] The symptoms also may suggest an asthmatic attack, possibly connected with repression of angry feelings.[16] Even Louis's contemporaries, as we have seen, made such connections between unexpressed "chagrin" and illness. Furthermore, there were examples of such symptoms within Louis's ken: The duc d'Epernon was known at court to have recently had a seizure or fit from chagrin at the defiant behavior of his son in converting to Protestantism.[17] The same duke had had a similar attack while in the bridal party en route to Bordeaux in 1615. According to De Thou, that earlier seizure was feigned and expressed emotional rather than physical upset.[18] This may have been suggestive to Louis.

Whatever its nature, the crisis in Louis's health could not fail to raise questions about what might happen if he were to die. He was now fully grown by the standards of the time, and certainly at an age at which he could be expected to be increasingly unmanageable by others. His brother, on the other hand, was only eight years old—the same age at which Louis had begun his long dependency as king. It was plausible that Ancre might prefer the younger brother as king in order to continue his domination of the state, and Louis may even have imagined that Marie might support her Florentine compatriot in this ambition. Yet the queen mother would have had to be entirely lacking in realism to believe that she could have commenced a new regency with the support she had had for the first one. Fontenay-Mareuil's asessment is more credible: he believed Marie was genuinely alarmed that Louis might die, if only because she knew that never again could she become regent.[19]

Where the Maréchal himself was concerned, the direst suspicions found ample nourishment in court and country. The Italian had long been the focus of rumors surrounding the death of Louis's father. Any assassination of an important figure gives rise to thoughts of conspiracy, and this had been especially true of the murder of the great Henri. Concini's spectacular and sudden rise, through what seemed an inexplicable preference of the queen mother, made him a natural target for suspicions of complicity in the affair. Condé had cultivated the rumor that Marie and her favorite, together with the Spanish faction in the French court, had been involved in Henri's assassination. One who could believe this could certainly believe that a similar conspiracy was possible against the king's heir.

The weak affectional bonds between Louis and his mother must have been significant for the king's own suspicions. There was, as has been seen, a belief at court that Marie favored Gaston over Louis, and it was thought that dire developments flowed from such maternal favoritism. Court legend had it that Catherine de Medici had poisoned her son Charles IX from a similar set of sentiments, in order to promote Henri III to the throne. Bassompierre relates a conversation with Louis suggesting that the young king believed this story.[20]

Marie's increasing intervention in the treatment of Louis's illness did not reassure either the patient or his doctor. Héroard may well have felt uneasy that the queen mother, who had formerly championed him, now seemed to lack confidence in him. Leonora and the queen had medical advisors who were not from Héroard's circle—Petit and Delorme, who had long standing at court,[21] Marie's surgeon, Ménard, who had done the bleeding, and several of exotic origins to whom Louis's physician never refers by name.[22] The doctor of the Spanish duke of Monteleone seems also to have been significant in medical counsels at court, assisting at the bleeding of Anne in the spring of 1617.[23] Spanish physicians were not likely to have been on very good terms with the Protestant-reared Héroard, who was no friend of Spain and, moreover, had counseled Louis to continue abstaining from sexual contact with his Spanish bride. The Spanish government wished, on the contrary, to encourage the couple to procreate as soon as possible.

Ten days after Louis's crisis, Marie tried to take over his medication. The boy feared "black medicines"—those containing senna—apparently the kind favored by Marie's doctors. Nevertheless, Héroard tells us, he was presented with a concoction of almond milk infused with senna for purgation "following the command of the queen, his mother."[24] Héroard may have tacitly encouraged Louis in his adamancy. The doctor reports that the king "sends it back, and it was never possible to dispose him to take it." A few days later Louis told Héroard gleefully that his mother had relieved him greatly by promising that the medicine he would take the next day would only contain almond milk, "like the ones" writes the doctor, "I had made him used to taking."[25]

Cause for Suspicion

Louis's fears that others might do him harm were usually near the surface; in his weakened and painful condition they became stronger. In any case, it was customary, when the powerful fell ill, to suspect foul play.[26] Louis now found new cause to fear others' malign intentions toward him; he had good reason to think that Ancre aimed to alienate some of his most intimate servitors.

We have already noted reports that Concini offered rewards to some of those in Louis's entourage who would pledge him their loyalty; Du Ruau writes that the boy's "dear chevalier de Vendôme" as well as his "faithful Luynes" were targets for the maréchal's lures.[27] Montpouillan, the king's companion since childhood, reported that the Florentine tried to buy his favor with a lavish pension.[28] Pasquier confirms Ancre's designs toward Luynes and adds that Antoinette Joron, Louis's childhood nurse, who was still close to his person, was "won over" by Concini—presumably through a settlement of property on her—and induced to leave the court with her family.[29]

Perhaps the most disturbing rumor of those on the maréchal's list concerned Héroard himself. According to Arnauld, "they" made use of the first physician's absence at the beginning of October to try to "do him a bad turn." And even after the king began to recover, the same observer reports, "they" continued their efforts against Héroard. So serious was this enmity, according to that source, that the physician offered his resignation to Louis through Luynes. Louis was "extremely irked" by this suggestion and said he would never hear of his physician's leaving him.[30]

Louis's mistrust was further aroused by several reports that Marie had been advised of the possibility of a recurrence of the king's illness, which Héroard had minimized, in the springtime. Presumably the physicians who made this prediction had diagnosed his seizure as epileptic.[31] To Louis, anticipation of such a recurrence had a sinister implication: forecasting dire developments could easily be interpreted as designing to bring them about. At the same time the queen mother intensified her surveillance of her son, watching him take nourishment after his seizure, appearing at some of the frequent enema times, and forcing him, despite the earlier concessions, to swallow the hated black medicines, although "he says he has a horror of them."[32]

It may have been at this time that the young king became cautious about taking nourishment in Marie's apartments. Vauquelin claims that Héroard warned Louis (in a whisper) against eating or drinking anything while visiting his mother,[33] and the doctor's diary provides some support for this contention. An enigmatic entry describes Louis as leaving the queen's quarters one afternoon that winter and "going up to his office because he was hot and, from that, thirsty." At supper later, the king was not hungry and, the doctor says, "tells me what he had done at teatime, and the reason." Héroard does not pass the reason on to us. A few weeks later Louis had another unpleasant experience in the queen mother's chambers. This time, he assured, Héroard, he would have fallen had he not been supported. This episode, too, was followed by acute thirst and loss of appetite.[34] In these episodes there seems to be much that Héroard does not divulge.

TARGETS FOR RAGE

Whatever the nature of Louis's illness, its crisis in late October appears to have marked a turning point in his state of mind as well as in his physical well being. His fears and suspicions had been multiplied and intensified by the apparent threat to his life. His successful struggle to survive his malady may have helped convert suppressed feelings of rage and acceptance of abuse and denigration into planning for vengeance.

Marie and Concini

In the following year, 1617, Pierre Matthieu, a royal historian, was to write an account of the coup against Ancre for which Louis himself was probably one informant. Matthieu affirms that the king decided to "rid himself" of the maréchal six months before the deed was accomplished. This would place the decision in the latter half of October 1616, at about the time of his seizure.[35] Thus, Louis's determination to seize the leadership of his state apparently took shape at the beginning of his convalescence.

As Louis's slow recovery progressed he was encouraged to get out of bed if he felt able and willing to be dressed and active. Although his malady returned from time to time in more moderate form, he was therefore seen by courtiers in the autumn and winter of 1616 following a more or less usual routine.

On previous occasions Héroard had noted Louis's occasional irritation with his mother's favorite. During Concini's October visit, however, the king began to show his hostile feelings more openly. All the court became aware of an encounter in which Concini pressed Louis for compensation of the damages he had suffered in the sack of his house. It was effrontery for one who owed everything to the Crown to say, as Arnauld reports the Italian did, that "he had lost much" in the pillage for the sake of the king's service. Louis turned away from this plea in stony silence. Nevertheless, money was paid to Ancre. When Louis learned of this he was heard to complain that "they" were able to find 150,000 livres for the maréchal but there was no money in the royal treasury when the king himself wanted a warrant to spend thirty francs.[36]

Marie gave her son new reason for displeasure by welcoming the returning maréchal with enthusiasm. Furthermore, she tolerated from him a familiarity that others felt was repugnant to the dignity of the Crown. Arnauld notes that Concini responded with impudence to Marie's reception and ironically describes him "doing the honors" of the Louvre to the duc de Guise.[37] No one was more sensitive than the young king to subordinates' deficiencies in the courtesy due to royalty, and Concini was casual in observing these niceties. Two years later Richelieu, who was always ceremonially scrupulous, would recall that he had warned the Florentine against familiarity with "Their Majesties."[38]

Marie also allowed Ancre's intervention in political affairs in which he had no official standing. She tolerated his intrusion into meetings of the council of finances. And it was she who assented to the proposition that had so disgusted Louis: she instructed her minister of finance, Barbin, to reimburse Concini for his losses in the looting of his house.[39]

By the end of October Louis's displeasure with the maréchal had become obvious even to the queen. As usual she attributed it to the bad influence of members of his entourage. Thus, as she had done in threatening to disrupt Louis's intimate circle, she made herself one with Ancre in implicitly deprecating Louis's independence.[40]

Ministers of State

The onset of Louis's illness had virtually coincided with the beginning of important changes in the government of France. By the end of 1616 holdovers from earlier councils had been replaced by three new chief ministers, who owed their promotions solely to the Concinis and the queen mother. With the qualified exception of the thirty-one-year-old bishop Richelieu, who had firm connections at court dating from before Henri's time, these new managers were persons of slight status—"*gens élevez de peu,*" as Condé called them. As secretary of state the young bishop himself replaced Villeroy, an old confidant and advisor of Henri, who had been the only one in

Marie's cabinet to enjoy familiar terms with Louis, acting in some respects in loco parentis to the child king—sometimes even lecturing him on his responsibilities.[41]

The arrest of Condé and the dismissal of the old ministerial leadership marked a new departure in government policy. So long as the prince and Villeroy were influential, the queen's course called for propitiating demands of the *grands* for an ever-greater share in state power and wealth. After the palace revolution, however, vacillation and weakness at the top seemed to end. The new cabinet had ambitions to restore the state to solvency and to suppress rebellious activities of the great lords. Richelieu, the most articulate and ambitious of the new leaders, took the initiative in announcing an intention to restore royal control. For those disposed to listen, his instructions to Schomberg after Condé's arrest struck a resounding note of authority on behalf of the king that had not been heard since the death of the great Henri.[42]

Lacking political sophistication, however, Louis was not likely to catch the significance of these efforts of his new secretary of state. Others at court also assumed that Richelieu, as a former representative of the clergy at the Estates General and as one who had achieved his promotion through the favor of the queen mother, was linked to Ultramontanist views and the interests of Spain.[43] The young bishop had no more sympathy with either of these causes than with the pretensions of the native *grands*, but even Marie, to whose favor he owed his promotion, was probably unaware of this.[44]

The queen mother's expectations of others often unrealistically reflected her own desires. She had believed, for example, that the Guises would welcome Condé's arrest, whereas instead the event alarmed them enough to make them flee the court.[45] In any case, she herself remained infatuated with her papal and Spanish connections: as has been noted, Ubaldini, though recalled to Rome, delayed his return to continue as her advisor, and the Spanish ambassador, Monteleone, was a member of her intimate circle, with access to the Louvre at any hour, unlike all other foreign emissaries.[46] Marie's correspondence with Philip III shows her conviction that in arresting Condé she was following a policy that would give "satisfaction" to His Most Catholic Majesty.[47] As opposition to her government strengthened among the princes, she began to plan, with the help of the Spanish emissary, to call upon Philip III to send forces from across France's northern border to aid her.[48] When, at Soissons, princely dissent turned to organized arms, Ancre hired Liégeois mercenaries from the Spanish Netherlands to attack the rebels. After the maréchal's death this became a major charge against him: "He recruited for his army 3000 Liégeois infantry and 500 cavalry, all foreigners; the former led by Spaniards, the others by Italians."[49] Given Louis's interest in military matters, we may suspect his personal indignation in the terms of this denunciation.

Thus Louis's growing mistrust of his mother's motives toward him could find reinforcement from his detestation of Spain, his fear and hatred of Ancre, and his suspicions of the new government leadership.

REBELLIOUS TEMPTERS

The *grands*, for their part, sought to win Louis's favor at Marie's expense. They found means to ingratiate themselves with the young king all the while they were organizing armed opposition to his government's authority. At the height of his illness, word reached him of their solicitude and good wishes for his recovery. Witnesses testify to the gratification he showed on receiving this message.[50] His pleasure at such professions of personal attachment suggests how complete was his disaffection from his mother. It is noteworthy, however, that for four or five years after Henri's death court opinion still tended to discount Louis's political intentions and interests and to suppose that Marie would be able to exercise power in his name indefinitely. Those who did not know the young king intimately regarded him as innocuous.

This impression was reinforced by the fact that the functions of the Luynes brothers were apparently confined to facilitating Louis's amusements. In this capacity, however, they performed some of the same tasks that Héroard and other intimates carried out. Thus one day Louis was on a bird-hunting expedition at Bourg-La-Reine, with a new captain of guards in charge of his protection. Luynes had to initiate the newcomer and order him " 'not to let many people come near me while I'm hunting. But tell him not to be bothered if I sometimes get angry with him.' "[51] Delegating authority to Luynes to protect Louis's pleasures, at the same time presenting his hot temper in the most favorable light possible, was a practice that would later be applied to more momentous matters of state concern.

The *grands* had always pretended that their legitimate complaints never reached the ears of the king. A constant theme in the letters of the rebel duc de Nevers, for example, is that the king was prevented from seeing communications addressed to him containing vital information about his realm. The duke's biographer is convinced that Louis was never shown the declaration that caused Nevers to be accused by the Crown of lèse majesté, for in it he exonerated Louis from blame for the policies of his government.[52] In the many proclamations and open letters issued by renegade lords at the beginning of the winter of 1616–1617, Concini remained the overt target of attack. But these princes were, like Louis, aware that Marie's support was responsible for the role played by the maréchal.

Ancre himself seems to have been perversely oblivious to Louis's sensibilities. On November 12, 1616, when Louis was still convalescent, his physician reports the king's entrance into the great gallery, accompanied only by a guard and a few dignitaries. Aware of Louis's concern lest his cortège desert him, Héroard notes that the king "looked around at every step to see whether he was followed" by attendants as he stationed himself at one of the first windows overlooking the river. At this moment Concini entered, accompanied by more than a hundred persons; he also stopped before one of the windows, without going toward the king, "having everyone pay him court with bared head"—homage owed only to royalty. Héroard regards Ancre's behavior as a deliberate affront since "he knew very well that the king was there because he had been told so, having inquired in the [king's] chamber." Louis withdrew to the Tuileries, "his heart full of displeasure."[53]

This was the last occasion on which the court would witness the young king's outrage with the maréchal. Thereafter, rather than express his displeasure for all to see, Louis was to make his plans in private.

CHAPTER FOURTEEN

Rite of Passage:
The Killing of Concini

The worst thing he did in all his life, being an act fitter for the seraglio than his Castle of the Louvre.[1]

On April 24, 1617, Concino Concini, Maréchal d'Ancre, was shot and stabbed to death as he was about to enter the Louvre courtyard. The deed was done by soldiers under the direction of the baron de Vitry, captain of the king's guards. Louis, awaiting news of the encounter upstairs in his antechamber, was at last head of his state in fact.

To plot the murder of an enemy, even an enemy of the state, is not a proper activity for one who is called "Very Christian king of France." The seemly way for Louis, as chief dispenser of justice in his realm, to be rid of Ancre would be to have him taken into custody and prosecuted for treason. Not surprisingly, therefore, the *Mercure* declares that this was indeed his intention: After taking counsel from those entitled to give it, the government register relates, the king decided to have the maréchal arrested and turned over to Parlement for trial. Thus the official explanation of the killing maintains that Ancre was shot while resisting arrest.[2]

Another version embellishes the story: The king, "resolving for good and all" to take the reins of government in his own hands, "commands the sieur de Vitry . . . to arrest . . . Ancre and . . . make him prisoner . . . in order to carry the legal procedure against him and his accomplices through to its conclusion." Unfortunately, the account continues, these law-abiding intentions had to be suspended because, when confronted by the guards captain, the maréchal started to draw his sword.[3]

At the time, many disbelieved this account. Some, seeing the young king as merely the instrument of courtiers' ambitions, credited the deed to the planning of his intimates. Others, like Howell, knew of Louis's long-standing detestation of Ancre and saw the murder as the king's work. Another contemporary reports several versions of the event, including the official denial that Louis himself intended the killing and also considers whether Concini's death may have been planned by Luynes. He adds, however, an afterthought concerning the king: "It is true that he always had a fundamental aversion to him."[4]

While some, like Howell, deplored the lawlessness of the act that disposed of Ancre, others regretted the delay of so welcome an event, blaming Luynes's timidity or even Louis himself. At Louis's *coucher* on the evening of the murder, one pamphlet has it, "happiness made him utter these words: 'It wasn't on account of me that this didn't happen sooner; it was Luynes who never could resolve upon it—he's such a poltroon.'"[5]

Who were the parties to the plans to be rid of Concini? When did these plans take shape? What, when, and how were the means decided upon? What was Louis's part in the assassination? In searching for answers we shall follow evidence on the king's behavior in the months leading up to the coup d'état. What light has so far been thrown on Louis's character should contribute something further to our understanding.

CONSPIRING

Parties to successful conspiracies usually cover their tracks. Prior to the dénouement, secrecy is essential; afterward, publicity may nullify the desired effects. Sometimes, therefore, only clues to what went on can be detected, even with painstaking examination of evidence.

Clues

For information on the plot against Concini, the source that has up to now yielded so much—Héroard's diary—changes its character. The doctor who watched his patient so carefully and was so meticulous in recording his daily actions no longer gives us the account we have come to expect. The reasons for this change seem to lie partly in the king's dissimulation, partly in Héroard's care to guard the secrecy of his patient's plans. Thus, to get at the truth of the matter, it is helpful to read between Héroard's lines—noting what he does *not* say—as well as to search in other sources.

Until this time Louis had kept few secrets from his physician. Now, however, he did not confide his intentions toward Ancre. A remark reportedly made by the king to a co-conspirator as the time for the act approached shows that Louis believed he had kept Héroard in the dark. He told Cadenet, one of Luynes's younger brothers, that he had spent a sleepless night worrying about the outcome: "If my anxiety continues I don't know what I can tell my *premier médecin,* for although I'm not ill, I can't get any repose."[6]

It is easy to understand why Louis would attempt to conceal the conspiracy even from his faithful physician. Despite his oneness with his patient's interests, Héroard had heretofore also been loyal to Marie, to whom he owed much. Although the young king had confidence in his doctor and felt a need for him, he could be made suspicious of anyone—at least some of the time. Moreover, Louis had—as Héroard himself had repeatedly noted with pride—a gift for secrecy, and he took pleasure in using it. He could enjoy fantasizing concerning his capacity to retain secrets, as when he remarked to Cadenet, "So determined am I to let nothing out [*à ne rien déclarer*] that even were I dying they could not pull one word from my mouth."[7]

It was one thing, however, for the young king to conceal his plans from Héroard and another for him to deceive the doctor successfully. Héroard had devoted years of observing his patient; like Louis, he was exceptionally able to keep silent about what he knew. Further, it was Louis's practice to apportion confidences among his intimates. Thus, even though Luynes was certainly the confidant of many of his young master's secrets, he was unlikely to have been told all his thoughts and plans. On the other hand, the king may well have confided in Héroard notions that he did not wish to reveal to others.

Héroard's diary, as it has been preserved, suggests attempts to conceal what he had learned concerning Louis's intentions. At some point in November 1616, he seems to have suspected the direction in which the king's thoughts were tending and apparently retraced his entries to disguise or erase telltale pointers.

As we have seen, Héroard reports Louis's "displeasure" at being upstaged by Ancre on November 12. Certainly the doctor shared Louis's anger (*déplaisir* was a strong word at that time) at this scene in the Louvre gallery and gave special recognition to its significance: the marginal "*Na [Nota]*," which customarily emphasizes events in his manuscript, is doubled here. He adds an exceptional "*Notandum.*"[8] Indeed, both Héroard and Louis may have recalled the fantasy they had once shared in which Henri admitted the dauphin as his companion in the same gallery—"his beautiful hall in The Louvre"—in which Ancre had just snubbed the king. If so, their anger would probably have been intensified by the fact that Henri's heir was once again the unfavored one as he had so often been when Henri was alive.

Louis's displeasure with Concini could not have diminished in the ensuing months. In fact the maréchal was responsible for certain subsequent events that had even more potential for irritating Louis. But from the day Ancre publicly slighted the young king, Héroard remains silent on these matters.

On November 21, for example, Bompar, the first page assigned to the king as a child, to whom he had been very close, was murdered by a former page of Leonora, promoted to the officer class by Ancre.[9] Louis must have learned of this; yet Héroard's journal reports nothing about it. Instead, after the king's return from a three-day visit to Saint-Germain en Laye, on November 17, signs of hasty recopying begin to appear on various pages of the diary. It may be that Louis's reception of the news of Bompar's death has been excised by the physician; a long sequence of dates has been entered wrongly and corrected. Most of the entries are shorter than before. The elaborate page that begins the year 1617 is mistitled "*An mille six cent sept.*"[10]

Other facts connect Héroard's editing with some knowledge of the conspiracy that was hatching. At the height of Louis's illness the doctor, always watchful of his patient's sleeping behavior, tells us that in the early morning hours of November 4, the king got up restlessly, went to the little room where Luynes stood guard, and lay down on the cushions on which his favorite slept, saying, "Come on, Loïnes, everyone gets his turn." He remained there without sleeping for a short time, then went through the same pattern on his valet's pallet. This routine was repeated for the next few days.[11] Planning for the move that would liberate Louis from his mother and Ancre could have taken place in such sessions, either after the king's formal *coucher* in the evening or before his official rising, when he could converse privately with intimates. Héroard ceases to mention such nocturnal ramblings, however, after the report of the great gallery scene with Ancre. Nevertheless, they seem to have continued.[12]

Cadenet's account gives substance to these conjectures. After the coup was arranged, Luynes's brother relates, he came to see Louis before his formal *lever*. Louis, still in bed though awake, asked him in a whisper, "Is there any news?" When Cadenet gave a negative reply Louis said, "Come close, because I don't want Hurles [a valet] to hear me."[13] It was Héroard's duty to know of these matutinal comings and goings; after the first week in November, however, he tells us nothing more about them.

Actions are one thing; dreams another. Clues to Louis's plans may be found in some of Héroard's reports of Louis's dreams. But even here the doctor is sometimes circumspect in a way that gives rise to the suspicion that he dissimulates. On the afternoon of November 7, for example, the king awakens after a nap: "He reasons lucidly [*nettement*], remembers everything he has dreamed, saying, "I was really dreaming," and tells what the words were."[14] But the diarist does not pass the words along to us as he has done before. Perhaps something made them unacceptable for general knowledge.

Dreams with a mythical content seem to be safer. Toward the end of November Louis had such a dream. For days, he has been rehearsing a ballet that he is obliged to put on, "the first he has danced as king." It will be recalled that this was a form of court entertainment that gave Henri much pleasure, that César de Vendôme excelled in it, but that the dauphin had participated only reluctantly. Just before the first evening performance Louis awakens from a nap "with a start": he is "angry, demanding his sword to combat Abimilech, and shouts, 'There! There! Abimilech,' at which he begins to laugh."[15] Abimilech was the illegitimate son of Gideon who usurped authority over Israel by killing all but the youngest of Gideon's legitimate sons. It was the curse uttered by this last "dauphin" that caused the tyrant's eventual downfall.[16]

If this dream was indeed an expression of anger at Concini, the usurper of Louis's legitimate power, it is further evidence that, in the king's mind, the maréchal was linked with César de Vendôme, and perhaps with other hated and loved rivals of Louis's childhood.

Louis versus the Government

During these weeks a new royal council, unaware of Louis's hopes and plans, was trying to stamp out the princes' insurrection. A new and more effective Crown strategy began to bring results in military as well as in civil fields. This was owing partly to Richelieu, who acted as secretary of both state and war. At the same time that the cleric took action to reassure, and thus neutralize, Protestant anxiety in Normandy,[17] he was seeking, successfully, to prevent British intervention from bringing aid to the rebellious princes. On December 29 a long set of instructions went out to Maréchal Schomberg, ambassador in Germany:[18] the *grands* were to be pursued relentlessly with every arm of state power.

In mid-January of 1617 Richelieu launched his political campaign against the rebels. A proclamation over Louis's signature declared the duc de Nevers, chief organizer of the rebellion, guilty of treason. It was verified by Parlement on January 17. At the end of the month the duke addressed a public reply to the king, attacking Ancre and the new ministers. A few days later other dissident *grands* added their own manifesto complaining about the Ancres and deploring the departure of the "old councillors" from the king's cabinet. Richelieu's retaliatory *Déclaration du roy* denounced the rebels in language demonstrating a new decisiveness in royal authority.[19] At the same time the besieged *grands* at Soissons were increasingly cut off from outside contacts and support. The new government had begun to take a hard line against those who acted as couriers to the rebel princes, informing them on royal policy.

During this winter, however, as Richelieu and others labored to bring the *grands* to heel once and for all, the young monarch was secretly aiming to subvert their intentions. The first plan formed by Louis and his friends to overturn the government led by the queen and Concini seems to have been to leave Paris for a reunion with the self-exiled princes, who were gathering at Soissons in defiance of the Crown's proclamations. Louis apparently thought that once he had joined his rebellious subjects, all resistance would cease, lords and followers alike would rally to their legitimate leader, and Ancre's strength would fall away as his soldiers deserted him to join the service of their king. Together king and princes would redirect their forces against the hated Italian, who would be killed or at least driven from the kingdom, followed only by his foreign troops, running for their lives. The emancipated monarch would lead a victorious band back to the Louvre to restore his father's government.

The site originally chosen for a rendezvous with the princes may have been Courcelles, near the Pont de Neuilly on the way to Saint-Germain en Laye. Héroard reports that Louis purchased the property on December 18, 1616, and began to build a fort on the summit. During the rest of the month he visited it frequently, bringing armaments and rehearsing battle strategy, mounting sentry during the process of construction. Once he received his young queen there with ceremony, wining and dining her before taking her on a tour to show her the order of the guard.[20]

On the other hand, it is possible that the plot was not yet serious: as a royal historiographer later wrote, "the king pretended to be a child out of a marvelous prudence, in order to trap him [Concini] more easily."[21] There was certainly a good deal of play in Louis's behavior concerning the fort, as when he imagined pitting himself against enemies who might besiege him. In any case, we hear no more of Courcelles after about the first of the year. Other developments would have made a plan to use it for a rendezvous superfluous.

Marie unwittingly played into Louis's strategy for overcoming Concini. By February, government plans were being implemented to send Louis north at the head of his armies to confront the rebel *grands*. Richelieu mentions in a letter of February 22, 1617, that Louis was planning a trip to Rheims about a week later to be closer to his army.[22] The bishop, as secretary of war as well as of state, was optimistic regarding the probability of success in quelling the insurrection and eager to be aggressive. He concentrated his strategy on mustering the utmost power against the insurgents, ignoring signs of Louis's less than wholehearted approval. Richelieu's obliviousness to Louis's contrary intentions can be explained not only by the king's deliberate dissimulation but also by Marie's credulity.

Marie was easily deceived when she wanted to be. Nicolas Pasquier describes a scene at this time during which she was impervious to Louis's sentiments. Ancre, Barbin, Mangot, Richelieu, and the queen mother were present at a conference on war strategy against the *grands*: "The king wanted to get nearer to hear what was being discussed, but the queen, coming forward, asked him to go off and play . . . from which he conceived an extraordinary displeasure [*merveilleux mescontentement*]."[23]

Louis, of course, was a master of deception and a paragon at keeping secrets. But not all the parties to the conspiracy were the equals of the king and his physician in discretion. Luynes in particular, it was later to be said, lacked this necessary quality of a conspirator. Thus, news of the plot being hatched in the king's circle became widely diffused. Several of the dissident nobles were informed about the king's intentions. Cardinal de Guise in Paris was one link for communicating with the rebels at Soissons. They asked him to arrange with Luynes for Louis's defection. The duc de Mayenne, a leader of the Soissons resistance, learned of the plan through a courier sent from the capital.[24] Villeroy, former secretary of state, was another who was kept posted, via the young Loménie, who carried messages for Louis.[25] The insurgents were informed that the place of the planned rendezvous was now to be Compiègne, a town south of Amiens, Ancre's headquarters, and also near Soissons, in order to facilitate rallying the *grands* to the royal standard when the young king should appear. The Marquis de Beauvais-Nangis, a courtier of long standing, was approached by Luynes for assurance of his loyalty to Louis, a sign to that officer that a contest was about to reach its climax.[26]

An incident took place at this time that may be related to the clandestine traffic then current between Louis's entourage and the embattled *grands*. Among the king's official protectors were companies of Swiss and Scottish guards, originally assigned to the royal person because their nationality was supposed to assure their independence of local factions and their unconditional loyalty to their master. But such independence seems to have been little appreciated by Marie and her friends. After Henri's death the English ambassador was instructed by his government to resist the French government's proposal for a reduction of the king's Scottish guards.[27] The attempt to deprive the king of these loyal defenders was one of the sins of which Concini would be accused after his death.

Sometime during February 1617, a certain "Seigneur Struard" (probably Stuart), one of the Scots, was accused of having secret dealings with the "perturbers of the State" at Soissons. Héroard identifies the crime as having bribed soldiers to defect to the insurgent side.[28] Informed of this, Marie, on the advice of her council, ordered the guard put in the hands of the *prévôt de l'hôtel,* who had him decapitated in front of the Louvre on February 27 to serve as an "example and a terror to all who might desire to undertake like enterprises."[29]

On that morning Louis had awakened early, reporting that he had "dreamed all night that he had a sword in his hand." According to his doctor, the king had learned of the impending execution while he was out hunting birds on the Vaugirard plain. He sped back to town at a gallop with the intention of forestalling it but arrived too late.[30] Louis's behavior suggests that whatever traffic with the "enemy" Struard had been engaged in had been in concert with the king's plans to defect to the princes' side. It is possible that Louis's failure to prevent the execution was not fortuitous.

The *Mercure* says nothing of the royal rescue effort but reports that the "tall Scot" denied his guilt to the end.[31] He may have had reason to expect the king's grace. If so, this was the first instance in which Louis's inaction—or insufficient action—allowed a head to fall.

At this time Ancre seems to have become apprehensive about his own security. According to most reports, he no longer had confidence that his wife would support him with Marie. Contemporaries agree that Leonora felt that his grasp for power had reached too far and that his ambitions would lead them both to ruin. Pasquier, who was close to the insider Mangot, attests that she warned Marie, "You favor that madman, but he will ruin us all."[32] His behavior in the six weeks before his death was a mixture of apprehension and reckless disregard of all hazards.

Concini's apprehension was demonstrated by his behavior as a commander in the field. He seems to have feared to keep a rendezvous with the king and his armies in the place that had been agreed upon, near Soissons. A letter from him to Richelieu on March 13, 1617, indicates that the bishop, in Louis's name, had been pressing the maréchal to proceed to Pont Saint-Maxence, on the Oise, at the earliest possible moment. But Ancre demurred, claiming that "despite all diligence" in complying with the royal council's order, he first had to meet with his troops, the Liégeois, who needed help in crossing the river in order to join him. Therefore he could not possibly be at Saint-Maxence before March 25, a delay of more than a fortnight. Furthermore, it would be best if the king did nothing before he, Concini, arrived, as only then could military action give the greatest surprise to the enemies. The Florentine seems to have had some thought of defending himself against the accusation that he lacked ardor in the royal cause by publishing, on the same day, a letter addressed to Louis, taking credit for having raised, "at his own expense," an army of mercenaries to do battle for the king. According to one informant, Richelieu had expressed to the queen his dissatisfaction with Ancre's insistence on pursuing a private action to confiscate property he believed was owed him by the duc de Montbazon. Concini's self-indulgence at the expense of the young king's treasury was a public scandal. In the maréchal's open letter he implicitly denied cupidity and proclaimed his high public purpose.[33] The protestation of self-sacrifice from one who owed all he had to the Crown further inflamed feeling against him.

The maréchal's suggestion that he delay proceeding to the rendezvous with the king until he had met the Liégeois contingent was rejected by a letter from Louis sent the next day and countersigned by Richelieu: "I send this courier by coach to let you know by this letter that I desire that as soon as you receive it you proceed . . . [to Saint-Maxence] with all the cavalry and infantry you have to wait there for the said Liégeois, since I fear that Auvergne [commander of the forces besieging Soissons] may not be strong enough without you."[34] The admonition, of course, was sent not by Louis but by Marie, undoubtedly on the advice of Richelieu and the new council. Richelieu himself sent a separate letter to the maréchal, probably by the same courier, telling him that although "they" had very seriously weighed all the reasons Ancre had given for delay in his letter, diligence seemed paramount: "The queen has commanded me privately [to instruct you to proceed at once] and the king [so] orders you."[35]

If Ancre had been apprehensive about what might happen when he arrived at Saint-Maxence, he was not reassured by Richelieu's letter. A letter from the maréchal from Nesle on March 20 shows him still caviling at the instructions he has received. He has learned that the "enemies plan to attack the Liégeois" who are coming to join him; he is therefore on his way to Breteuil to await the king's instructions before crossing the Oise.[36]

Richelieu and Barbin had apparently gained enough of Marie's confidence to increase Ancre's apprehension, for reliable reports circulated that the maréchal had decided to try to replace them with two new ministers, who would be more compliant. Although the queen mother is said to have resisted Concini's pressures on this score, nevertheless, by Easter Monday, March 27, the decision had been made not to send Louis to Saint-Maxence after all.

This change of plans was a sudden one; the guards assigned to accompany the king had already departed when Louis's expedition was called off. Explanations for the decision vary. The *Mercure* declared that the "Sovereign Companies" and the "Corps de Ville" of Paris had petitioned the queen not to allow the king to expose himself. Not only danger to the royal person may have been in question. Leaving the capital without a resident monarch when enemies were so near evoked other fears: Parisians have always become apprehensive when hostilities approached the city. This was the case in March 1617, with the princes encamped at Soissons and Ancre seeking foreign troops to combat them. Furthermore, gallows began to appear in public squares about the capital city. This, and the execution of the Scottish guardsman, increased fears that the government, under Ancre's influence, was following a new policy of oppression, out of fear of enemy subversion.[37]

Some memoirists, writing after the assassination, claim that Marie canceled the plan for Louis to join the campaign because she discovered his intention to adhere to the princes and that thereafter she restricted his activities to the confines of the Louvre and the Tuileries. There is no indication, however, that the king's freedom was reduced to this extent or that Marie was aware of his plans.[38] On the contrary. While Louis's military excursion was being planned, Marie confided in Guido Bentivoglio, the new papal nuncio. He mentioned the pope's concern that the princes aimed to separate her son from his mother. She replied that success in this attempt was impossible, as Louis had just assured her that he wished to remain united with her against the *grands* and did not yet feel himself capable, because of age and lack of inclination, to assume the heavy burdens of government.[39]

Final Decision

Beginning in the first week in March, at the time Louis's trip north was being planned, Héroard's daily entries show signs of extensive editing and recopying.[40] Increasingly, Héroard's accounts become minimal and unrevealing. Except for persistent toothache, which occasionally troubled his sleep, the king's routine during most of March was a regular one: visits to his mother and occasionally to his wife, frequent excursions, and participation in the observances ending Lent. Nevertheless, one change in habit is perceptible: Every evening the doctor notes a substantial interval between Louis's retirement and the time of his falling asleep: "put to bed at. . . . Conversed with [*entretenu*] until. . . ." These entries differ from those of the preceding month, when the notation had more often been that Louis had played "quietly" or "gaily" or "diversely" after being put to bed.[41] This older form of entertainment—not conversation but diverse amusement"—again became the rule on March 24, about the time Louis's military excursion was canceled. Thereafter the description becomes a mechanical notation: "amused in diverse ways"—but the time interval covered is often two or more hours. The change suggests either that Louis successfully concealed nightly conferences from Héroard or, more likely, that Héroard deliberately concealed the conspiratorial conclaves for fear that an unauthorized reader might find the journal. That Héroard was capable of such dissimulation there can be no doubt. For example, Arnauld d'Andilly writes that, just after Ancre's murder, Louis reported that he had not slept for five nights. Héroard must have been aware of this, but, contrary to his usual practice, he does not report a single episode of wakefulness on the part of the king.[42]

On April 17 Concini returned to Paris unexpectedly, apparently—so Arnauld tells us the court believed—because he had learned that Leonora was counseling peace negotiations with the *grands*. Indeed, there are signs that their capitulation was imminent. Arnauld reports that Barbin told him he virtually had the rebels' surrender in his pocket.[43] Since February, British government correspondence had revealed fears that the princes were being "left to destruction" and the belief that the only hope of preventing the French Crown from exterminating the Huguenots once it had suppressed the rebellion, would lie in uniting foreign and domestic Protestants on peace terms.[44]

Ancre had good reason to fear that with the vigorous new leaders in the government he was being left out of consideration. After the assassination Marie told Bartolini that she had not wanted the maréchal to return; she believed that he could no longer remain in France. Leonora herself felt that her husband was reaching too high and that his days of eminence were numbered. She had already taken steps to withdraw to Italy.[45]

Ancre's appearance at court on April 17 may have been a surprise to some courtiers, but his impending return is likely to have been known by the royal family and council for at least several days. On the preceding Thursday Héroard mentions, exceptionally, both Louis's attendance at the council meeting, held in his mother's apartments, and two visits to the bedroom of "Loïnes" afterwards, one of long duration in the evening. These visits to Luynes plus another on the following morning suggest urgent conferences between the two, possibly in anticipation of Ancre's arrival. Héroard does not inform us that Louis visited his favorite again before the murder. Yet, as will be seen, at least one such visit took place. Héroard's transcription of his journal has several unusual mistakes on April 15 and 16, just prior to Ancre's return—of which he makes no note!—and then becomes uninformative.[46]

The prolonged consultation of Louis and Luynes on April 13 and 14 may be explained by their fears that the princes' opposition to Ancre would collapse, as was anticipated in the council. The prospect of Ancre's return to court may also have seemed to necessitate changes in their strategy of joining with the princes to turn on the maréchal. Perhaps they feared Concini had discovered their plot against him. Louis may have become convinced that the Florentine's presence was a sign of designs on his own person. It seemed a sinister fact that some of Louis's guards had been sent away earlier because of the royal trip that was subsequently cancelled; thus his protection was not at full force. Suspicion was further fueled by Ancre's arrival from Amiens in the remarkable time of only one day. It was later charged against him that this "invention" was an affront to the Crown; no French king had ever ventured to cover that distance in so short a time.[47] This unprecedented haste seemed to confirm the existence of a threat to Louis's safety. The king feared that the Maréchal had got wind of the conspiracy brewing against him.[48]

With such suspicions in Louis's mind, Ancre's murder would seem not only justified but necessary. On Wednesday morning, April 19—two days after Ancre's return—a new conference took place between Louis and his favorite "after six": "The king had gone to Monsieur de Luynes's room, and finding that he had not yet got up, seated himself on his bed and conversed with him a good [*grosse*] hour, talking very softly the whole time . . . and it is believed that it was then that the final undertaking on the maréchal was definitely resolved upon."[49]

If Ancre had been worried about the possibility of Louis's anger when he rushed back to Paris, on his arrival he was persuaded by the king's dissimulation that he had no grounds for such apprehension. When Marie warned the Italian of her son's hostility toward him Concini was outraged that she

could suggest such a thing, according to the Florentine resident's report, because the king had just been extremely cordial to him—"*lui avoit fait de très-
grandes caresses.*"[50] Such behavior on Louis's part meant that Ancre's fate
had been decided upon.

DISSIMULATION

Ancre assured Marie of Louis's good feeling toward him on Sunday evening, April 23. On Monday, Arnauld d'Andilly reports: "The maréchal
d'Ancre killed by order of the king." He goes on to list the "execution-
ers"—all from among Louis's guards—and the handsome rewards they received from their commander, the king.[51] Although there was no doubt in
Arnauld's mind that Louis had ordered Ancre's execution, some later versions of the event tended to exonerate the king. Marie is reported to have
exclaimed, when she heard the news, "What counsel!" as though Louis
could have taken such a step only on the advice of others.[52] When the finger of blame was pointed it was most often directed at Luynes.[53]

Did Louis intend Ancre's murder, or was it, as the maréchal d'Estrées
later speculated, an action counseled by another—Luynes—who, withal,
had "very gentle inclinations"?[54] Fontenay-Mareuil puts Louis at two re-
moves from the deadly deed, saying that it was Luynes "who got the king"
to issue the fateful command but that this was "assuredly not that he be
killed." In this view of the matter, the deadly outcome was intended by neither Louis nor his favorite.[55]

The young Henri de Loménie, apparently less impressed by Luynes's
gentleness, believes that Louis "did not command" Vitry to kill Maréchal
d'Ancre but only to "take him prisoner [*s'assurer de sa personne*]." It was
Luynes "who made the king fall into the trap he had laid for him" by asking
what Vitry was to do in case Ancre defended himself. Louis, obliged to answer, said "if that happened" Ancre would have to be killed.[56] It seems,
however, that Loménie was not among the conspirators and that Fontenay-
Mareuil was in an even worse position to determine responsibility, since he
was besieging Soissons at the time. Apparently these three memoirists,
who tend to pass the blame to Luynes, were themselves at some distance
from the event.

The report attributed to Montpouillan puts the matter in a different light.
It must be given some weight, for this age-mate of Louis was one of his
companions of longest standing and certainly was in his confidence. Yet
since his memoir was transcribed after his death by his brother, it cannot be
trusted in all details. According to this account, Montpouillan himself was
assigned by Louis to seize the maréchal in the king's *cabinet d'armes* several
days before the assassination took place. He understood, Montpouillan
said, that his orders to "get rid of him" meant that murder was authorized.

It was not Louis whose resolution faltered he claims, but Luynes. Indeed, since there were three Albert brothers, of whom Luynes was the eldest, it should have been they who were assigned the deadly task, but they lacked the "boldness" to undertake it, actually panicked as Montpouillan was about to execute the king's orders, and sent in Brantes, one of the three, to stay the assassin's hand at the last moment.[57]

Only two accounts of the conspiracy have come from full participants in it. Both of these, moreover, were apparently (one avowedly) written to satisfy Richelieu's omnivorous desire for information. Their fidelity to the truth must have been constrained by the possibility, after the cardinal's return to favor in 1624, that the king himself might have had access to them. One is the contribution made by Cadenet, later duc de Chaulnes, which has already been discussed.[58] The other comes from Guichard Déageant, an intimate of the Luynes brothers at the time of Ancre's murder and later an aide to Richelieu.

In Déageant's version, the killing was not designed by Louis, although he gives the king credit for skill in helping to plan it and in keeping the plot secret. According to him, the plan was to arrest both Concinis. It was believed that there would be enough evidence of their criminal connivance with the Spanish power to convict them in court. Perhaps Déageant gives away more than he intends, however, when he relates that, on the day of the coup, Louis, waiting upstairs, was told that his guards had "missed" the maréchal d'Ancre, who was on his way upstairs with his retainers, sword in hand. According to this account, Louis then asked for his sword and calmly received the advice of a dauphinois guard at his side to "pass them through the stomach with it."[59]

The account by Chaulnes, Luynes's brother and co-conspirator, substantially supports Montpouillan's assertion that Louis was the driving force behind the plan to kill Ancre. This report forms the first part of the published *Relation exacte*. Chaulnes quotes Louis's avowal of "the resolve I have taken" and "rid myself" of the maréchal [*m'en défaire*] and contrasts this with the rejected strategy of arresting and trying the hated Concini. Although Chaulnes has Vitry play the role Caumont claimed for Montpouillan, he confirms the earlier attempt on Ancre's life in the king's arms cabinet and, like Caumont, depicts Luynes as vacillating and apprehensive.[60]

Two semiofficial versions of the drama appeared within a year of the event. Both have Louis authorizing the killing. In Matthieu's account the coup was first planned for Thursday, April 20. The king is said to have "commanded" Vitry to "seize Concini and, if he resisted, to put him to death."[61] The other chronicle admits that Vitry promised to deliver the maréchal to his monarch "dead or alive."[62]

Chaulnes's part of the *Relation exacte* explains, moreover, why imprisonment could not be contemplated. If Concini continued to live, he writes, the queen would exert intolerable pressure on Louis because she would feel the need to demonstrate her own power to intervene for her "creature." The king clearly saw the need to put this possibility out of her reach.[63]

Probably Louis tried, in giving orders for the murder, to avoid being explicit. Vitry, on the other hand, had good reason to persuade his master to be specific in authorizing him to kill. When the commission was given him he made sure witnesses were present. Without definite orders, Chaulnes explains, those who were to act for Louis risked having their actions repudiated later. The king might give in to Marie's desire for vengeance, for example, and deny that he had commanded the killing: "Princes, to protect themselves from the bad outcomes of great plans, very often blame them on those who got involved only . . . out of . . . obedience. . . . In such cases the service one has rendered becomes instead a crime."[64] That those commissioned to kill Ancre insisted that Louis authorize the deed is confirmed by the memoirs of Montpouillan. According to him, when Vitry and his brothers asked the king what they were to do in case Ancre defended himself, Luynes and his brothers "did not dare open their mouths." Montpouillan himself, however, on terms of long-standing familiarity with Louis, is said to have answered boldly, "The king understands that he [should] be killed." Vitry then said to the king, "Sire, do you command me to do this?" To which Louis replied, "Yes, I command you."[65]

The very fact that the task of confronting Ancre was assigned to Vitry signified to some that the orders came from Louis and that the King's intention was that the maréchal be killed. The baron, captain of Louis's bodyguards, had been committed to him for many years. It was Vitry, it will be remembered, who was charged by Marie to safeguard the new king immediately after Henri's murder, when fears for Louis's safety were running high. When Leonora learned that Vitry had commanded the group that murdered her husband, she exclaimed, "Then it is the king who killed him!"[66] Vitry was, moreover, known to be among the most violent men at court, responsible for at least two recent murders. One victim was a very good friend.[67] Antoine Aubéry, who, perhaps of all seventeenth-century historians, had the greatest access to secret papers, concludes that the maréchal "was killed by the king's express orders."[68]

THE DEED DONE

After at least one aborted attempt to "be rid of" Ancre, a new trap was laid for him on the morning of April 24, a Monday. Louis remained in his first-floor apartments while, in the courtyard below, an elaborate scheme of signals was to alert those awaiting Concini's impending arrival.[69] The ambush was headed by Baron de Vitry, his brother, Du Hallier, and another of the king's guards. Several others were in attendance.

Reports agree on most details of the confrontation. As Ancre entered by a drawbridge leading from the street to the Louvre, Vitry took hold of his arm and announced, "The king has commanded me to arrest you [*me saisir de vostre personne.*]" The maréchal replied, in Italian, "What, me?" and Vitry rejoined, "Yes, you!" upon which someone was heard to cry, "Kill! Kill!"[70] A few contemporary accounts report that Ancre's hand moved in a way that could have been interpreted as reaching for his sword. The fact seems to be, however, that Vitry moved in on him so closely and swiftly that none of these reports can be taken as first-hand testimony. Henri de Loménie made inquiries to get at the truth of the matter. "It has been said," he sums up, that Ancre "was reaching for his [sword], but none of those who bore witness has agreed to this privately."[71] One who was present says Vitry pushed Concini against the railing of the bridge and struck him with a sword in the stomach.[72] Another says that Vitry shot him. In all, three or four bullets were fired, two striking Concini in the head.[73] But the distinction of having finished off the Florentine was disputed:

> Perray thought he was the first; Morsain did too, and Guichaumont more than all the others. [He] seemed to have the best case inasmuch as he was dressed in mourning, and that made him more noticeable. [Several others] wanted to take part as well. Sarroque gave him a sword's blow in the side, under the nipple—he had offered himself to the king to make the strike more than a month before. Taraud gave two sword blows, one of which was in the neck. The others gave some too, but he was already dead. There were so many that he fell to his knees, supported by the railing, and Vitry, shouting "*Vive le roy,*" gave him a sword's blow that succeeded in laying him out on the ground.[74]

According to a provincial visitor who happened to be in the Louvre courtyard for a meeting of tax officials, "Vitry then walked into the court to inform His Majesty, whom he found on the balcony adjoining the queen's bedroom." Thereupon the king called to the captain to ask if "he were dead, whom, having answered 'Yes,' he thanked with open arms."[75]

According to Chaulnes's account, Louis had that morning gone to his third-floor arms cabinet, where he had charged "forty or fifty little muskets, in case he might have need of them." Descending briefly to station Colonel Ornano in the *grande salle* overlooking the main court, he went back upstairs, accompanied by Luynes, to his arms cabinet, from which there was no view of the murder scene. Later, hearing the tumult below, he started to descend. Ornano, who had witnessed the coup from his post, came to meet him and told him, "'Sire, Baron de Vitry has just killed the maréchal.' 'Sir,' replied the king, 'it was by my command. That is why I am going down there—to approve the deed he has done and the service he has rendered me.' "[76] The king then entered his bedroom, whereupon his *huissier de chambre,* made anxious by all the drawn swords, closed the door brusquely behind them. Louis "ordered him to reopen it, telling him that now that he had rid himself of the maréchal d'Ancre, he no longer had any enemies." Leaving his bedroom he went to a window of the *grande salle,* from which he could see Vitry and a crowd of gentlemen in the court below "all with sword or carbine in hand. [He] shouted to them all four times, very loudly, 'Baron de Vitry, I acknowledge [*advoue*] the action you have taken and that it is by my command that you have killed the maréchal d'Ancre.' "[77]

No autopsy could have verified the cause of death. Although Concini's body was hastily interred in Saint-Germain de l'Auxerrois, across the street, the remains were repossessed the next morning by a mob that dragged them through the streets until, desecrated hundreds of times over, they were divided and redivided, and finally scattered. Bishop Richelieu, who was on his way to see the nuncio, found his coach's progress obstructed by a crowd "drunk with fury" as they "wrought every imaginable indignity" upon the maréchal's body.[78]

Perhaps for him, as for many who had known Ancre well, it was hard to understand the frenzied hatred of the crowd for the amiable, easygoing maréchal. Estrées was led to reflect on his strange fate: "He was himself benevolent by nature, and since he had disobliged few people, it must have been his star, or the nature of affairs, that caused so many to rise up against him."[79]

It is, of course, in "the nature of affairs" that one who has risen by personal favor rather than sanctioned authority should be a focus of blame for all the ills of a state. In Ancre's case, however, it was his fate not only to play this role but also to become the target for desires, hatreds, and fears of his young monarch that he had taken no part in engendering but had unwittingly helped to redirect toward himself.

CHAPTER FIFTEEN

A New Order?

Never was France more peaceful and gay, nor the king more absolute.[1]

A few months before Ancre was assassinated, Louis rebuked a courtier who gleefully reported a rumor that either Vendôme or Bouillon had been killed. "The king said, coldly and seriously," reports the faithful Héroard, "'I do not rejoice at the death of another!'"[2] Now, learning of the death of his mother's deputy, he belied those words, giving unrestrained signs of a joy greater than any he had experienced before.

LOUIS REJOICING

As soon as the maréchal's death was confirmed the young king appeared at a second-story window overlooking the courtyard, sword raised high, and cried: "Be of good cheer, my friends! Now I am king!" He was greeted with acclaim by those below.[3] The Orléans deputy who, happening to be in the courtyard, saw the king thank Vitry for doing the murder, noted that he did so "with open arms, as though embracing him."[4] Louis then went into the great gallery, where the crowd of noble well-wishers soon became so large that he was helped up onto the billiard table to receive them, "with a highly assured and happy countenance."[5] In the afternoon, he again received a long parade of celebrants, to whom he repeated the words "Now I am king, I am your king!" in a voice "mixed with tears and delight." He added, with a bit more circumspection, "I have been that, but now I am, and shall be with God's help, more than ever."[6]

Yet, as the British ambassador wrote to his government, perhaps it was not altogether seemly for the king of a great country to preempt the legal process in so violent a manner and then to rejoice so openly at the death of another.[7] The Venetian ambassador reported, possibly with similar misgivings, that Louis was unable to restrain his joyous laughter during an audience and "had to put his hand over his mouth so that his interior hilarity could not be seen."[8]

At the time, Louis did not hesitate to take credit for the murder. Arnauld tells us that in his first euphoria the king, with "tears of joy in his eyes," told the group that rushed to surround him that in order to "forestall the evil intentions" Ancre had harbored toward him and his state, "he had been obliged to have him die."[9] Later Louis told Villeroy and other former ministers of state that "he had had the maréchal d'Ancre killed, as guilty of treason."[10] Villeroy, indeed, made his appearance so promptly as to confirm other evidence that he had been kept closely informed about the conspiracy's progress. He and his former colleagues—Jeannin, Sillery, Du Vair—were told by Louis that day to resume their old posts in a council that would now be headed by the king alone. Significantly, Louis addressed Villeroy as "*mon père,*"[11] an appellation that he rarely used except to a priest. The king then delivered a prepared address to the reinstated officials, expressing his intention to restore the felicities of his father's regime.[12]

Claude Barbin, the favorite of Marie and Leonora and sponsor of Richelieu, was not only the first minister to be deprived of his charge (as superintendant of finance); he was also put under arrest, certainly on orders of the king. Soon thereafter Louis sent Luynes to retrieve the seals that had been surrendered by the ousted chancellor, Mangot. These acts gave special pleasure to the young king, who had suffered from feeling that the resources of his treasury were slipping away. "Now that we have the seals," he exulted, "we shall have finance; I shall give them to someone who is my good servitor."[13]

Armand de Richelieu, bishop of Luçon, had been fast becoming the most influential member of the council appointed by the queen. During the previous few months his passionate prosecution of the war against the princes had led to increasingly militant declarations and strategic directives issued over his signature in Louis's name. On the afternoon of the assassination, the young king, standing on the billiard table above the crowd, caught sight of the bishop and shouted, "Well, Luçon, at last I've escaped from your tyranny! Go away! Go away! Get out of here!"[14] It apparently was not part of Luynes's plans to dispense with the bishop's useful services, however, and a few confidential asides between the favorite and the king were sufficient to moderate the youth's damning words for one he felt had "tyrannized" him. Yet that spontaneous and fervent outbreak against Richelieu seems to show not only Louis's dislike for the policy followed against the princes but his sense of chafing under the prelate's domination.

For, after all, the king of France was still only fifteen years old. On the afternoon of this triumphant day Cardinal de La Rochefoucauld called upon him and, observing the political demands pressed on him from all sides, which prevented his continuing a conversation he had been having with one of the young courtier companions of his childhood, remarked to him that he would be restricted much more in the future than he had been up to now. "No!" replied Louis staunchly, "I was much more restricted playing at being a child than I am by all these affairs." Then, turning to another attendant, he added, "They made me twiddle my thumbs [*fouetter les mulets*] for six years in the Tuileries; it's high time I did my job."[15]

Yet it was not so easy to become adult all at once. During a round of receiving petitioners the king was obviously thinking of something else. While receiving President Miron he started to play on a spinet that was on the table. Someone asked, "What are you doing there, Sire?" Louis replied, "I'm being a child." The reporter of this exchange, reminded perhaps of some comment by Henri on the dauphin's musical cleverness, recalls, "The late king used to call him *Maistre Mouche*."[16]

The same reporter, apparently present at meetings of the royal council, followed the adolescent king's official conduct with critical attention during the next few days and found it, on the whole, exemplary. At a council meeting on April 26, he concludes, "No proposition was made on which His Majesty didn't offer some *bon mot*, and one worthy of what he was." And, when Louis took his leave, says this observer, he did so with "highly commendable grace and simplicity [*honnesteté*]."[17]

In these days following the murder, the king, still exulting, began to put his feelings in writing. A proclamation announced his "resolution to take care myself" of the affairs of the realm.[18] In a letter he acknowledged congratulations from the duc Du Maine—who only two days before had been struggling against the forces of the Crown—by telling him that he found his words "very pleasant." Past resistance would be forgiven when the duke returned; then would Louis "deliver my realm from the miseries of war." To the duc de Guise he was more joyous still at his coup, "since it has pleased God to deliver me from the Marquis d'Ancre, who by his insolence and violence troubled the peace of the realm, kept its princes and *grands* divided, and everyone in a state of discontent and mutual mistrust." We may note here that Louis refrains from honoring the dead Concini with the title of maréchal.[19]

Louis was eager to have *les siens* restored to him. One of his deepest grievances against Concini had been that the Florentine was better accompanied than his monarch, always followed by numerous attendants and waited upon by petitioners who made a veritable court out of his private dwelling. After the coup, the young king's desire to have a full suite of courtiers was at last gratified. From the moment of the murder the press to wait upon him was overwhelming and the "quantity of nobility" to be found in the Louvre "unbelievable."[20]

One morning, however, Louis was up and about so early that he found himself in the great gallery unattended except for the captain of his guards.

Jokingly, he pretended that he was being pressed by a crowd, saying to the lone guardsman, "Du Hallier, you seem very hampered there, why don't you have me give you more room?" Then, carrying the fantasy further, he suggested, "They ought to resuscitate Concini, in order to keep the court at his house." The reporter, no doubt aware of the king's usual taciturnity and his tendency to stutter, comments: "He chats with great ease when he gets involved [*s'en mesle.*]"[21] Involved indeed was Louis: anger had held him in silent thrall; Concini's death liberated his tongue.

HÉROARD'S TRIUMPH

Between the notation of Ancre's murder at 11:00 A.M. on April 24 and the notation of his patient's dinner at noon, Héroard leaves two-and-a-half blank pages. Perhaps he meant to fill them in later with some account of the high excitement of the last hour of that morning. Why he did not do so—at least, not in the diary version that is known to us—remains mysterious. Yet it is clear that, next to the young king himself, no one exulted more in Louis's triumph than Héroard. For fifteen years the doctor had pictured himself as grooming his young master for a great role. It must have seemed that the glorious day had arrived at last when he reports, on April 25, that his patient goes to council where his secretaries of state were," and adds, "It is the first time, all alone."[22]

It may have been soon after this that Héroard drew up an account of an earlier royal plot he had witnessed at court—the assassination of the duc de Guise and his brother, the cardinal—in 1588. The quotation from Tasso that Héroard chose to preface his report on this killing presumably refers to the ambitions of the Guises, but it seems less applicable to them than to the more lowly born Concini:

> *Ai voli troppo alti e repentini*
> *Sogliono precipiti esser vicini.*
> Those who fly too high, too suddenly,
> Are wont to be near precipitate falls.[23]

There were many points of comparison between the earlier double murder, effected by the orders of Henri III, and that of Concini. Some of the features of the earlier killing emphasized by Héroard throw light on how he valued his young master's conduct. "Good King Henri," for example, had made the signal error of allowing himself to be drawn from his capital city. Louis, we have seen, had planned to leave Paris for the north but later had rejected the idea of such "desertion." Further, Héroard could take pride in the fact that Louis was both discreet and unshakable in his resolve to be rid of one who obstructed his authority. Henri, on the other hand, had been anything but intrepid. The doctor reports him as fearfully agitated at the very

hour of the deed, expressing his apprehension of the difficulties of overcoming the powerful duke. As he waited for Guise to fall into the trap his nerve
began to fail: "He is tall; he is powerful," Héroard reports him as saying; "He
will be exasperated [*marri*] by it" — presumably, by the assault upon him.[24]

One feature the first coup shared with the second — the presence in the
background of a queen mother — is treated by Héroard in a way that suggests an implicit analogy. When the murder of the Guises took place Catherine de Medici, Henri III's mother, had been excluded from councils of state
for some time through the influence of Epernon, the king's favorite. Marie
de Medici, on the other hand, was an important potential impediment to her
son's plans. There may be a link between the fact that Héroard takes special
note of Henri's solicitousness for Catherine — he was anxious not to disturb
her sleep (her bedroom was beneath the scene of the crime) by undue noise
during the murder — and by the doctor's own long-standing sympathy for
Marie and concern for her welfare.[25] A similiar report exists of Louis's pro-
tectiveness of his mother's repose. According to this, the opportunity presented itself to seize Ancre in the queen mother's quarters, but the king ve-
toed the idea, presumably on grounds of principle, or sentiment, or both: " 'I
don't want anything to be undertaken . . . in the bedroom of my mother the
queen,' he said," this contemporary account reports. Howell agrees that
Vitry had orders "not to touch" the maréchal "in Marie's lodgings."[26] If
these reports are accurate, however, they are virtually the only evidence that
concern for Marie de Medici figured in any of Louis's calculations. Indeed,
his ruthless treatment of his mother in the murder's aftermath astonished his
contemporaries.

A MOTHER BANISHED

Before the body of the murdered duc de Guise was burned by Henri III's instructions, some said that it was thrown out of a window of the château of
Blois. Perhaps Marie de Medici was recalling this reported insult to the
corpse of the earlier royal rival when, after Concini's death, she told the Florentine emissary that the maréchal had been "so odious to her son" that Louis
had planned for some time to have him killed and then to have his body
defenestrated.[27] Following the coup, Marie may have suspected that she herself was scarcely less odious to her son. Many of those who excused his extreme measures against Concini were stunned to see the harsh measures he
took against his mother. Louis's severity, said Mathieu de Morgues, a confidant of Marie in her days of exile, "flung her into the strangest grief that
had ever been inflicted upon a queen." Morgues's sense of outrage at
Louis's mistrust of Marie is evident when he reports that after the coup the
king's officers searched the queen mother's rooms, "even to the point of
looking under her bed."[28] Indeed, not only Marie's supporters but also inti-

mates of Louis were surprised; they seem to have expected that his filial feelings for Marie would make him weak where she was concerned. Since the beginning of Marie's leadership of the state, publicity had stressed Louis's high respect for Marie.[29] Instead, immediately after the maréchal's death, the king had his mother put under virtual house arrest and substituted his own guards for hers. Her nearest advisors and her other children were at first forbidden access to her, and the king himself refused her pleas to see him from the day of the murder to the day of her departure, on May 3. What communications he deigned to have with her were cryptic, carried on through third persons, and not reassuring. Bishop Armand de Richelieu was sometimes the appointed messenger.

On the evening of the day after the coup Marie and her maids were disturbed by the noise of axe-wielding Swiss guards demolishing the drawbridge that gave upon her private garden. The king had already sent for the keys to her outside doors. Later, all but one of these were walled up.[30] Writing home to the grand duchess of Tuscany, the Florentine representative compared Louis to Nero, declaring that his behavior showed "enormous barbarity."[31]

The queen mother's treatment, in fact, was worse than that given some treacherous princes—Vendôme and Condé, for example. This difference gave rise to fears that Marie's fate would ultimately be harder than theirs had been.

When Marie's removal from court was decided upon and the place of her exile negotiated, the fact that she would continue to be under Louis's surveillance and restraint was made clear. Just before her departure she was allowed to meet with her son, in a staged encounter for which a script had been drawn up beforehand. During the few minutes it took to say the lines, Louis remained formal and unyielding. Only one exchange in the scene was unscheduled—Marie's plea for the release of Barbin. To this her son responded evasively that she had already been told he would try to satisfy her in every way, including the fate of the former minister. It was now time for farewell: "Then the queen, unable any longer to hold back her tears, came up to the king, weeping bitterly, and kissed him on the mouth without embracing him. And the king, who had been entirely steadfast during the interview, withdrew, but not without shedding a few tears." Louis did not wait to see eight-year-old Gaston make his short speech of farewell, which caused Marie to dissolve in tears once again. She kissed and embraced him as well.

After a short exchange with Luynes, the queen mother went straight to her carriage, while Louis moved to a balcony over the courtyard to watch as his mother and her suite ceremonially departed in a train of horse-drawn coaches. He then transferred to the great gallery to see the procession cross the Pont Neuf. Immediately after it disappeared from view Louis also departed, with his queen, for the Bois de Vincennes.[32]

An excursion to the eastern forest had been planned for the same day as Marie's departure in order, as one account tells us, to facilitate housecleaning of the Louvre. "Some say," however, the same report continues, that it was also scheduled to allow the king's men "to search thoroughly throughout in order to make sure that no 'maréchalist rascal' had put [gun] powder in some corner, or prepared some other mischief."[33] One of Marie's ladies of honor claimed to have been told by one of Louis's searchers that they were looking in the chamber above the queen mother's for a powder keg intended to blow up the king.[34] We may recall Louis's own fantasy, as a child, of blowing up Madame de Montglat; perhaps now he feared that his mother might do the same to him. In any case the precaution seems to reflect the depth of Louis's mistrust of his mother.

ADDITIONAL VICTIMS

Marie's continued presence in the Louvre after the maréchal's murder had given pause to the *grands*, who would otherwise have flocked back to the court in even greater numbers. Within an hour after her departure on May 3 Louis repaired to Vincennes with his suite where in the next fortnight he received avowals of renewed allegiance from many of the nobles who had not previously put in appearances.

The king, who had proclaimed his intention to exercise his authority fully, continued to attend council meetings and conduct state business in that wooded refuge. But on the second day after his arrival he also created another occupation more in keeping with his long-standing tastes. The fort he had had built a few months earlier at Courcelles, near the Pont de Neuilly, perhaps with the intention of rallying the *grands* to his side there, was now reproduced in the woods of Vincennes. He began to design the plans on May 5, and from then on he visited the site several times a day, braving inclement weather. He scoffed at violent rainstorms, his proud doctor tells; "He endures everything with ease." Louis attended the afternoon council meeting for an hour; his play in the park had occupied three.[35]

After council on May 10 we find him playing sentinel before the fort while one of his young companions attacked it. The players were diverted, however, by the sound of trumpets heralding the signing of a truce with the rebellious princes.[36] It had been necessary for Louis to send money to Soissons to enable the formerly insurgent leaders to pay off their troops, the lords would not renew their allegiance to the Crown until they could induce the king to produce the wherewithal to persuade their soldiers to go home.

The *Mercure* was to rejoice that, with Concini's demise, peace had been restored to France in a "wink of the eye."[37]

The same day that Louis interrupted war games with his age-mates in order to give attention to the agreement whereby the *grands* laid down their arms, Alphonse Du Travail was executed in the Place de Grève, where Leonora Galigai would follow him two months later.

Du Travail

No fate worse than exile was to befall Marie de Medici, but certain evidence suggests that her son indeed entertained thoughs of having her killed. The facts connected with the prosecution and conviction of Alphonse Du Travail are especially suggestive.

Du Travail had been one of the intimate circle that plotted the murder of Concini,[38] although testimony against him later held that "he insinuated himself" in the undertaking with such "artfulness" that the conspirators "had been constrained to let him know about it." The author of the *Relation exacte* says that Du Travail had offered to get rid of Ancre all by himself while the king was out hunting and to conceal the deed for twenty-four hours by some means. The same writer reports that Du Travail had the "effrontery" to repeat his proposal to the king himself. Yet certainly Louis must have been willing to hear such an offer, already presented to Luynes. After all, the king was actively entertaining various strategies to dispose of the maréchal, and several others had offered their services for the task.

"They" tried to "be rid of" Du Travail, the same account continues, presumably because Louis and his intimates had already decided upon an assassination plan of their own. Nevertheless, the man persisted, proposing to perform another service for the king—to dispose of his mother. This proposal, too, may have been made before Ancre's death; Louis seems to have heard it also without taking immediate action against Du Travail. On May 2, however, a week after the murder and one day before Marie's departure, Du Travail was imprisoned and charged with treason.

The case was pushed with urgency from the Louvre. Louis took a personal interest in bringing about a conviction; Déageant later wrote Richelieu that "His Majesty has taken great pains [*un grand soing*] in this affair."[39] On May 5 Luynes joined two other courtiers, Bressieux,[40] and L'Espinette, in testifying against Du Travail. The verdict was expected the next day, a Saturday, but was postponed, possibly because of differences within the court. This is suggested by the fact that a parliamentary delegation of the "king's men" called upon Louis at Vincennes on May 6, apparently to consult with him on the progress of the trial.[41]

The decision on the case was finally reached on Wednesday, May 10, as Déageant announced in his letter to Richelieu at Blois. Du Travail was to be judged that day, he wrote, and it was expected that he would be found guilty, condemned to death, and executed. The royal prosecutors, he added, were demanding that he be burned alive.[42] The more usual punishment was to strangle the condemned person before igniting his body; the proposal to deny this mercy to him may have been made on Louis's suggestion or with his concurrence.[43]

Suffering preliminary torture, Du Travail was said to have confessed to "most" of the accusation and to have remarked "that he would have made no difficulties over killing his own father and mother for the good of the state."[44] Did he also resolve to die for the state without revealing the extent to which intimates of the king, and perhaps the king himself, had been party to his murderous plans? Luynes's and Louis's part in the prosecution suggest this possibility, although their assiduity had been explained by the claim that the protection of Marie herself made it necessary to punish such *complots* ruthlessly. The execution of Du Travail served to advertise the king's concern for his mother's welfare.

It did not, however, lay to rest popular suspicions of the former regent. More than a month after Du Travail's death, an Italian commuter between Paris and Blois wrote to Richelieu that just the day before a man had been arrested for saying that the queen mother had only to return to Paris in order to bring off [*achever*] the murder of the king according to plans she had laid for this purpose.[45] Apparently the notion persisted in some quarters that Marie was part of the conspiracy that the Ancres were supposed to have formed against Louis. And, as we have seen, Louis himself seems to have shared this view at least part of the time.

Nevertheless, asserting Louis's solicitude for Marie had now become important in order to defend the king against the charge of callousness in her regard. On the day Du Travail was executed Luynes wrote Richelieu to express happiness at learning of Marie's safe arrival in Blois. The favorite assured the bishop of Louis's deep concern for his mother's welfare and reported that the king had taken care, on each day of her journey, to inquire of her health from persons arriving in court who had passed her party on the road.[46]

Leonora

No document suggests that the queen mother was at all interested in the alleged crimes of the doomed Du Travail. It was otherwise, however, with her concern for her friend the maréchale d'Ancre. But the court had made it clear that any attempt to intervene in Leonora's fate would be useless and damaging to Marie herself. And certainly, whatever the queen's deficiencies of insight may have been, she no longer underestimated her eldest son's obduracy.

Almost immediately after Concini was killed, his widow was placed under arrest and isolated in the Louvre. During the next few days, she was subjected to indignities associated with the search and seizure of her belongings. She seems to have realized Marie's powerlessness to help her virtually from the beginning. Learning that her royal patron was isolated and detained in her own apartments, she said, in a mixture of Italian and French, "Poor woman—I have been the cause of her downfall! [*Je l'ai perdoua!*]"[47]

In detailing his complaints against Concini to visiting members of Parlement, Louis had accused Leonora of having participated in plans "to make me die and to keep my mother always dependent on her will."[48] One of the charges brought against the maréchale was that her great influence over Marie had been acquired by magic. Richelieu, who apparently played a part in persuading the queen not to attempt to rescue her friend, may have realized that any such effort would have been counterproductive, if only because it would have indicated that Marie was not yet freed from Leonora's "spell." This was the accusation of Père Coton, the maréchale's former friend. He wrote the Marquis de Nerestang that he now hoped the case against "*La Conchine*"—a derogatory designation—would disclose the "Jewish charms" that she had used to keep Marie in thrall so that that "good princess" could be released from her companion's sorcery, but that this would be impossible so long as the bewitcher, who was possessed by a demon, continued to live.[49] In the same letter the priest reported that the imprisoned Leonora had made derogatory remarks about her mistress. In fact, such allegations were baseless; there is considerable evidence that the matron of honor remained loyal to the queen mother to the end.[50]

Nor does Marie's silence concerning the fate of her friend seem to indicate a betrayal on her part. If Richelieu contributed to this silence it was because of the clear signs from Louis's entourage that the king would interpret any intervention from his mother on Leonora's behalf as an action inimical to himself.[51] Marie was by no means averse to pleading for clemency for her own creatures; her efforts on Barbin's behalf had been vigorous. The former finance minister, however, was not only a person with a reputation for probity but also an outsider for whom Louis could have been expected to have few intense feelings. Leonora, by contrast, had been a familiar of the royal household since before the young king's birth, and her high degree of intimacy with all his family could not have left Louis indifferent. However great her loyalty to all of them, she, like her husband, had become enormously rich in their service.

During the first days of her captivity, Leonora showed that she expected to benefit from benevolent feelings that she believed the king had for her. Oblivious to his ill will, the queen's old friend appealed to him more than once, referring to the intimate and rather amiable footing on which their relationship had been based. While she was still held in the Louvre, a servitor suggested that she give him something from her remaining treasures because eventually everything would be taken from her. She refused with these words: "You think the king would want to take away my dress? I don't believe it!"[52] Yet the king was ready to do that, and worse.

A few days later, on April 28, Leonora was deprived of almost all her servants and portable possessions (she was left without even a change of undershirt)[53] and was imprisoned in the Bastille. When Du Hallier, the new captain of Louis's guards, arrived to escort her to the dread fortress, she begged him to remind his master that "she had formerly seen him [Louis] emerge from his mother's womb."[54]

When Louis's first joyous exuberance at Ancre's death had subsided, he claimed to some that he had intended to bring the maréchal to trial and allow justice to run its course. Now the young king proposed to rectify his departure from this plan by following it in Leonora's case, as well as by trying the "memory of Concini" through a posthumous legal process. In a letter patent to the court of Parlement on May 9, charges against the dead man were coupled with new ones against his widow. It declared that she had been a "participant" in her husband's "crimes and conspiracies" against "our person and our state" and called for her indictment and trial "according to the laws and ordinances of our realm."[55] In her case, however, the forces of "justice" were not to be allowed to proceed without direct participation by Louis himself.

Thirty-six hours after Louis signed the inculpating letter, his guards captain arrived in the middle of the night to conduct the Florentine woman from the Bastille to a "nasty little cell" in the Conciergerie. There she remained under close guard until, ten days later, she was brought for the first time before the magistrates appointed to judge her.[56] In the days of questioning that followed, this court asked Leonora to respond to accusations that she had been an accomplice in the alleged crimes of her husband: usurpation of the king's authority and trafficking with foreign powers. Both these offenses constituted "human" treason; like the "divine" variety, they were capital offenses. Leonora's testimony in her defense was cogent. She scoffed at the accusation that she had practiced magic and consorted with sorcerers; her powers over Marie were owed to nothing more than her ability to serve. And she insisted that if her husband had had treacherous designs against the state or the king she had known nothing of them.

Evidence that there had been attempts to exorcise Leonora, who had suffered from nervous disorders for more than a decade, brought out nothing that was obviously incompatible with Catholic ritual, especially Italian ritual, of the time. Testimony at the trial gave details about the religious rites that had been held for her. Some of these had taken place at an Augustinian monastery under the sponsorship of its prior, Père Roger Girard. It gradually appeared that Girard was a doctor of theology of notable reputation. Before 1600, while sojourning in Italy, he had been appointed confessor to Marie de Medici herself and assigned to accompany her on her removal to

France. He had not become Leonora's confessor until her marriage to Concini. Again, it was Marie who had imported a group of Italian Ambrosian monks who were specialists in exorcising rites.[57]

Further evidence indicated that Leonora's "Jewish connection" was also effected by the queen mother. Montalto, a noted Jewish physician, had been called in to treat Leonora in 1607 while he was stopping in Paris on his way to Italy. The treatment seemed a great success; the patient was cured. Montalto went on to Florence, where he became physician to the grand duke, Marie's uncle. It was Marie who invited the doctor to come to the French court in 1612. She had recently lost some of her own medical staff and asked Duke Ferdinand to release Montalto and send him to her. She also wrote to the pope to ask for his approval of the doctor's entering her service for the sake of her health and that of her household.[58] After Montalto's death, efforts were made to replace his counsel by consulting other Jewish scholars on the Hebrew texts he had used. One such scholar was found, through Elisabeth's Spanish almoner, to be living with David Rivault de Fleurance, Louis's tutor at the time and another figure closely connected with Marie. Such high sponsorship tended to make it difficult to inculpate Leonora for illegal magical practices.[59]

As for "human" treason, letters of courtesy exchanged between her and the duke of Lerma and other Spanish notables were brought as evidence of treacherous behavior although these, too, were certainly exchanges on behalf of Marie, whose enthusiasm for Spanish links has already been remarked.[60] Further, the maréchale's demand that the charge of her political crimes be considered separately from those laid at the feet of Concini was backed by the general awareness that the couple had lived apart for several years,[61] a fact of which Louis was certainly aware. Even the prince de Condé, himself imprisoned in the Bastille, presumably by Concini's orders, expressed pity, before Leonora's trial, for the injustice done her. "It was not she who was guilty of the ills of France," he asserted, "but her husband."[62]

In view of the problematical nature of the charges against Leonora it is not surprising that some who were well-informed on secular legal procedure did not believe that the evidence against her supported a capital sentence. Soon after her imprisonment Déageant's letter to Richelieu, who was with the queen mother at Blois, also showed some uncertainty: "They're working on the trial of the 'better half [*la moitié*],' and believe that they'll find enough to pull if off with [*à quoi en venir à bout*]."[63]

How then was her condemnation achieved?

Some sources alleged that Luynes persuaded one or more of the crown prosecutors to demand the death penalty by promising that the king would subsequently grant grace to the maréchale.[64] At the same time, according to one informant, Louis's favorite was said to have visited each of the judges privately to warn them of danger to the queen mother should Leonora continue to live.[65] As in the case of Du Travail, some of those close to Louis found it expedient to suggest that sinister powers around the court threatened the life of Marie de Medici. And Louis's suspicions may have provoked a last-moment attempt by Leonora's judges to get her to admit some complicity in the assassination of Henri. "I know nothing about that!" the unfortunate woman replied angrily to her interlocutor.[66] The attempt to inculpate her on this score, however, seems to have been no more than half-hearted.

While legal formalities were observed in Leonora's case, the outcome was the same as that of the more summary procedure that ended her husband's life: on the same day that the court found her guilty of treason, both "divine and human," she was taken in a cart across the river to the scaffold in front of the Hôtel de Ville. There, before an enormous and hushed crowd, she was decapitated and her body burned, following out the sentence the judges had pronounced.[67] Almost to the end, apparently, Leonora disbelieved in Louis's ill will toward her. About to be executed, she asked one of her interrogators, Voisin, "If you see the king, I pray you to tell him that I beg him to leave to my son and my brother the properties that I have in France."[68]

The calm and dignity with which Leonora met her execution excited widespread appreciation. Her resignation and decorum tended to bely the official image of her—apparently the public had expected to witness the burning of a witch. The *Mercure* reported, however, that although the condemned woman had a dark [*noir*] complexion and her face was wrinkled and freckled, the great crowd found that she "did not seem as ugly as they had imagined."[69] Leonora, in turn, cried to God, "I forgive the king and the queen [presumably Anne], and all these people who wish me ill."[70]

Leonora had been surprised by her sentence of death; Louis was not. On the day of the execution he hunted stag at Saint-Germain. He was in at the kill. In the evening he had himself put to bed at about the same time the maréchale was mounting the scaffold. According to Héroard, "they" had talked about the event to him so much that he was in "continual apprehension," unable to fall asleep until half past three in the morning.[71] It is not clear to what this apprehension was due. It may have been a fear that could be calmed only by Leonora's death. Indeed, Morgues reported that her judges had been told "*de la part du Roy*" that Louis feared for his life if Leonora was not condemned.[72] At the least, Louis's part in bringing about her condemnation had been considerable. Nor had he done anything to prevent the execution by granting his mother's former companion the grace of pardon and exile.

The accused woman's last plea at her interrogation probably seemed justified to those best informed in the matter: "I don't deserve to die. I wouldn't have minded if they had found me [guilty of] something, perhaps that I was too curious [*fort curieuse*] [about occult practices], but that doesn't deserve death. If they sent me back to my country without a scrap of clothing [*tout nue*] it wouldn't bother me that they'd taken everything—I would still be able to earn my living again."[73] Against the combination of emotions and interests that brought Leonora to the scaffold, however, the truth was of no avail.

DIVIDING THE SPOILS

As a foreigner in France, Leonora, unlike many of the *grands* who were to suffer from the Crown's justice in the coming years, had no powerful supporters willing to make her case their own. And, as she pointed out during her captivity, there were some at court who expected to benefit from confiscation of the Concinis' many properties. She complained of her judges: "They are making me die because I am a foreigner. They are wicked people who make me die to have my property."[74]

Indeed, the process of seizing and redistributing the Ancres' possessions had begun with the looting, by soldiers and courtiers, of Concini's dead body as it lay in the courtyard of the Louvre. Later, Du Hallier, Vitry's brother, discovered a box of valuable jewels the Florentine marshal had left with an apothecary for safekeeping. This Louis "bestowed" upon the guards captain, sight unseen, without requiring him to account for its contents.[75] As for Vitry himself, "they couldn't recompense enough the executive of the king's vengeance." He claimed some of the Concinis' liquid possessions on May 2, before the maréchale had come before any judge.[76] But there were many other properties that were not so easily transferred. To such transfers, moreover, Leonora's continued existence constituted a legal obstacle. The marquisate of Ancre, for example, was in her name, like many other valuable assets that she possessed by virtue of the queen mother's favor. Apparently, a number of these were assigned to various members of Louis's circle even before judgment had been pronounced on their owner. In fact, the attribution of a good many of her possessions "was known in advance."[77] The main beneficiaries of these transfers of assets were Vitry, those, like Du Hallier, who had helped execute the coup, and Luynes and his brothers.

On the night of Ancre's murder a group came to the king's *coucher* "to ask him for the unfortunate man's spoils." Among these was Louis's half brother the chevalier de Vendôme, who asked for the abbey of Marmoustier, one of the richest in France. Its abbot was Leonora's brother, who was accused of no crime. Nevertheless, the prize was accorded to the petitioner, "in case it became vacant."[78] Thus, when Leonora, about to mount the scaffold two months later, pleaded for conservation of her brother's rights, she was unaware that he had long since been ousted from his principal holding in favor of Louis's intermittently loved and hated childhood companion, Alexandre de Vendôme.

The most powerful office Concini left vacant was that of maréchal. Two days after the murder of the Florentine, the assassin Vitry took the oath, at Louis's hands, of maréchal de France. One Sieur de Géran had much earlier been promised the first vacancy in this high post, but now he was told that this was no normal vacancy—that "it was not reasonable that Vitry should have killed Conchino for him."[79] Luynes took the office that had given Ancre title to be on intimate footing with the king—first gentleman of the chamber. Ancre had already bought the survivance of this post for his only son, Henri, now thirteen years old, but neither legal niceties nor his condemned mother's plea served the child any better than they had his father or his uncle. The expropriation was validated retroactively by the same order that condemned Leonora to death: punishment for the parents' "crimes" was visited upon the son: all his titles to property and nobility were revoked. After Leonora's execution Louis issued a decree, validated by Parlement on July 22, awarding the remainder of Henri Concini's confiscated property and posts to that other godson of Henri IV, Charles de Luynes.[80] Without this measure, the young Henri would have been entitled to compensation for his losses; his father had no doubt paid high prices to obtain his son's succession to his many offices.

Henri Concini's fate attracted a certain attention. It does not seem to have provoked comment, however, that he had been familiar to the fifteen-year-old monarch since babyhood. The pathos of the boy's position is accented by the subservience he showed where Louis was concerned. His docility is evocative of the behavior of another childhood servitor of the young king—and still another namesake and protégé of the great Henri—Henri de Verneuil, Louis's young half brother. When, soon after his mother's arrest, the Concini child was discovered in the Louvre hungry and abandoned, he was reported to have said, "Miserable as you see me today, I still had the honor to present the king with his shirt four times and to take the oath for the office of his First Gentleman of the Chamber."[81]

Despite allegations to the contrary,[82] Henri Concini persisted in this deferential attitude toward Louis during his short lifetime, even after he had taken refuge in Florence from the wretched legacy of his parents' reputations. When French armies had passed into Italy after defeating the defenders of La Rochelle and lifting the siege of Casal, Henri Concini wrote Richelieu, now Louis's prime minister, asking his advice on how to gratify his "passionate desire to serve the king."[83] It is not clear whether or not the Ancres' son owed his escape from France with his life to any clemency of Louis. One of the tracts about the ill-fated Florentine favorites that flooded French presses in 1617 has their "shades" rejoicing that their son "did not follow our fatal path"; the shade of Concini observes, "The king has always been sweet and kind to him."[84] On the other hand, a letter exists from Richelieu, then in the queen mother's service, to Puisieux, one of Louis's ministers of state, thanking him on behalf of Marie for having been instrumental in securing the freedom of the Concinis' only surviving child. It is unlikely that Marie dared intervene directly on behalf of Henri Concini, and it is not clear whether Louis was willing to do anything for him either—except to take credit for being so lenient as to allow him to live.[85]

LIKE FATHER, LIKE SON?

Louis returned with his court to the Louvre late on May 13 to prepare for Pentecost and also for the solemn rite that was performed each May 14— the commemoration of the murder of his father. The present occasion was especially memorable, for Cardinal Du Perron, whose ecclesiastical and political roles had been so intertwined with Henri's establishment of the Bourbon dynasty, conducted the ceremonies as *grand aumônier*. Indisposition had prevented him from doing so for the previous several years.

Now that the war was over, the *noblesse* turned out in huge numbers. Attendance at the afternoon ceremony of thaumaturgy was also spectacular. The record crowd formed a parade so long that it stretched almost the whole length of the great gallery of the Tuileries.[86] The king touched eight hundred and twenty-six subjects who presented themselves as suffering from scrofula. Such ritual touching was a royal function that had been given renewed importance during Henri's lifetime.

In the general euphoria after Ancre's death the name of Henri IV was often evoked. For many, as for Bassompierre, the new court held out the promise of a return to the happy days of the *vert galant*. Older courtiers were delighted that Louis knew how to reproduce the informal ways of his father. When, for example, he returned to Saint-Germain to hunt, for the first time since his coup, he joined a group of nobles at the supper table in a surprise visit. Refusing to permit them to rise for him, he seated himself between the dukes of Rohan and Mayenne, old companions of the *vert galant*, and, after receiving their toasts, "supped with the whole company, and allowed them all sorts of liberty."[87]

In one matter Louis's behavior was known to be unlike his father's. The young king's marriage had still to be consummated, unless we accept the report he made to Héroard on his wedding night. In any case, he had not shared a bed with *"la petite reine"* since that time nearly two years before, although Anne was allowed to follow him on some of his excursions and to join in some of his play. A court historian later explained that "those who were responsible for the physical care of his majesty [feared] . . . that in the tenderness of his age . . . regular knowledge of his wife would harm his health, exhaust his strength, and prevent him from growing and perfecting his natural vigor."[88] A sixteen-year-old's abstinence, of course, was unlikely to raise anxiety among his subjects, except possibly for the contrast it presented with the sexually precocious Henri.

But this was, after all, only a matter of style. What might, with more prescience, have excited some concern were signs of how policy might be conducted in the future. On this point Louis tried to give the impression that he would tread the path blazed by his revered father. Among his first words had been his call for the "old servitors of the late king, my father." "By their counsel," said he, "I wish henceforth to govern myself."[89] His words were immediately belied by the fact that Sully, prominent among his father's old counselors, was not among those whom Louis had chosen for his new council. As the situation developed, it presented other features that did not suggest that the course of affairs under Louis would follow the same direction in Henri's reign.

A rather curious report may be further evidence that following his father's example was not always in Louis's mind. In the written communications he exchanged with his mother while he held her under house arrest, he is said to have claimed, "God had me born a king"[90]—a statement at variance with the facts, as the queen mother knew at least as well as anyone! Marie herself, of course, had had little influence on state affairs while Henri lived and was now banished. The emotional significance of this for Louis may have been that, since his mother had come to represent his father, her removal caused a renewal of those pleasant feelings that had followed his liberation by Henri's death. Richelieu, whose "tyranny" Louis had exulted in escaping, had accompanied the queen mother in her exile, having replaced Concini as her chief political advisor. He therefore had seemingly not only stepped into the shoes of the Florentine, but also, as Concini had done before him, into those of Henri himself. For Louis, this could be a double reason to keep the ambitious prelate at a distance. And, indeed, the king soon asked him to remain in his priory at Coussaye, away from the queen. A further command from Louis banished the bishop from the realm itself, exiling him to the papal city of Avignon. Voluminous correspondence aimed at reinstating Richelieu in favor at court failed to have an effect, despite the apparent support given to the effort by Luynes and several of his friends. One who followed these thwarted attempts at a comeback came to the conclusion that it was the unwillingness of Louis himself to have the bishop return that accounted for the failure of these persistent efforts.[91]

More significant still may have been the fact that Père Coton, Louis's confessor since his first communion, was banished soon afterward. This priest had also been Henri's confessor, an apparently complaisant monitor of those royal sins that an earlier confessor had dared denounce from the pulpit.[92] Père Jean Arnoux, who was chosen to replace Coton, was known as one of the "roughest adversaries of Protestantism in France."[93] This Jesuit priest's especially fiery attacks in June 1617 aroused deeper anxieties among the Protestant ministry than had been felt since the death of their protector, Louis's father. Coton, on the other hand, was credited with exceptionally pleasing manners. That the young king decided to dispense with his services suggests that he meant to be governed by a conscience, however stringent, that was less closely associated with Henri le Grand and to lend himself to religious aims that Henri had rejected.

Sojourning at Fontainebleau at the beginning of the summer, the court was "so swollen [*grosse*]" that it comprised as many as thirty-four princes. But whereas his father had had informal relations with his retinue, Louis doubled the number of his guards in spite of warnings that this might make the *grands* uneasy. "He said that wherever he went he wanted to be master," Robert Arnauld reports,[94] possibly with some misgivings. Perhaps the intent of this precaution was to put to rest Louis's lifelong feeling—not shared by his father—that an inadequate train of *suivants* might diminish his sense of completeness.

On the whole, observers rejoiced at the apparent course of events in the first few months after Louis's triumph. Yet there were a few—very few—reservations. The jurist Nicolas Pasquier gave his private appraisal of Louis in a letter to a friend written soon after the coup. He acclaimed the king's "sound and level-headed" resolve, but he was not without doubts about the future. Power was a heady intoxicant, he reflected, and he was wary lest the young king, beginning his active rule with such an overwhelming stroke, might overreach the proper limits and pursue violent aims. He should heed the voice of the people, through which God speaks, and its demand for peace, which is the main objective of governments.[95] A widely distributed periodical sounded a similar warning: the sovereign is "guardian of the republic," and though it is not for subjects to question the will of the prince, he must remember that the state is perpetual, that the people never die; consequently he holds his authority only in trust.[96]

Such twinges of apprehension might have been stronger had the sources of Louis's hatred for Ancre been better understood. We have noted that part of Louis's resentment derived from jealousy of the Florentine's military pretensions. A royal historian in the young king's confidence would later explain that his animosity toward Ancre was partly owed to the obstacles Concini put in the way of Louis's demonstrating his personal courage, presumably in battle.[97] Opportunities for such brave displays would soon arrive for Louis—but they would also be cause for public regret that the peace that had arrived in a "wink of the eye" had not been somewhat more durable.

Another private letter a few months after Ancre's death described Louis to an old follower of Henri, the sieur de Mirancourt, then in Venice. It noted virtues in the adolescent ruler that were already well advertised: his fitness and endurance, his skill and knowledge in horsemanship and military arts, the temperance of his habits—abstinence at the table and modesty in dress—his religious zeal, his intelligence and good judgment, his sagacious restraint. "We owe the fortunate success of the coup that he had struck last year to his wise . . . silence." Perhaps even the stutter was an advantage, for "facility" in a monarch is unfortunate: "Louis XIII will never be fairly accused of that failing."

The writer, Bellemaure, then remarks on other characteristics bearing little resemblance to those that made Henri beloved. The young son of the still-mourned *"père du peuple"* is "extraordinarily jealous" of his authority, and it would be an "audacious subject who did not comply when he assumes the tone of master." Furthermore, "one sees his edicts more religiously observed than those of any of his predecessors . . . even than of his father," whose clemency was, however, a safeguard against abuses. Yet perhaps the son's greater severity is a virtue too. With him, "the example of two or three heedless ones . . . dragged ignominiously [through the streets] quite dead, sets a brake."[98] The king who is here described might have reminded Bellemaure, as he seems sometimes to have reminded Héroard, more of Henri III than of Henri IV.

On the day after his murder Louis's father had been officially acclaimed as "Henri le Grand." The clement king's reign had ended with his death through the violent act of another. Louis justified the act of violence that began his own rule partly as a vindication of his murdered predecessor. His historiographer writes: "The people, remembering the condition to which [Ancre] . . . had brought France, forcing the princes to take refuge . . . and the continuation of the war . . . , recognized an act of justice in the death of that *ambitieux* and gave much praise to the king, and it was chiefly then that they began to give to our great Louis the title of Just."[99] Bellemaure, too, agrees that the title of "Just" is appropriate for Louis. He concludes: "He lets regular justice take its course, having learned that the best cement of his law is the blood of those who scorn it."[100] The first part of this affirmation seems more doubtful than the second.

As time passed, another difference began to be noticed between "Louis le Juste" and "Henri le Grand." Louis's father, in contrast to his Valois predecessor, had been known for not relying on favorites for political decision making. In the first celebration of Ancre's murder Louis, too, had announced his resolution to "take care of the affairs of my realm myself."[101] But within a few weeks of the coup, Louis's dependence on Luynes had become evident to many. As new, and bloodier, civil wars broke out in the next few years, surreptitious pamphlets would begin to liken the new first gentleman of the king's chamber to his predecessor, whose recent murder had been hailed as inaugurating a more peaceful era, and to say that "little had been gained by the change."[102] From many sides Louis would once again be exhorted to take the affairs of his realm into his own hands.[103] And some time after Luynes's death in 1621, Louis would tell yet another alter ego—Richelieu—that he had never wished his former falconer to have the highest military post in France, that he had bestowed it on him against his will as a result of trickery [*"par art"*],[104] just as he had told those who gathered around him after the coup against Ancre that he had never wanted Concini to be maréchal de France.

But in that summer of 1617—the most joyous of the reign—the era of favorites had barely begun.

EPILOGUE

Louis's feelings of strength and dominance, raised high by his triumph over the Ancres and the exile of his mother and Richelieu, were reinforced in the months that followed. Less than a week after Leonora's execution, the king was to stage-manage the imprisonment and decapitation of an insubordinate great lord of Brittany, foiling, by dissimulation, a scheme of his own half brother César de Vendôme to arrange the rebel's rescue.

But in matters of great moment it was Luynes who was to dominate state affairs in the four years ahead. The former falconer sometimes repaid the honor, wealth, and power that Louis continued to heap upon him by measures that increased the king's self-confidence. One of these measures was taken when Louis was seventeen. In large part through Luynes's encouragement and facilitation, the young king was finally able to consummate his marriage—an act that had only been symbolized by the ritual of 1615. Further, with Luynes guiding policy, Louis was able, in 1620, to lead his armies into Béarn and Navarre, the Protestant homeland of his father, where he easily reestablished the authority of the Crown and the privileges of the Catholic church—an achievement that had eluded his father (or that had been avoided by him).

As Luynes's power grew, however, he became overbearing and less heedful of Louis's dignity. The king's feelings for the older man were increasingly colored by the jealousy and spite that had been ingredients of most of his childhood loves. Nor were all succeeding campaigns against rebel Huguenots as successful as the first ones, and Luynes, now constable of France by virtue of Louis's favor, was held responsible for military setbacks. The favorite was reproached, from one side, by Ultramontanist factions for excessive compromising with the Huguenots and, from the other, by the Huguenots themselves, for persecuting them. Such criticisms of his regime gave Louis additional reasons to despise his creature. Luynes's death, at the end of 1621, was felt as a release by the king, whose continuing romantic relations with Anne and pride in his military enterprises were evidence of a new-found sense of autonomy. Thus, for a time, he was able to resist the efforts of his mother, who had been formally reunited with her son in 1620, to regain a place in the council of state.

During his period of dominance, Luynes, preoccupied by growing domestic unrest, had permitted successful challenges by the Spanish Habsburg powers to France's influence in the states on her eastern border. Louis's ever-present anxiety that his possessions might slip away was rekindled by these trends. The queen mother, advised by Richelieu, courted her son by stressing the threat such trends posed to the kingdom's reputation and Louis's glory. She urged him to be militant. This approach succeeded: in 1622 Richelieu was finally made a cardinal and Marie was readmitted to the council.

In the same year the king's brief experience of domestic happiness came to an end when Anne suffered the first of several miscarriages. Louis blamed her and her friends for the loss. His anger and disappointment were expressed by renewed mistrust of his wife and the reestablishment of an emotional distance from her, although then, as throughout most of the rest of his life, he continued to perform his conjugal duties fairly regularly.

Once more lacking the power or the perseverance to control events, Louis gradually lowered his defenses against his mother and her advisor. In April of 1624 the cardinal entered the council of state. Quickly acquiring preeminence in the direction of state affairs, Richelieu showed himself to be more effective than Luynes had been in implementing Louis's demand for authority over rebellious subjects. In 1627 the cardinal successfully directed the reinforcement of bastions against English forces off the coast of La Rochelle; in the following year he brought the long siege of that Protestant stronghold to a conclusion. Héroard died during the siege, in February 1628, at the age of seventy-seven. To the last he had tried to record and to preside over the health of his master and also to organize medical care for the encamped French troops. On learning of his death Louis is said to have expressed regret because he felt a continued need for his oldest intimate retainer. In fact, Héroard's disappearance was soon followed by Louis's increased dependence upon Richelieu and his expression of warmer feelings toward the cardinal.

For the cardinal had been slow to win the king's personal trust. The fear and animus paternal figures sometimes aroused in Louis had been aroused by Richelieu, although the fact that the older man was a priest seems to have mitigated somewhat Louis's feelings of being threatened by him. During the course of the campaign against La Rochelle, moreover, the prime minister proved that he was adept in showing off his ruler to best advantage and also in facilitating the hunt and the military excursions and exercises that were necessary to prevent the king from succumbing to black moods and lassitude. Further, no sooner had Louis made his triumphant entrance into the ruined city of La Rochelle and accepted the obeisance of its survivors than the cardinal showed his readiness to take aggressive action in order to expel outsiders from French areas of commitment beyond the eastern frontier. He turned immediately to the task of warding off further intrusions from the powers allied with Spain.

Marie had always been drawn to just those powers; she had not understood Richelieu's deeply Gallican sentiments, and she now increasingly aligned herself against the cardinal on the side of a faction in the government that was willing to take its lead from the pope, in favor of staying at peace with Spain and its allies in return for concessions to them. With whatever help could be provided by Anne, her Spanish daughter-in-law, she struggled to turn her son against his prime minister.

Instead, Louis warmly endorsed Richelieu's warlike purposes and enthusiastically supported his project for an alpine campaign. Together, in midwinter, they were able to lift a siege of Casal by Spanish-supported forces and reinstall a French garrison there. In the following months the king continued to support the cardinal in resisting Habsburg threats and in seeking allies among Protestant powers. Louis also agreed to renew religious guarantees of the Edict of Nantes for Huguenot cities that put down their arms.

Thus, when, in 1630, Marie forced her son to choose between herself and Richelieu, the king rejected her a second time. For Louis, at last, the enemies of France, and of himself, had once more become the "enemies of Papa"—Spain, the empire, and the Ultramontanists. The queen mother was barred from the court and soon fled to Brussels. Despite her efforts, she was never permitted by Louis to return to France until her death, in 1642.

The twelve years of collaboration between Richelieu and the king that followed Marie's banishment have been called a "bicephalic" monarchy. Without intensive examination of each major decision it is often difficult to distinguish the respective roles of king and cardinal in shaping policy. But documentary evidence shows that the reputation for rigor won by their regime was due at least as much to Louis's dispositions as to his minister's. The executions and imprisonments that were ordered after the defeat of the queen mother's party had the king's active support; his implacability in the face of his younger brother's rivalry, his mother's petitions, and the challenges of rebellious noblemen was at least as great as Richelieu's. Louis's antipathy to Spanish pretensions and his indifference to papal claims for authority were of long standing and owed nothing to his minister's influence.

The role taken by the king in managing state affairs is fairly easy to identify. In the war against Spain—openly declared in 1635—we see Richelieu planning grand strategy, foreseeing contingencies, offering the king alternative courses of action. Louis reviews his minister's proposals, usually ratifying them but sometimes hardening them; considers in detail the minutiae of military planning, particularly concerning the care of the troops and appointment of personnel; and, when he is permitted, takes a personal part in the life of his soldiers.

He dutifully and diligently performs the ceremonial role of king. But also, especially in army matters, he is, as before, the corporal rather than the commander. As the years pass, his affective relationship with Richelieu becomes more intense; he is dependent upon the older man for the recreations so necessary to him, for his domestic peace, and for approval and admiration.

Although Louis's romantic relationship with the queen had been replaced by habitual mistrust and estrangement, the couple's sexual relations continued to be exclusively with each other. The reward for this fidelity, after twenty-three years of marriage, was the birth of a dauphin in 1638. The continuity of the dynasty was further ensured by the birth of a second royal prince two years later. Though Louis was gleeful at the effect of these events in dashing the hopes of Gaston, his younger brother, to succeed to the throne, they did not transform him into a solicitous, loving father. His indifference to his queen's devotion to her children was also evident. The birth of the future Louis XIV, indeed, coincided with the commencement of Louis's passion for an eighteen-year-old guardsman, Henri d'Effiat, marquis de Cinq-Mars.

For it was not the queen but a series of young men (and, less intensely and more briefly, two young women) who were the objects of Louis's love. His infatuation with such favorites seemed to vary directly with the amount of suffering he experienced at their hands; Cinq-Mars, the last one, was the one who caused him the most pain. Although after Luynes Louis did not again delegate political power to one of his personal favorites, they had importance for state affairs, both by affecting the king's moods and by becoming focal points of court factions, usually directed against Richelieu's influence. Further, the king often confided his own critical thoughts of Richelieu to his loves of the moment.

Louis's modus vivendi with his prime minister never became easy or free of conflict. La Rochefoucauld's aphorism is apt: "He wanted to be ruled, but supported being so impatiently." He could be a brutal master, but he was also a fractious slave. Since he was no more inclined than he had ever been to tolerate adverse public opinion, he was most restive under Richelieu's leadership when military reverses, diplomatic setbacks, or public unrest gave fuel to the regime's critics. The king even encouraged Cinq-Mars in expectations that led him to seek support from the Spanish enemy in order to overthrow the cardinal. But when Richelieu exposed the treachery, Louis was at least as ruthless as his minister in ensuring that his former favorite and co-conspirator went to the scaffold.

Richelieu's death in December 1642 was not followed by a change in policy. The rigor of the regime, which had executed, banished, or imprisoned so many, continued. And so did the war. At the age of six Louis had told Madame de Vitry, "When I grow up, I want to go to war all the time." For almost all of his long reign he had his wish.

But without the support of Richelieu, the king's physical powers soon began to fail. Since childhood his life had been marked by periodic crises in health, mostly of a gastroenteric nature. In February 1643 he took to his bed with a persistent dysentery. The illness had ups and downs, but by April the king seemed resolved to die. He assured attendants that he set no value upon life—that he had never passed a day without some mortification, had never experienced an unalloyed joy. From then on he concentrated on dying with full observance of church requirements. He organized the mechanics of his physical care, lovingly designed all details of rituals accompanying his decline, and vigilantly supervised their performance. For these final days he was installed, not in his apartments in the old château at Saint-Germain en Laye, but in the king's chambers in the Château Neuf, where he had visited his father as a child. After May 7 he was given up for dead several times. On May 13 he was not expected to last the day. But he did not die until early in the morning of May 14, 1643, thirty-three years to the day after the murder of his father. The immediate cause of death was ulcerative colitis, the symptoms of which Héroard had described many years before.

Abbreviations

AMRE   Archives du Ministère des Relations Extérieures (France)

AN   Archives Nationales (France)

BL   British Library

BN   Bibliothèque Nationale (France) Département des Manuscrits

S. & B. Jean Héroard, *Journal de Jean Héroard sur l'enfance et la jeunesse de Louis XIII*, ed. Eudore Soulié and Edouard de Barthélemy, 2 vols. (Paris, 1868)

Notes

PREFACE: METHODS AND SOURCES

1. Hardouin Le Bourdays, *Discours sur l'ordre tenu de Leurs Majestes en entrant dans la ville du Mans . . .* (Le Mans, 1614), unpaginated.
2. John Morley, *The Life of William Ewart Gladstone,* 3 vols. (Macmillan, London: 1903), I, 10.
3. Etienne Baluze's handwritten inventory, "Catalogus librorum mss. bibliothecae Colbertinae," is Bibliothèque Nationale (hereafter cited as BN), nouvelle acquisition française (n. a.) 5692. In it, Héroard's diary is numbered 2601–2606.

CHAPTER 1: INTRODUCTION

1. Gérard de Contades, "Trois lettres de Nicolas de Vauquelin, sieur Des Yveteaux," *Bulletin de la Société Historique de l'Orne,* 8 (1889), 475–482.
2. See chapter 7, "Louis's Religion."

CHAPTER 2: THE FIRST FAMILY OF LOUIS XIII

1. Jean Héroard, *Journal de Jean Héroard sur l'enfance et la jeunesse de Louis XIII,* ed. Eudore de Soulié and Edouard de Barthélemy, 2 vols. (Paris, 1868), hereafter cited as S. & B., I, 367. October 20, 1608.
2. A list of the officers of the dauphin's household for his first year, dated April 13, 1602, names his nurse, Madame Bocquet (known as Doundoun—see below), third, after his governess and Mademoiselle Piolant, his sub-governess. Fifth on the list is Mademoiselle Le Mercier, chambermaid for serving him (*pour bailler*), followed by his chaplain-almoner, Monsieur Louis Boulongne, and his physician, in that order. Archives du Ministère des Relations Extérieures (hereafter cited as AMRE), Mémoires et documents 764, fol. 160 and 160v.
3. Joseph A. Schumpeter asserts of the Medicis: "They are the only merchants that ever rose to a footing of equality with the uppermost stratum of the feudal world." *Capitalism, Socialism and Democracy* (New York: Harper and Bros., 1947), 12f. n.
4. *Lettres missives du roi Henri IV,* ed. Berger de Xivrey and J. Guadet, 8 vols. (Paris, 1850–1873), V, 249. April 11, 1600.
5. Marie was born on April 26, 1573.

6. Archivio Gonzaga (Mantova), Francia, Correspondenza Estera (Serie E) 627, fol. 533. January 1, 1601. (Misdated 1608.)

7. Alexandre was also a name in the Bourbon family; it had been the name given Henri III by his godfather, Antoine de Bourbon, Henri IV's father. See Pierre Champion, *La jeunesse de Henri III* (Paris: Grasset, 1941), 8 n.

8. Quoted in Louis Batiffol, *La vie intime d'une reine de France* (Paris, 1906), I, 204.

9. A portrait of a woman in profile drawn by Marie as an adolescent shows her skill. It was presented by her to Philippe de Champaigne, the noted portraitist of Louis XIII's court, and is held by the Bibliothèque Nationale, Cabinet des Estampes. Her father, Grand Duke Francesco II, had been a passionate art patron and collector.

10. Accounts of these scenes, drawing on dispatches of various representatives at court, are in Berthold Zeller, *Henri IV et Marie de Médicis* (Paris, 1877), 99–118, 189–212. See also *Négociations diplomatiques de la France avec la Toscane,* ed. Giuseppe Canestrini and Abel Desjardins, 5 vols. (Paris, 1875), V, 458–462, 475–477, 496, 509, and Maximilien de Béthune, duc de Sully, *Mémoires,* 6 vols. (Paris, 1822), IV (1604–1606), 212; V (1607–1610), 111–114.

11. S. & B., I, 2–6. September 27, 1601.

12. Louise Bourgeois, *Récit véritable des naissances de messeigneurs et dames les enfans de France* (Paris, 1626), 116–120. This midwife's story that she teased the king by concealing the neonate's sex for a few minutes is not confirmed by any other observer.

13. S. & B., I, 20. March 19, 1602.

14. *Ibid.,* 7. October 5, 1601.

15. Adrien Blanchet, "Un médaillon de Jean Héroard," *Revue numismatique,* 11 (1893), 252–258, pl. 4.

16. Elizabeth W. Marvick, "The Character of Louis XIII: The Role of His Physician in Its Formation," *Journal of Interdisciplinary History,* 4 (1974), 347–374. Sources for the present discussion can be found in this article, unless otherwise noted.

17. Jean Héroard, *Discours des droits appartenans à la maison de Nevers es Duchés de Brabant, Lembourg et Ville d'Anvers, avec une table de la généalogie de ladicte maison pour la déclaration d'iceux* (Paris, 1581), unpaginated.

18. S. & B., I, 2. September 21, 1601. Officially, although he was the dauphin's "first" physician, he was only a *médecin ordinaire* in rank — that is, while Henri IV lived, subordinate to the king's first physician and, most likely, to several other doctors at court. See AMRE, Mémoires et documents 764, fol. 160v.

19. Musée de Chantilly, Bibliothèque Condé, "Hippostéologie," fol. 3.

20. Bound with Laurent Joubert, *Erreurs populaires* (Bordeaux, 1579), Bibliothèque Municipale de Montpellier, Réserve 30444.

21. S. & B., I, xlviif.

22. Louise Bourgeois, *Observations diverses sur la stérilité, perte de fruict, fécondité, accouchements et maladies des femmes et enfants nouveau naiz* (Paris, 1609), dedicatory page.

23. Bibliothèque Nationale, Imprimés Lb 35. 1053 (n. p., n. d.), folio.

24. *Lettres de Peiresc,* ed. Philippe Tamizey de Larroque, 7 vols. (Paris, 1880–1898), VII, 542; VI, 169. October 26, 1621; May 2, 1625.

25. S. & B., II, 330f.

26. Bibliothèque Nationale, Manuscrits, français 4022, fol. 2v. January 1, 1605.

27. For a comparison of Héroard's practices with ones then prevalent, see my "Character of Louis XIII," 357f.

28. S. & B., I, 7.

29. René Spitz, *The First Year of Life* (New York: International University Press, 1967), 64–67.

30. S. & B., I, 8. October 10, 1601.

31. Simon de Courtaud, "Journal de Jean Héroard," BN, n. a. 13008, fol. 12v. October 2,

1601, *et seq.* This contemporary abridgment of the first three-and-a-third years of Héroard's journal, for which the original is missing, gives many details omitted in the published version that is based upon it.

32. *Ibid.*, 13v. October 10–11, 1601.

33. S. & B., I, 7. October 5, 1601.

34. *Ibid.*, 16. December 27, 1601.

35. BN, n. a. 13008, fol 20. December 25, 1601.

36. *Ibid.*, fols. 13, 13v. October 6–14, 1601.

37. See, for the term and also for description of the experience, Donald W. Winnicott, "The Depressive Position in Normal Development," *Collected Papers* (London: Tavistock, 1968), 271.

38. See James Moloney, "Some Simple Cultural Factors in the Etiology of Schizophrenia," *Child Development*, 22 (1951), 163–183; Donald W. Winnicott, *The Child, the Family, and the Outside World* (Harmondsworth: Penguin, 1964), 43; Andrew Peto, "Body Image and Archaic Thinking," *International Journal of Psychoanalysis*, 40 (1959), 223–237.

39. See Donald W. Winnicott, "The Depressive Position" and "Primitive Emotional Development," *Collected Papers*, 262–273, 145–156.

40. BN, n. a. 13008, fol. 23v. February 16, 1602.

41. Spitz, *First Year*, 51f.

42. BN, n. a. 13008, fol. 22. January 15, 1602.

43. BN, fr. 10321, fol. 2. This very brief undated manuscript is mostly repetitive of Courtaud's. The detail just given, however, and a few others not to be found in Courtaud suggest that the author, like Courtaud, had access to the original version.

44. BN, fr. 4022, fol. 40. March 19, 1605. This is the first volume of what survives of Héroard's original manuscript. It commences on January 1, 1605.

45. *Ibid.*, fol. 224v. April 10, 1606.

46. S. & B., I, 195. June 27, 1606.

47. For a discussion of infant symbiosis and the conditions of early "hatching," see Margaret S. Mahler, Fred Pine, Anni Bergman, *The Psychological Birth of the Human Infant* (New York: Basic Books, 1975), 43–55. On the relationship of time of weaning to transitional objects, see Benjamin Spock, "The Striving for Autonomy and Regressive Object Relationships," *Psychoanalytic Study of the Child*, 18 (1963), 361–364.

48. BN, fr. 4022, fol. 50. April 3, 1605.

49. *Ibid.*, fol. 47v. March 31, 1605.

50. Eugène Griselle, ed., *Supplément à la maison du roi Louis XIII* (Paris: Editions de Documents d'Histoire, 1912), 34.

51. BN, Cinq cents Colbert 98, fols. 186–187.

52. S. & B., I, 22f. April 13, 1602. This routine handling probably frequently included the child's penis. Héroard does not, however, usually describe his own actions. An exception is a comment on the birth of Louis's first full brother, whom he observes to have an erection when he was about to be dressed for the first time. ".I felt it," the doctor reports. *Ibid.*, 258. April 16, 1607. (Note also the relationship between the familiar word for that member, "*guillery*"—literally, "pecker"—and "*le petit oiseau*" in the pulse.)

53. Héroard's first description of Louis was a head-to-toe "catalogue." (See BN, n. a. 13008, fols. 4f.) A reader notes, "One would have thought that the lord of Vaugrigneuse [Héroard's country estate] was taking inventory of his domain." C. Rossignol, *Louis XIII avant Richelieu* (Paris, 1869), 11.

54. See Mahler et al., *Psychological Birth*, 290.

55. BN, n. a. 13008, fols. 58v., 38v. March 26, 1603; February 9, 1604.

56. *Ibid.*, fol. 145. February 29, 1604.

57. BN, fr. 4022, fol. 245v. May 14, 1606.

58. *Ibid.*, fol. 211. February 20, 1606.
59. BN, fr. 10210, fol. 4. Another version of this manuscript, apparently copied somewhat later, is in BN, Cinq cents Colbert 98, fols. 177–213. The version edited by Georges Mongrédien, *Oeuvres complètes de Nicolas Vauquelin* (Paris: Picard, 1921; Slatkine reprint, Geneva, 1967), 156–177, does not follow either one with absolute fidelity.
60. For the possible significance of this designation, see below, chapter 3, "Encouraging Genitality," note 10.
61. BN, fr. 4022, fol. 275, 275v. July 21, 1607.
62. S. & B., I, 272. July 1, 1607.
63. *Ibid.*, 66. May 15, 1604.
64. *Ibid.*, 60. January 7, 1604.
65. BN, n. a. 13008, fol. 86. March 4, 1604.
66. BN, fr. 4022, fol. 40. May 19, 1605. Héroard was not alone in equating stubborn bad humor with the withholding of faeces—and words. An observant father of the time wrote to a relative that his little daughter was again taking the "path of internal closure" [i.e., constipation]: "stubborn . . . and taciturn." Henri Drouot, ed., "Un père de famille sous Henri IV: Lettres domestiques d'Etienne Bernard, 1598–1609," *Annales de Bourgogne,* 24 (1952), 161–175.
67. "Hippostéologie," quoted in La Croix Du Maine et Du Verdier, *Les bibliothèques françaises* (Paris, 1772), 444f.
68. BN, n. a. 13008, fol. 32v. May 11, 1602.
69. *Ibid.*, fol. 95; S. & B., I, 74f. May 17, June 12, July 2, 1604.
70. BN, fr. 4022, fol. 87v. June 25, 1605.
71. S. & B., I, 190. June 6, 1606.
72. *Ibid.*, 87, 137; BN, fr. 4022, fol. 68. September 12, 1604; May 21, June 23, 1605.
73. *Ibid.*, BN, fr. 4022, fol. 33. March 8, 1605.
74. See, for example, the struggle on August 19, 1604. BN, n. a. 13008, 118v.
75. *Ibid.*, fol. 79. January 8, 1604.
76. BN, fr. 4022, fol. 3v. January 8, 1605.
77. *Ibid.*, fol. 410. May 6, 1607. The case history of a child whose bowel movements were controlled by enemas from the age of three weeks shows comparable effects in stimulation of "anal libido" and evocation of recalcitrance to toilet training. See Editha Sterba, "Psychogenic Constipation in a Two-year-old," *Psychoanalytic Study of the Child,* 3–4 (1949), 227–252.
78. BN, n. a. 13008, fols. 158v., 130, 151–151v. December 2, 1604; September 23, 1604; November 14, 1604.
79. *Ibid.*, fol. 80. January 12, 1604.
80. "Anecdotes de l'histoire de France . . . tirées de la bouche de M. Du Vair," in *Mémoires de Marguerite de Valois,* ed. Ludovic de Lalanne (Paris, 1858), 295.
81. Edward, Lord Herbert of Cherbury, *Autobiography* (London: Walter Scott, 1888), 136.
82. BN, n. a. 13008, fol. 39. July 22, 1602.
83. *Ibid.*, fols. 159, 128v. December 3, 1604; September 18, 1604.
84. *Ibid.*, 163v.; S. & B., I, 263. December 14, 1604; May 7, 1607.
85. BN, n. a. 13008, fols. 145v., 160. October 30, December 6, 1604.
86. S. & B., I, 425. February 21, 1610.
87. BN, n. a. 13008, fol. 159v. December 5, 1604. Compare "little George's" preoccupation with wooden beads in a similar context. Sterba, "Psychogenic Constipation," 227–252.
88. *Lettres missives,* VI, 530f. September 28, 1605.
89. BN, n. a. 13008, fol. 118v. August 18, 1604.
90. S. & B., I, 71. June 16, 1604.
91. *Ibid.*, II, 325.

CHAPTER 3: TEMPTATIONS AND FEARS

1. S. & B., I, 118. March 2, 1605.
2. A panegyric to the queen on the occasion of Louis's birth urged her to follow this advice while waiting for him to grow up: "Oh blessed Queen, make us a world of little kings; may your abdomen be always filled with this royal *germe*." BN, fr. 15534, fol. 410v.
3. S. & B., I, 5. September 27, 1601.
4. *Ibid.*, 31, 45, 36. July 24, 1602; April 3, 1603; November 5, 1602.
5. *Ibid.*, 50. July 29, 1603.
6. *Ibid.*, 30. June 22, 1602.
7. *Ibid.*, 35. September 30, 1602. For a clinical description of such genital exhibitionism, see Rose Edgcumbe and Marion Burgner, "The Phallic Narcissistic Phase: A Differentiation between Preoedipal and Oedipal Aspects of Phallic Development," *Psychoanalytic Study of the Child,* 30 (1975), 161–190.
8. S. & B., I, 34, 38, 100. September 11, December 12, 1602; November 3, 1604.
9. *Ibid.*, 97. October 25, 1604.
10. Compare Freud's interpretation of the "Wolf-man's" nightmare of white wolves in "From the History of an Infantile Neurosis," *Collected Papers,* III, 508.
11. S. & B., I, 327f. March 28, 1608.
12. BN, n. a. 13008, fol. 151v. November 16, 1604.
13. S. & B., I, 100. November 3, 1604.
14. *Ibid.*, 123. April 4, 1605.
15. *Ibid.*, 117. February 14, 1605.
16. *Ibid.*, 105. December 1, 1604.
17. *Ibid.*, 104. November 29, 1604.
18. *Ibid.*, 350. August 11, 1608.
19. BN, fr. 4022, fols. 54v., 119v. April 16, August 22, 1605.
20. S. & B., I, 134. June 11, 1605.
21. BN, fr. 4022, fol. 13v. January 18, 1605.
22. BN, n. a. 13008, fols. 98, 152, 155–156. June 3, November 14, November 23 *et seq.,* 1604.
23. *Ibid.*, fols. 166, 104. December 23, 1604.
24. S. & B., I, 113f. January 6, 1605.
25. BN, fr. 4022, fol. 35v. March 12, 1605.
26. For the effects of such experience on prematurely stimulating castration fears, see Herman Roiphe, "On an Early Genital Phase, with an Addendum on 'Genesis,'" *Psychoanalytic Study of the Child,* 23 (1968), 348–365.
27. British Library (hereafter cited as BL), Additional MS 14840.
28. S. & B., I, 50f., 32. July 29, 1603; August 7, 1602.
29. *Ibid.*, 32. August 2, 1602.
30. *Ibid.*, 44. February 13, 1603.
31. BN, n. a. 13008, fol. 65. June 22, 1603. Héroard also notes that the dauphin stutters on the following August 27 (fol. 69v.) but apparently has forgotten these observations by the following January when he first takes official notice of it.
32. S. & B., I, 55. November 7, October 9, 1603.
33. *Lettres missives,* VII, 385. November 14, 1607.
34. BN, n. a. 13008, fols. 79, 79v. January 3–7, 1604. See also S. & B., I, 60.
35. *Ibid.*, 60f. January 12, 1604.
36. S. & B., I, 269, 65. June 15, 1607; May 13, 1604.
37. BN, n. a. 13008, fol. 143. October 25, 1604.
38. BN, fr. 4022, fol. 118v. August 21, 1605.
39. BN, n. a. 13008, fol. 168v., 167v., 118v. December 31, 28, August 19, 1604.

40. BN, fr. 4022, fol. 118 v. August 21, 1605.
41. *Ibid.,* fol. 56 v. April 20, 1605.
42. *Ibid.,* fol. 84v. June 24, 1605.
43. S. & B., I, 275. July 17, 1607.
44. See *ibid.,* lxviii. When he did start to prescribe frequent enemas he chose milder ingredients than those preferred by other court doctors. See below, chapter 13, "Deepening Suspicion."
45. BN, n. a. 13008, fol. 54. January 17, 1603.
46. BN, fr. 4022, fol. 33v. March 9, 1605.
47. BN, Cinq cents Colbert 98, fols. 177–213.
48. BN, n. a. 13008, fol. 123. September 3, 1604. A curious note much later is prompted by Louis's excretion of a six-inch-long dead worm. Héroard seems to express pride when he writes, "It is the first one he has ever made." (BN, fr. 4024, fol. 98v. September 3, 1608.)
49. BN, n. a. 13008, fol. 168v. December 29, 1604.
50. BN, n. a. 13008, fol. 153. November 19, 1604.
51. BN, fr. 4022. fol. 56. April 20, 1605.
52. S. & B., I, 76. July 7, 1604.
53. BN, fr. 4022, fols 7, 60v. January 9, April 29, 1605.
54. S. & B., I, 84f. September 3–5, 1604.
55. *Ibid.,* 95f. October 23, 1604.
56. *Ibid.,* 98. October 29, 1604.
57. *Ibid.,* 64f. April 21, 1604.
58. BN, n. a. 13008, fol. 85. February 22, 1604.
59. *Ibid.,* fol. 124. September 5, 1604.
60. *Ibid.,* fol. 144, 151v. October 26, November 15, 1604.
61. S. & B., I, 101. November 6, 1604.
62. BN, n. a. 13008, fol. 157. November 28, 1604.
63. *Ibid.,* fols. 246–247. May 15, 1606.
64. *Ibid.,* fol. 276. July 10, 1606.
65. Compare the case of "Johnny," "restless and hyperactive," whose father had played "overexciting and overstimulating games with his children." This child was "haunted" by the sight of his mother's genitals; both his homosexual and heterosexual fantasies were sadomasochistic. For him, "aggressive and erotic drives existed in the same fantasy," and "self-punitive symptoms appeared when his behavior made him a successful rival of his father. . . . Experiential factors contributed toward making a normal developmental conflict (the oedipus complex) into a much more acute phenomenon which Johnny could not master without developing symptoms." Alex Holder, "Theoretical and Clinical Notes on the Interaction of Some Relevant Variables in the Production of Neurotic Disturbances," *Psychoanalytic Study of the Child,* 23 (1968), 71–78. Compare also "Jerry," whose "elimination was controlled by suppositories in the first months of life," and was, at fifteen months, "constantly in motion." Cited by Edith Buxbaum and Susan S. Sodergren, "A Disturbance of Elimination and Motor Development," *ibid.,* 32 (1977), 115f., from Samuel Ritvo et al., "Some Relations of Constitution, Environment, and Personality as Observed in a Longitudinal Study," in Albert J. Solnit and Sally A. Provence, eds., *Modern Perspectives in Child Development* (New York: International University Press, 1963), 197.
66. S. & B., I, 107f. December 24, 28, 1604.
67. *Ibid.,* 108. December 29, 1604.
68. BN, fr. 4022, fol. 11v. January 16, 1605.
69. *Ibid.,* fol. 199v. January 20, 1606.
70. *Ibid.,* fol. 115v. August 17, 1605.
71. S. & B., I, 176. February 17, 1606.

72. In Latin the doctor reports Louis "blushing" from "modesty" at Henri's saying to the child, as he brandishes his penis after urinating in the garden, "There's the sort of stuff with which you were made!" *Ibid.,* 267 n. May 28, 1607.
73. *Ibid.,* 335, 194. May 2, 1608; July 26, 1606.
74. BN, n. a. 13008, fol. 122v. September 3, 1604.
75. S. & B., I, 205f. August 12, 1605.
76. *Ibid.,* 137; BN, fr. 4022, fol. 85v. June 24, 1605.
77. S. & B., I, 293. November 2, 1607.
78. *Ibid.,* 168f., 306. January 5, 1606, 1608.
79. *Ibid.,* 377. January 5, 1609.
80. BN, fr. 4022, fol. 554. April 16, 1605.

CHAPTER 4: MIXED FEELINGS: LOVES AND HATES

1. Gédéon Tallemant Des Réaux, "Louis Treiziesme," *Les historiettes,* ed. Louis de Monmerqué and Paulin Paris, 6 vols., 3d ed. (Paris, 1863), II, 83.
2. S. & B., I, 179. March 15, 1606.
3. Chrestienne arrived at Saint-Germain on March 11, 1606.
4. BN, fr. 4022, fols. 240v., 241. May 8, 1606.
5. *Ibid.,* fol. 238. May 4, 1606.
6. *Ibid.,* fol. 242. May 10, 1606.
7. S. & B., I, 191. June 6–8, 1606.
8. *Ibid.* June 8, 1606.
9. BN, fr. 4022, fol. 266v. June 19, 1606.
10. S. & B., I, 194. June 26, 1606.
11. This was Louis's name (with the accent on the last syllable) for his governess.
12. BN, fr. 4022, fol. 264. June 10, 1606.
13. S. & B., I, 218. September 30, 1606.
14. BN, fr. 4022, fol. 285v. July 26, 1606. Compare the case of the "wolf-man": "The form taken by the anxiety, the fear of 'being eaten by the wolf' was only the . . . transposition of the wish to be copulated with by his father." Sigmund Freud, "From the History of an Infantile Neurosis," *Collected Papers of Sigmund Freud,* 5 vols. (London: Hogarth Press, 1949), 517.
15. S. & B., I, 186; BN, fr. 4022, fol. 239v. May 7, 1606.
16. *Moses and Monotheism* (New York: Alfred A. Knopf, 1939), 11.
17. BN, n. a. 13008, fol. 139. October 17, 1604.
18. In this, he writes, she resembled her husband. (Quoted in S. & B., I, 4 n.) The baron de Montglat was anathema to Héroard as well.
19. See, for example, S. & B., I, 242. January 11, 1607. The five-year-old Elisabeth gives an amusing imitation of her speech, which Héroard carefully transcribes. BN, fr. 4022, fol. 228. September 23, 1607.
20. Affects felt toward the mothers were visited on their children. Louis is intolerant of Mamanga's requests for benefits to her two daughters, but he is fiercely protective of Doundoun's two children, Charles and Louise. See, for examples, BN, n. a. 13008, fol. 154; *idem,* fr. 4022, fol. 42. November 20, 1604; March 23, 1605.
21. S. & B., I, 176. February 16, 1606. Alternatively this represents gossip he may have heard concerning possible infidelities of the baron.
22. S. & B., I, 95f.; BN, n. a. 13008, fol. 142. October 23, 1604.
23. *Ibid.,* fol. 156. November 27, 1604.
24. Madame de Montglat's correspondence with the duc de Montmorency, Connétable of France, shows her intense efforts to avoid becoming the butt of Henri's rage by anticipat-

ing his wishes and acquiescing in them in advance. For example, Bibliothèque Condé, XCIII, fol. 146. September 12, 1608.

25. S. & B., I, 100. November 4, 1604.
26. BN, fr. 4022, fol. 60v. April 29, 1605.
27. S. & B., I, 136. June 18, 1605.
28. BN, fr. 4022, fols. 415v., 416. May 17–18, 1606.
29. S. & B., I, 345. June 27, 1608.
30. BN, fr. 4023, fol 13v.; S. & B., I, 349. January 28, August 6, 1608.
31. *Ibid.*, 373. December 7, 1608.
32. *Ibid.* Thus he also "castrates" Madame de Montglat. Compare "An 'Anal Hollow-Penis' in Woman," Sandor Ferenczi, *Further Contributions to the Theory and Technique of Psychoanalysis* (New York: Basic Books, 1959), 317.
33. Louis's later letters to Mamanga show this lack of warmth. For example, in one consoling her for the death of her son in a duel says that he is worried about the state in which this event will find her, "the more so since I fear that this loss may be followed by another, greater one, which would be of you yourself." BL, Additional 14840, fol. 11. January 8, 1615.
34. BN, fr. 4022, fol. 83. June 16, 1605.
35. *Ibid.*, fol. 245. May 14, 1606.
36. S. & B., I, 269. June 17, 1607.
37. *Ibid.*, 69, 74, 119. June 9, 21, 1604; March 4, 1605.
38. *Ibid.*, 329. March 30, 31, 1608.
39. *Ibid.*, 279. August 10, 1607.
40. *Ibid.*, 333. April 25, 1608.
41. Louise Boursier, *Les six couches de Marie de Médicis,* ed. Achille Chéreau (Paris, 1875), 122f.
42. Pierre L'Estoile, *Journal pour les règnes de Henri III, de Henri IV, et du début du règne de Louis XIII,* ed. Louis-R. Lefèvre and André Martin, 4 vols., (Paris: Gallimard, 1943–1960), I, 472; II, 5. January 23, 1596; February 8, 1601.
43. George Carew, "A Relation of the State of France (1609)," in Thomas Birch, *An Historical View of the Negotiations between the Courts of England, France, and Brussels, from the Year 1592 to 1617* (London, 1749), 493.
44. *Journal du règne de Henri IV,* III, 432. February 1609.
45. BN, Cinq cents Colbert 98, fol. 117.
46. S. & B., I, 69. June 10, 1604.
47. *Ibid.*, 73, 98f. June 20, October 30, 1604.
48. *Ibid.*, 93, 120f. October 3, 1604; March 15, 1605.
49. BN, n. a. 13008, fol. 127. September 14, 1604.
50. S. & B., I, 191, 345. June 9, 1606; June 26, 1608.
51. BN, fr. 4023, fol. 68; S. & B., I, 382. June 26, 1608; February 6, 1609.
52. S. & B., I, 192. June 9, 1606. This dangerous junction was a perennial hazard to travelers.
53. *Ibid.*, 206, 261, 227, 321. August 16, 1606; April 23, 1607; November 18, 1606; February 29, 1608.
54. AMRE, Mémoires et documents 767, fol. 123.
55. BN, fr. 4023, fol. 63. May 31, 1608.
56. S. & B., I, 378. January 11, 1609.
57. *Ibid.*, 311, 338, 329. January 23, May 3, March 31, 1608.
58. *Ibid.*, 319. February 22, 1608.
59. *Ibid.*, 414. November 26, 1609.
60. BN, fr. 4023, fol. 64, 64v. June 18, 1608.
61. S. & B., II, 27. October 8, 1610.
62. *Ibid.*, I, 42. January 23, 1603.

63. BN, fr. 4022, 25v. February 17, 1605.
64. BN, n. a. 13008, fol. 126. September 14, 1604.
65. Watching him at table one evening, Louis warns the chevalier, "You hardly eat anything; you'll always be little!" BN, fr. 4022, fol. 16. January 25, 1605.
66. *Journal du règne de Henri IV*, III, 137; Berthold Zeller, *Marie de Médicis et Villeroy* (Paris, 1897), 141f. June, 1610.
67. S. & B., II, 19, 73. September 30, 1610; August 4, 1611.
68. Carew, "Relation of the State of France," 493.
69. S. & B., I, 383. February 9, 1609. So long as children only were concerned, Marie seems to have fallen in with her husband's desires good-naturedly. She wrote Madame de Montglat referring to "our little troop"; "the whole gang"; "my Vendôme and Verneuil daughters." BN, fr. 3649, fol. 44; Cinq cents Colbert 87, fols. 142, 288.
70. Zeller, *Henri IV et Marie de Médicis,* 348f. Quoted from a dispatch of Giovannini, March 8, 1604.
71. AMRE, Mémoires et documents 767, fol. 124.
72. S. & B., I, 143. August 6, 1605.
73. *Ibid.,* 264. May 9, 1607.
74. BN, fr. 4023, fol. 32v. March 15, 1608.
75. S. & B., I, 308. January 11, 1608.
76. *Ibid.,* 100, 252. November 5, 1604; February 15, 1607.
77. *Ibid.,* 341. May 18, 1608.
78. *Lettres missives,* VI, 664. September 15, 1606.
79. BN, fr. 4022, 90v. June 30, 1605.
80. S. & B., I, 158. October 25, 1605.
81. AMRE, Correspondance diplomatique, Rome, XXIII, fol. 180.
82. It is a peculiarity that may derive from Héroard's antipapism that he cites Cardinal de Joyeuse himself as the *parrain,* without alluding to the pope. S. & B., I, 211. September 14, 1606.
83. BN, fr. 3798, fol. 32. Undated.
84. S. & B., I, 297. December 4, 1607.
85. *Ibid.,* 308. January 12, 1608.
86. *Ibid.,* 212, 195. September 14, June 28, 1606.
87. It is also, as has been noted, a name Louis used for his penis and, a few days before, for the switches with which he had just been whipped.
88. S. & B., I, 196. July 1, 1606.
89. *Ibid.,* 234, 250. December 15, 1606; February 12, 1607.
90. BN, fr. 10201, 12. A search in Héroard's diary for the exact occasion of the Vincennes episode seems fruitless, since he rarely gives a complete roster of persons in attendance. Louis made several excursions to Vincennes in the late summer and autumn of 1609, however, during periods when both Héroard and Vauquelin were performing their duties.
91. S. & B., II, 40; BN, fr. 4023, 367v. December 2, 1610.
92. See Jean H. Mariéjol, "La réforme et la ligue," *Histoire de France,* ed. Ernest Lavisse, VI:1 (Paris: Hachette, 1904), 218f. Héroard himself, as one of that king's physicians, had been witness to intimate scenes in Henri III's life. See chapters 14 and 15 below.
93. S. & B., I, 272. July 1, 1607.

CHAPTER 5: BECOMING BRAVE: FORTITUDE AND SKILLS

1. Carew, "State of France," 493.
2. Georges d'Avenel, *Richelieu et la monarchie absolue,* 4 vols. (Paris, 1895), I, 308.
3. *Négociations avec la Toscane,* V, 497, 519. June 8, 1602; November 17, 1603.

4. In his *L'institution des prince,* S. & B., II, 361.

5. Quoted by Zeller, *Marie de Médicis et Villeroy,* 69.

6. Avenel, *Richelieu et la monarchie,* I, 308.

7. BN, n. a. 13008, fol. 169. December 29, 1604.

8. BN, fr. 4022, 30v. March 2, 1605. It is interesting that Héroard's nineteenth-century editors chose not to reproduce these negative evaluations of a future king's courage.

9. *Ibid.,* fol. 276v.; S. & B., I, 224. July 10, November 6, 1606. Water-connected hazards seem to have aroused particular anxieties in Louis. A page's torn sleeve makes him think that the fish will eat him up when he goes swimming "all naked." Put in a bath for the first time with his sister Elisabeth, he is anxious, when about to sit down, at the thought of water entering his rectum: "Hey! My God! Water will get into my anus [*cu*]!" And when he goes swimming with his father for the first time he fears to join the king in drinking water from the Seine because Henri has urinated in the river. On that occasion, however, he wins a bet made by the *grand écuyer* that he would be afraid to try to swim and withstands teasing by Henri, who dumps hatfuls of water on his head. BN, fr. 4022, fol. 122, fr. 4024, fol. 81; S. & B., I, 400. August 26, 1605; August 2, 1608; July 22, 1609.

10. S. & B., I, 224. November 6, 1606.

11. BN, fr. 4022, fols. 14v., 30, 30v. January 19, March 2–3, 1605.

12. BN, fr. 4023, 5v. January 8, 1608.

13. Queens, however, were supposed to be like other princes, and while Marie de Medici was said to lack many good qualities, she was never faulted on physical courage. Once, when Henri IV went walking with the treacherous Biron, Marie had the notion of following closely behind in order to throw herself upon the maréchal if he made a false move. See Zeller, *Marie de Médicis et Sully,* 142.

14. BN, n. a. 13008, fol. 154v. November 20, 1604.

15. BN, fr. 4022, fol. 127. September 15, 1605.

16. *Ibid.,* fol. 115. March 1, 1605.

17. S. & B., I, 353. August 20, 1608.

18. Alphonse Thibaudeau, ed., *Catalogue of the Collection of Alfred Morrison,* 1st series, 6 vols. (London, 1883–1892), III, 206. End of August, 1609 (undated).

19. S. & B., I, 317. February 14, 1608.

20. BN, fr. 4022, fol. 116v. August 18, 1605.

21. S. & B., I, 416f. December 22, 1609.

22. Baguenauld de Puchesse, ed., "Vingt-quatre lettres de'Henri III à Gilles de Souvré," *Annuaire-bulletin de la Société de l'Histoire de France,* 390 (1919), 131, and Thomas Pelletier, *Discours sur la mort de feu M. de Souvré* (Paris, 1626), 11.

23. L'Estoile, *Journal pour le règne de Henri IV,* III, 175. August, 1610.

24. S. & B., II, 98. January 26, 1612.

25. *Ibid.,* I, 184; BN, fr. 4022, fol. 32. April 20, 1606.

26. BN, fr. 4022, fol. 56v. April 21, 1605.

27. S. & B., I, 345; BN, fr. 4023, fol 68. June 26, 1608.

28. BN, fr. 4022, fol. 4. January 4, 1605.

29. *Ibid.,* fol. 4v. January 5, 1605.

30. *Ibid.,* fol. 115. August 18, 1605.

31. S. & B., I, 185f., 346. May 4, 1606; July 2, 1608.

32. *Ibid.,* 387. March 16, 1609.

33. *Ibid.,* II, 83; BN, fr. 4024, fol. 113, 113v. October 20, 1611.

34. BN, fr. 4022, fol. 7. January 11, 1605.

35. *Ibid.,* fol. 223. April 6, 1606.

36. *Lettres missives,* VII, 752f. August 17, 1609.

37. BN, fr. 4022, fol. 30. March 2, 1605.

38. *Ibid.*, fol. 117v. August 21–22, 1605.
39. *Ibid.*, fols. 462–463. August 10, 1605.
40. *Ibid.*, fol. 46. March 27, 1605.
41. *Ibid.*, fols. 228, 228v. April 19, 1606.
42. S. & B., I, 395. June 1, 1609.
43. BN, fr. 4022, fol. 229. April 20, 1606.
44. *Ibid.*, fol. 228v. April 19, 1606.
45. S. & B., I, 282. August 19, 1607.
46. *Ibid.*, 283. August 24–25, 1607.
47. *Ibid.*
48. BN, fr. 4023, fol. 55. May 19, 1608.
49. Armand Baschet, *Le roi chez la reine,* 2d ed. (Paris, 1866), 229f.
50. S. & B., II, 79. September 23, 1611.
51. *Ibid.*, I, 412f. November 15, 1609..
52. Charles d'Arcussia, Seigneur d'Esparron, *La fauconnerie du roy* (Rouen, 1644), 163.
53. Baschet, *Le roi,* 228.
54. BN, fr. 4024, fol. 148. January 25, 1612.
55. S. & B., II, 97f.; BN, fr. 4024, fol. 143v. January 10, 1612.
56. Arcussia, *La fauconnerie,* 169.
57. BN, fr. 4024, fol. 143v. January 11, 1612.
58. *Ibid.*, fol. 143. January 8, 1612.
59. *Ibid.*, fol. 122v. November 14, 1611.
60. Arcussia, *La fauconnerie,* 170.
61. S. & B., I, 32, 69. July 29, 1602; June 8, 1604.
62. *Ibid.*, 366. October 18, 1608.
63. *Ibid.*, 118. March 2, 1605.
64. *Ibid.*, 327. May 24, 1608.
65. BN, n. a. 13008, fol. 116. August 7, 1604.
66. BN, fr. 4022, fol. 47. March 30, 1605.
67. S. & B., I, 226. November 12, 1606.
68. BN, fr. 4022, fols. 227, 228. November 19, 1606.
69. BN, fr. 3798, fol. 33. Undated.
70. BN, fr. 4023, fols. 71v., 72. July 9, 1608.
71. S. & B., I, 125. April 16, 1605.
72. *Ibid.*, 219. October 3, 1606.
73. *Ibid.*, 351f. August 15, 16, 1608.
74. *Ibid.*, II, 58. March 28, 1611.
75. *Ibid.*, I, 274, 320. July 8, 1607; February 23, 1608.
76. Héroard often shows Louis arranging singing parts and directing them. See also the *Mercure françois,* 14 (1629), 619. A contemporary has him singing "almost without a false note." Le Sieur de Bellemaure, *Le pourtraict du roi envoyé au sieur de Mirancourt,* 1st ed. (Paris, 1618); Danjou and Cimber, eds., *Archives curieuses de l'histoire de France,* 2d. series, 27 vols. (Paris, 1834–1840), I, 406. Marin Mersenne asserts that he composed the words for "Amaryllis," while others put it to music. See his *Harmonie universelle,* 2 vols. (Paris, 1636), II:6, 391.
77. BN, fr. fols. 462, 463. August 10, 1607.
78. Gérard de Contades, "Trois lettres de Nicolas Vauquelin, Sieur Des Yveteaux," *Bulletin de la Société Historique de l'Orne,* 8 (1889), 479.
79. S. & B., I, 183. April 16, 1606.
80. BN, fr. 4022, fol. 55. April 17, 1605.
81. BN, fr. 10210, 8f.

82. See, for example, BN, fr. 4023, fol. 90. August 18, 1608.
83. Contades, "Trois lettres de Vauquelin," 479. May 6, 1609.
84. S. & B., II, 83–85. October 23–24, November 2, 1611.
85. Cherbury, *Autobiography,* 136.
86. S. & B., II, 26. October 3, 1610.
87. See Abel Lefranc, "Louis XIII, a-t-il appris l'espagnol?" *Mélanges Fernand Baldensperger,* 2 vols. (Paris: Champion, 1930), II, 37–40.
88. *La vie de Louis XIII* (Paris: Grasset, 1943), 250f. Héroard's editors misread the entry for April 13, 1621. Compare BN, fr. 4026, fol. 431v. with S. & B., II, 256. April 10, 1621. For Louis's single Spanish utterance, see *ibid.,* 185. November 21, 1615.
89. *Ibid.,* I, 83. August 31, 1604.
90. BN, fr. 4022, fols. 53, 39v. April 15, March 18, 1605.
91. *Ibid.,* fol. 7. January 9, 1605.
92. S. & B., I, 427. March 8, 1609.
93. *Oeuvres,* III, 131. January 11, 1610.

CHAPTER 6: HENRI'S LEGACY

1. Guido Bentivoglio, *Lettres* (Paris, 1680), 180f. June 8, 1617.
2. S. & B., I, 376. January 1, 1609.
3. *Ibid.,* II, 320.
4. BN, fr. 4022, fol. 122. August 26, 1605.
5. S. & B., I, 426. February 23, 1610.
6. *Ibid.,* 406. September 16, 1609.
7. *Ibid.,* 197. July 16, 1606.
8. *Ibid.,* 215f. September 23, 1606.
9. *Ibid.,* 297. December 4, 1607.
10. Quoted at the head of this chapter.
11. BN, fr. 4022, fol. 24v. February 15, 1605.
12. *Négociations avec la Toscane,* V, 546–548, 587. September 19, 1604; September 16, 1608. Edmund H. Dickerman argues for a change in the direction of recklessness in the king's last years of life. See his "Henry IV and the Juliers-Clèves Crisis: The Psychohistorical Aspects," *French Historical Studies,* 8 (Fall, 1974), 626–653. Patterns of conduct seemingly aimed at warding off depression, however, had been characteristic of Henri since his youth.
13. S. & B., II, 354.
14. *Ibid.,* I, 69, 160f., 173. June 2, 1604; November 19, 1605; January 24, 1606.
15. Jacques Nompar de Caumont, Duc de La Force, *Mémoires du duc de La Force et de ses deux fils,* 4 vols. (Paris, 1843), I, 44f.
16. S. & B., II, 325, 331.
17. *Négociations avec la Toscane,* V, 592. May 26, 1609.
18. Quoted from BN fr. 10321 in S. & B., I, lxviii.
19. BN, fr. 4022, fol. 74. June 14, 1605.
20. Quoted by Félix Rocquain, *Notes et fragments d'histoire* (Paris, 1906), 348.
21. Zeller, *Henri IV et Marie de Médicis,* 192, 348. March 8, 1604.
22. S. & B., I, 3; II, 327.
23. *Négociations avec la Toscane,* V, 531. May 16, 1604.
24. BN, Cinq cents Colbert 86, fols. 275, 277. 1605.
25. S. & B., II, 327.
26. *Ibid.,* I, 379. January 24, 1609. Emile Magne provides insight into Madame de Montglat's parsimonious nature (although he misnames her Françoise de Longuesac instead of Lon-

guejoue). She had a "real head for business," he writes, even while she was Louis's governess, and accumulated a considerable fortune from inheritances and speculation as well as
gifts from the king. She continued to live in a little house provided by him until she died,
when it was found that though she possessed every kind of luxury and household supplies
of all kinds she lacked any facilities for sharing her comforts and riches with guests. *La vie
quotidienne au temps de Louis XIII* (Paris: Hachette, 1942), 145–149.

27. BN, fr. 4023, fol. 74. July 15, 1608.
28. BN, Cinq cents Colbert 98, fol. 197. Fr. 10210 has *"habitudes vertueuses"* instead of *"tortueuses,"* 9.
29. *Journal du règne de Henri IV,* II, 432. February, 1609.
30. L'Estoile is also at pains to cite the failure of César's education to improve his character.
See *ibid.* Héroard's hostile reports may have been a cue not only for the famous diarist but
also historians of later generations to conclude that Louis XIII's education was sorely neglected. Louis himself, of course, provided post facto recriminations for his own purposes.
See below, chapter 8, "A Difficult Taskmaster."
31. S. & B., I, 393, 404; II, 20; BN, fr. 4023, fol. 334v. May 2, September 7, 1609; September
3, 1610.
32. L'Estoile, *Journal du règne de Henri IV,* II, 433. February, 1609.
33. Quoted from *Mémoires d'Estat, recueillis de divers manuscrits à la suite de ceux de Monsieur de
Villeroy* (Paris, 1645), III (Arsenal MS 5925h), in Georges Mongrédien, *Etude sur la vie de
Nicolas Vauquelin* (Paris: Picard, 1921), 114.
34. S. & B., II, 71. July 25, 1611.
35. See below, Chapter 8, "Distant Objects and Schoolroom Politics."
36. BN, fr. 4023, fol. 120. November 4, 1608.
37. S. & B., I, 392. April 27, 1609. Louis has graduated from being switched to being lashed.
38. *Ibid.,* 407; BN, fr. 4023, fol. 218. September 25, 1609.
39. *Ibid.,* fol. 42. April 14, 1608.
40. S. & B., I, 339; BN, fr. 4023, fol. 53v. May 15, 1608.
41. *Ibid.,* fol. 82. August 3, 1608.
42. S. & B., I, 375f., 378. January 1, 10, 1609.
43. In minor as well as major ways, Henri gave mixed signals to his heir. For example, the
form of address that he instructed Louis to use with him was exceptionally familiar for
monarchs—"Papa" rather than "Sire" or *"Monsieur mon Père,"* but he was also sometimes
insistent on formal signs of deference. Both demands are illustrated by a little postscript of
the seven-and-a-half-year-old Louis to a letter from Henri to Marie: "Papa has permitted
me to add a few words." *Lettres missives,* VII, 688. March 22, 1609.
44. S. & B., I, 255f.; April 11–12, 1607; April 16, 1609. On the following Holy Thursday,
too, "the king finds himself unwell," according to Héroard. The alert editors of the journal
note on this occasion, "It is remarkable that Henri IV is often ill on the day of this ceremony." *Ibid.,* 430. April 8, 1610.
45. *Ibid.,* 396. June 2, 1609.
46. *Ibid.,* 423. January 26, 1610.
47. BN, fr. 4023, fol. 89. August 17, 1608.
48. S. & B., I, 407. September 27, 1609.
49. *Journal du règne de Henri IV,* III, 91. May 15, 1610.
50. *Ibid.,* II, 4; BN, fr. 4023, fol. 292v. May 14, 17, 1610. Héroard finds this remark "memorable."
51. S. & B., II, 4, 57. May 18, 1610; March 15, 1611. Louis occasionally had himself taken into
Souvré's bed at night, as he had done with his nurse and his governess and her husband.
52. *Ibid.,* 79, September 26, 1611.
53. BN, fr. 4024, fol. 111. October 13, 1611.

54. See above, chapter 3, "Encouraging Genitality."
55. Recall, also, his competition with César to put the capons on the spit in readiness for Henri's return from the hunt. See above, chapter 4, "The Vendômes."
56. S. & B., II, 81. October 14, 1611.
57. BN, fr. 4024, fol. 11v. October 14, 1611.
58. S. & B., II, 2; BN, fr. 4023, fol. 297. May 15, 26, 1610.
59. L'Estoile, *Journal du règne de Henri IV*, III, 89. May 15, 1610.
60. S. & B., II, 42, 37. December 15, November 14, 1610.
61. BN, fr. 4023, fol. 337. September 10, 1610.
62. François-T. Perrens, *Les mariages espagnols* (Paris, n. d.), 310.
63. Cited by Zeller, *Marie de Médicis et Sully*, 127–129. Dispatch of September 12, 1610.
64. BN, fr. 4024, fol. 226. S. & B., II, 109. September 26, 1612.
65. *Journal du règne de Henri IV*, III, 137.
66. "La mort de Henri IV," *Documents d'histoire*, 3 (1912), 229f.

CHAPTER 7: ROYAL NORMS AND LOUIS'S TEMPERAMENT

1. Letter of Nicolas Vauquelin, "Trois lettres," 479. May 6, 1609.
2. S. & B., II, 320. Indeed, the doctor had claimed of the four-year-old, "Loved to question and never stopped inquiring until his mind was satisfied." The following spring a note remarks, "Wanted to know everything." BN, fr. 4022, fols. 116, 240. August 18, 1605; May 7, 1606.
3. S. & B., II, 320.
4. BN, fr. 3840, fol. 44.
5. Compare Darricau's list, which adds to piety the requirement that the prince be "prudent," as well as "just and strong" and "temperate," and Tyvaert's survey of seventeenth-century history books, in which he finds wisdom to figure after piety, valiance, and justice, in that order, but before temperance. Also featured on the historians' lists is love of the people and of letters, arts, and sciences. Raymond Darricau, "La spiritualité du prince," *Dix-septième siècle*, 52–53 (1964), 77; Michel Tyvaert, "L'image du roi: légitimité et moralité royales dans les histoires de France au XVIIe siècle," *Revue d'histoire moderne et contemporaine*, 21 (1974), 531–538.
6. *La royale réception de leurs maiestez très-chrestiennes en la ville de Bourdeaus ou le siècle d'or ramené par les allians de France et d'Espaigne* (Bordeaux, 1615), 137–213.
7. Preface to *De l'art de régner* (Paris, 1658).
8. J.-Philippe Varin, *L'heureuse . . . entrée de Louis le Juste* (Lyons, 1622), 14.
9. Jean de Viguerie, "Les serments du sacre des rois de France," *Hommage à Roland Mousnier: Clientèles et fidélités en Europe à l'époque moderne*, ed. Yves Durand (Paris: Presses Universitaires de France, 1981), 58–61.
10. See Chapter 5.
11. Claude Seyssel, *The Monarchy of France*, ed. J. H. Hexter, tr. Donald R. Kelly (New Haven: Yale University Press, 1981), 53f.
12. BN, fr. 3649, fol. 68. September 6, 1606.
13. The first time this occurred was on November 1, 1606. See S. & B., I, 223.
14. *Ibid.*, 48. June 15, 1603.
15. *Ibid.*, II, 84. October 25, 1611.
16. *Ibid.*, 27. October 6, 1610.
17. BN, fr. 4022, fol. 52v. April 8, 1605.
18. Père Le Moyne cites this practice of Henri IV as designed to "atone for his sinfulness." *L'art de régner*, 609.
19. S. & B., I, 147; BN, fr. 4022, 113v. August 14, 1605.

20. *Ibid.,* 312. January 29, 1608.
21. La Mère Pommereuse, *Les chroniques de l'Ordre des Ursulines* (Paris, 1673), III, first treatise, 51.
22. Gabrielle M.-L.-E. Guedré, *Au coeur des spiritualités: Catherine Ranquet, mystique et éducatrice, 1602–1605* (Paris: Grasset, 1952), 14, 90.
23. S. & B., I, 124. April 5, 1605.
24. BN, fr. 4022, fol. 52v. April 14, 1605.
25. S. & B., I, 391; BN, fr. 4023, fol. 168. April 16, 1609.
26. S. & B., II, 110, 159. October 23, 1612; October 1, 1614.
27. Letter of Père Joseph Du Tremblay in *Revue rétrospective,* 1st series, 2 (1885), 253. However, this seems to have been a widespread ritual before the consummation of a marriage, as Orest Ranum has called to my attention in a personal communication.
28. BN, fr. 4022, fols. 54v., 116. April 17, August 19, 1605.
29. BN, fr. 10210, fol. 5.
30. BN, n.a. 13008, fol. 11.
31. S. & B., II, 350.
32. Charles Bernard, *Histoire du roy Louis XIII* (Paris, 1646), 6.
33. See chapter 5, "Formal Instruction."
34. On speed of responses among stutterers see Ira B. Keisman, "Stuttering and Anal Fixation," Diss., New York University, 1958.
35. BN, n. a. 13008, fol. 109; fr. 4022, fols. 329v., 475v. July 1, 1604; October 6, 1606; September 9, 1607.
36. S. & B., II, 10f. June 25, 1610.
37. *Ibid.* BN, fr. 4023, fol. 96v. August 31, 1608.
38. S. & B., I, 340. May 16, 1608.
39. Louis's intense interest in everything to do with his hunting makes this seem likely. By 1625 a similar proclamation doubles the price paid for taking these animals, "so that no just complaints may arise from it." Eugène Griselle, *L'écurie du roi Louis XIII* (Paris: Editions de Documents d'Histoire, 1912), 40.
40. BN, fr. 4023, 139v. April 24, 1609.
41. See chapter 5, "Birds and Beasts."
42. BN, fr. 4022, fol. 230v. April 24, 1606.
43. S. & B., II, 9. June 14, 1610.
44. *Ibid.,* 116; BN, fr. 4024, fol. 275v. January 11–12, 1613. It is typical of Héroard that he does not tell us the outcome of Louis's effort.
45. BN, n. a. 13008, fol. 156. November 26, 1604.
46. S. & B., I, 382, 380. February 6, January 27, 1609.
47. *Journal du règne de Henri IV,* I, 504.
48. AMRE, Mémoires et documents 767, fol. 2v.
49. S. & B., I, 374. December 21, 1608.
50. *Ibid.,* II, 94f; BN, fr. 4024, fol. 140. December 31, 1611.
51. BN, n. a. 13008, fol. 144. October 26, 1604.
52. BN, fr. 4022, fol. 24. February 14, 1605.
53. S. & B., I, 385. March 2, 1609.
54. For example, BN, fr. 4022, fol. 12v. January 17, 1605.
55. *Ibid.,* fols. 2v., 19. January 1, February 2, 1605.
56. BN, n. a. 13008, fols. 156v., 155. November 28, 24, 1604.
57. S. & B., II, 48; BN, fr. 4024, fol. 3. January 5, 1611. We also noted above, chapter 3, "Fears," that this prize was a mixed attraction for Louis.
58. S. & B., I, 287; BN, fr. 4022, fols. 479v., 33, 21. September 18, 1607; March 3, February 11, 1605.

59. S. & B., II, 102. April 17 (misdated April 7), 1612.
60. *Ibid.,* 19. September 29, 1610.
61. BN, fr. 10210, fol. 13.
62. BN, n. a. 13008, fol. 70. September 7, 1603.
63. BN, 4022, fols. 13v., 123. April 4, August 5, 1605.
64. *Lettres missives,* VI, 530f. September 28, 1605.
65. BN, fr. 4022, fol. 123. August 5, 1605.
66. See chapter 8, "A Difficult Taskmaster."
67. S. & B., II, 50. January 13, 1611. In the margin Héroard notes his restraint. BN, fr. 4024, fol. 6.
68. S. & B., II, 98; BN, fr. 4024, fol. 148v. January 26, 1612.
69. BN, fr. 4022, fol. 51; S. & B., I, 80. April 5, 1605; August 4, 1604.
70. BN, fr. 4022, fol. 41v. March 21, 1605.
71. S. & B., I, 121. March 15, 1605.
72. BN, fr. 4023, fols. 91, 91v. August 20, 1608.
73. See chapter 3, "Conflicting Passions."
74. BN, fr. 4022, fol. 30; 4024, fols. 16v., 82. March 2, 1605; February 3, August 3, 1608.
75. See S. & B., I, 328. March 29, 1608.
76. BN, fr. 4025, fol. 3v. January 6, 1611.
77. BN, n. a. 13008, fol. 119. August 19, 1604.
78. *Ibid.,* fol. 124, 124v. September 5, 1604.
79. BN, fr. 4022, fol. 47v. March 31, 1605.
80. S. & B., II, 323.
81. *Oeuvres,* III, 130. January 11, 1610.
82. S. & B., II, 65. June 28, 1611.
83. *Ibid.,* 122; BN, fr. 4024, 100v. June 23, 1613; September 17, 1611.
84. *Journal du règne de Henri IV,* II, 440.

CHAPTER 8: WIDENING PERSPECTIVES: THE BOY KING AND OTHERS

1. Vauquelin, *Oeuvres,* 166f.
2. S. & B., II, 30. October 16, 1610.
3. Bernard, *Histoire du roy Louis XIII,* 8–15.
4. S. & B., II, 31. October 17, 1610.
5. Bernard, *Histoire du roy Louis XIII,* 14f.
6. S. & B., II, 32f. October 21, 1610.
7. On the whole, however, Héroard was highly satisfied with his performance on this occasion. *Ibid.,* I, 81f. August 29, 1604.
8. *Ibid.,* 211f. September 14, 1606.
9. *Ibid.,* 255–257. April 12, 1607.
10. BN, n. a. 13008, fol. 24. February 26, 1602. This rash also caused consternation to Madame de Montglat, who blamed it on teething: "Mgr. le Dauphin is very well, except for the scales on his face, of which he has a quantity. But I hope this will make for better health after his teeth are all in. . . . I wish very much it could be before the king arrives in order for him to be prettier." Archives Condé (Chantilly), CVIII, fol. 19.
11. BN, fr. 4025, fol. 162. April 9, 1616.
12. S. & B., II, 24, 111. September 24, 1610; October 31, 1612. The first rejoinder brings three marginal "*Notas*" from Héroard "for his temperament [*humeur*]." BN, fr. 4023, fol. 341v.
13. S. & B., II, 171f. January 3, 1615.
14. *Ibid.,* I, 425; II, 77. February 21, 1610; August 30, 1611.
15. *Journal du règne de Henri IV,* III, 156.

16. See chapter 4, "Brothers."
17. S. & B., II, 73. August 4, 1611.
18. Shortly after the death of his first brother, Louis sent Haran (Héroard writes "Haranc") ahead to meet Gaston, the only surviving one, with his little chariot pulled by mastiffs. "He [Gaston] will be so delighted, he'll die from it," speculated Louis. BN, fr. 4024, fol. 127. November 25, 16ll.
19. "Anecdotes de Monsieur Du Vair," 296f.
20. "And goes off," Héroard appends after his report of the king's remark. S. & B., II, 51; BN, fr. 4024, fol. 12. January 29, 1611.
21. *Marie de Médicis et Sully*, 224.
22. Sully had frequently visited the infant Louis, often in company with Henri. When Héroard first notes the baby's coolness to the finance minister, Louis is two-and-a-half years old. S. & B., I, 67. May 24, 1604.
23. Malherbe, *Oeuvres*, III, 131. January 11, 1610.
24. Sully was associated with doling out money to Louis in the form of coins. The child's distaste was often expressed in refusal of such offers. This may have arisen from resentment at what he perceived as the minister's preemption of his father's (and ultimately his own) money. Or it may have been Sully's association with "filthy lucre" that accounts for the revulsion that Héroard depicts clearly. When, for example, the seven-year-old Louis was told that he would be presented with a diamond-studded ribbon by his father's finance minister, he reacted with scorn: "And he wouldn't even pay for the horses for my cart!" It is Louis's "nature," Héroard remarks, that he "doesn't like to be turned down." But he has told us nothing about the circumstances of that refusal. See S. & B., I, 394; BN fr. 4023, fol. 179. May 16, 1609. It is also plausible that the duke, as Henri's boon companion, was subjected to anger that the child could not express directly at the king. A significant scene where both men were present took place on June 26, 1608. Again, on May 9, 1610, Louis gave a disdainful response ("*per contemptum*," as Héroard says) to Sully's offer of cash, made in Henri's presence. S. & B., I, 345, 434.
25. On Sully's courtship of Louis see Edmund Dickerman, "The Man and the Myth in Sully's *Economies royales*," *French Historical Studies*, 7 (1972), 307–331. On Louis's rejection of Sully's services, see below, chapters 14 and 15.
26. See below, "Distant Objects and Schoolroom Politics."
27. L'Estoile is cited in a note to S. & B., II, 71, where Héroard's observation also appears. July 25, 1611. Georges Mongrédien notes the continuing correspondence between Louis and his former tutor in Vauquelin, *Oeuvres*, "Preface." Apparently Richelieu believed, early in his own rise to power, that it was worthwhile to cultivate Vauquelin's good will. See *Lettres, instructions et papiers e'Etat du cardinal de Richelieu*, ed. Denis-Martial Avenel, 8 vols. (Paris, 1853–1877), II, 12. May 1624. In 1642 Louis's first tutor seems to have been employed by the cardinal, reporting to Charpentier, Richelieu's secretary, on affairs in the southwest of France. BN, Baluze 337, fols. 172–176.
28. BN, Cinq cents Colbert 98, fol. 188.
29. S. & B., II, 73, 80. August 4, September 26, 1611. Nicolas Le Fèvre is said to have accidentally gouged out one of his eyes as a young man, while whittling a pen. His one-eyedness is not likely to have improved his reception by Louis. Paulin Paris, *Les manuscrits français de la Bibliothèque du Roi* (Paris, 1840), III, 361.
30. *Ibid.*, 111 n. November 4, 1612.
31. *Oeuvres*, III, 262. The poet had scant esteem for the tutor's literary imagination. His own hopes to succeed him were disappointed.
32. BN, fr. 4024, 246v. October 22, 1612.
33. He was author of *Elements de l'artillerie* (Paris, 1608) and, at about the time of his promotion, of several other works designed to flatter Marie de Medici. See Auguste-François

d'Anis, *Etude littéraire et historique: David Rivault de Fleurance et les autres précepteurs de Louis XIII* (Paris, 1893), 100.

34. Vauquelin, *Oeuvres,* 176. Fleurance died in 1616. The coincidence of Vauquelin's description with the circumstances of Le Fèvre's fate suggests that Louis's first tutor, writing some years later, may have confused the two.

35. Louis de Rouvray, duc de Saint-Simon, *Parallèle des trois rois Henri IV, Louis Treize, Louis Quatorze* (Paris: Jean de Bonnot, 1967), 7.

36. For examples see S. & B., II, 32, 75–79, 113. October 19, 1610; August–October, 1611. Typical is an occasion when he makes Souvré do a geometry assignment: "Doing it badly he [Louis] laughs at him." BN, fr. 4024, fol. 260. November 29, 1612.

37. Guy Patin, *Lettres choisies* (Paris, 1692), 122. A lengthy medical history of Louis, for which this physician, Bouvard, was apparently the source, credited him with a fortunate natural endowment that had been ruined in his youth by Héroard's poor therapeutic stratagems. Robert Lyonnet, *Brevis dissertatio de morbis haereditariis* (Paris, 1647), 11–19.

38. Robert Stoller, citing Theodor Reik, finds the revenge fantasy "at the root of masochism." *Sexual Excitement* (New York: Pantheon, 1979), 127f.

39. Perrens, *Les mariages espagnols,* 309. The anti-Spanish bias in the nursery made its influence felt on all the children—even Gaston, who in later life was willing to ally himself with Spain against his brother's policies. When the Spanish marriages were being arranged during a visit of the duke of Pastrano, Louis's five-year-old brother was heard to say "in a nice manner," that "he was astonished to see that he was not black like other Spaniards." *Mercure françois,* 2 (1615), 470. August 16, 1612.

40. BN, fr. 4022, fols. 8v., 9. January 1, 1605.

41. *Ibid.,* fol. 25v. February 16, 1605.

42. BN, n. a. 13008, fol. 155v. November 24, 1604.

43. S. & B., I, 246. January 29, 1607.

44. BN, fr. 4022, fol. 12v. January 17, 1605.

45. BN, fr. 4023, fol. 14; S. & B., I, 312. January 29, 1608. Also at about this time, however, the Venetian ambassador reports Louis to have shown "much scorn" for the idea of marrying an infanta. Perrens, *Les mariages espagnols,* 309.

46. S. & B., I, 347; BN, fr. 4023, fol. 76. July 18, 1608. See also the message Louis devises for a German gentleman's collection of autographs, to be read in "all of Germany" alongside inscriptions from Maurice of Nassau, the earl of Essex, Henry, Prince of Wales, and Lord Cecil. S. & B., I, 352. September 30, 1610.

47. Interestingly, Héroard's report includes an oversight. The book modified by Louis bore the name of the emperor, as well as that of the pope, before that of the king of Spain. The child's alteration allowed both of those precedents to stand. *Ibid.,* II, 25; BN, fr. 4023, fol. 345. September 30, 1610.

48. S. & B., I, 262. April 29, 1607.

49. BN, fr. 4023, fol. 98. September 3, 1608.

50. S. & B., I, 359. September 20, 1608.

51. BN, n. a. 13008, fols 145, 152v. October 29, November 18, 1604.

52. *Ibid.,* fol. 119v. August 12, 1604.

53. S. & B., I, 148f., 331. August 17, 1605; April 13, 1608.

54. *Ibid.,* 148, 207, 289. August 15, 1605; August 23, 1606; October 14, 1607.

55. *Ibid.,* II, 43, 103. December 19, 1610; April 22, 1612. Henri IV may unwittingly have conveyed to his son his lack of confidence in the reforming powers of Coton. In a letter from Henri to Marie, apparently responding to her report that Coton was drawing large crowds to his Paris sermons, he expresses doubt that these audiences are sincerely interested in virtuous behavior. *Lettres missives,* VII, 857. March 12, 1610.

56. S. & B., I, 274, 321, 331. July 7, 1607; March 2, April 13, 1608.

57. *Ibid.,* II, 51. January 27, 1611.
58. *Ibid.,* I, 175. February 12, 1606.
59. *Journal du règne de Henri IV,* III, 175. August, 1610.
60. Héroard's account of this part of the lesson is in a marginal note added later—possibly much later. S. & B., I, 386; BN, fr. 4023, fol. 157v. March 6, 1609.
61. S. & B., II, 24. September 24, 1610. As we saw above, chapter 7, "Temperance", Vauquelin also tried to encourage Louis to enter the debate over conciliar versus papal supremacy. It was a heated issue after William Barclay's *De potestae papae* (1607) had been countered by Bellarmin's Ultramontanist *De potestate summi pontifici in rebus temporalibus* (1610).
62. Edmond Richer maintains that the preceptor tried to exert a pro-Gallican influence on the administration during his short tenure. Villeroy, however, had denounced Vauquelin to the queen for having, among other travesties, averred to Louis that the "greatness of Spain had been acquired by the 'fleshly lance'" (i.e., by marriage alliances) rather than military skill and might, and had recommended the Ultramontanist cardinal Du Perron himself as a suitable preceptor for Louis. *Histoire du syndicat* (Paris, 1753), 99, *Mémoires d'Etat de Monsieur de Villeroy* (Paris, 1725), V, 201–203. Chancellor Sillery, who presented Le Fèvre to the queen and praised him to Louis (S. & B., II, 75f.), was closely allied to Villeroy by marriage.
63. The year Rivault succeeded Le Fèvre, 1612, was the year his second book appeared, ingratiatingly dedicated, like the first, to Marie. See Anis, *Fleurance et les autres précepteurs,* 115.
64. Letter of January 17, 1613, cited by Jean-Marie Prat, *Recherches historiques et critiques sur la Compagnie de Jésus . . . au temps du père Coton* (Lyons, 1876), III, 469, 486f.
65. Shortly after Henri's death, Souvré and his family received several notable clerical benefices.
66. Héroard's eventual conversion is certain: he was buried in the Catholic church of Vaugrigneuse. His *L'institution du prince* was published by a Protestant publisher in 1609 (perhaps indicating his continuing fidelity to that persuasion), but the fact that an anti-Huguenot work was dedicated to him on November 18, 1618 seems conclusive evidence that he was known as a convert to Catholicism at least a year or so before that date. See Jacques Pannier, *L'église réformée de Paris sous Louis XIII (1610–1621)* (Paris: Champion, 1922), 27, 403.
67. *Histoire du syndicat,* 342f.
68. S. & B., II, 117; BN, fr. 4024, fol. 284. February 2, 1613. The Protestants Montpouillan, son of the duc de La Force, and Henri de Beringhen were favorites in Louis's court of honor.
69. S. & B., II, 187. December 4, 1615.

CHAPTER 9: QUEEN MARIE'S COURT: 1610–1614

1. S. & B., II, 84; BN, fr. 4024, fol. 116, marginal note. October 27, 1611.
2. See, for example, the young Armand de Richelieu's remarks in his harangue to the clergy in the closing sessions of the Assembly of the Estates General in 1615. *Mémoires du cardinal de Richelieu,* 10 vols. (Paris: Société de l'Histoire de France, 1908–1929), I, 340–365.
3. Berthold Zeller, *Richelieu ministre: 1616* (Paris, 1899), 173.
4. Mathieu Molé, *Mémoires,* 4 vols. (Paris, 1855), I, 51.
5. Zeller, *Marie de Médicis et Villeroy,* 188. March 15, 1614.
6. On the circumstances of this *sacre* see Marie Thiroux d'Arconville, *La vie de Marie de Médicis,* 3 vols. (Paris, 1774), I, 111–113.
7. Archivio Gonzaga, Francia (Correspondenza Estera, serie E) 628, fol. 52. August 11, 1610.
8. Contemporaries do not agree on all the details of Leonora's origins. For a summary of

most of the facts, and for an acute insight into Marie's relationship to the maréchale, see Louis Batiffol, *La vie intime d'une reine*, I, 1–7, 48f.

9. "L'ami estraordinarissimamente, e che sia come innamorata di lei." Matteo Botti in *Négociations avec la Toscane*, V, 639. June 10, 1610.

10. For some details see Malherbe, *Oeuvres*, III, 413; Fernand Hayem, *Le maréchal d'Ancre et Leonora Galigai* (Paris: Plon, 1910), 192, 165, 208.

11. See Batiffol, *La vie intime*, I, 48. Many suggested that Marie preferred her youngest son, who was later to ally himself sporadically with her. If there was a difference between her feelings for Louis and for Gaston, however, it is difficult to detect. Her letters to and concerning all her children mostly deal with practical matters—as in the case of the five-year old Gaston: "The doctors advise that it is necessary to make him take an enema and a small medicine, and for that my presence is absolutely necessary. Today I made him take the enema, but force was required, and I had him taken by five or six persons, who had a hard time holding him. He will take his medicine Saturday, and I'm afraid I shall have to take the same pains." BN, fr. 10241, fol. 55. October 17, 1613. The need for her presence in this case is in suggestive contrast with her relation to Louis, for whom her presence was never a necessity. Her tone is somewhat softer in correspondence concerning her daughters.

12. Claude Malingre, *Histoires tragiques de nostre temps* (Rouen, 1641), 64.

13. S. & B., I, 436; II, 88f.

14. "Anecdotes de Monsieur Du Vair," 295f.

15. S. & B., II, 8. June 12, 1610.

16. *Ibid.*, 6, 110. Another notation by Guérin—substituting for Héroard—is, "Wakened, whipped," made on March 10, 1611. There is no explanation for this, neither on this day nor on the preceding one. Héroard, recopying later, left four-and-a-half blank lines after the "foueté" but failed to fill them in. *Ibid.*, 126; BN, 4024, fol. 27v. September 29, 1613.

17. *Ibid.*, 126. It may also be, of course, that the scene he is here forbidden to witness evoked anxiety associated with watching or imagining comparable forbidden scenes between adults during his childhood.

18. A Florentine emissary wrote home regretfully, "She is a woman who remembers things only while one is talking about them to her." Quoted by Berthold Zeller, *Marie de Médicis et Villeroy*, 144. She would happily interrupt consultations on important political matters to consider decorations for her palace. See Zeller, *Marie de Médicis et Sully*, 320–322.

19. Molé, *Mémoires*, I, 22. The young Robert Arnauld d'Andilly was also a witness to Marie's choleric outbursts. See his *Journal inédit, 1614–1620* (Paris, 1857), 18, 92f.

20. S. & B., II, 22. September 15, 1610.

21. Nicolas Vauquelin, who reports this incident, believed that Louis's mistrust of his mother could be traced to it. *Oeuvres*, 173.

22. S. & B., II, 22, 53, 129. September 15, 1610; February 9, 1611; January 1, 1614.

23. Quoted by J.-B. H.-R. Capefigue, *Richelieu, Mazarin, et la fronde* (Paris, 1848), 359f.

24. Malherbe, *Oeuvres*, III, 285; Zeller, *Marie de Médicis et Sully*, 253. January 21, 1613; January 26, 1611.

25. Prat, *La Compagnie de Jésus*, V, 318.

26. Zeller, *Marie de Médicis et Villeroy*, 149.

27. S. & B., II, 109; BN, fr. 4024, fol. 26. August 25, 1612. S. & B., II, 89. November 19, 1611.

28. S. & B., II, 221; BN, fr. 4024, fol. 107. August 16, 1612.

29. See Giovannini's dispatches to the grand duke of Tuscany, *Négociations avec la Toscane*, V, 459–464. February 16–May 3, 1601.

30. S. & B., I, 43. January 2, 1603.

31. BN, fr. 4024, fol. 79. April 24, 1612.

32. Hayem, *Le maréchal d'Ancre*, 51.
33. S. & B., I, 29. June 10, 1602.
34. *Ibid.*, 43, 53, 74. February 1, September 7, 1603; June 22, 1604. There is an ingratiating letter to the governess from Concini in BN, fr. 3818, fol. 22. Undated.
35. BN, fr. 3818, fol. 24. April 18, 1614. When Elisabeth, en route to be married, was recovering from smallpox in Poitiers, Leonora and her favored physician, Montalto, were apparently attending her. Both the favorite and the Italian Jewish doctor received a letter of courtesy from Madame de Montglat, according to a letter of the queen mother's secretary, Phélypeaux, to the former governess. Institut, Godefroy 268, fol. 30. September 4, 1615.
36. BN, fr. 4023, fol 345; S. & B., II, 36. June 24, 1608; November 9, 1610.
37. Scipion Dupleix, *Histoire de Louis le Juste* (Paris, 1633), 98.
38. Pierre Matthieu, *La coniuration de Conchine* (Paris, 1618), 34.
39. Scurrilous literature of the time that linked Concini romantically to Marie has been categorically repudiated by Louis Batiffol, who summarizes the evidence that Marie's attachment was to Leonora, not to her husband. See "Le coup d'Etat du 24 avril 1617," *Revue historique*, 95 (1907), 297–302. Batiffol does not offer the complementary conclusion: in Marie such dalliance was inconceivable; she was not sensually attracted to any man.
40. S. & B., II, 87. November 8, 1611.
41. *Ibid.*, 25. September 27, 1610.
42. It took place in the office of the queen, whom Louis visited several times on this day, though Héroard, for reasons of his own, makes no mention of it. BN, fr. 4024, fol. 2.
43. *Marie de Médicis et Sully*, 184.
44. S. & B., II, 58. March 28, 1611.
45. BN, 4024, fol. 33. S. & B., II, 58. March 28, 1611. *Vilanie(s)*, the word used here, is an alternate form of the old *vilenie*, given this meaning by Littré.
46. S. & B., II, 62. May 14, 1611.
47. *Ibid.*, 116. January 11, 1613.
48. Quoted by Zeller, *Marie de Médicis et Villeroy*, 71f. October 26, 1612.

CHAPTER 10: INTERREGNUM: PLEASURES AND PAINS

1. Nicolas de Neufville, Sieur de Villeroy, "Discours présenté à la Reyne-mère . . . 1612," in *Memoires d'Estat de Monsieur de Villeroy* (Paris, 1725), 207.
2. S. & B., II, 69. Héroard adds, *"Nota: serius et facetum responsum."* BN, fr. 4024, fol. 71. July 6, 1611.
3. S. & B., II, 49. January 12, 1611.
4. *Ibid.*, 56. March 8, 1611.
5. BN, fr. 4024, fol. 57. May 30, 1611.
6. S. & B., II, 15, 110. August 10, 1610; September 18, 1612.
7. *Ibid.*, 105. June 23, 1612.
8. *Ibid.*, 141. June 5, 1614.
9. *Ibid.*, 61f. April 25, May 1, 1611.
10. BN, fr. 23048. "Discours des favoris fait par M. de Nangis," fol. 19, 19v.
11. Ed. Tartarin, "Roger de Termes, Duc de Bellegarde," *Société des Etudes Historiques* (1892), 378–392. This affinity of taste in companions between Henri III and Louis was not the only characteristic shared by the two kings.
12. S. & B., I, 331, 335, 406. April 17, 30, 1608; July 22, 1609.
13. *Ibid.*, II, 32, 100, 168. October 18, 1610; March 17, 1612; November 21, 1614.
14. Courtenvaux enters Héroard's diary as a facilitator of one of Louis's favorite pleasures: he presented the three-year-old dauphin with a pair of spurs. See *ibid.*, I, 93. October 10, 1604.

15. BN, fr. 4024, fol. 118. November 1, 1611.

16. Charles Bernard, *L'histoire des guerres de Louis XIII* (Paris, 1636), 77.

17. S. & B., II, 159, 164, 168. October 1, 24, November 28, 1614.

18. Quoted by Zeller, *Marie de Médicis et Sully*, 90. July 24, 1610.

19. Bernard, *Histoire des guerres*, 243.

20. Berthold Zeller, *Le connétable de Luynes*, (Paris, 1879), 28.

21. Baptiste Legrain, *La décade commençant l'histoire du roy Louis XIII, 1610–1617* (Paris, 1618), 269; Bassompierre, *Mémoires*, II, 139 n.

22. Perhaps they entered it somewhat later. A son of the comte Du Lude became Louis's *enfant d'honneur* in 1609. This child's prior acquaintanceship with the Luynes brothers may have been their entrée to Louis's ken. See Griselle, *Etat de la maison de Louis XIII*, 49. A memoir of the comtesse Du Lude supplies dates of the Luynes's service in that household. *Collections des inventaires sommaires des archives départementales antérieures à 1790. Archives civiles (Maine et Loire)* (Paris, 1863), I, 243.

23. Arcussia, *La fauconnerie du roy*, 166.

24. Zeller, *Marie de Médicis et Sully*, 128.

25. S. & B., I, 333. April 25, 1608.

26. See above, chapter 6, "Aftermath of Murder."

27. S. & B., II, 81f. October 18, 1611.

28. *Ibid*.

29. *Ibid*., II, 91; BN, fr. 4024, fol. 128. November 28, 1611.

30. "A person . . . used to experience feelings, exercise functions, and execute actions in one's own stead." Martin Wangh, "The Evocation of a Proxy: A Psychological Maneuver; Its Use as a Defense; Its Purpose and Genesis," *Psychoanalytic Study of the Child*, 17 (1962), 451–469.

31. Bassompierre, *Mémoires*, II, 139f. n.

32. *Autobiography*, 137.

33. Arcussia, *La fauconnerie du roy*, 171.

34. Héroard reports the king amusing himself by making verses about this nose. (S. & B., II, 169.) Zeller reproduces a contemporary medallion of Luynes as the frontispiece to *Le connétable de Luynes*. A bust by François Rudé, showing the same youthful rotundity, but also considerable voluptuousness, is reproduced in Pierre Chevallier, *Louis XIII* (Paris: Fayard, 1979), between 316–317.

35. *Histoire du règne de Louis XIII*, I, 95. A later rival, Richelieu, refers in passing to his "good nature." *Lettres*, VII, 514. Late 1621.

36. James Howell, *Lustra Ludovici* (London, 1646), 38.

37. *Mémoires de Messire François Duval, Marquis de Fontenay-Mareuil*, ed. Joseph-François Michaud and Jean-Joseph-François Poujoulat (Paris, 1837), 127–129.

38. *Letters to the Duke of Monteleone* (London, 1753), 143. March 27, 1619.

39. Richelieu, *Lettres*, VII, 514f.

40. *Mémoires*, 129.

41. Michel Baudier, *Histoire du maréchal Toiras* (Paris, 1664), 31.

42. The Venetian ambassador, quoted by Zeller, *Le connétable de Luynes*, 268. December 24, 1621.

43. Héroard once records that Louis pretended to beat on the tambourine, using the hands of a Swiss guard. S. & B., II, 104. June 9, 1612.

44. Héroard claims that Louis was unconscious of making a pun in using the word *fredon*, which the editors take as evidence that Littré's linking of the word to *fredaine*, a youthful transgression, is justified. *Ibid*., 166f. n.

45. *Ibid*., 166f. November 6, 1614.

46. *Ibid*., 49; BN, fr. 4024, fol. 3v. January 8, 1611.

47. S. & B., II, 50; BN, fr. 4024, fol. 6v.
48. *Ibid.*, fols. 17v., 35v.; S. & B., II, 59. February 12, April 3–4, 1611.
49. BN, fr. 4024, fols. 27, 122v., 157v. February 22, November 11, 1611; February 22, 1612.
50. *Ibid.*, fol. 212v.; S. & B., II, 144; BN, fr. 4025, fol. 67v. July 27, 1612; July 8, 1614.
51. S. & B., II, 9f.; BN, fr. 4023, fol. 306v. June 20, 1610.
52. Zeller, *Marie de Médicis et Sully*, 257; S. & B., II, 55f.; BN, fr. 4024, fol. 25v. March 3–4, 1611.
53. *Ibid.*, 324v.; S. & B., II, 122. May 28–29, 1612.
54. S. & B., II, 62, 64; BN, fr. 4024, fols. 48–49v., 51v. May 7–10, 15, 1611. See also above, chapter 6, "Aftermath of Murder."
55. BN, fr. 4024, fols. 157–158. February 20–21, 24, 1612.
56. S. & B., II, 100; BN, fr. 4024, fols. 168–169v. March 7, 25–30, 1612.
57. See *Mercure français*, 2 (1612), 334ff.
58. S. & B., II, 101. April 12, 1612.
59. BN, fr. 4024, fol. 179v. April 14–15, 1612.
60. *Ibid.*, fols. 175v, 176. April 15, 1612.
61. *Ibid.*, 179v. April 26, 1612. Héroard marks each renewal with a marginal "R."
62. *Ibid.*, fols. 216, 216v. August 4, 1612.
63. Young Verneuil minimized the gap between the two kinds of unions. He replied, "Master, excuse me, there's certainly a different ceremony to go through." *Ibid.*, fol. 220. August 12, 1612.
64. *Mercure français*, 2 (1612), 465f.
65. S. & B., II, 108. August 24, 1612.
66. BN, fr. 4024, fol. 228v. September 3, 1612.
67. S. & B., II, 110; BN, fr. 4024, fol. 235. September 21–23, 1612.
68. *Ibid.*, 245v. October 18, 1612.
69. *Ibid.*, fols. 245v., 292. October 18, November 7, 1612.
70. *Ibid.*, fols. 273–289v.
71. *Ibid.*, fol. 337. July 4, 1613. One may only conjecture how this report could have meaning in "dream logic" if, instead of six hundred (*six cents*), we understand the near homologue sixty (*soixante*). (The product of 15x12 is 3x60). It is three years since Henri died; when he died he was three years short of being sixty. At the time of this dream Louis is actually three years short of being fifteen. The "comte de Maure" (*Maure* or *More*—literally Moor—had an invidious connotation of half-breed or "nigger") suggests the near homonym, Moret, family name of his youngest half brother who, it will be remembered, came after *merde* in Louis's estimation. (See above, chapter 4, "Lesser Breeds.") Louis was five when this last visible evidence of Henri's promiscuity was born. Louis's marriage actually took place in 1615, and there may have been talk around him at the time of the probable union that year. "*Maure*" also could have the significance of Spaniard.
72. *Ibid.*, fols. 353–355.
73. Compare Freud: "The orginal form of the unconscious male fantasy was not . . . 'I am being beaten by my father,' but rather 'I am loved by my father. . . . The beating fantasy has its origin in an incestuous attachment to the father." *Collected Papers*, II, 194f.
74. BN, fr. 4024, fol. 385v. November 18, 1613.
75. *Ibid.*, fols. 394–402.
76. *Ibid.*, 395v., S. & B., II, 128f. December 13, 1613; January 3, 1614.
77. BN, fr. 4024, fol. 388v. On apathy as a defense against dangerous desires see Ralph Greenson, "The Psychology of Apathy," *Psychoanalytic Quarterly*, 18 (1949), 290–302.
78. BN, fr. 4024, fol. 395v. December 12, 1613.
79. S. & B., II, 127. November 19, 1613.
80. BN, Dupuy 661, fol. 148.

CHAPTER 11: COMING OF AGE

1. Malherbe, *Oeuvres*, III, 399. February 20, 1614.
2. Berthold Zeller, *Marie de Médicis et Villeroy* (Paris, 1897), 170.
3. Robert Arnauld d'Andilly, *Journal inédit, 1614–1620*, 4. January 9, 1614.
4. S. & B., II, 49f. January 13, 1611.
5. *Oeuvres*, III, 375. January 16, 1614.
6. BN, fr. 4025, fol. 6; S. & B., II, 130. January 13, 1614.
7. BN, fr. 4025, fols. 6–8. January 14–21, 1614.
8. Arnauld, *Journal, 1614–1620*, 9. February 11, 1614.
9. *Oeuvres*, III, 399. February 20, 1614.
10. BN, fr. 4025, fol. 17. February 19, 1614.
11. Malherbe is precise in these details, recorded the next day. (*Oeuvres*, III, 396f., February 20, 1614.) Zeller reports the day of escape as Thursday, February 29 (*Marie de Médicis et Villeroy*, 173), an error perhaps due to misreading of the Italian ambassador's correspondence, but one that has been followed by Pierre Chevallier in *Louis XIII*, 82. Even had 1614 been a leap year, February 29 would have fallen on a Saturday.
12. BN, fr. 4025, fol. 17v.
13. S. & B., II, 134; BN, fr. 4025, fol. 22v. March 6, 1614.
14. Cited from an Ammirato dispatch of February 15, 1614, by Zeller, *Marie de Médicis et Villeroy*, 171f.
15. Malherbe, *Oeuvres*, III, 400. February 20, 1614.
16. Louis's first almoner, who was often with him at bedtime prayers, was bishop of Bayonne. His name was Bertrand Des Chaux, or de Chaux, as Héroard and Tallemant call him, conceivably providing additional dream material as a condensed form of *chapeaux*. The dream may also disguise the more obscure, passive wish to have "dispatches" opened by Henri/César.
17. *Histoire de Louis XIII*, I, 68.
18. BN, fr. 4025, fols. 31v., 41. April 2, 29, 1614.
19. *Ibid.*, 36 v., S. & B., II, 137. April 15, 1614. Héroard writes in the margin: "*Na. pietas.*"
20. BN, fr. 4025, 34v., 40v.; S. & B., II, 136–138. April 11, 22, 28, 1614.
21. Zeller, citing the Venetian ambassador's dispatch of May 7, 1614, *Marie de Médicis et Villeroy*, 208f.; Griffet, *Histoire de Louis XIII*, I, 68.
22. Although Louis adds "it was nothing but water," Héroard notes marginally: "Dreams they are drawing his blood." BN, fr. 4025, fol. 43; S. & B., II, 138.
23. Zeller, *Marie de Médicis et Villeroy*, 208f. The Venetian ambassador was not always well-informed. He believed that Villeroy, secretary of state, was among those who had always advised war to the queen (*ibid.*,) while Joseph Nouaillac has shown otherwise. Compare the latter's "Avis de Villeroy à la reine Marie de Médicis, 10 mars 1614," *Revue Henri IV*, 2 (1908), 79–81.
24. S. & B., II, 138f. May 15, 1614.
25. *Ibid.*, 139–143; BN, fr. 4025, fols. 50v.–55. May 26–June 15, 1614.
26. Cited in S. & B., II, 140 n. May 31–June 1, 1614.
27. S. & B., II, 86; BN, fr. 4024, fols. 119v., 362. November 6, 1611; September 6, 1613.
28. Claude Malingre, *Entrée magnifique du roi . . . en sa ville d'Orléans, 8me juillet 1614*.
29. His mixed feelings concerning immersion on the occasions of his first bath and his first swim may be recalled. See chapter 5, "Repression and Denial," note.
30. BN, fr. 4025, fol. 77v.
31. S. & B., II, 149f.
32. *Ibid.*, 150. Héroard was himself born in a province on the Atlantic coast, according to Louise Flattet, *Le pays de Tancrède: Hauteville la Guichard (Manche)* (Saint-Lo, 1938), whose

source is a transcription of departmental archives, now lost, in *L'annuaire de La Manche* of 1830. This obscure connection may explain why the doctor makes a special note of this "first" for Louis: "At dinner he had a little sole from the tidewater of La Rochelle. It is the first time that he has eaten from that coast." BN, fr. 4025, 72v. July 25, 1614.

33. S. & B., II, 148; BN, fr. 4025, fol. 76v. August 4, 1614.
34. S. & B., II, 153; BN, fr. 4025, fol. 83v. August 26, 1614
35. S. & B., II, 154; BN, fr. 4025, 84v. August 29, 1614.
36. Héroard reports a similar one at Tours on July 23. S. & B., II, 146.
37. Le Bourdays, *Discours sur l'ordre tenu . . . dans la ville du Mans.*
38. Richard Daniell to John Egerton, September 29, 1614. Huntington Library, HM1658.
39. BN, fr. 4025, fols. 87, 88. September 6–8, 1614.
40. *Ibid.*, 89v.; S. & B., II, 158; September 15, 1614. The doctor's small château, today a training center for camp counselors, was built on land belonging to his wife, Marguerite Du Val, with funds provided by Louis, in a village near Limours, about forty kilometers from Paris.
41. *Ibid.*, 158f. September 16, 1614.
42. *Ibid.*, 159f. October 2, 1614.

CHAPTER 12: REHEARSALS FOR KINGSHIP

1. Malherbe, *Oeuvres*, 496. March 23, 1615.
2. "Discours particulier de la mort des duc et cardinal de Guyze tuez à Blois le 23e décembre 1588," BN, fr. 16806 (ancien St.-Germain 1398), fols. 75–90. This manuscript, although not in Héroard's handwriting, is identified at the beginning as *"par le sieur Héroard, médecin de S. M. et le Sr. Miron, depuis Lieutenant Civil, amis intimes en quy le Roy confioit."* Internal evidence suggests it was solicited by a friend of Héroard, perhaps some connection of the Dupuy brothers. A manuscript copy of it, with some alterations, is to be found in the hand of Pierre Du Puy in BN, Depuy 480, where, however, it is attributed to Miron alone. It was published in this form by Antoine Aubéry, *L'histoire des cardinaux françois* (Paris, 1644), 550, where it is again identified as François Miron's work without mention of Héroard, whose perspective, as it appears in the original manuscript, is discussed in chapter 15, "Additional Victims."
3. AMRE, Mémoires et documents 769, fol. 227. January 5, 1615. Mathieu Molé also recounts this scene, but does not quote Louis directly. *Mémoires*, I, 27.
4. For example, he attributes to Du Perron (whom he knew well) remarks that Arnauld (who was probably present, as Héroard certainly was not) attributes to Cardinal Sourdis of Bordeaux. BN, fr. 4025, fol. 124v. January 8, 1615. Du Perron was also present, however, and, according to Arnauld, joined Sourdis in casting aspersions on Condé's loyalty. *Journal, 1614–1620*, 26.
5. "Balzac inconnu," *Documents d'histoire*, 1 (1910), 161. February 21, 1616.
6. "Lettre de Jacques-Auguste de Thou . . . sur la conférence de Loudun," in *Histoire universelle de J.-A. de Thou* (London, 1734), XV, 554f., 568f.; Joseph Nouaillac, *Villeroy: Secrétaire d'Etat et ministre* (Paris: Champion, 1909), 537f.
7. S. & B., II, 172.
8. Arnauld, *Journal, 1614–1620*, 26f.
9. BN, fr. 4025, fol. 124v. The published version is different enough to obscure the meaning of this exchange and, inexplicably, the editors give the date as Tuesday, January 6, 1615. S. & B., II, 172.
10. A few weeks later Sourdis gave the Florentine resident an account of another altercation, said to have have taken place between Marie and the prince. The report was that on this occasion Louis was prevented from speaking, but later said that, had he been allowed to do

so, he would have come to the defense of his mother and "had he had his sword, would have run it through the prince's body." If Louis did indeed make this remark, Héroard does not report it. On the day in question he describes Louis hunting, painting, playing a game, and visiting his mother twice, but gives no details of anything politically significant. Though such an omission is not conclusive, another explanation of the discrepancy may fit. Perhaps Condé's earlier words menacing Sourdis in the manner described by Arnauld had reached the cardinal's ears, and he turned them back toward his enemy, the prince, by putting them in Louis's mouth instead. In any case, Marie's compatriot, who gave this version, had an interest in reporting to the Tuscan grand duke that Louis had defended his mother against Condé's insults, rather than that he had taken the side of the prince against his mother's clerical friends. Berthold Zeller, *Marie de Médicis: Chef du conseil* (Paris, 1898), 78.

11. "Prédication: La politique en chaire," *Documents d'histoire*, 1 (1910), 121–123.
12. Arnauld, *Journal, 1614–1620*, 37. January 22, 1615.
13. Paul Phélypeaux de Pontchartrain, *Mémoires*, ed. Joseph-François Michaud and Jean-Joseph-François Poujoulat (Paris, 1837), 340.
14. *Journal, 1614–1620*, 44. February 5, 1615. According to Conrart's manuscript account, his words were: "You are my king; you are my master. I will shed my blood for your service to the very last drop. But as for the queen, I do not say the same." Cited by Aumale, *Histoire des princes de Condé*, III, 43.
15. Quoted by Zeller, *Marie chef du conseil*, 25. November 10, 1614.
16. Bassompierre maintains that Souvré was motivated in this by his ambitions for his own son continuing in the king's favor. *Mémoires*, II, 139f. Courtenvaux, as already noted, was a *bon compagnon* of long standing.
17. S. & B., II, 164. October 29, 1614.
18. *Relation exacte de tout ce qui s'est passé la mort du maréchal d'Ancre*, ed. Joseph-François Michaud and Jean-Joseph-François Poujoulat (Paris, 1837), 451–484. This source is discussed below, in chapter 14, "Conspiring," note. See also *Mémoires de Richelieu*, I, 307.
19. *Journal, 1614–1620*, 59f. The same source claims that Vendôme, too, had a part in it, whether in his capacity as governor of Bretagne, in the thought of improving himself in Louis's graces, or both.
20. *Mercure françois*, 4 (1615), 27–29; Zeller, *Marie, chef du conseil*, 114f.
21. Arnauld, *Journal, 1614–1620*, 41. January 29, 1615.
22. S. & B., II, 105. May 20, 1612.
23. *Ibid.*, I, 391. April 16, 1609. For documentation on Richelieu's family history and early life, see my *The Young Richelieu: A Psychoanalytic Approach to Leadership* (Chicago: University of Chicago Press, 1983), *passim*.
24. *Mémoires de Richelieu*, I, 359–361.
25. *La vénalité des offices sous Henri IV et Louis XIII* (Rouen: Maugard, 1945), 589.
26. *Mercure françois*, 4 (1615), 144–147. August 9, 1615.
27. Arnauld, *Journal, 1614–1620*, 32. Héroard has Louis visiting his mother in the morning and afternoon of that day. BN, fr. 4025, fol. 4 v. January 11, 1615.
28. Zeller, *Marie de Médicis et Villeroy*, 135f.
29. *Oeuvres*, III, 360. November 27, 1613. The gift to Anne, however, would revert to the Crown of France. See Ruth Kleinman, *Anne of Austria* (Columbus: Ohio State University Press, 1985), 292 n.
30. *Mercure françois*, 4 (1615), 282f. See also *Céromonies et magnificences observées . . . au mariage de Madame* (Bordeaux: 1615).
31. Quoted by Zeller, *Marie, chef du conseil*, 106. Dispatch of March 17, 1615.
32. See, for example, letters from Aix of Guillaume Du Vair to Villeroy, secretary of state. *Revue d'histoire littéraire de la France*, 2 (1900), 603–623.

33. Humbert de Terrebasse, *Antoine de Pluvinel, dauphinois* (Lyons: L. Brun, 1911), 15. Nothing gives a better picture of Louis's equestrian recreations and the court social life surrounding them than Antoine de Pluvinel, *Le manège royal* (Paris, 1623), illustrated with engravings by Crispin de Passe. (Reprinted by Henri Veyrier, Madrid, 1974, from the German edition of 1625.)

34. S. & B., II, 178. July 6, 1615. His assurance encourages doubts about possible earlier insincerities!

35. Bellemaure, *Le pourtraict du roi* (Paris, 1618), 23.

36. S. & B., I, 396. July 4, 1609.

37. BN, fr. 4025, 185v. August 22, 1615. Antoinette Joron had given birth to a boy, baptised Louis, eighteen months previously. Queen Marguerite de Valois and César de Vendôme were godparents. Auguste Jal, *Dictionnaire critique de biographie et d'histoire* (Paris, 1872), 920.

38. S. & B., II, 179. July 29, 1615.

39. *Journal, 1614–1620*, 92. Héroard reports Marie's diarrhea and "bloody stools." BN, fr. 4025, 187v. July 28, 1615.

40. S. & B., II, 180. Zeller, *Marie, chef du conseil*, 152. August 16, 1615.

41. *Ibid.*, 106. Dispatch of March 17, 1615.

42. S. & B., II, 180f.

43. *Ibid.*, 183.

44. Bernard, *Histoire du roy Louis XIII*, 60.

45. S. & B., II, 183. October 21, 1615.

46. *Ibid.*, 183f.; BN, fr. 4025, fols. 213v., 214. October 21, 1615.

47. *Ibid.*, fols. 214–217v. October 25–November 3, 1615.

48. *Ibid.*

49. Anne's departure from Spain and arrival in France have been authoritatively described by Ruth Kleinman in *Anne of Austria*, 22–27. I am indebted to Professor Kleinman for an early opportunity to read a part of her manuscript.

50. S. & B., II, 184f.

51. Palma Cayet, *Chronologie septenaire*, ed. J.-A.-C. Buchon (Paris, 1875), 295.

52. Philip II of Spain and a duke of Tuscany also practiced this ritual, according to François Garasse, *La royale réception de Leurs Majestez très chrestiennes en la ville de Bourdeaux ou le siècle d'or ramené par les allians de France et de l'Espagne* (Bordeaux, 1615), 100.

53. S. & B., II, 185f.

54. Bernard, *Histoire du roy Louis XIII*, I, 60. Letter quoted by Baschet, *Le roi chez la reine*, 172.

55. *Mercure françois*, 4 (1615), 340.

56. *Ibid.*

57. Baschet cites a contemporary to the effect that the nurse of each was stationed in the bedchamber. *Le roi chez la reine*, 198.

58. BN, fr. 4025, fol. 224.

59. Indeed, one of Condé's arguments against the marriage had been that sexual contact in one so young as the king would sap his strength as well as jeopardize his hope of progeny and France's hope of stable succession. "Manifeste . . . par M. le Prince," August 9, 1615. *Mercure françois*, 4 (1615), 178f. Howell, also, reports that he had "bedded with the queen" for only two hours at Bordeaux "for fear it should hinder his growth and enervate his strength." *Lustra Ludovici*, 43.

60. "Lettre de Loudun," 549.

61. S. & B., II, 197. April 28, 1616.

62. Quoted by Zeller, *Marie, chef du conseil*, 262. Dispatch of May 16, 1616.

63. S. & B., II, 198. June 8, 1616.

64. Zeller, *Marie, chef du conseil*, 263.

65. *Ibid.*, 252.
66. Henri de Loménie, comte de Brienne, *Mémoires,* ed. Joseph-François Michaud and Jean-Joseph-François Poujoulat (Paris, 1838), 11.
67. Zeller, *Marie, chef du conseil*, 309.
68. S. & B., II, 201f.; BN, fr. 4025, fol. 308.

CHAPTER 13: MOTIVES FOR MURDER

1. Le Bourdays, *Discours sur l'ordre tenu . . . dans la ville du Mans.*
2. *Mercure françois*, 4 (1616), 200–204.
3. Scipion Dupleix, *Histoire de Louis le Juste* (Paris, 1637), 87.
4. Nicolas de Verdun, *Récit véritable de ce qui s'est passé au Louvre depuis le 24 avril jusques au départ de la reyne mère du roy* (Paris, 1617), 8.
5. *Mercure françois*, 4 (1616), 217.
6. Zeller, *Marie, chef du conseil*, 44 n., citing dispatch of October 11, 1616; Pontchartrain, *Mémoires*, 373.
7. Héroard had left a "M. Bodinet" on diary duty in his absence. BN, fr. 4025, fols. 318, 318v. October 5, 1616.
8. BN, fr. 4025, fols. 322–323.
9. *Ibid.*, fols 320v., 333. October 10, November 7, 1616.
10. See chapter 3, "Conflicting Passions."
11. BN, fr. 4025, fol. 328v.
12. Héroard says that six glasses of blood were taken and that Louis watched the procedure without alarm. BN, fr. 4025, fol. 329. November 1, 1616.
13. *Journal, 1614–1620*, 224.
14. [Le docteur] Trenel, "L'épilepsie de Louis XIII," *Aesculape*, 19 (1929), 125–196.
15. BN, fr. 4022, fol. 229v. April 20, 1606.
16. See H. Flanders Dunbar, "Psychoanalytic Notes Relating to Syndromes of Asthma and Hay Fever," *Psychoanalytic Quarterly*, 7 (1938), 25–68; Lucie Jessner, John Lamont, Robert Long, et al., "Emotional Impact of Nearness and Separation for the Asthmatic Child and his Mother," *Psychoanalytic Study of the Child*, 10 (1955), 353–375.
17. Pontchartrain, *Mémoires*, 350.
18. *Histoire universelle*, XV, 548f.
19. *Mémoires*, 117. Marie has of course been represented as deficient in the political insight that would have made this obvious to her.
20. *Mémoires*, II, 154.
21. They made a judgment that Louis's urine was "colored" during his illness. BN, fr. 4025, fol. 318. October 3, 1616.
22. Francisque Alvarez, a Portuguese, was physician to the queen mother at this time. He also treated Leonora on occasion. "Perhaps Jewish," he was said to be a member of the "Faculty of Medicine"—probably of Paris—and therefore from a group inimical to the *montpellérain* Héroard. Robert Lavollée cites depositions given by Alvarez and others at Leonora's trial (transcribed in BN, Cinq cents Colbert 221) in "La mort de Conchine et Léonore," *Le correspondant*, 4 (1909), 539f.
23. Héroard leaves his name blank; Soulié and Barthélemy, exceptionally, misread "Monteleone" as "Mantoue." Compare BN, fr. 4025, fol. 389v.; S. & B., II, 210.
24. BN, fr. 4025, fol. 321. October 13, 1616.
25. *Ibid.* See also, S. & B., II, 202f. October 13, 16, 1616.
26. I believe it would be difficult to find any case of a serious illness of a royal person in seventeenth-century France where suspicion of poisoning or deliberate exposure to infection by

malevolent others was not reported by some chronicler. My more limited reading in accounts of the English court would lead me to guess that the same would be found true there.

27. Florentin Du Ruau, *Propos dorés sur le glorieux règne de Blanche de Médicis ou Tableau de la régence* (Paris, 1618), 30f.

28. "The marquis . . . had Montpouillan offered 16,000 livres of pension, his plan being to leave him with the king, in order to render him [Ancre] good offices and warn him of all that happened there." Caumont, *Mémoires du duc de La Force*, IV, 23. Montpouillan was close to Louis at this time. After his death in 1622 his memoirs were drawn up by his brother, presumably on the basis of recollected confidences.

29. Nicolas Pasquier, *Lettres* (Paris, 1623), 556. Antoinette gave bedside consolation to Louis during his illness; Héroard shows her telling him stories on November 2, 1616. S. & B., II, 203. According to records published by Griselle, her court service terminated in 1618. See *Etat de la maison de Louis XIII*, 292.

30. *Journal, 1614–1620*, 224f.

31. This is Marie Thiroux d'Arconville's interpretation of the advice. *Marie de Médicis*, II, 285f.

32. BN, fr. 4025, fols. 330v., 346v. November 4, December 15, 1616.

33. BN, Cinq cents Colbert 98, fols. 177–213.

34. BN, fr. 4025, fols. 339, 346. November 24, December 12, 1616.

35. *La coniuration de Conchine*, 164. Matthieu declares he was ousted as Henri IV's "trumpet of glory" by Concini; apparently he was reinstated after the Florentine's murder.

36. Arnauld, *Journal, 1614–1620*, 221.

37. *Ibid.*, 217.

38. Richelieu, *Lettres*, VII, 418.

39. Arnauld, *Journal, 1614–1620*, 221.

40. Berthold Zeller, *Richelieu ministre, 1616* (Paris, 1899), 44. Venetian dispatch of October 25, 1616.

41. Pierre Matthieu, *Considerations on the Life and Services of Monsieur Villeroy* (London, 1638), 65. Trs. by Thomas Hawkins of *Remarques d'Estat et d'histoire sur la vie et les services . . . de M. de Villeroy* (Rouen, 1618).

42. Zeller, *Richelieu ministre, 1616*, viif. Jean Mariéjol, *Louis XIII et Henri IV*, vol. VI of *Histoire de France*, ed. Ernest Lavisse, 187.

43. The Venetian ambassador wrote home, "The rumor is current here that he draws a pension from Spain." Quoted by Zeller, *Richelieu ministre*, 52. November 29, 1616.

44. On Richelieu's real views at this time see Marvick, *Young Richelieu*, 201f.

45. Zeller, *Marie, chef du conseil*, 311f.

46. This was under pretext of serving the reigning queen, young Anne, as major domo. When Louis discovered this, shortly after Concini's death, he immediately annulled the privilege. See *Relation exacte*, 470.

47. Cited in Richelieu, *Lettres*, I, 193. October 15, 1616.

48. This was reported by both Venetian and Tuscan representatives. See Zeller, *Richelieu ministre, 1616*, 39.

49. Pierre Boitel de Gaubertin, *Histoire générale des guerres et choses mémorables arrivées sous le règne très-glorieux de Louis le Juste . . . jusques . . . à 1624* (Rouen, 1624), 281.

50. For example *Mémoires du maréchal d'Estrées*, ed. Joseph-François Michaud and Jean-Joseph-François Poujoulat (Paris, 1854), 417.

51. BN, fr. 4024, fol. 123; S. & B., II, 171f. January 3, 1615.

52. Emile Baudson, *Charles de Gonzague, duc de Nevers, de Réthel et de Mantoue* (Paris: Perrin, 1947), 143; AMRE, Mémoires et documents 771, fol. 5. December 15, 1616.

53. BN, fr. 4025, 334v. Soulié and Barthélemy mistakenly date this scene November 22. S. & B., II, 204.

CHAPTER 14: RITE OF PASSAGE: THE KILLING OF CONCINI

1. Howell, *Lustra Ludovici*, 38 v.
2. *Mercure françois*, 4 (1617), 198.
3. Boitel de Gaubertin, *Histoire générale des Guerres . . . de Louis le Juste*, 324.
4. Estrées, *Mémoires*, 419.
5. *Le comtadin provençal* (n. p., n. d.), 12.
6. *Relation exacte*, 454. When this most detailed account of the conspiracy was first published in Leiden, in 1659, as the last chapter of Pierre Dupuy, *Histoire des plus illustres favoris*, it was attributed to Michel de Marillac. There is no internal or external evidence to support this attribution. The most plausible explanation for it is that the source of the Leiden version credited a "M. de Marsillac" with authorship and that this was later misread as Marillac, the better-known name, by editors. François V, prince de Marsillac and comte de La Rochefoucauld, a member of Louis's inner circle after 1611 and a partisan of Marie de Medici against Condé in 1615, seems to have been of an age and in a position to be the possible author. See S. & B., II, 191; Griselle, *Etat de la maison*, 11; Fontenay-Mareuil, *Mémoires*, 83. Because a partial version of the *Relation* in the archives of the French foreign ministry is attributed to "Monsieur de Chaulnes," one of the younger brothers of Luynes, and because it contains passages in which Chaulnes (at the time Cadenet) played a central part in the plot, Louis Batiffol concluded that the whole account was Chaulnes's work. What appears to be an original manuscript of the *Relation*, however, BN, Dupuy 661, fols. 127–179v., does not contain these passages and, moreover, contains others, omitted or mangled by the Leiden publication, which suggest that Chaulnes was not the author of any except the AMRE version, even though that account precedes the Dupuy 661 one in the Leiden version. That combination of the two accounts was reproduced under the same title by Michaud and Poujoulat (Paris, 1837), 451–484. Citations are made to it here when possible.
7. *Relation exacte*, 454.
8. BN, fr. 4025, 334v. November 12, 1616.
9. Arnauld, *Journal, 1614–1620*, 233.
10. BN, fr. 4025, fols. 339–359. There is a corrected entry for January 1, 1617, but the discarded one was also bound into the BN volume (fols. 353, 354).
11. *Ibid.*, fols. 330v., 332v.
12. See also below, "Final Decision."
13. All versions of the Cadenet-amplified account wrongly identify Hurles as "Durles."
14. BN, fr. 4025, fol. 332v.
15. S. & B., II, 204. November 27, 1616. Remarkably, Héroard's nineteenth-century editors connect Louis's bellicose dream about the "savage Judge of Israel" with murderous feelings towards Concini.
16. Judges 9:1–57.
17. See the correspondence with Schomberg, AMRE, Correspondance diplomatique, V, Allemagne, fols. 344f., explaining, for the benefit of the ambassador to the Protestant German powers, a new authoritative policy in domestic politics. Note also his efforts to reassure the Huguenots, as in the Vignolles mission. BN, Clairambault 372, fol. 43. February 4, 1617.
18. *Lettres de Richelieu*, I, 208–235.
19. *Mercure françois*, 4 (1617), 32–86; *Lettres de Richelieu*, I, 301–316. February 18, 1617.
20. BN, fr. 4025, fols. 348–350v. December 18–23, 1616. Héroard's editors misread the notation as merely a wish to buy. S. & B., II, 205.
21. Matthieu, *La coniuration de Conchine*, 34.
22. *Lettres*, VII, 352.

23. *Lettres*, 556.
24. Estrées, *Mémoires*, 417.
25. *Mémoires du comte de Brienne*, 10.
26. *Mémoires du marquis de Beauvais-Nangis* (Paris: Société de l'Histoire de France, 1862), 151.
27. *Calendar of State Papers,* domestic series, IX, 85. November 7, 1611.
28. BN, fr. 4025, fol. 372v. February 27, 1617.
29. *Discours sur le sujet de la mort du Sgr. Struard, escossois* (Paris, 1617), 8.
30. BN, fr. 4025, fol 372v. February 27, 1617.
31. *Mercure françois*, 4 (1617), 115.
32. *Lettres,* 558.
33. *Mercure françois*, 4 (1617), 155f.
34. Bibliothèque de l'Institut, Godefroy 268, III, fol. 156.
35. BN, fr. 5131, fol. 16. (Misdated May 1617.)
36. BN, Fichier Charavay. March 20, 1617.
37. *Mercure françois*, 4 (1617), 115.
38. Héroard shows him on hunting excursions to Madrid, "in back of Montmartre" on March 27, in Vincennes on March 29, and in Colomb on the first of April. BN, fr. 4025, fols 382–383. Courcelles may have been declared off limits for him, however; these visits seem to have ceased abruptly at the beginning of 1617.
39. *La nunciatura di Francia del cardinale Guido Bentivoglio: Lettere a Scipione Borghese,* ed. Luigi di Steffano, 2 vols. (Florence, 1863), I, 127. February 28, 1617. In the same letter the nuncio reports that in this conversation Marie again compared her position with that of Catherine de Medici—"the other queen mother of her House and of the troubles that she had to endure, and of the schemes that the malcontents of those days had to take her children from her." Marie's secretary, Phélypeaux, also gives no hint in his memoirs that the queen was aware of Louis's plans.
40. For example, half of one day's routine affairs are added in the margin, presumably from having been omitted in the process of recopying. The following day is abnormally short. BN, 4025, fol. 375v. March 7, 8, 1617.
41. For example, *ibid.*, fols. 368–369v. February 13–15, 1616.
42. *Journal, 1614–1620,* 282.
43. *Ibid.*, 285. A letter of Mme. de Nevers promising to surrender her besieged duchy to the royal forces is evidence of the effectiveness of the government in negotiating capitulation. It is dated "*le . . . [sic] jour d'avril, 1617,*" certainly before the overthrow of Ancre, since the acceptance by the king, "assisted by the queen his mother," had also been prepared. AMRE 771, fols. 107–108.
44. *Calendar of State Papers*, domestic series, IX, 434. February 12, 1617.
45. Documents were to show that some of her fortune had already been transferred. Her testimony at the trial that she had counseled her husband to relinquish his claims to power put her on the side of the new counselors to the queen who had persuaded Marie that Concini had become a liability to royal authority. The court knew that Leonora and her husband were no longer on good terms. (See below, chapter 15, "Additional Victims," note.) The only one to represent Leonora, rather than Concino, as the one reluctant to bow out is Bassompierre, in his *Mémoires,* 134f. Père Griffet offers an explanation for this—in his view—falsification. *Histoire de Louis XIII,* I, 166f. It might also be noted that Bassompierre wrote down his recollections in prison, after the banishment of Marie, and long after the execution of Leonora. Hoping for a pardon from Louis, it is understandable that he did not want to represent the queen mother as heeding prudent advice from her long-standing favorite or that favorite as essentially innocent of the charges that later led to her execution.
46. BN, fr. 4025, fols. 388–389v. April 13–17, 1616.
47. Matthieu, *La coniuration de Conchine,* 33.

48. Guichard Déageant, sieur de Saint-Martin, *Mémoires envoyés à Monsieur le cardinal de Richelieu*, vol. III of *Mémoires particuliers pour servir à l'histoire de France* (Paris, 1756), 40.
49. BN, Dupuy 661, fols. 127, 127v.
50. Zeller, *Richelieu ministre, 1616*, 173.
51. *Journal, 1614–1620*, 283.
52. *Ibid.*
53. Robert Lavollée accepts this interpretation. See "La mort de Conchine et Léonore," *Le correspondant*, 237 (1909), 326f.
54. Estrées, *Mémoires*, 419.
55. *Mémoires de Fontenay-Mareuil*, 114.
56. Brienne, *Mémoires*, 12.
57. Caumont, *Mémoires du duc de La Force*, IV, 23–25.
58. See above, note 6.
59. Déageant, *Mémoires*, 43–45.
60. *Relation exacte*, 451–453.
61. Matthieu, *La coniuration de Conchine*, 264.
62. Baptiste Le Grain, *La décade commençant l'histoire du roy Louis XIII* (Paris, 1618), 387.
63. *Relation exacte*, 453f.
64. *Ibid.*, 454.
65. Caumont, *Mémoires du duc de La Force*, IV, 33.
66. *Relation exacte*, 458. The manuscript gives Leonora an Italian accent that is lost in the publication. BN, Dupuy 661, fol. 131.
67. The editor of Arnauld, *Journal, 1614–1620*, 130 n., cites Père Anselme (VIII, 796) to the effect that the young baron de Montglat, killed by Vitry in December, 1615, was one of his best friends.
68. *Histoire du cardinal-duc de Richelieu*, 2 vols. (Cologne, 1656), I, 22.
69. Déageant claims that Louis remained in his chambers on the pretext that he had taken a purgative. *Mémoires*, 42. This seems unlikely, both because Héroard would have had to be a party to such a pretext and because the king would have remained in semiundress, whereas when he received news of the murder he was dressed as though prepared for outdoor sport. This fact coincides better with reports that he had announced his intention to go hunting that day. It may be significant, moreover, that this was the same strategy he had rehearsed with the seizure of Condé.
70. Déageant, *Mémoires envoyés*, 45. Matthieu says it was Vitry who gave this order. *La coniuration*, 265.
71. *Mémoires*, 12.
72. Adrien Blanchet, ed., "Un récit inédit de la mort du maréchal d'Ancre," *Bulletin de la Société de l'Histoire de Paris et de l'Ile de France* 27 (1900), 135–141.
73. Jean Boucher de Guilleville, *Concino Concini . . . sa mort*, ed. Jules-Stanislas Doinel (Orléans, 1883), 5f.
74. BN, Dupuy 661, fol. 128v.
75. *Ibid.* An engraving of the time shows Louis on his balcony watching Concini's murder in the court below. Since the assault took place on the drawbridge, however, outside the yard, it is not likely that the king could have seen it even if he were looking.
76. AMRE, Mémoires et documents 364, fol. 93.
77. *Ibid.*, fols. 93–95.
78. *Mémoires de Richelieu*, II, 195. Maximin Deloche gives reasons for believing that this is an authentic reminiscence of the future cardinal. "Les vrais mémoires du cardinal de Richelieu," *Revue des questions historiques*, 109 (1928), 297. Ritualistic aspects of these desecrations are discussed in Orest Ranum, "The French Ritual of Assassination in the Late Sixteenth Century," *Sixteenth Century Journal*, 11 (1980), 63–82.
79. *Mémoires*, 419.

CHAPTER 15: A NEW ORDER?

1. "Remarcques de Monsieur de Bassompierre sur les vies des Roys Henry IV et Louis XIII de Dupleix," in *Mémoires de Beauvais-Nangis* (Paris, 1665), II, 224.
2. S. & B., II, 202. October 8, 1616.
3. Arnauld, *Journal, 1614–1620*, 282f. The same words are attributed to him by an English reporter and by the Venetian emissary. See *Calendar of State Papers*, domestic series, IX, 461; BN, italiens 1771, fol. 81.
4. Boucher de Guilleville, *Concino Concini*, 6.
5. Arnauld, *Journal, 1614–1620*, 282f.
6. Molé, *Mémoires*, I, 144–146.
7. Cited in note 1 of chapter 14 above.
8. Quoted by Gabriel Hanotaux, *Histoire du cardinal de Richelieu*, 2 vols. (Paris, 1896), II, 214.
9. *Journal, 1614–1620*, 283.
10. Pontchartrain, *Mémoires*, 387.
11. Boucher de Guilleville, *Concino Concini*, 6.
12. *Life and Services of Monsieur Villeroy*, 68, trs. from *Remarques . . . sur . . . Monsieur de Villeroy*.
13. *Relation exacte*, 461.
14. *Ibid.* 461. While this source is seemingly the only one to report these words of Louis rejecting Richelieu, the observer's apparent impartiality and the fact that it was written within two months of the events give it credibility. The author could not have guessed at the bishop's future role, nor did he bear a grievance against Ancre, about whom he writes with neutrality. The published version is misleading on this last point: where the manuscript calls Concini "*le mareschal*," for example, the printed relation has changed the words to "*ce monstre.*" Compare BN, Dupuy 661, fol. 166v. and *Relation exacte*, 477.
15. *Relation exacte*, 462.
16. BN, Dupuy 661, fol. 139 v.
17. *Relation exacte*, 467.
18. BN, fr. 17363, fol. 230.
19. *Ibid.*, fol. 227, April 26, 1617, and fol. 228 (misdated April 17).
20. Arnauld, *Journal, 1614–1620*, 283. April 24, 1617.
21. BN, Dupuy 661, fol. 170v.
22. S. & B., II, 210; BN, 4025, fol. 393.
23. BN, fr. 16806, fol. 75.
24. *Ibid.*, fol. 87v.
25. *Ibid.*, fols. 85v., 87.
26. *Relation exacte*, 455; *Lustra Ludovici*, 139.
27. Lavollée, "La mort de Conchine," 327. Dispatch of May 5, 1617.
28. *Les deux faces de la vie et de la mort de Marie de Médicis* (Antwerp, 1643), 10.
29. For example, Du Ruau, *Propos dorés sur . . . la régence*, 64, who compared it to the reverence of Saint Louis for his mother, Blanche de Castille.
30. BN, Dupuy 661, fol. 142v., italien 1771, fol. 94, dispatch of May 2, 1617; *Relation exacte*, 464.
31. Lavollée, "La mort de Conchine," 338.
32. *Relation exacte*, 473f.
33. *Ibid.*, 471.
34. Mathieu de Morgues, *Lumières pour l'histoire de France* (n. p., 1636), 52.
35. BN, fr. 4025, fol. 398.
36. *Ibid.*, fol. 398v.; S. & B., II, 211.
37. *Mercure françois*, 4 (1617), 193. This virtually instantaneous cessation of hostilities may have seemed magical to some, including perhaps Louis himself. Only four hours after Ancre's

death one nobleman declared that the king was already "being obeyed by all people of good will" and that so few of the other kind were apparent that "it seems as though they never had any other intention." Archives Nationales, K111.

38. *Relation exacte*, 472; Déageant, *Mémoires*, 36.
39. AMRE, Mémoires et documents 771, 112v. May 10, 1617.
40. This officer had served as intermediary between Louis and the queen mother in the days after Ancre's assassination. See *Relation exacte*, 461.
41. *Ibid.*, 475.
42. AMRE, Mémoires et documents 771, 112v.
43. In the event, the judgment of May 10 ordered that the arms and legs of the living man be broken on the scaffold and "afterwards his dead body . . . burned." It later specified that "having received two blows" (presumably with the aim of breaking his limbs) "he would be strangled first." AN, X2a 198, fol. 24v.
44. *Relation exacte*, 475f.
45. AMRE, Mémoires et documents 771, fol. 134. June 19, 1617.
46. *Ibid.*, fol. 114. May 10, 1610.
47. BN, Dupuy 661, fol. 147v.
48. "Récit véritable depuis le 24 avril," 9f.
49. Institut, Godefroy 15, fol. 52. June 9, 1617.
50. Philippe Tamizey de Larroque, "Un mot apocryphe de la maréchale d'Ancre," *Revue des questions historiques,* 6 (1869), 545–549.
51. See Richelieu's letter to Déageant in *Lettres,* VII, 383f., and Déageant's side of the correspondence in AMRE, Mémoires et documents 771, fol. 118v. May 10–19, 1617.
52. *Relation exacte*, 464.
53. *Ibid.*, 475.
54. *Ibid.*, 470f.; BN, Dupuy 661, fol. 153v.
55. The letter patent is reproduced in Hayem, *Le maréchal d'Ancre,* 217f.
56. Lavollée, "La mort de Conchine," 310f, 531f.
57. BN, Cinq cents Colbert 221, fols. 84, 86v., 87; Hayem, *Le maréchal d'Ancre,* 104f. Hayem's partial transcription of the testimony recorded in the Cinq cents Colbert manuscript is used wherever possible.
58. Hayem, *Le maréchal d'Ancre,* 98, 272f.
59. Although evidence was also heard that Leonora had corresponded with suspected sorcerers, little was made of this in her sentencing. Convictions on accusations of sorcery were outmoded by 1617, particularly in the first court of the realm: since 1610 there had been no execution on those grounds as a result of an appeal to the Paris Parlement. See Alfred Soman, "La décriminalisation de la sorcellerie en France," *Histoire, économie et société,* 2 (1985), 187f., 197.
60. BN, Cinq cents Colbert 221, fol. 23. Letters from Leonora and her husband were written to Leonora in January 1615, when the Spanish marriages were being planned. AN, K1454a, 60, no. 8.
61. Pasquier, *Lettres,* 566.
62. *Relation exacte*, 475. An additional bit of evidence that the authors of the so-called Richelieu *Mémoires* lacked firsthand grasp of the politics of these years is their attribution to Condé of bad feelings towards Leonora. (See II, 212.) So far as is known, the Florentine favorite had always kept the promises she made to the prince, and nothing in his behavior indicates that he was ungrateful for this.
63. AMRE, Mémoires et documents 771, fol. 118v.
64. *Mémoires de Richelieu,* II, 222.
65. Lavollée, "La mort de Conchine," 556.
66. Arsenal 4110, fol. 1155.

67. Leonora's friend, the Florentine Philippe de Gondi, left one of the most interesting of eyewitness accounts. See "Relazione della morte della mareschialla d'Ancre," *Archivio storico lombardo,* 4 (1877), 39–42.
68. Lavollée, "La mort de Conchine," 561.
69. *Mercure françois,* 4 (1617), 232.
70. Arsenal 4110, fol. 1160. One of those who admired her courage on the occasion was Henri de Richelieu. This cavalier wrote his youngest brother, Armand, by then isolated in his diocese of Luçon, a letter praising the Christian steadfastness with which the maréchale met her hard fate. *Ibid.,* fol. 155. July 12, 1617.
71. BN, 4025, 419v.; S. & B., II, 213. July 8, 1617.
72. *Lumières,* 52.
73. Arsenal 4110, fol. 1155.
74. *Ibid.,* fol. 1153.
75. *Relation exacte,* 465.
76. Robert de Crèvecoeur, *Un document nouveau sur la succession des Concini* (Paris, 1891), 251.
77. *Ibid.*
78. BN, Dupuy 661, fol. 143v.
79. *Relation exacte,* 467.
80. Lavollée, "La mort de Conchine," 562.
81. Arnauld, *Journal, 1614–1620,* 290.
82. For example, Lavollée, "La mort de Conchine," 334, citing a letter to Marie de Medici of December 6, 1628 in BN, fr. 3689.
83. Fichier Charavay (Ancre). April 10, 1629.
84. *La magicienne estrangère par un bon françois nepveu de Rotomagues* (Rouen, 1617), 29.
85. Eugène Griselle, *Louis XIII et Richelieu* (Paris, 1911), 167f.
86. *Relation exacte,* 477f.
87. *Ibid.,* 482.
88. Scipion Dupleix, *Histoire de Louis le Juste* (Paris, 1633), 170.
89. *Relation exacte,* 458.
90. *Ibid.* 459.
91. A letter from one of Richelieu's professed supporters, Tantucci, came to that conclusion. It was summarized for the bishop by his personal secretary. See AMRE, Mémoires et documents 771, fols. 343–345 (undated). Louis's command to Richelieu to remain in his diocese, away from the queen mother, is dated June 15, 1617. *Ibid.,* 244, fol. 2.
92. Paul Jacquinet, *Des prédicateurs du XVIIe siècle avant Bossuet* (Paris, 1885), 67–69, 87–90.
93. Ernest M. Rivière, "Le père Arnoux, controversiste, 1613–1618," *Documents d'histoire* 1 (1911), 169f.
94. *Journal, 1614–1620,* 306. June 10, 1617.
95. *Lettres,* 563–570.
96. *Mercure françois,* 4 (1617), 161.
97. Bernard, *Histoire du roy Louis XIII,* Part I, 77.
98. Bellemaure, *Le pourtraict du Roy,* 407f.
99. Bernard, *Histoire du roy Louis XIII,* I, 81.
100. *Le pourtraict du Roi,* 408.
101. BN, fr. 17363, 230.
102. Bernard, *Histoire du roy Louis XIII,* Part I, 81.
103. One anti-Luynes pamphlet even went so far as to suggest that the connétable had been, like the maréchal, a foreigner, because he was a provençal from Mornas! See *Le comtadin provençal,* 1.
104. *Les papiers de Richelieu.* Section politique intérieure, ed. Pierre Grillon, 5 vols. (Paris: Pedone, 1975–1982), II, 567. October 6, 1627.

Bibliography

References to works bearing on psychological research are to be found in the notes; only a selection from historical writings consulted is cited here. A fuller bibliography for the history of France, 1600–1620, is to be found in my *The Young Richelieu*.

MANUSCRIPTS

Archives du Ministère des Relations Extérieures (AMRE)

Mémoires et documents, France, 243–246, 364, 373, 764, 767, 769, 771.
Correspondance diplomatique, Rome, 23, Allemagne, 5.

Archives Nationales (AN)

V5 270, K111, K1454a, X2a 198, X2a 979.

Institut de France

Godefroy, 15, 268.
Musée de Chantilly, Bibliothèque Condé, 93, 108, 337, I:8, M:1, L:83.

Bibliothèque Nationale (BN)

Arsenal 2648, 4110, 5925h.
Baluze 145, 337.
Béthune 9299.
Cinq cents Colbert 86–89, 98, 221.
Clairambault 372.
Dupuy 39, 480, 658, 767, 853.
Fichier Charavay.
Fonds français (fr.) 3445, 3649, 3689, 3798, 3818, 3826, 3840, 4022–4027, 5131, 10201, 10210, 14423, 15534, 16806, 17308, 17363, 19076, 21448, 23200, 23251.
Nouvelles acquisitions françaises (n. a.) 5130, 13008.
Pièces originales 1516.

Archives de l'Ecole de Médecine de Montpellier

D42, H3, H4, M.

Archivio Gonzaga (Mantua)

Francia, Correspondenza Estera (Serie E) 627, 628.

British Library (BL) (London)

Additional, 14840.

PUBLISHED CONTEMPORARY SOURCES

Arnauld d'Andilly, Robert. *Journal, 1614–1620.* Edited by Achille Halphen. Paris, 1857.

Arcussia, Charles d', seigneur d'Esparron. *La fauconnerie du roy.* Rouen, 1621.

Aubéry, Antoine. *L'histoire des cardinaux françois.* Paris, 1644.

———. *L'histoire du cardinal-duc de Richelieu.* 2 vols., Cologne, 1666. Vol. I.

Bassompierre, François de. *Mémoires.* Edited by Claude-Bernard Petitot. 3 vols. Paris, 1822–1823. Vol. I.

———. "Remarcques de Monsieur de Bassompierre sur les vies des roys Henry IV et Louis XIII de Dupleix," in *Mémoires de Beauvais-Nangis.* 2 vols., Paris, 1665. Vol. II.

Beauvais-Nangis, Nicolas de Brichanteau, marquis de. *Mémoires du marquis de Beauvais-Nangis.* Edited by Monmerqué and Taillandier. Paris, 1862.

Bellemaure, le sieur de. *Le pourtraict du roi envoyé au sieur de Mirancourt.* First edition. Paris, 1618. Also in Danjou and Cimber, editors, *Archives curieuses de l'histoire de France.* 27 vols. Paris, 1834–1840. 2d. series, vol. I.

Bentivoglio, Guido. *La nunziatura di Francia de Cardinale G. Bentivoglio: Lettere a Scipione Borghese.* Edited by Luigi de Steffani. 2 vols. Florence, 1863. Vol. I.

Bernard, Charles. *L'histoire des guerres de Louis XIII.* Paris, 1636.

———. *Histoire du roy Louis XIII.* Paris, 1646.

Blanchet, Adrien, editor. "Un récit inédit de la mort du maréchal d'Ancre," *Bulletin de la Société de l'Histoire de Paris et de I'lle de France,* 27 (1900), 135–141.

Boitel de Gaubertin, Pierre. *Histoire générale des guerres et choses mémorables arrivées sous le règne très-glorieux de Louis le Juste . . . jusques . . . à 1624.* Rouen, 1624.

Boucher de Guilleville, Jean. *Concino Concini . . . sa mort.* Edited by Jules-Stanislas Doinel. Orléans, 1883.

Bourgeois (or Boursier), Louise. *Observations diverses sur la stérilité, perte de fruict, fécondité, accouchements et maladies des femmes et enfants nouveau naiz.* Paris, 1609.

———. *Récit véritable des naissances de messeigneurs et dames les enfans de France.* Paris, 1626.

———. *Les six couches de Marie de Médicis.* Edited by Achille Chéreau. Paris, 1875.

Brienne, Henri Auguste de Loménie, comte de. *Mémoires du comte de Brienne.* Edited by Joseph-François Michaud and Jean-Joseph-François Poujoulat. Paris, 1838.

Bufalo, I. del. *Correspondance du nonce en France, 1601–1605.* Edited by Bernard Barbiche. Vol. IV of *Acta Nunciaturae Gallicae.* Rome: Gregorian University, 1964.

Calendar of State Papers. Domestic series, vol. IX (1611–1618). *Reign of James I.* Edited by Mary Green. London, 1858.

Carew, George. "A Relation of the State of France (1609)," in Thomas Birch, *An Historical View of the Negotiations between the Courts of England, France and Brussels, from the Year 1592.* London, 1749.

Catalogue of the Collection of Alfred Morrison. Edited by Alphonse Thibaudeau, First series, vols. I–VI. London, 1883–1892.

Cayet, Palma. *Chronologie novenaire et septenaire.* Edited by J.-A.-C. Buchon. 2 vols. Paris, 1836–1875.

Cherbury, Edward, Lord Herbert of. *Autobiography.* London, 1888.

Le comtadin provençal. Anon. N. p., n. d. (ca. 1617).

Coton, Pierre. *Lettre dédicatoire des pères Jésuites . . . à la reyne mère suivie de l'anticoton et réponse à l'anticoton.* Paris, 1610.

Déageant, Guichard de, sieur de Saint-Martin. *Mémoires envoyés à Monsieur le Cardinal de Richelieu.* Vol. III of *Mémoires particuliers pour servir à l'histoire de France.* Paris, 1756.

Des Yveteaux, Nicolas Vauquelin, sieur. *Oeuvres complètes de Nicolas Vauquelin.* Edited by Georges Mongrédien. Paris: Picard, 1921; Geneva: Slatkine, 1967.

———. "Trois lettres de Nicolas Vauquelin, sieur Des Yveteaux." Edited by Gérard de Contades. *Bulletin de la Société Historique de l'Orne,* 8 (1889), 475–482.

Dupuy, Pierre. *Histoire des plus illustres favoris, anciens et modernes.* Leiden, 1659.

Dupleix, Scipion. *Histoire de Louis le Juste,* Paris, 1633.

Du Ruau, Florentin. *Propos dorés sur le glorieux règne de Blanche de Médicis ou Tableau de la régence.* Paris, 1618.

Estrées, François-A., duc d'. *Mémoires du maréchal d'Estrées.* Edited by Paul Bonnefon. Paris: Société de l'Histoire de France, 1910.

Fontenay-Mareuil, François Duval de. *Mémoires.* Edited by Joseph-François Michaud and Jean-Joseph Poujoulat. Paris, 1837.

Garasse, François, Père. *La royale réception de leurs maiestez très-chrestiennes en la ville de Bourdeaus ou le siècle d'or ramené par les allians de France et d'Espaigne.* Bordeaux, 1615.

Gondi, Philippe de. "Relazione della morte della marescialla d'Ancre." *Archivio Storica Lombardo,* 4 (1877), 39–42.

Griselle, Eugène, editor. *Documents d'histoire.* 4 vols. Paris, 1910–1913.

———. *Formulaires de lettres de François I à Louis XIV et Etat de la France dressé en 1642.* N. p., n. d.

———. *L'écurie du roi Louis XIII.* Paris: Editions Documents d'Histoire, 1912.

———. *Etat de la maison du roi Louis XIII.* Paris: Editions Documents d'Histoire, 1912.

———. *Supplément à la maison du roi Louis XIII.* Paris: Editions Documents d'Histoire, 1912.

Henri IV. *Lettres missives du roi Henri IV.* Edited by Berger de Xivrey and J. Gaudet. 8 vols. Paris, 1850–1873.

Héroard, Jean. *Journal de l'enfance et de la première jeunesse de Louis XIII.* Edited by Eudore Soulié and Edouard de Barthélemy. 2 vols. Paris, 1868. (This edition reprints, in vol. II, 320–392, the first—and French—version of *L'institution du prince,* presented to the dauphin Louis in 1609.)

————. *Discours des droits appartenans à la maison de Nevers es Duchés de Brabant, Lembourg et Ville d'Anvers, avec une table de la généalogie de ladicte maison pour la déclaration d'iceux.* Paris, 1581.

Howell, James. *A Brief Admonition of Some of the Inconveniences of All the Three Most Famous Governments.* London, 1659.

————. *Familiar Letters.* 2 vols. Boston: Houghton Mifflin, 1908.

————. *Lustra Ludovici.* London, 1646.

Joubert, Laurent. *Erreurs Populaires.* Bordeaux, 1579.

La Force, Jacques Nompar de Caumont, duc de. *Mémoires du duc de La Force et de ses deux fils.* 4 vols. Paris, 1843. Vols. I, IV.

Le Bourdays, Hardouin. *Discours sur l'ordre tenu de Leurs Majestés en entrant dans la ville du Mans. . . .* Le Mans, 1614.

Legrain, Jean-Baptiste. *Décade commençant l'histoire du roy Louis XIII.* Paris, 1619.

Le Moyne, Pierre, Père. *L'art de régner.* Paris, 1658.

L'Estoile, Pierre. *Journal pour les règnes de Henri III, Henri IV, et du début du règne de Louis XIII.* Edited by Louis-R. Lefèvre and André Martin. 4 vols. Paris: Gallimard, 1943–1960.

Louis XIII. *Lettres de la main de Louis XIII.* Edited by Eugène Griselle. Paris: Société des Bibliophiles Français, 1914.

Lyonnet, Robert. *Brevis dissertatio de morbis haereditarius.* Paris, 1647.

La Magicienne estrangère, par un bon François nepveu de Rotomague. Rouen, 1617.

Magnificences observées . . . au mariage de Madame . . . le dimanche 18 octobre 1615. Anon. Bordeaux, 1615.

Malherbe, François de. *Oeuvres.* Edited by Ludovic Lalanne. 4 vols. Vols. III, IV. Paris, 1862.

Malingre, Claude. *Histoire du règne de Louis XIII.* 2 vols. Paris, 1646.

————. *Histoires tragiques de nostre temps.* Rouen, 1641.

Matricule de l'université de médecine de Montpellier, 1503–1599. Edited by Marcel Gouron. Geneva: Droz, 1957.

Matthieu, Pierre. *Remarques d'Estat et d'histoire sur la vie et les services . . . de M. de Villeroy.* Rouen, 1618.

————. *La coniuration de Conchine.* Paris, 1618.

Mémoires d'Estat, recueillis de divers manuscrits à la suite de ceux de Monsieur de Villeroy. 4 vols. Vol. III. Paris, 1645.

Mémoires du cardinal de Richelieu. 10 vols. Paris: Société de l'Histoire de France, 1908–1931. Vols. I, II.

Mercure françois. Edited by Estienne Richer. Vols. I–IV. Paris, 1611–1617.

Mersenne, Marin, Père. *Correspondance.* Edited by Paul Tannery. 6 vols. Paris: Centre Nationale de la Recherche Scientifique, 1932–1960.

————. *Harmonie universelle.* 2 vols. Paris, 1636; Antwerp, 1633.

Molé, Mathieu. *Mémoires de Mathieu Molé.* Edited by Aimé Champollion-Figeac. 4 vols. Paris, 1855–1857.

Montglat, François de Paule de Clermont, marquis de. *Mémoires de Montglat.* Edited by Joseph-François Michaud and Jean-Joseph-François Poujoulat. Paris, 1881.

Morgues, Mathieu de. *Les deux faces de la vie et de la mort de Marie de Médicis.* Antwerp, 1643.

————. *Lumières pour l'histoire de France. . . .* N. p., 1636.

Négociations diplomatiques de la France avec la Toscane. Edited by Guiseppe Canestrini and Abel Desjardins. 6 vols. Vol. V. Paris, 1875.

Pasquier, Nicolas. *Lettres.* Paris, 1623.

Patin, Guy. *Lettres choisies.* Paris, 1692.

Peiresc, Fabri de. *Lettres.* Edited by Philippe Tamizey de Larroque. 7 vols. Paris, 1888–1898.

Pluvinel, Antoine de. *Le manège royal.* Paris, 1623.

Propos dorés sur l'autorité tyrannique de Concino. (Anonymous.) N. p., 1617.

Pommereuse, Marie [Mère]. *Les chroniques de l'Ordre des Ursulines.* 2 vols. Paris, 1673. Vol. III.

Pontchartrain, Paul Phélypeaux de. *Mémoires de Pontchartrain.* Edited by Joseph-François Michaud and Jean-Joseph-François Poujoulat. Paris, 1837.

Puységur, Jacques de Chastenet de. *Mémoires.* 2 vols. Paris, 1883. Vol. I.

Relation exacte de tout ce qui s'est passé à la mort du maréchal d'Ancre. Edited by Michaud and Poujoulat. Paris, 1837. (See text and notes of chapter 14, "Conspiring," for attribution.)

Relazioni degli stati europei: Lettere al senato degli ambasciatori veneti nel secolo XVIIo. Edited by Guglielmo Berchet and Nicolo Barozzi. 3 vols. Venice, 1857. Second series, vol. I.

Richelieu, Armand-Jean Du Plessis, Cardinal de. *Lettres, instructions et papiers d'Etat du cardinal de Richelieu.* Edited by Denis-Louis-Martial Avenel. 8 volumes. Paris, 1853–1877.

———. *Les papiers de Richelieu.* Section politique intérieure. Edited by Pierre Grillon. 6 vols., 1 vol. index to vols. I–III. Paris: Pedone, 1975–1985.

———. *Les papiers de Richelieu.* Section politique extérieure. L'empire allemand: 1619–1629. Edited by Adolf Wild. Paris, Pedone, 1982.

Richer, Edmond. *Histoire du syndicat d'Edmond Richer.* Avignon, 1753.

Saint-Simon, Louis de Rouvray, duc de. *Parallèle des trois premiers rois Bourbons.* Paris: Bonnot, 1967.

Seyssel, Claude de. *The Monarchy of France.* Edited by Donald R. Kelly. Translated by Jack H. Hexter. New Haven: Yale University Press, 1981.

Sully, Maximilien de Béthune, duc de. *Mémoires du duc de Sully.* 6 vols. Paris, 1822–1827.

Tallemant des Réaux, Gédéon. *Les historiettes.* Edited by Louis-Jean-Nicolas de Monmerqué and Paulin Paris. 6 vols. Paris, 1862.

Thou, Jacques-Auguste de. *Histoire universelle.* 15 vols. London, 1735. Vol. XV.

Valois, Marguerite de. *Mémoires.* Edited by Ludovic de Lalanne. Paris, 1858.

Varillas, Antoine. *La pratique de l'éducation des princes.* Paris, 1685.

Varin, J.-Philippe. *L'heureuse . . . entrée de Louis le Juste dans la ville de Lyon. . . .* Lyons, 1622.

Verdun, Nicolas de. *Récit véritable de ce qui s'est passé au Louvre depuis le 24 avril jusques au départ de la reyne mère du roy.* Paris, 1617.

Villeroy, Nicolas de Neufville, Seigneur de. *Mémoires servant à l'histoire de notre temps.* Edited by Joseph François Michaud and Jean-Joseph-François Poujoulat. Paris, 1822.

———. *Mémoires d'Estat de Monsieur de Villeroy.* Paris, 1725.

SECONDARY WORKS

Books

Anis, Alphonse-François d'. *Etude historique et littéraire: David Rivault de Fleurance et les autres précepteurs de Louis XIII.* Paris, 1893.

Arconville, Marie Thiroux d'. *La vie de Marie de Médicis.* 3 vols. Paris, 1774.

Aumale, Henri d'Orleans, duc d'. *Histoire des princes de Condé.* 8 vols. Paris, 1863–1896. Vols. III, IV.

Avenel, Georges d'. *Richelieu et la monarchie absolue.* 4 vols. Paris, 1895. Vol. I.

Barbiche, Bernard. *Sully.* Paris: Albin Michel, 1978.

Baschet, Armand. *Le roi chez la reine.* Paris, 1866.

Batiffol, Louis. *Le Louvre sous Henri IV et Louis XIII.* Paris: Calmann Lévy, 1930.

———. *Le roi Louis XIII à vingt ans.* Paris: Calmann-Lévy, 1934.

———. *La vie intime d'une reine de France.* 2 vols. Paris: Calmann-Lévy, 1906.

Baudson, Emile. *Charles de Gonzague, duc de Nevers de Rethel et de Mantoue (1580–1637).* Paris: Perrin, 1947.

Bayley, Peter. *French Pulpit Oratory.* Cambridge: Cambridge University Press, 1980.

Belvederi, Raffaele. *Guido Bentivoglio e la politica Europea del suo tempo.* Padua: Liviana, 1962.

Blet, Pierre. *Le clergé de France et al monarchie.* 2 vols. Rome: Gregorian University, 1959. Vol. I.

Bloch, Marc. *Les rois thaumaturges.* Strasbourg, 1924; Paris: Colin, 1961.

Bontems, Claude, Raybaud, Léon-Pierre, and Brancourt, Jean-Pierre. *Le prince dans la France des XVIe et XVIIe siècles.* Paris: Presses Universitaires Françaises, 1965.

Buisseret, David. *Sully.* London: Allen and Unwin, 1968.

———. *Henri IV.* London: Allen and Unwin, 1984.

Capefigue, Jean-B.-H.-R. *Richelieu, Mazarin et la Fronde.* Paris, 1848.

Champion, Pierre. *La jeunesse de Henri III.* Paris: Grasset, 1941.

Chérot, Henri. *Le père du grand Condé.* Paris, 1892.

———. *Trois éducations princières au 17e siècle.* Lille, 1896.

Chéruel, Alphonse. *Dictionnaire historique des institutions de la France.* 2 vols. Paris, 1874.

Chevallier, Pierre. *Louis XIII.* Paris: Fayard, 1979.

Crump, Lucy. *Nursery Life 300 Years Ago.* New York: Dutton, 1930.

Dainville, François de. *Les Jésuites et l'éducation de la société française.* Paris: Beauchesne, 1940.

Daniel, Charles. *Une vocation et une disgrâce.* Paris, 1861.

Daniel, Marc. *Hommes du grand siècle: Etudes sur l'homosexualité sous les règnes de Louis XIII et de Louis XIV.* Paris: Arcadie, 1957.

Daussy, Henri. *Histoire de la ville d'Albert (autrefois Encre) jusqu'à la révolution de 1789.* Albert (Somme), 1895.

Delumeau, Jean. *Naissance et affirmation de la réforme.* Paris: Presses Universitaires Françaises, 1965.

Dhotel, Jean-Claude. *Les origines du catéchisme moderne.* Paris: Aubier, 1967.

Druon, Henri-V.-M. *Histoire de l'éducation des princes dans la Maison des Bourbons de France.* Paris, 1897.

Flandrin, Jean-Louis. *Familles: Parenté, maison, sexualité dans l'ancienne société.* Paris: Hachette, 1976.

Fromilhague, René. *La vie de Malherbe: Apprentissage et luttes (1555–1610).* Paris: Colin, 1964.

Godard de Donville, Louise. *La signification de la mode sous Louis XIII.* Aix-en-Provence: Edisud, 1978.

Griffet, Henri [Père]. *Histoire du règne de Louis XIII.* 3 vols. Paris, 1756. Vols. I–III. (Vols. XIII–XVI of *Histoire de France.*) Edited by Gabriel Daniel. 17 vols. Paris, 1755–1757.

Griselle, Eugène. *Louis XIII et Richelieu.* Paris: Leclerc, 1911.

——. *Profils de jésuites du 17e siècle.* Paris: Desclée-Brouwer, 1911.

Guedré, Gabrielle M.-L.-E. *Au coeur des spiritualités: Catherine Ranquet, mystique et éducatrice, 1602–1605.* Paris: Grasset, 1952.

Hanley, Sarah. *"Le Lit de Justice" in Early Modern France.* Princeton: Princeton University, 1983.

Hanotaux, Gabriel. *Histoire du cardinal de Richelieu.* 2 vols. Vol. I., second edition. Paris: Firmin-Didot, 1911. Vol. II, first edition. Paris, 1896.

Hayden, J. Michael. *France and the Estates General of 1614.* Cambridge: Cambridge University Press, 1974.

Hayem, Fernand. *Le maréchal d'Ancre et Leonora Galigai.* Paris: Plon 1910.

Hinrichs, Ernst. *Fürstenlehre und politisches Handeln im Frankreich Heinrichs IV.* Göttingen: Vamdemjoeck and Ruprecht, 1969.

Hunt, David. *Parents and Children in History.* New York: Basic Books, 1970.

Jackson, Richard A. *"Vive le roi!" A History of the French Coronation from Charles V to Charles X.* Chapel Hill: University of North Carolina Press, 1984.

Jacquinet, Paul. *Des prédicateurs du XVIIe siècle avant Bossuet.* Paris, 1885.

Jal, Auguste. *Dictionnaire critique de biographie et d'histoire.* Paris, 1872.

Jegou, Marie-Andrée. *Les Ursulines du Faubourg Saint-Jacques à Paris: 1607–1662.* Paris: Presses Universitaires Françaises, 1982.

Kleinman, Ruth. *Anne of Austria.* Columbus: Ohio State University Press, 1985.

La Ferrière, Hector de. *Deux années de mission à Saint Petersbourg.* Paris, 1867.

Magne, Emile. *La vie quotidienne à Paris au temps de Louis XIII.* Paris: Hachette, 1942.

Major, J. Russell. *Representative Government in Early Modern France.* New Haven: Yale University Press, 1980.

Mariéjol, Jean H. *Henri IV et Louis XIII (1598–1643).* Paris: Hachette, 1911. (Vol. VI of *Histoire de France.* Edited by Ernest Lavisse. 18 vols.)

Marvick, Elizabeth W. *The Young Richelieu: A Psychoanalytic Approach to Leadership.* Chicago: University of Chicago Press, 1983.

Mastellone, Salvatore. *La reggenza di Maria de' Medicie.* Florence: D'Anna, 1962.

Méthivier, Hubert. *Le siècle de Louis XIII.* Paris: Presses Universitaires Françaises, 1971.

Mongrédien, Georges. *Etude sur la vie de Nicolas Vauquelin.* Paris: Picard, 1921.

Mousnier, Roland. *L'assassinat d'Henri IV.* Paris: Gallimard, 1964.

——. *La famille, l'enfant et l'éducation en France et en Grande-Bretagne du XVIe au XVIIIe siècle.* Paris: Centre de Documentation Universitaire, 1975.

——. *Les institutions de la France sous la monarchie absolue.* 2 vols. Paris: Presses Universitaires Françaises, 1974–1980.

———. *La plume, la faucille et le marteau*. Paris: Presses Universitaires Françaises, 1970.

———. *La vénalité des offices sous Henri IV et Louis XIII*. Rouen: Maugard, 1945.

———, et al. *Le Conseil du Roi de Louis XIII à la révolution*. Paris: Presses Universitaires Françaises, 1970.

Mouton, Léo. *Le duc et le roi: D'Epernon, Henri IV, Louis XIII*. Paris: Perrin, 1924.

Muchembled, Robert. *Culture populaire et culture des élites*. Paris: Flammarion, 1978.

Nouaillac, Joseph. *Villeroy: Secrétaire d'Etat et ministre*. Paris: Champion, 1909.

Pannier, Jacques. *L'église réformée de Paris sous Louis XIII (1610–1621)*. Strasbourg: Istra, 1922.

———. *L'église réformée de Paris sous Louis XIII, 1621 à 1629 environ*. Paris: Champion, 1932.

Perrens, François T. *Les mariages espagnols*. Paris, n. d.

Pillorget, René. *La tige et le rameau: Familles anglaise et française, 16e–18e siècles*. Paris: Calmann-Lévy, 1972.

Prat, Jean-Marie. *Recherches sur la Compagnie de Jésus*. 5 vols. Lyons, 1876–1878. Vols. III–V.

Ranum, Orest. *Artisans of Glory*. Chapel Hill: University of North Carolina Press, 1980.

———. *Paris in the Age of Absolutism*. New York: Wiley, 1968.

———. *Richelieu and the Councillors of Louis XIII*. Oxford: Oxford University Press, 1963.

———, editor. *National Consciousness, History, and Political Culture in Early Modern Europe*. Baltimore: Johns Hopkins University Press, 1975.

Rocquain, Félix. *Notes et fragments d'histoire*. Paris: Plon, 1906.

Rossignol, C. *Louis XIII avant Richelieu*. Paris, 1869.

Rowen, Herbert H. *The King's State: Proprietary Dynasticism in Early Modern France*. New Brunswick: Rutgers University Press, 1980.

Siri, Vittorio. *Mémoires secrets*. 8 vols. Paris, 1776. Vol. IV.

Taylor, Ida A. *The Making of a King*. London: Hutchinson, 1910.

Terrebasse, Humbert de. *Antoine de Pluvinel, dauphinois*. Lyons: L. Brun, 1911.

Vaunois, Louis. *La vie de Louis XIII*. Paris: Grasset, 1943.

Vermeylen, Alphonse. *Sainte Thérèse en France au XVIIe siècle, 1600–1660*. Louvain: Presses Universitaires de Louvain, 1958.

Zeller, Berthold. *Le connétable de Luynes*. Paris, 1879.

———. *Henri IV et Marie de Médicis*. Paris, 1877.

———. *Marie de Médicis: Chef du conseil*. Paris, 1898.

———. *Marie de Médicis et Sully*. Paris, 1892.

———. *Marie de Médicis et Villeroy*. Paris, 1897.

———. *Richelieu ministre*. Paris, 1899.

Zeller, Gaston. *Aspects de la politique française sous l'ancien régime*. Paris: Presses Universitaires Françaises, 1964.

Articles

Bailey, Donald A. "Les pamphlets de Mathieu de Morgues (1582–1670)." *Revue française de l'histoire du livre*, 18 (1978), 1–18.

Louis Batiffol, "Marie de Médicis et les arts." *Gazette des Beaux-Arts,* 34:2 (1905), 441–460; 35 (1906), 223–243.

Blanchet, Adrien. "Un médaillon de Jean Héroard." *Revue numismatique,* 11 (1893), 252–258, pl. 4.

————, editor. "Un récit inédit de la mort du maréchal d'Ancre." *Bulletin de la Société de l'Histoire de Paris et de l'Ile de France,* 27 (1900), 135–141.

Blet, Pierre. "Libertés gallicaines et Jésuites en 1611." *Archivum historicum Societatis Iesu,* 24 (1955), 165–188.

Cappelletti, Licurgo. "La sorella di latte di Maria de Medici." *Ressegna nazionale,* 173–174 (1910), 544–560, 3–20.

Choublier-Myszkowski, Noëlle. "L'education du prince au XVIIe siècle d'après Héroard et La Mothe Le Vayer." Paris: Hachette, 1976. (Microfiche of an FNSP *mémoire de maîtrise.*)

Darricau, Raymond. "La spiritualité du prince," *Dix-septième siècle,* 52–53 (1964), 78–111.

Deloche, Maximin. "Les vrais mémoires du cardinal de Richelieu." *Revue des questions historiques,* 109 (1928), 297.

Dickerman, Edmund S. "Henry IV and the Juliers-Clèves Crisis: The Psychohistorical Aspects." *French Historical Studies,* 8 (1974), 626–653.

Drouot, Henri, editor. "Un père de famille sous Henri IV: Lettres domestiques d'Etienne Bernard, 1598–1609." *Annales de Bourgogne,* 24 (1952), 161–175.

Gougenheim, Philippe, "L'observation du langage d'un enfant royal du XVIIe d'après le journal de Héroard." *Revue de philologie française et provençale,* 43 (1913), 1–15.

Hamy, Ernest-Théodore. "Les faucons du roy Henri IV." *Bulletin du Musée d'Histoire Naturelle* 14 (1908), 195–210.

————. "Jean Héroard: Premier surintendant du Jardin Royal." *Bulletin du Musée d'Histoire Naturelle* 2 (1896), 1–12.

Himelfarb, Hélène. "L'apprentissage du mécénat royal: Le jeune Louis XIII face au monde des arts et des lettres dans le journal d'Héroard." *L'age d'or du mécénat (1598–1661).* Edited by Roland Mousnier and Jean Mesnard. Paris: Centre Nationale de la Recherche Scientifique, 1985, 25–36.

————, and Michèle David. "Une Observation directe au XVIIe siècle: Le journal de Héroard." *Nouvelle revue de psychanalyse,* 19 (1979), 270–330.

Lavollée, Robert. "La Mort de Conchine et Léonore." *Le correspondant,* 237 (1909), 320–341, 531–562.

Le Franc, Abel. "Louis XIII, a-t-il appris l'espagnol?" *Mélanges Fernand Baldensperger,* 2 vols. (Paris: Champion, 1930), II, 37–40.

Le Roy Ladurie, Emmanuel "La monarchie française classique." *Commentaire,* 7 (1984), 418–429.

Major, J. Russell. "The Crown and the Aristocracy in Renaissance France." *American Historical Review,* 69 (1964), 631–645.

————. "Henri IV and Guyenne: A Study Concerning Origins of Royal Absolutism." *French Historical Studies,* 4 (1966), 363–383.

Marvick, Elizabeth W., "The Character of Louis XIII: His Physician's Role in its Formation." *Journal of Interdisciplinary History,* 4 (1974), 347–374.

————, "Childhood History and Reasons of State: The Case of Louis XIII." *Journal of Psychohistory*, 2 (1974), 135–180.

————, "Nature versus Nurture: Trends and Patterns in Seventeenth-Century French Childrearing." Lloyd Demause, editor. *The History of Childhood*. New York: Harper, 1976, 259–301.

Nouaillac, Joseph. "L'affaire de Mantoue en 1613." *Revue historique*, 98 (1910), 63–83.

————, "L'avis de Villeroy sur la paix: 3 octobre 1614." *Revue Henri IV*, 2 (1908), 79–81.

Pichon, Jérôme. "Jean et Nicolas Vauquelin." *Bulletin du bibliophile* 1 (1846), 554–721, 512–526, 601–627, 663–676, 721–727.

Pigallet, Maurice. "Etude sur Concini: 14 mai 1610–8 juillet 1617." Ecole Nationale des Chartes: Positions de Thèses, 1902. (The thesis could not be located.)

Prätorius, Num. "Des Liebesleben Ludwigs XIII von Frankreich," Abhandlungen aus dem Gebiete der Sexualförschung, 2:6 (1919–20).

Ranum, Orest. "The French Ritual of Tyrannicide in the Late Sixteenth Century." *Sixteenth Century Journal*, 11 (1980), 63–82.

————. "Guises, Henri III, Henri IV, Concini: Trente ans d'assassinats politiques." *Histoire* 51 (1982), 36–44.

Samaran, Charles. "Cursives françaises des XVe, XVIe et XVIIe siècles," *Journal des Savants* (July/Sep. 1967), 129–153.

Soman, Alfred. "La décriminalisation de la sorcellerie en France." *Histoire, économie et société*, 4 (1985), 179–203.

————. "La sorcellerie vue du Parlement de Paris au début du XVIIe siècle." *Actes du 104e congrès national des sociétés savantes*, 2 vols., Section d'histoire moderne et contemporaine. Bordeaux: Centre Nationale dela Recherche Scientifique, 1979, II, 393–405.

————. "Les procès de sorcellerie au Parlement de Paris." *Annales*, Ecomonies Sociétés Civilisations, 32 (1977), 790–814.

Tamizey de Larroque, Philippe. "Un mot apocryphe de la maréchale d'Ancre." *Revue des questions historiques*, 6 (1869), 545–549.

Tartarin. "Roger de Termes, duc de Bellegarde." *Revue de la Société des Etudes Historiques*, 4th series, 9 (1892), 378–392.

Tyvaert, Michel. "L'image du roi: Legitimité et moralité royales dans les histoires de France au XVIIe siècle." *Revue d'histoire moderne et contemporaine*, 21 (1974), 531–538.

Viguerie, Jean de. "Les serments du sacre des rois de France." *Hommage à Roland Mousnier: Clientèles et fidélités en Europe à l'époque moderne*. Edited by Yves Durand. Paris: Presses Universitaires Françaises, 1981, 58–61.

Index

Abimilech, Old Testament figure, 189
Agnès Sorel, 142
Aiguillon, duc d', 128
Albret, Jeanne d', 6
Alvarez, Francisque, 254n22
Amboise, fortress of, 148–49, 161
Ammirato, Scipione (the younger), 110
Ancre, Concino Concini, maréchal d': early relations of with Louis, 126–28; made maréchal, 144; and Luynes, 162; dwelling of looted, 175; as military commander, 182, 192; murdered, 199–200; posthumously indicted for treason, 211
Ancre, Leonora Galigai, maréchale d': Marie de Medici's attachment to, 8, 121–22; marriage of, 125; early relations of with Louis XIII, 126–27; doctors of, 178; relations of with husband, 192, 257n45; "Jewish connection" of, 210; courage attributed to, 261n70
Anjou, duc d'. *See* Gaston, duc d'Orléans
Anne de Saint-Benoist, Ursuline, 94
Anne of Austria, queen of France, 24–25, 62, 101; arrival and marriage in France, 170–71, 253n49; entertained by husband, 190; husband's relationship with, 223
Ariès, Philippe, xviii–xix
Arnauld, Isaac, 167
Arnauld d'Andilly, Robert, 160, 161, 181, 246n19, 251n4
Arnoux, Père Jean, confessor of Louis XIII, 217–18
Assassination rituals, 258n78

Baluze, Etienne, xvii
Balzac, Guez de, 159
Bar, Catherine, duchesse de, sister of Henri IV, 24, 47
Barbin, Claude, 157, 173, 181, 190, 193, 202, 206, 210
Barthélemy, Edouard, xvii–xviii, xix
Bartolini, Mattei, Tuscan ambassador, 194
Bastille, the, 147, 150, 211, 212
Batiffol, Louis, xviii
Bayonne, bishop of. *See* Des Chaux, Bertrand
Beauchamp, comte de, xviii
Beauvais-Nangis, Nicolas de, 191
Bélier, Geneviève Robert, dame du, 141, 142
Bellarmin, Cardinal Robert, 158
Bellegarde, Roger de Termes, duc de, 133
Bentivoglio, Guido, papal nuncio, 193, 200
Beringhen, Pierre de, 119, 129
Bermond, Françoise de, 94
Bernard, Charles, xvi, 114
Bérulle, Cardinal Pierre de, 158
Bettelheim, Bruno, 61
Bible, the, 101
Bocquet, Jacques, 36. *See also* Joron, Antoinette
Bompar, Charles de, page of Louis XIII, 46–47, 137, 187
Bongars, court mason, 31, 32, 33
Bordeaux, royal journey to, 169–70
Bouillon, Henri de La Tour d'Auvergne, duc de, 146, 201

Index